Intelligence Requirements for the 1980's: Counterintelligence

CONSORTIUM FOR THE STUDY OF INTELLIGENCE

Intelligence Requirements for the 1980's: Counterintelligence

Edited by
Roy Godson

Published by
National Strategy Information Center, Inc.

Distributed by
Transaction Books
New Brunswick (USA) and London (UK)

Intelligence Requirements for the 1980's
NUMBER THREE
Counterintelligence

Published by
National Strategy Information Center, Inc.
1730 Rhode Island Avenue, N.W.
Washington, D.C. 20036

LC 80-84005
ISBN 0-87855-829-2

Printed in the United States of America

Table of Contents

Preface

This is the third volume of a continuing series under the blanket title and from the unifying perspective of *Intelligence Requirements for the 1980's*. Herein, the Consortium for the Study of Intelligence explores systematically and in depth what has heretofore been the dark continent of the intelligence universe. Counterintelligence has not been without its popularizers to be sure. Masterman's absorbing account of British success in World War II, *The Double Cross System*, convinces the layman of the tangible military benefits to be gained from "turning" enemy agents. In the realm of fiction, LeCarré is only the latest in a tradition that includes Ambler, Greene, Maugham and E. Phillips Oppenheim; and such CI terms of art as "moles" and "doubles" and "penetrations" have worked their way into the vernacular of mass communications—even into prime-time television.

But if counterintelligence has been partially explored, it is doubtful that it has yet been understood, simultaneously in its conceptual simplicity (to "counter" the efforts of adversary intelligence services) *and* in the infinite subtlety and complexity of its ways (which range from protective security to the deliberate manipulation of adversary services into affirmative instruments of one's own purposes). In this volume the Consortium attempts to contribute to both levels of understanding. To a very considerable degree it succeeds.

Let us focus here on a relatively narrow issue—but one, as is so typical of CI, that at once broadens out to encompass the fundamental question of the role of all of intelligence in a society of laws and of constitutionally-protected personal liberties. The issue is that of intrusive investigatory techniques *versus* privacy, of CI *versus* civil liberties. (Note that this singular but widely used formulation is a mark of the extent to which the avowed enemies of a "full service" US intelligence capability have been able to prejudice the public debate and throw the intelligence community on the defensive.)

It must be frankly conceded that intelligence in general and CI in particular manifestly threaten some privacy and put some civil liberaties at a degree of risk. Indeed they must—and CI, to repeat, in particular. It is the hallmark of the "CI mentality," and of its operating methods, to view almost every given with skepticism, to prod and pry at targets of opportunity, including targets of unwitting innocence concerning their own tangential involvement with agents and operations hostile to US security interests. And to this end, the techniques of intrusion into personal privacy—close surveillance, electronic intercepts, "black bag" operations at the extreme—are CI stocks-in-trade. Effective CI necessitates *sometimes* and under *rigorous self-imposed professional discipline* engaging in activities that from a purist, civil libertarian perspective are simply not "nice." (For that matter, it is also "not nice" for innocent millions of American women to have the privacy of their handbags invaded by airport control on the remote chance that one may be a potential skyjacker. If we learn to live with the humiliation of body and baggage search to avert the inconvenience of airline detour to Cuba, perhaps it is not intolerable to suffer comparable "indignities" to frustrate KGB freebooters who may aspire to skyjack freedom itself.) "CI *versus* civil liberties." More than a fashion, it is now the prevailing intellectual predisposition ("bias" might be the more appropriate word) to state this relationship as either-or.

In the introductory essay that follows, Roy Godson acknowledges the state of perpetual tension. But he rightly rejects the either-or relationship: "civil liberties," he argues at one point, "are best served by effective CI *as well as* by the safeguarding of our constitutionally-protected freedoms." The emphasis is his—but, in my judgment, he is not nearly emphatic enough. "Effective CI" as the paradigm of an effective national intelligence capability generally is not merely to be tolerated as a "servant" of civil liberties: it must be seen as an unequivocally indispensable precondition to the maintenance of our evolving free society in a largely unfree world and thus to the luxury of having any civil liberties to safeguard in the first place. The tension is not dissolved thereby. But the burden of proof shifts from "how can you have it both ways?" to "how can you *not*?"

At another point, Dr. Godson observes that, "The proposition that CI is essential to the maintenance of democratic processes and human liberties *usually does not have to be demonstrated*." Here the emphasis is not his but mine—possibly no more than a difference between us of nuance, but what a nuance! It is precisely my point that his assertion not only has to be demonstrated "usually" but over and over again. Given the prevailing tilt of our communications and culture, this proposition never goes without saying. Quite the opposite: the built-in presumption is that the CI operative who wants to engage in "intrusive investigatory techniques"—even if only in a preliminary, exploratory way, simply to establish that a potentially ''interesting'' target may turn out to be a legitimate target indeed—must always be prepared to demonstrate the *bona fides* of the investigation (usually at an implausibly high level of substantiality), must as a general rule assume a weighted burden of proof, and is probably (so goes the presumption) pushing the matter to the extreme anyway. This, if anything, is what ''usually does not have to be demonstrated''—not that the CI enterprise in particular or the intelligence enterprise in general is essential to the preservation of our liberties and indeed of our society.

In recent years those who profess to be more ''chilled'' by the misdemeanors and malfeasance of the CIA than the high crimes of the KGB in expanding the Gulag, have been dangerously successful in casting the US intelligence community in the role of the heavy—the ''rougue elephant'' running out of control, *prime facie* the willful ''invader'' of privacy, the needless ''intruder'' into personal liberties, the gratuitous ''underminer'' of our democratic way of life. As if no guard dog were needed in a wilderness of bears and jackals. There are some few and fitful signs that the balance is now beginning to shift a bit the other way. But given the extraordinary license we now grant the Soviet, Czech, East German and Cuban intelligence services to probe our society, surely Dr. Godson is oversanguine to a fault. The demonstration of the centrality of an effective national intelligence (and CI) capability to, in the most literal and fundamental sense, the defense of our ''value infrastructure'' would appear to be an effort never overdone and never lightly left to chance.

The Consortium for the Study of Intelligence, a project of the National Strategy Information Center, was formed in the Spring of 1979 to provide an institutional focus for (as the prospectus put it) ''a balanced, coherent understanding of the role of intelligence in a free society.'' In all of its activities and publications so far, the Consortium has responded to that intimidating mandate in good measure. This time, it comes closer still—with literal spadework in largely unexplored territory.

Frank R. Barnett, President
National Strategy Information Center
October 1980

CHAPTER ONE

Counterintelligence: An Introduction

Roy Godson

Counterintelligence (CI) is perhaps the least understood component of intelligence. It is probably also the most mysterious as well, even within the intelligence community itself and among some practitioners of the more self-evident disciplines of collection, analysis and covert action. Yet CI remains an absolutely essential element, a prerequisite, for an effective intelligence capability generally. And even while there may have been substantive improvements in some aspects of US counterintelligence in the 1970's, it is far from clear that this country has the CI capabilities it will need to meet the growing challenges of the 1980's.

To review these future CI needs, and to assess their implications for public policy, the Consortium for the Study of Intelligence convened a three-day colloquium in April 1980. This volume, the third in the series, *Intelligence Requirements for the 1980's* is the result of a meeting of over sixty academics, current and former CI practitioners from the US and abroad, and congressional staff specialists on intelligence.

This introduction anticipates the major conclusions of the volume first by briefly defining CI and summarizing its significance for the other component elements of US intelligence. It then reviews the dimensions of the major CI threat in the 1980's—that posed by the Soviet Union and its allies. Finally, it considers the current US capability to cope with this threat. The pervasive question is this: to what extent do we have the organization, the laws and guidelines and the personnel to meet these critical challenges?

It is not easy to define counterintelligence. Its practitioners themselves disagree about the meaning of the concept. At a minimum, however, CI can be defined as the identification and neutralization of the threat posed by foreign intelligence services, and the manipulation of these services for the manipulator's benefit. Some say CI is more all encompassing: That it should deal with a wider range of threats to a nation's security, from that posed by adversary states in their totality, rather than by their intelligence services alone, as well as threats posed by such non-governmental forces as terrorist groups and internationally-organized crime. But the "minimalist" focus on the threat posed by foreign intelligence services is almost universally shared, as a starting point at least.

Few also would disagree that CI is important not only to the nation's security but to the effective functioning of the nation's apparatus for intelligence as well. The public is reasonably well aware that CI exists to prevent spies, foreign and domestic, from penetrating our government, armed forces and intelligence agencies. There is even widespread recognition that this country should not be without means to safeguard the security of the high technology produced by our industry, and that nations cannot deal with terrorist organizations, or with large-scale internationally-organized crime, by *ad hoc* investigations alone, subsequent to the event.

Essential to dealing with all of these threats is information that can be obtained only by clandestine technical and human means, by a panoply of what have come to be called "intrusive techniques," often involving audiovisual surveillance. Nor is there much need to argue that if the US is going to discover the "illegals" whom the Soviet Union has sent to this country for purposes of long-term infiltration, the systematic counteraction must comprise sophisticated analysis as well as investigation. There are those—among them the leaders of the American Civil Liberties Union—who have urged the virtual abolition of all CI and clandestine collection from human sources, both home and abroad (see, for example, Ernest Lefever and Roy Godson, *The CIA and the American Ethic,* Washington, D.C.: Ethics and Public Policy Center, 1979). But the proposition that CI is essential to the maintenance of democratic processes and human liberties usually does not have to be demonstrated.

It is far less clear, however, except to specialists, that CI is essential to the success of all other components of intelligence. Neither collection nor analysis can produce reliable results, nor can covert action be effectively conducted without constant attention to what hostile (and even friendly) services might do to turn our intelligence activities to their advantage.

The security of the processes by which we collect intelligence is often precarious. For example, it is impossible to know *a priori* whether any human source is actually working for us or is feeding us false or doctored information. Intelligence services traditionally, wisely and necessarily employ a variety of techniques to investigate and, above all, to test their human sources. Technical sources also can be used by hostile services to deceive us. Telemetry (the signals emitted by missiles in test flight) is an obvious example of information that the adversary knows we are capable of picking up. It would be uncharacteristic, at the very least, if the adversary failed to take this into account in planning the format and content of the telemetry of its test platforms. We also must assume that the adversary is aware of its potential vulnerability to other methods of technical collection and is doing the utmost not only to deny us data but to bias the data we do get. We always can try to minimize our vulnerability to countermeasures by keeping our collection activities as secure as possible. But the collection system has yet to be devised that will be able completely to neutralize the adversary's efforts to deny and to misinform. Therefore, CI experts must constantly devise and carry out tests to determine how, and how well, the adversary is coping with our collection activities.

Covert action couples the promise of significant gains for our country with the real prospect of embarrassing failure and the waste of precious assets. This century is replete with examples of covert political and paramilitary activity turned to the initiator's disadvantage. Among the major methods of determining if a covert action is about to be "turned" are painstaking, skeptical analysis of all the information connected with the operation and the subtle, constant, testing of both assets and opponents. Only by working hand-in-glove with CI, as a general rule, can those in charge of covert action maximize their chances of success.

Analysis may be the most important and is surely one of the most vulnerable components of the intelligence process. Analysts are required to answer difficult questions on the basis of usually limited data. Thus they are frequently tempted to accept data more or less at face value. The active involvement of CI specialists can be very helpful in assisting analysts to deal with the adversary's efforts to confuse them or lead them deliberately to the wrong answers. CI specialists, by highlighting the activities of foreign services, may also be able to provide positive information of extraordinary value to analysts. The down side is that excessive concentration on CI can sterilize the analytical process. But, at its effective best, CI not only protects analysts against deception but provides them with a vital increment of in-depth knowledge of their subject.

The Soviet KGB and other hostile intelligence services pose a broad-gauged threat both to our country and to our intelligence, considered organizationally and substantively. The KGB, the largest and most centralized major intelligence service in the world, has excelled over the years in traditional espionage and the penetration of Western services. The number of intelligence officers under legal cover in Soviet embassies and official missions in the US and other countries grew considerably in the 1970's. In addition, unlike many of the Western services that operate against the Soviet Union, the KGB does not limit itself to sending out "legal" intelligence officers to recruit agents and sources. The KGB and other bloc services make extensive use of "illegal" agents, who are infiltrated into target countries until ordered into action, sometimes years later and after thoroughly establishing their local credentials. The Soviet services also have demonstrated a facility to use the considerable assets of the world's Communist parties and front groups both for collection and for covert action.

Given the nature of open societies in the West and the ready supply of Moscow's human assets, the Soviet Union does not have to put particular emphasis on sophisticated and expensive means of technical collection. It is likely, however, that the Soviets realize that the US has had to rely (or even over-rely) on precisely these means. Thus, the Soviets have the incentive, and may have developed the means to bias the results of US technical collection. Indeed, there is considerable evidence that they devote significant resources and senior personnel to deceiving their adversaries at almost every level of competitive endeavor, from infantry tactics to international trade, to missilery.

Powers hostile to the US, and especially the Soviet Union, also have developed impressive capabilities for unconventional warfare and for training and supporting terrorist organizations. The transnational movement of paramilitary forces, terrorists and members of their support groups, poses a serious challenge to US counterintelligence. These groups frequently are organized and do much of their work prior to the actual initiation of hostilities or violent terrorist acts. Insofar as such paramilitary forces and terrorists become involved in bolstering political movements friendly to the Soviet bloc and undermining pro-western governments and nongovernmental forces such as democratic trade unions, co-operative movements and the independent press in many parts of the world, the US is obliged to treat these activists as challenges to itself. And, CI must begin to identify and prepare to neutralize these forces before they strike.

Even under the best of circumstances, however, our ability to cope with the direct threats of hostile services is open to question. In addition to the growing capabilities of adversary services, it also should be noted that CI has never been our strongest suit. Americans frequently have either misunderstood or distrusted CI, primarily because of a well-founded distaste for anything that resembles a political police or that may be used as an instrument of partisan influence. As a result, historically, we have kept our CI components small, and divided the CI task into domestic and foreign components among many agencies. Even as analytical intelligence has become increasingly centralized, there has been a reluctance to centralize the various CI disciplines and component elements. Limited coordination does take place at times. But it is far from clear that interagency coordination wholly overcomes the disadvantages of fragmentation. After all, CI work does not really begin until it is determined that a matter is of CI interest; and it is often difficult to cross that critical initial threshold until the full range of intelligence activity and information is reviewed.

Another major problem in US CI stems from the widespread confusion, which grew worse in the 1970's between CI and law enforcement. It has become commonplace in some quarters to regard investigation as a hard-to-justify burden that should not in any case be imposed on any US person unless that person has committed—or is about to commit a crime. According to this view, almost any kind of surveillance or investigation, even to the keeping of files from open sources, constitutes a virtual "search and seizure" under the Fourth Amendment or an inhibition on First Amendment freedoms. Because CI consists in substantial part of investigations, sometimes of completely unwitting persons who have come innocently into contact with the intelligence activities of foreign powers or terrorists, a web of "standards" has grown up around it, the purpose of which is to ensure that these constitutionally-protected freedoms are not violated. One by-product of this eminently defensible purpose is to inhibit CI.

The path to ensuring effective CI is not found in any particular doctrine. No *a priori* means have yet been discovered for determining how skeptical an intelligence system ought to be about its sources or how wary about its adversaries' attempts at disinformation. Similarly, the way in which tasks are assigned in government ought not to depend wholly on tradition or ideology but also—and simultaneously—on assessments of what is needed to do the job for which government exists. Thus, the cause of civil liberties would best be served by effective counterintelligence as well as the safeguarding of constitutionally-protected freedoms. The need to balance dangers, costs and risks is perpetual.

What then is counterintelligence? Practitioners have debated this subject endlessly but it has received almost no serious consideration in the voluminous literature of intelligence. In Chapter two, Arthur Zuehlke, Jr., who taught at the Defense Intelligence School for several years and who is presently a research analyst in the Soviet and Warsaw Pact Division of the Defense Intelligence Agency, considers various concepts of counterintelligence. He opts for an approach midway between the minimalist and the most expansive definitions and goes on to suggest that the definition of CI in President Carter's Executive Order 12036 is perhaps a positive step, embodying a more sophisticated understanding of the concept than has often been the case in the US government. Newton "Scotty" Miler, the former Chief of Operations of CIA's CI staff, who retired in 1974, believes Zuehlke's concept may not be sufficiently precise and that E.O. 12036 does not go far enough in providing the kind of centralized CI that is necessary to deal with the KGB's strategy. Major General Edmund Thompson, the Army's Assistant Chief of Staff for Intelligence, agrees with Zuehlke's emphasis on the "multidisciplinary" nature of CI, but opposes the specific proposals the paper advances for the reorganization of the Department of Defense CI structure.

What are the likely dimensions of the CI threat in the 1980's? In Chapter three, Dr. William R. Harris, an international lawyer and Harvard Ph.D. in history now with the Social Science Department of the Rand Corporation, considers CI problems that arise from our utilization of technical means of collection. Harris suggests that the Soviets may have intentionally deceived us in the sixties and seventies and that improved US analysis requires an increased emphasis on CI in technical collection, as well as extending coordinated CI jurisdiction to technical as well as human means of collection.

Rear Admiral Donald P. Harvey (USN Ret.), Chief of Naval Intelligence from 1976-1978 and now with TRW, Inc., is not convinced that we were in fact deceived and thus doubts that the steps Harris suggests are necessary. Dr. Roland Herbst, on the other hand, believes that we were vulnerable to Soviet deception about the accuracy of their ICBMs. A physicist by training, Herbst specializes in strategic and space systems and served as chairman of the ICBM Accuracy Panel of "B Team" established by CIA Director George Bush in 1976.

The evolution of and the significance the Soviet leadership attaches to its paramilitary forces are analyzed in Chapter four by Dr. John Dziak, a Ph.D. in history from Georgetown University. Dr. Dziak has taught at the Defense Intelligence School and George Washington University and is now a senior Soviet specialist with the Defense Intelligence Agency. Lt. Colonel John Guenther, Special Assistant to the Director of Intelligence, US Marine Corps, and Lt. General William Odom, Military Assistant to the Assistant to the President for National Security, agree that the role of Soviet paramilitary forces, and particularly the KGB's *Spetsnaz* forces, has not received adequate attention up to now.

The threat posed by insurgency and terrorism in the 1980's is the focus of an essay by Major General Schlomo Gazit, Director of Israeli Military Intelligence, 1974-1979, and Dr. Michael Handel, a research associate at Harvard's Center for International Affairs. General Gazit and Dr. Handel have written a manual, almost a textbook, on intelligence, insurgency and terrorism. In their paper and in additional remarks, General Gazit and Dr. Handel distinguish, perhaps for the first time in intelligence literature, two types of counterterrorist strategies involving intelligence, a "defensive passive" strategy and an "active counter" strategy.

Robert Chapman, a former CIA Station Chief who was responsible for collection in various regions of the world and who specialized in terrorism and counterterrorism, discusses almost the identical use of terrorism by urban guerrillas on several continents to weaken governments and create insurgencies, and the US inability to deal with it. Dr. Abram Shulsky, a professional staff member of the Senate Intelligence Committee, suggests that the US does not have the intelligence capability to implement either the "defensive passive" or "active counter" strategies outlined by Gazit and Handel.

The Soviet intelligence threat in the US is taken up by Herbert Romerstein in Chapter six. Mr. Romerstein, who has investigated and studied Soviet and Communist activities in the US for several decades, and who is now a professional staff member of the House Intelligence Committee, focuses on the Soviets' ability to collect information in the US. He maintains their most striking successes have come from "ideological spies" in periods of relatively relaxed relations between the US and the USSR.

William Branigan, a former FBI Chief of Soviet Counterintelligence who retired in 1976, agrees with Romerstein's overall conclusions. However, he believes the Soviets have been able to do considerable damage to the US by recruiting "mercenaries" as well as ideological spies and doubts that the FBI currently has the capability to deal adequately with the growing Soviet presence in the US. Professor Allen Weinstein of Smith College is not sure we know enough about past Soviet behavior in the US to reach firm conclusions at this point. He suggests that, for the most part, studies have been limited, of necessity, to public sources and defectors and, above all, to knowledge of Soviet failures rather than successes. He suggests that additional information should be obtained from newly-available archival sources, defectors, former dissident communists and others who might have special knowledge of Soviet activities, and that a special effort be made to maintain an "institutional memory" so that accumulated knowledge of the past can be applied to future problems.

Further to amplify the challenge of the 1980's, Appendix I contains an imaginary "Directive" from the KGB in Moscow to the Chief of its London station. The "Directive" was written by John Bruce Lockhart, a former senior member of the British Foreign Service who concentrated on intelligence matters. While the "Directive" is purely imaginary, Mr. Lockhart believes, based on his experience, that it illustrates important (and very real) aspects of the relationship of the Soviets with revolutionary movements in various parts of the world and the nature of the tasks assigned to major KGB stations.

To what extent do we have the organization, personnel and legal procedures to meet these challenges? Chapter seven focuses on the organizational relationship of CI with the other components of intelligence. Norman Smith, who retired as Deputy Chief of Operations of the CIA's CI staff in 1976, begins by describing the merits and effectiveness of the two types of CI organization, in broad terms, centralized and decentralized, that have existed in the CIA. He concludes that, in view of the likely threats in the 1980's, the current decentralized staff organization is inadequate.

Donovan Pratt, former Director of Research on the CIA's CI staff, is even more emphatic on the need to reorganize the intelligence community and create a new "clandestine service which will conduct only clandestine missions." He believes that, to conduct both positive intelligence and CI, it is ncessary to separate secret from essentially non-secret tasks, something that has not been done in the omnibus organization of the CIA, where clandestine and non-clandestine officers share literally the same parking lot.

Eugene Burgstaller, who served as a CIA Station Chief, most recently (until 1979) in Paris, believes the creation of a more decentralized staff in the mid-1970's may have had some negative effects but also, based on his experience with the new system, important positive benefits as well. However, he urges more coordination among the various component elements to ensure more effective CI.

David Ignatius, who specialized in intelligence matters for the *Wall Street Journal,* highlights the dispute between those who believe the pre-1974 CI organization, the centralized line unit, was too powerful and detrimental to the overall intelligence mission, and those who believe the newer decentralized system has so degraded CI that overall intelligence effectiveness has been impaired. He also endorses the proposal to create a genuine clandestine service but is not sanguine about our ability to do so.

Chapter eight takes up the question of what kinds of personnel should be recruited and how they should be trained to meet future needs. Kenneth deGraffenreid, a professional staff member of the Senate Select Committee on Intelligence, believes that current recruiting and training are inadequate. He spells out some measures that he judges are necessary to ''a national program of strategic multidisciplinary CI.''

Dr. Robert Nisbet, former Albert Schweitzer Professor of Sociology, Columbia University, and Resident Scholar at the American Enterprise Institute, feels that there is a great potential reservoir of talent that can fulfill the CI mission, especially at non-Ivy League schools and among young people grounded in ''traditional'' values. Lawrence McWilliams, who retired in 1977 as the FBI's Chief of Foreign Counterintelligence Training, believes our performance has not been as poor as deGraffenreid suggests and, consequently, sees less need for major reform. He does, however, suggest that much more coordination among agencies would be beneficial.

The final chapter focuses on legal constraints and incentives. Dr. Arnold Beichman and this writer examine the effects of various laws, court cases, executive orders and guidelines on professional intelligence officers working in CI, as well as on their agents abroad and informants at home. We conclude that the current ''rules'' and (possibly even more important) the perceptions of them are having a negative effect: that to protect American civil liberties and to ensure more effective CI performance quite different incentives ought to be operating.

Professor Antonin Scalia of the University of Chicago Law School, who as Assistant Attorney General in the Ford Administration helped develop many of the "rules," agrees with many of our recommendations for change. He maintains, however, that our essay misinterprets and misconstrues important statutes, court decisions and guidelines. Professor James Q. Wilson of Harvard University, who specializes in the study of law enforcement agencies, is not convinced that the rules themselves create a disincentive to effective performance but believes instead that the perception of the rules is indeed a major problem. He agrees, however, that greater emphasis on training and organizational incentives is likely to improve performance.

While a broad consensus was reached on many issues in the course of the colloquium, the views expressed in the papers and the comments of the discussants are those of the individuals alone. This is particularly true of current US Government employees, whether in the executive or legislative branches, whose views in no way should be taken to represent those of the individual agency, department or committee. Nevertheless, the papers and discussion summarized here, necessarily greatly compressed, add to public understanding of counterintelligence and its symbiotic relationship with other components of intelligence, as well as the major dimensions of the CI threat in the 1980's and future US needs.

CHAPTER TWO

What is Counterintelligence?

Paper:

Arthur A. Zuehlke, Jr.

Discussants:

Mr. Newton S. Miler

Major General Edmund R. Thompson

Perspectives on Counterintelligence

Ambiguity and confusion surround this concept which denotes a function deemed essential by most nation states to the effective pursuit of both their national interest and national security. Differing perspectives and contrary assumptions about counterintelligence (CI) have contributed to the "porosity" of this concept or rubric, which subsumes a variety of intelligence activites. These activities range widely in nature and purpose: from aggressive to strictly defensive, from the collection of information to its protection, and are carried out in both the home territory and abroad, even within the ranks of an adversary state's intelligence and security service.

Counterintelligence is fundamentally directed at coping with or countering threat. This threat may be immediate, latent, or potential, and originates or emanates from foreign sources. The hostile "entity" may be individuals or organizations, which may or may not be under the control or direction of an adversary state. In the effort to protect against the hostile entity, CI has acquired its characterization as a "defensive" function. While this view of CI as a protective, defensive function offers an abstract notion of its ultimate purpose, it falls short of conveying the truly broad scope of CI activities and value of CI operations. CI is, in effect, relegated to the role of "negating" and countering an adversary's hostile actions, thus putting CI in almost dialectical opposition to the aggressive, "positive" intelligence activity of the hostile entity. An unfortunate consequence of this view is that CI operations are often deemed apart from or incongruent with such positive intelligence activities as collection and analysis. Sherman Kent, for example, with his dichotomy between Security Intelligence and Positive Intelligence, would likely place CI squarely in the former category which he views as "basically the intelligence behind the police function. Its job is to protect the nation and its members from malefactors who are working to our national or individual hurt. . . . By and large, security intelligence is the knowledge and the activity which our defensive police forces must have before they take specific action against the individual ill-wisher or ill-doer."[1] He cites the detection of "clandestine agents sent here by foreign powers" as Security Intelligence in one of its "most dramatic" forms.

Another example of CI as essentially a defensive, security function is found in Harry Howe Ransome's *The Intelligence Establishment* (1970). He describes CI narrowly as intelligence activity "devoted to countering the effectiveness of hostile foreign intelligence operations."[2] Ransome goes on to depict CI as "essentially a police function" which protects against espionage including hostile infiltration of friendly intelligence operations, and secures installations from sabotage. He maintains that CI is, "in a sense, a negative, defensive, function." Ransome does allow, however, that CI may "turn up information of significance to those concerned with 'positive intelligence'." From this negative, defensive perspective, CI is said to be important to positive intelligence in that it provides revelations of the adversary's "information gaps as well as his intentions and capabilities."[3] What Sherman Kent virtually excludes, Ransome underemphasizes: namely, that CI is critically important to the generation of positive intelligence about the adversary. Far from being divorced from positive intelligence, CI directly contributes to it. It plays a substantial role in positive intelligence collection.

The famous cases of Penkovskiy and Philby, both high-level penetrations of intelligence services, while relatively rare, represent Security Intelligence "nightmares". From a strictly security perspective, a penetration or "mole" on the order of a Kim Philby can do inestimable harm to the victimized service through compromise of its operations and personnel over an extended period of time. The damage can extend beyond the "mole's" tenure, given the possibility of his recruiting additional agents from the service's personnel. Moreover, such penetrations illustrate the vital contribution to Positive Intelligence that CI can make. When CI succeeds in "turning" or recruiting an officer of a hostile intelligence service in his own country or abroad, he may continue to operate under the control of a CI case officer. The potential always exists for this "turned" officer to develop into a "mole" of the dramatic stature of a Philby. The intelligence data at his command concerning his nation's strategic intentions, policies, military plans, operations, and capabilities may far surpass in importance the compromise of his own intelligence and security service. Thus the Positive Intelligence activities of CI should not be underemphasized, and as the subsequent treatment of counterespionage, security, and types of CI operations will show, a key role can be played by CI in the collection of foreign intelligence (FI). If Sherman Kent's dichotomy were applied to contemporary intelligence activities, both in the United States and abroad, CI would be found to have an important share in both categories.

Another important feature of CI that rarely receives the attention it deserves is that essential corollary to CI activity, Counterintelligence Information. Most descriptions of the CI function tend to concentrate on CI "activity." Sherman Kent, however, even in his primitive categorization of Security Intelligence, shows an awareness of this vital feature by mentioning "the knowledge and the activity" that must precede action taken against the threat. He is alluding to the process of gathering, compiling, analyzing, and using CI information to support the countering operation. Allen Dulles identifies CI Information in a very different way in describing the nature of counterintelligence. He refers to protective operations devoted to identifying a hostile intelligence service's targets, methods, and personnel as belonging to the field of counterespionage, and "the information derived from them is called counterintelligence."[4] Thus CI information is the "product" of counterespionage operations. Dulles further emphasizes the requirement for "rapid dissemination of CI information" among the various US agencies assigned the mission of counterespionage. Finally, he mentions "CI specialists" in the study of the Redl Case, 1902-1913—an extraordinary penetration of the Austrian military intelligence service's counterespionage branch by the Russian Okhrana: its chief, Alfred Redl, was a Russian agent. From this it might be inferred that CI information is a body of knowledge enriched through the patient analysis of key espionage cases of the past as well as the present. CI information then, as we know it today, is produced from basic analysis as well as from counterespionage itself. It is an essential input to the planning, execution, and subsequent evaluation of CI activity—an important component of which is counterespionage.

As Miles Copeland accurately observes, instructors in intelligence schools "argue endlessly" over the various definitions of counterespionage activities, and then for good reason: precise operational definitions of CI concepts have so far eluded its practitioners; the result is ambiguity and absence of uniform CI doctrine. By offering several prevalent but differing interpretations, Copeland illustrates the "porosity" of CI as a concept. CI is sometimes employed as an "inclusive" term denoting activities ranging from penetration of a hostile service to provision of physical security. At one end of this spectrum CI is viewed as essentially counterespionage (CE), which means "the penetration and manipulation of foreign espionage services;" at the other extreme, CI is deemed "straight security" denoting "purely defensive measures." Finally, there is the restricted notion of CI as the investigative activity conducted with respect to espionage cases.[5]

Counterespionage, Counterintelligence and Security

In the discussion so far, the effort has been made to illustrate that CI transcends the defensive notion of security and should be understood to include an aggressive and positive function as well. Much of the tension in the challenge of defining the concept of CI seems to have arisen because CI is often equated, in the main, with counterespionage. Dulles, as noted above, depicts CI as merely the "information derived" from counterespionage. The real battle lines form not around CI vs. Security, but because of the operational cross purposes that can arise between counterespionage (CE) and Security. In some intelligence institutions a "CI mentality" connotes an officer's obsessive security interest, whereas in others, the "CI mentality" refers to the individual's interest in a counterespionage approach. A comparison of the two will help clarify the dichotomy between CE and Security.

Christopher Felix provides an excellent discussion of CE drawing a sharp contrast with Security. In distinction to Security whose chief purpose is apprehending adversary intelligence agents (catching spies), "CE is an offensive operation, a means of obtaining intelligence about the oppostion by using—or, more usually, attempting to use—the opposition's operations."[6] Noting that successful CE operations require controlled, continual contact with (and ideally penetration of) the hostile intelligence service, Felix contrasts Security as "a defensive operation which seeks to destroy the enemy's operations and cut off all contact with him as dangerous."[7]

As CE acts to penetrate and exploit a hostile intelligence service's HUMINT operation, it is "controlling" it and thus neutralizing the threat it poses. Simultaneously, the CE operation creates the opportunity for collecting positive foreign intelligence. This intelligence may be of a relatively low order, such as observation of increased collection activity as a possible indicator of policy change and impending adversary behavior. Or it may be extremely sensitive data derived from a high-level penetration located close to the adversary's national decisionmakers.

Security, on the other hand, devotes its efforts to preventing hostile intelligence services from operating against the targets it is assigned to protect. On detection of a hostile HUMINT operation, Security seeks to identify all its personnel and then swiftly eliminate it. It does not share CE's concern for the potentially valuable information that could be derived from the hostile operation.

Those who see a dichotomy between CI and Security often identify this as a real "problem" because their concept of CI is limited primarily to CE activities. In their perspective, CI is seen to be generally offensive and positive, much of its value stemming from its utility for intelligence collection rather than merely from its defensive and protective function. This perspective on CI is not shared by all its practitioners; however, virtually all would agree that CE is an important activity—one of many that must be accomplished by CI.

In the contemporary practice of CI in the US Armed Forces, the "CE-dominant" perspective is balanced by concern with several other CI activities deemed vital to the continued effectiveness of military plans and operations, as well as the defense of military installations, personnel, and sensitive equipment. The sharp contrast that Felix draws between CE and Security is not evident in the military definition of CE. In JCS Pub. 1, for example, CE is defined as an "aspect of CI" in broad terms: "designed to detect, destroy, neutralize, exploit or prevent espionage activities through identification, penetration, manipulation, deception, and repression of individuals, groups, or organizations conducting or suspected of conducting espionage activities."[8] This definition is significant in that it incorporates a defensive mission and some of what Felix might term "aims" of security, yet also specifies a variety of positive, offensive CE actions to accomplish the mission.

So CE represents one of the "active" components of CI. The scope of CI activity also includes legitimate functions and activities that are essentially "passive" with respect to the hostile entity. They do not require direct contact with and penetration or control of the hostile entity. While not constituting Security or security measures *per se*, this "passive" component of CI activity nonetheless contributes directly to the maintenance of security.

It may thus be useful to adopt the "active-passive" terminology with respect to CI activity, for while rather general, these terms avoid such limited and distorted contrasts as "CE vs. Security." Because of the varied nature of its activity, its multiple purposes, and the application of the information it generates to positive intelligence as well as to CE and Security, CI transcends "protection" and "defense." Its functions may be more usefully defined as threefold: aggressive, preventive, and defensive.

It should be noted that the "issue" of CE vs. Security is not universal among the many intelligence and security services operating today. As a consequence of their fundamental *raison d'etre* and primary mission, the Soviet intelligence and security services do not reflect any such dichotomy. The principal service, the KGB, since its inception as the VCheka, has had as its primary mission that of internal security and maintenance of the regime (i.e., the rule of the CPSU). From its early activities directed at internal political foes, the scope of its mission has broadened, but political security remains as the fundamental one. An appraisal of the KGB reveals that by far the bulk of activity and resources is committed to the mission of maintaining the security of the Party's control and of carrying out its will, both at home and abroad. Thus the KGB earns its title as the "Sword and Shield" of the CPSU. The sword and shield is a metaphor, in effect, for the CI function. For the Soviets it is both aggressive and defensive, active and passive. As CI comprises the functional core and purpose of KGB activity, its operational philosophy reveals an unbroken continuum from Security to foreign intelligence collection.

The Current Threat: Multidisciplinary

Another important conceptual problem concerning the nature of CI stems from the traditional assumption that CI is counter-HUMINT. This assumption is related to the view that CI is almost solely CE, or should be—a misapprehension no doubt fostered by a long history of espionage, whereas technical means of collection are a relatively recent phenomenon. In today's intelligence environment the threat is much broader in scope than that posed by agent operations. So, while Soviet intelligence continues to emphasize HUMINT as a collection means, its capability in the other collection disciplines is formidable.

The "threat" is multidisciplinary, encompassing SIGINT, PHOTINT, and HUMINT. While much of the collection activity of a hostile service may be by clandestine means, much effort is devoted to overt collection as well, and may include a wide variety of targets. The assumption that CI is essentially counter-HUMINT tends to circumscribe the realm of required CI activity. The multidisciplinary concept places the CI threat in a truer perspective, and because the worldwide threat emanates from all three collection disciplines, countering it requires knowledge and activity beyond that usually associated with CE. Multidisciplinary CI activities require "all-source" information from non-CI organizations in order to be effective. CI must therefore combine all the intelligence disciplines and posses personnel well-versed in them, in order to indentify and assess the threat and to design and execute counter-measures.

Counterintelligence and Deception

One issue not fully appreciated with respect to CI is deception. With the World War II legacy of the Double Cross System, deception is frequently related to CE operations. Deception is seen to be effected through double-agent operations and penetrations or, as in Double Cross, via an entirely-controlled enemy HUMINT apparatus. As Masterman and Montagu have illustrated, a principal channel for deception can be the enemy's HUMINT "doubled" by CE activity, but often the deception must be supported by other reinforcement measures susceptible to the enemy's SIGINT and PHOTINT. Montagu has indicated that the success of the Double Cross System was made possible in large part because ULTRA permitted almost continual monitoring of enemy reaction to the deception, and actions to correct deficiencies or ameliorate problems could be taken quickly. Today, deception efforts cannot rely on such "special" aids because of advanced encryption techniques.

If deception is viewed from another standpoint—that is, not as a "positive" CI activity made possible by CE successes, but rather as a threat that CI must counter—then a problem arises. Where does deception fit on the CI threat spectrum? Since deception programs are almost always multidisciplinary in nature, should CI share responsibility for exposing them? Is CI the appropriate function for analyzing adversary deception and developing countermeasures to include counterdeception? Deception can be directed at several targets, but in this discussion it will be assumed that the foreign intelligence collection element is the key one. And here, the role of CI in identifying and countering deception may create bureaucratic tension. CI could have the function of assessing foreign intelligence operations—to ascertain, for example, in the event they are HUMINT, whether they have been "doubled" and are in fact controlled by the adversary. This function might place CI at odds with the foreign intelligence collectors should CI discover reason to doubt but not convincingly determine the standing of their sources.

Additionally, the counterespionage operations of CI itself may provide a channel for adversary deception. This is essentially an operational problem for CI, which while probably infrequent, can prove to be potentially serious. Should the adversary detect a successful CE penetration or double agent operation, it has as an option the "redoubling" of the agent or agents involved for use as a deception channel. A possibly more potent threat is posed to CI by an adversary intelligence service defector used by that service to transmit the deception. The acceptance of the deception could be enhanced if the adversary service permitted CI *apparently* to recruit and "run" one of its officers for an extended length of time before arranging circumstances for a false defection (in a manner to further enhance the officer's *bona fides* in the eyes of his CI "case" officer). Then, buried among the mass of detail obtained from him in the post-defection interrogation, a subtle deception message is reinforced by a myriad of other details sent by other channels.

Given CI's experience in the conduct of counterespionage activities, including the mounting of deceptions, it seems clear that CI could play an important role in countering the deception threat at least in the exercise of active countermeasures themselves. Just as the counterespionage and other resources of CI may be used in deception, they may also be employed for counterdeception. For the task of identifying deception delivered through channels other than HUMINT, the role of CI becomes more problematical. Since CI must contend with a multidisciplinary threat, and assuming it is equipped with the skills necessary to identify if not always to counter it, CI seems a useful focal point for counterdeception activity. Endowed with the requisite analytical resources and supplied the necessary information, CI could in theory support or even manage the defense against deception. While a separate CI counterdeception analysis of intelligence would likely produce bureaucratic conflict with both the collection and analytical communities, such a "devil's advocate" role for CI may be a necessary price to pay if the threat of deception is taken seriously. A final argument favoring CI for this role concerns the professional orientation and perspective of the discipline. CI officers are more likley to possess the state of mind necessary for counterdeception analysis. Their outlook is tempered by long experience and close contact with a conspiratorial and clandestine enemy, and this endows them with greater potential sensitivity to deception than either the collector or the analyst.

US and Soviet Approaches to CI

A principal objective of this discussion is to assess the US CI program as it exists today as well as the new requirements deemed necessary for the decade of the 1980's. Thus a comparison of US and Soviet CI doctrine and operations is appropriate, for there is a very important factor affecting the conduct of CI that needs to be addressed. This factor exercises a continuing and shaping influence on the intelligence and security function in both authoritarian and democratic societies. It is the political and ideological milieu within which CI must operate. The differences between US and Soviet CI doctrine, operations, and organization sketched out below are deeply rooted in the political history and culture of the two societies. Out of these differences we can develop some useful insights about future requirements for US counterintelligence.

As noted already, the role of the KGB is to serve as the "sword and shield" of the Party. Its primary missions are internal security and the maintenance of Party rule, countering threats both foreign and domestic. While this essential political security mission dates back to the first days of the VCheka, it remains vital today and imparts to the KGB its fundamental character as a vast CI apparatus. Over the years following the Revolution, additional missions and activities have accrued to the KGB commensurate with the evolving international role of the USSR and the needs of successive Soviet leaderships. Of the KGB's many pursuits, foreign intelligence collection and the conduct of covert action abroad are perhaps the most visible and troublesome to western CI officers. As with the internal security missions, these activities also proceed from the basic Leninist ideological construct: the "life and death struggle" between the "two opposing world systems" of capitalism and socialism. In the sword and shield CI metaphor, the sword is the KGB's offensive component striking at enemies abroad and within, "protecting the Revolution." In the early days this involved only the defense of "the Socialist Motherland." Today the KGB assumes the offensive role of ensuring the "progressive and inexorable shift in the world correlation of forces in favor of the USSR and World Socialism."

The ideological milieu created by Marxism-Leninism fosters an integrated operational doctrine, spanning the broad range of the KGB's intelligence and security functions. The coordinated and mutually supportive activity of the KGB's foreign intelligence and CI elements reflect this doctrinal continuum.

The Committee of State Security, USSR, is the world's largest intelligence and security service. Centralized in the KGB are the various aggressive, preventive, and defensive CI functions. It is the only Soviet institution empowered to conduct CI activity. At home and abroad, the KGB has sole CI jurisdiction, exercising these powers over the Main Intelligence Directorate of the General Staff (GRU) and the Soviet Armed Forces as well.

Given the all-encompassing role of the KGB and its integrated operational doctrine, it is not surprising that this one entity should have responsibility for a range of intelligence activities that in the West, for example, are frequently divided among separate agencies. The KGB performs functions analogous to those of the CIA, FBI, NSA, Armed Forces CI elements, the Secret Service protective and many Treasury Department investigative functions, the Immigration and Naturalization Service's customs and border police functions, as well as many performed by the US Coast Guard.

The Soviet approach to intelligence and security is not without important drawbacks, as "The Great Terror" under Stalin illustrates. When the Soviet political system moves from Party control to control by one individual, the functions of the intelligence and security service are unimpaired—but the direction of its activity changes. When Stalin achieved plenary power, the service moved from the "action arm" of the Party to the "action arm" of Stalin himself. In the Soviet scheme there are no firm checks and balances that can inhibit the direction of the service's activity. The "organs of state security" have been described as a mindless monster—and whoever gives it a mind exerts control.

Another drawback implicit in the Soviet approach to the intelligence and security function stems from the close and currently almost symbiotic relationship between the KGB and Party leadership. Under these conditions, where the KGB enjoys an unparalleled status within the Soviet political system, a great potential exists for "politicization" of the intelligence process. One wonders to what extent intelligence products are made to reflect the preconceptions shared by Brezhnev and other Politburo consumers. How adequate and objective is the intelligence support for decisionmaking in policy arenas for which the KGB itself shares growing responsibility?

Finally, as noted earlier, the KGB emphasizes HUMINT as a collection means. Some observers argue that the Soviets prefer clandestinely-derived information over that gained through overt collection and analysis of open-source material. According to Alexander Orlov, a major Soviet intelligence and security service defector of the past, the Soviets regard as "true intelligence (razvedka)" only that "procured by undercover agents and secret informants in defiance of the laws of the foreign country in which they operate."[9] Perhaps the Soviet "conspiratorial" outlook on life gives more credence to the human collector in the traditional espionage role. The Soviet emphasis on agent operations is consistent with that essentially CI "ethos" infusing the KGB with its legacy of counterespionage activities.

Another and perhaps more disturbing interpretation of the KGB's interest in HUMINT is that in the relatively benign "operational climate" of western countries, this technique has proved to be a continually productive and rewarding collection means. Caution should be exercised in offering generalizations about any "emphasis" or "preference" for one means over another by a hostile service like the KGB. This service is highly competent in technical collection, and the generalization about HUMINT should not be permitted to divert attention from the essential fact that the threat faced by western CI is worldwide and truly multidisciplinary.

In comparison with the Soviet intelligence and security services, the US intelligence community differs in many important respects. Its collection techniques are multidisciplinary with important emphasis (and to some degree, reliance) on technical means (perhaps the old cliché about US fascination with technological gadgetry is of some significance). The pluralized US intelligence community comprises agencies that are in some ways functionally distinct. They do share significant areas of overlapping jurisdiction, however, and CI is one of them, creating fertile ground for difficulties in coordination. The political framework in which CI operates is quite contrary to that of the Soviet Union, and in some areas, US political values are viewed in real or potential conflict with intelligence activities. This controversy will not be addressed here. Suffice it to say, that, perhaps partly because of this tension and the community's decentralization, US intelligence doctrine is both ambiguous and fragmented. The problem is most pronounced in the arena of CI. At least four broad perspectives on the nature and purpose of CI are still manifest in the decentralized US intelligence community: (1) the "law enforcement" view (sometimes disparaged as the "cop mentality"); (2) CI as an "adjunct to collection" (emphasizing counterespionage for positive intelligence purposes); (3) CI to identify and neutralize hostile activity; and (4) CI to enhance operational security (to safeguard, for example, military operations and exercises, sensitive installations, personnel, and equipment).

United States Counterintelligence as Defined by Executive Order 12036

This typology by no means represents an exhaustive listing of current US CI perspectives, but it does serve as a useful backdrop for Executive Order 12036, "United States Intelligence Activities," in force since January 1978. The Order provides an important basic definition of intelligence—including *both* "foreign intelligence and counterintelligence." CI is thus distinct from foreign intelligence and, by inference, comprises half of the intelligence function. The inference is debatable, but the Order does support the contention that CI enjoys coordinate status with other intelligence disciplines and activities rather than the secondary one to which it is often relegated. The Order further describes CI as both "information gathered" and "activities conducted," the purpose of which is to "protect against espionage and other clandestine intelligence activities, sabotage, international terrorist activities or assassinations conducted for or on behalf of foreign powers, organizations or persons, *but not including personnel, physical, document or communications security.*"[10]

The explicit exclusion of the latter four activities is an important facet of the definition, for all save communications security were formerly provinces of CI. This step should help reduce ambiguity as to the true function of CI, because the past conduct of these activities by CI helped encourage the notion of CI as fundamentally a security function. An equally significant aspect of the definition is its provision that CI organizations and operations are to counter a broader spectrum of threats. Countering hostile foreign intelligence and security services is but one responsibility of CI. International terrorism and other hostile acts emanating from foreign sources are included as well. The definition makes clear that CI is directed against foreign threats only.

The Executive Order considerably expands the requirements placed on US CI, the exclusion of strict security functions notwithstanding. In addition to specifying a broader threat, the Order's definition of CI is unique in emphasizing the important concept of CI information. The mission statements for operational CI entities expand their role from simply conducting activities against the threat by explicitly charging them with "the production and dissemination of counterintelligence studies or reports." This is a new dimension for many of these entities, and requires the development of CI knowledge (versus action alone). By virtue of the Order, US CI must embrace the new role of producing intelligence based on the analysis of information generated by its own operations and from other sources. This change would seem to model CI on foreign intelligence and on the collection, production, and dissemination cycle.

This new emphasis on CI information is consistent with the Executive Order's treatment of the National Security Council Special Coordinating Committee's (NSC/SCC) responsibilities for CI. Beyond developing standards and guidelines for CI activities and resolving interagency differences over the implementation of CI policy, the NSC/SCC must also formulate and monitor guidelines governing the "central records" of CI information.[11] These central records (or data base) are essential to effective CI activities and proceed from data produced by operational CI. The production of CI information will support the NSC/SCC in one of its principal tasks—that of submitting to the President a periodic CI assessment of hostile threats and the effectiveness of CI activities taken to counter them.

The language of Executive Order 12036 is sensitive to many of the problems that have plagued US CI in the past. It has helped to redirect CI doctrine, which is now moving along a path toward a more coherent, cohesive, and standard form. The Order also has given the previously fragmented community definitive mission assignments, including both the conduct of CI activities and the production of CI reports and studies. With respect to the former, the Order provides the authority for CI entities to conduct, based on specified coordination, activities outside their areas of geographic primacy—thus ensuring some continuity of operations.

Active and Passive Components of Counterintelligence Activity

It was suggested earlier that it might be useful to describe the CI function as aggressive, preventive, and defensive. CI activities conducted in fulfillment of this threefold function have both active and passive components.

Passive Counterintelligence seeks to counter potentially hostile, concealed acts. In other words, it comprises measures undertaken to protect against what the adversary *may* do. Its function is essentially preventive and defensive. Typical of passive CI operations and activities are the following: (1) defensive source programs; (2) Technical Surveillance Countermeasures (TSCM); (3) Security Education; and (4) estimating or assessing the vulnerability of sensitive installations and activities to the CI threat. The first, defensive source programs, is a measure aimed at identifying possible "threat targets" among personnel and creating a program to monitor them. This activity involves developing a system of "sources" within the institution presumed under threat, to observe the actions of personnel deemed vulnerable to the hostile intelligence service or organization. Technical Surveillance Countermeasures refers to the set of measures employed to identify hostile technical devices planted by the adversary for collection purposes. A good example is the activity which led to the Great Seal Case—the discovery of Soviet acoustical devices (bugs) hidden within the ornamental Seal of the United States at the US Embassy in Moscow. Security Education is self-explanatory. It is aimed at heightening the security awareness of personnel and alerting them to the CI threat. By educating them as to the procedures to be followed should they be approached by a representative of a hostile service, or subjected to recruitment efforts, Security Education seeks to reduce the chances that such hostile actions will go unreported to CI authorities. Finally, estimating the vulnerability of installations and activities is conducted by CI to support the planning and implementation of security measures. A good past example is found in the US Army's "SAVE Program" or Senstive Activities Vulnerability Estimate. Because CI is knowledgeable as to the current threat (for example, the capabilities and presence of a hostile intelligence service or international terrorist organization in the locale or region concerned), it is well-equipped to estimate vulnerability and make recommendations to reduce it.

The CI activities described above are passive, aimed at forestalling or limiting the success of potential actions by the hostile entity. The four activities offered as examples are security-oriented, but even though they assist in enhancing security, they should not be regarded as security activities per se. They constitute CI activities because their execution requires substantial CI "knowledge" and information.

Active Counterintelligence differs from passive CI in that its fundamental purpose is to target and counter the *ongoing* threatening activity of the hostile entity. Operations conducted by CI to this end are of two types: investigative activity and countering activity. The former has as its purpose the identification of the ongoing hostile action itself as well as those persons employed in it. Active CI's countering activity—counterespionage (CE), countersabotage (CS), and counterterrorism (CT)—constitute CI's aggressive aspect, because they involve operations directed against the actions of the hostile entity. As the description of typical active CI operations will show, an effective counterespionage operation may counter the hostile action by "turning" it and using it against its originator to the benefit of friendly forces.

Specific Purposes and Operations of Active Counterintelligence

The "counters" all proceed on the basis of initial investigative activity. **Detection** is active CI's first phase and fundamental purpose. It seeks to identify the hostile activity and all individuals involved in it, and through investigations, to develop probative evidence. In the case of an adversary intelligence service, this would include its collection operation and intelligence targets, its officers and coopted personnel. CI investigations may be routine, aimed at identifying persons who are for various reasons vulnerable to entrapment or recruitment by a hostile service. Or these investigative activities may be aimed at the neutralization of personnel known to be in contact with or under the control of the hostile service. Both witting and unwitting agents are the targets of CI investigations.

Counterintelligence investigations are technically difficult and costly to mount. The basic tool of surveillance, employing human resources against a mobile target, requires a great deal of manpower to be effective. In some societies, laws respecting the privacy of individuals pose serious obstacles to CI investigations. The US Fair Credit Reporting Act, for example, effectively precludes the FBI from checking an individual's credit rating without alerting him to the investigation, for the FBI request is placed in his credit file. Therefore, CI investigations in the United States must be based on a standard of reasonable suspicion or cause.

Detection is one principal purpose of active CI because, on occasion, circumstances may dictate that further countering operations are inappropriate or unnecessary. Once the hostile operation is fully detected, minor steps may be taken to limit the scope of access of its coopted personnel (without either their or the hostile service's knowledge). Or, in the event that compromise of certain information to the adversary is deemed appropriate, the operation may be permitted to continue unhindered, albeit closely monitored. A nation may actually desire that a potential adversary know of a new military capability so as to enhance deterrence, and a given adversary may more readily accept and appreciate this capability should knowledge of it be acquired through clandestine means.

Active CI has two other main purposes besides that of detecting an ongoing hostile activity: **Neutralization** and/or **Manipulation** of that activity. CI operations pursuing these goals seek to capture, control, or "turn" the hostile activity against the hostile entity. The "ideal" way to turn the hostile activity is through what is generally referred to as double agent operations, a feature of counterespionage. In actuality, there are at least three distinct types of "doubling" operations that may be employed, but each has many esoteric variations. For the purpose of this discussion, Penetration, Double Agent, and Induced Double Agent operations will be described as clearly distinguishable examples of the neutralization and manipulation techniques of aggressive CI.

The penetration of a hostile intelligence service or international terrorist organization is accomplished through the "doubling" of its agents. That is to say, CI causes a defection or effects a "recruitment in place'' of the hostile entity's personnel—usually officers of a foreign intelligence service. Following his recruitment by CI, the individual continues to operate for the hostile entity but is really under the control of CI.

A double agent operation differs importantly from penetration. In this case, a representative of the hostile entity approaches an individual for the purpose of recruiting him and the individual reports the attempt. CI then mounts an operation wherein this individual permits his ''fake recruitment'' by the hostile service or entity. Thus the adversary's operation, with its apparent recruitment and penetration of friendly forces, is actually controlled by CI.

The third type of double operation, that which is ''induced,'' is also referred to as a ''Dangle'' operation. This variant involves the ''setting up'' of an individual by CI in such manner as to attract the hostile entity. CI thus lures a hostile intelligence service, for example, by ''dangling'' the bait before it with the hope of inducing an approach and recruitment. Once the adversary takes the bait and recruits the individual, the operation proceeds under the control of CI in the same manner as a regular double agent operation. The critical aspect of an induced double agent operation is obviously the credibility of the ''dangled'' individual—the type of bait and how it is presented by CI to its quarry.

Running a double agent is no simple matter. He must be provided with a continuing supply of ''feed'' material of sufficient accuracy and sensitivity to maintain credibility with the hostile service. The selection and preparation of a double agent's feed material must be carefully coordinated with parallel CI operations so that the adversary finds no contradictions in the information it is receiving. A serious contradiction could result in one or more double agents being compromised. Perhaps the best discussion of running double agents in wartime for deception purposes is found in Masterman's *The Double-Cross System* and Montagu's *Beyond Top Secret Ultra*.[12]

Basic Form and Common Features of Aggressive Counterintelligence Operations

In most cases the targets of operations like those illustrated above are hostile intelligence services or international terrorist organizations. The information generated from them is primarily of value to

CI, for it assists in the identification and countering of the ongoing threat from these entities. As was suggested earlier, however, aggressive CI operations may have positive intelligence targets as well. Penetrations may yield a rich bounty of foreign intelligence insofar as the doubled agent has access to it.

These operations have as their common purpose the detection, neutralization, and manipulation of the threatening entity or activity. The first two are essential to the CI mission. Manipulation is more difficult, but in wartime this may develop into the primary purpose of CI's double agent operations. Then, neutralization of an enemy service's HUMINT collection may be effected through the identification and arrest of enemy agents. If CI has a capability for thorough detection (and is confident in its ability to detect enemy agents), it may opt to "double" these agents, controlling them as a valuable deception channel. This may be easier to accomplish under wartime conditions because of the generally heightened security posture which reduces vulnerability to collection, the special wartime investigatory and detention powers of security agencies, and the fact that war has eliminated the legal presence of adversary intelligence personnel in the country.

In peacetime, neutralization measures may range along a wide spectrum depending on the political considerations at the time. At one extreme is arrest, indictment, and prosecution of hostile personnel and their cooptees; at the other is the quiet *persona non grata* expulsion of the foreign officer. Most neutralization activity takes place in the middle ground, where double agent operations and monitoring of cases are more typical.

Neutralization of a hostile collection threat in peacetime may also involve deception. Because the adversary's collection is most frequently multidisciplinary, and thus extraordinarily difficult to counter in all its forms, CI may choose deception as the most viable method. It is not always possible or even necessary to control the adversary's local collection apparatus in the fashion of the World War II Double-Cross System in order to carry out a deception, especially if the deception has as its aim the creation of ambiguity in adversary estimates. If CI cannot control the adversary's collection, it can nevertheless design a "feed" program corresponding to each collection discipline. This may mislead the adversary as to the real purpose or capability of an activity, installation, technology, or weapon system which CI seeks to protect.

The Value of Double Agent/Penetration Operations

There are a number of important "payoffs" that accompany aggressive CI operations, but two stand out. First, these operations will identify one or more hostile agents and provide insight into the *modus operandi,* tradecraft and paraphernalia, general targets, and desired information of the hostile intelligence service. Second, double agent and penetration operations "narrow" the threat by letting a case run on under control. This value rests on the assumption that it is generally too costly for the hostile intelligence service to provide multiple coverage of its targets. Agent networks are costly and hard to develop—valuable resources not likely to be wasted in duplicative efforts. The adversary's legal intelligence presence has an upper limit also, and these officers will, by this theory, be directed to collect against the widest possible array of intelligence targets. A potential problem exists with this general formulation, however. If the adversary service discovers its officers have been recruited or its agents doubled, it may attempt to "redouble" them. Should the adversary be successful at this, he will, in effect, be controlling the CI operation, not the other way around. The hostile service then may even induce, or more likely be content to control and monitor a CI penetration case, so that CI resources are spent in a blind alley. This frees the adversary service's other clandestine operations from CI attention, should CI be confident that it has detected and controlled all that hostile service's activity against a specific target. (While such permutations as these are easy to conjure up, they would be extremely difficult and dangerous to put in practice.)

Several other benefits accrue to CI from aggressive double agent operations. They permit the development of biographic and personality data on hostile personnel as well as general information about the behavior and operations of the hostile entity. This data provides key facts useful in the "spotting and assessing" of hostile personnel for the purpose of recruitment. It also assists in the important task of identifying and tracking hostile intelligence personnel or terrorists as they move about the world under fictitious identities and cover organizations.

An especially valuable aspect of double agent operations stems from their ability to support other aggressive CI operations. The double agent can provide a key mechanism by which CI can support a previously recruited penetration agent. This penetration agent may be recruited abroad, serve in his home country for a period of time, and then resurface in the field some years later. Contact with him may be broken in the interim. Once contact is reestablished with CI, a safe device is needed to provide for meetings with his CI contact and/or case officer. A double agent operation can be useful for this purpose. The penetration agent receives instructions and passes on intelligence to his controllers under the guise of a "meet" with one of his agents (actually one of CI's double agents). With the double agent installed as a "false" source providing the needed "feed" material, the penetration agent has more time to pursue the intelligence targets given him by CI, rather than those of his parent service. This latter burden is shouldered by his CI controllers and "satisfied" by the feed material transmitted via the "false" source or double agent. An interesting side benefit of this scheme is that CI can thus help enhance or at least maintain the status of its penetration agent within his parent intelligence service. The penetration agent's "false" source can pass "valuable" feed so as to heighten the credibility and perceived worth of both the source and the penetration who purports to run him.

Another general but very real benefit of aggressive CI comes as the consequence of successful induced double agent operations, or "Dangles." The intelligence service that has fallen victim to this ploy will likely exercise great caution when presented with recruitment opportunities that seem "too good to be true." Dangle operations can disrupt the confidence and thus the competence of the service in assessing "walk-ins" and apparent defectors. An individual with access to sensitive material who offers his services to a hostile entity can become an important "defector in place." If that hostile service has not previously assessed or approached the individual, his action in contacting them may be initially regarded as a CI provocation. Thus the potential traitor's first attempt at contact may be rebuffed, and his subsequent efforts to contact representatives of the hostile service may well bring him to the attention of CI. Like all good intelligence operations, the induced double agent operation buys time and opportunity to deal with the threat.

The inherent potential of double agent or penetration operations for positive intelligence collection has been mentioned earlier and needs no reiteration here. It may be observed, however, that the higher the penetration is placed, the grander the intelligence coup for the controlling service.[13]

A special benefit of aggressive CI operations stems from their peculiar feature of establishing a known channel of information to the hostile intelligence service, and thus ultimately to the consumers of that service's intelligence product. Such a channel may be used for a variety of purposes, including deception.

On the plane of more common CI pursuits and day-to-day problems of countering a hostile intelligence service's activities, aggressive CI operations have their chief value in neutralization. For closing down a hostile agent network and/or expelling a hostile intelligence officer, double agent operations are an essential tool. They provide the basis for *persona non grata* actions and create the opportunity to gather the probative evidence required for the arrest, indictment, and trial of hostile personnel and their cooptees.

Counterintelligence Analysis: Its Purposes and Products

This discussion of counterintelligence would be lacking if, after illustrating active and passive CI activity and aggressive CI operations, it failed next to focus on their "essential corrollary," CI information. It is not necessary here to argue the obvious requirement for a strong analytical capability in the intelligence community. It is important, however, to point out that the importance of intelligence analysis is not limited to the foreign intelligence community alone, but that CI too depends on the analysis, production, and timely dissemination of information.

In a fashion much like foreign intelligence collection, which provides the raw material for analysis, CI activities generate valuable information that also requires rigorous analysis. Similarly, both foreign intelligence collection and CI operations proceed from a preexisting information base (and knowledge of the threat) that directly affects their targeting, planning, execution, and subsequent evaluation. There are various kinds of CI information products with varying utility for other elements of the intelligence community.

One of the more regular and vital products of CI analysis is the threat assessment. Its purpose is to define and analyze the threatening capability of a hostile entity, a foreign intelligence service or an international terrorist organization. These assessments are designed to encompass all hostile collection and other activity and would likely incorporate all-source intelligence in analyzing the worldwide and multidisciplinary threat posed by an adversary service such as the KGB.

A wide variety of CI products are generated in this effort. They differ by topic and scope: some are special narrowly-focused studies and others may be general surveys. A special study may concern the operations of a hostile service in a given country or locale, against a specific set of targets. A survey may seek to aggregate the threat, for example, of the Soviet and Bloc intelligence and security services to NATO or the US Army in Europe.

These threat-oriented products have many consumers beyond those in the CI and foreign intelligence communities. They are employed in support of military operations and plans to assist, for example, in developing security measures. The data generated by threat analyses are incorporated in vulnerability assessments and protection programs (e.g., where and how best to test a new weapon system undergoing R&D, conduct a field maneuver, improve an installation's security, etc.).

Another very important purpose of CI production, aside from providing threat assessments, concerns the activity of CI itself. The examination of past operations, hostile and friendly, and the conduct of "post mortems" enables CI to measure and evaluate the effectiveness of its operations against the threat. A valuable consequence of these evaluations is the development of a data base and a fund of "operational experience" on hostile *modus operandi:* cover mechanisms, techniques of recruitment, funding, communications, personnel, training, etc. This data base is instrumental in supporting both ongoing CI activity and the training of CI officers. The fund of knowledge on *modus operandi,* behavioral profiles, and personalia can prove to be very important to efforts aimed at countering both international terrorism and hostile intelligence operations.[14]

Counterintelligence information also can be an important input to positive intelligence. Disregarding for the moment the special class of information potentially derived from a high-level penetration agent, it should be noted that more conventional counterespionage operations can also produce important insights into adversary intentions. Through contact with the hostile service, CI can assess the level of hostile intelligence activity, a useful indicator of intentions and a "tip off" of subsequent adversary behavior. Increased intelligence activity and hostile presence may be a clue to impending military action. CI information further contributes to positive intelligence through what is called basic encyclopedic production. The reports, studies, and appraisals of this nature are descriptive rather than analytical, and represent comprehensive source documents detailing the role, structure, functioning, personalities, logistics, training, locations, etc., of all foreign intelligence and security services. This data assumes greater importance, for example, with respect to a service like the KGB, because of its recent ascendancy and influential role in Soviet policy under the Brezhnev regime.

The discussion so far has been devoted largely to illustrating differing perspectives and important issues affecting the discipline of CI. The description of CI activity, some kinds of operations, and CI information has been included to give some flavor of the nature of CI. Throughout this discussion, CI has been approached in a generic fashion. That is, despite the occasional use of specific national examples, it should not be taken to represent a description or assessment of US CI in particular or, for that matter, any other nation's CI practices. This abstract orientation will now shift. In the concluding section, the intent is to suggest several measures to improve US CI in and for the future.

Measures to Improve US Counterintelligence in the Next Decade

As has been noted earlier in this discussion, and elsewhere by other observers, the US CI community is fragmented both philosophically and organizationally. No fewer than five operational entities engage in CI: elements of the CIA, FBI, Army, Navy, and Air Force. In this profusion of CI entities which also includes the non-operational CI components of OSD, DIA, and NSC/SCC, there is a wide divergence with regard to their CI philosophy and relationship with other elements of the intelligence community. Some of these operational CI entities are elements of organizations primarily concerned with law enforcement and criminal investigations. Their philosophy, institutional makeup, and commitment of manpower and other resources show they are not purely CI organizations. To a large extent they take a "law enforcement" approach to CI. Moreover, some of these CI organizations have little if any institutional affiliation or operational integration with the positive foreign intelligence elements of their parent organizations. The US CI community thus lacks unified doctrine and a consolidated institutional base with a true intelligence perspective. As these CI entities meet the threat individually, and occasionally in concert, they bring to bear a variety of procedures and philosophies, and greatly varying commitments of the resources needed for the overall effort.

Given this situation, Executive Order 12036 represents an important step toward meeting the worldwide, all-source, multidisciplinary CI threat faced by this country. It is only one step, however, along a continuum of actions needed to enhance the US CI effort. While the thrust of the Order is often viewed as preventing abuses of the privacy of US persons and organizations—such as had been alleged in connection with the acquisition and storage of information—its positive features also should be recognized and genuinely implemented. It contains valuable language designed to make available to the US intelligence community and its consumers all the bits and pieces of information developed by narrowly-focused organizations and operations. The important issue here is how to ensure that the information generated by traditionally operations-oriented CI entities is made available to the other CI consumers on a comprehensive and timely basis. The Executive Order with its new requirement of CI production and dissemination shows sensitivity to this issue. Moreover, its provision that the NSC/SCC develop and monitor guidelines governing the maintenance of "central records" of CI information indicates awareness of an additional and related issue for the US CI community. This is the question of how to develop from operational data and the narrow perspective of operational entities (many of which give low priority to CI and CI collection) a comprehensive, all-source, multidisciplinary CI data base with which to support the US intelligence community and its varied consumers—the operators, the commanders, and the policymakers. To address these issues effectively, Executive Order 12036 must be implemented in both spirit and letter, and new mechanisms and specific actions will be required to do this.

A first step that would provide fundamental benefits for US CI is the requirement to strip away from CI those functions and demands on resources that diffuse its efforts. CI must be clearly separated from law enforcement and criminal investigation. A sharp line should be drawn between the agencies, organizations, and elements engaged in CI activities and those concerned with security (specifically including operational security, OPSEC) and law enforcement. And in addition to this separation, CI must be closely integrated with the positive intelligence community. CI is an intelligence function, and only as an integral element of the intelligence community can it proceed as an all-source, multidisciplinary function with the high priority it deserves. A new focus on CI as an active production entity is required.

Another more specific institutional measure that could be taken to enhance the future US CI effort concerns the Defense Department. That would be the creation of a center in DOD (with powers and resources far exceeding the current CI Working Group) with which to provide a single focus for CI policy and management of CI resources among the armed services. It would serve to resolve the present differences in doctrine and procedures among the various military CI entities. This new agency would require JCS or OSD chartering and would concern itself solely with foreign CI. Along with the creation of the DOD CI agency, and subsumed under it, would be an all-source, multidisciplinary DOD CI Threat Analysis Center. This threat analysis center should be endowed with a CI data base and significant analytical resources of its own, focused on the totality of the threat to DOD, without regard to the parochial and fragmented perspectives of the military departments. An obvious requirement for such an organization is that it be staffed by professional intelligence analysts who have developed competence in all-source, multidisciplinary CI. The personnel selection would be difficult. Such experienced individuals are not in abundant supply, and neither the ranks of CI operators nor specialized analysts (i.e., in one intelligence discipline) provide ideal candidates.

Certain benefits of these suggestions seem evident—the potential for centralization and coordination of both operations and data in one entity. Such an arrangement would further heighten the supportive interaction between CI and foreign intelligence, with benefits for both. But several general issues would arise that, common as they are to institutional innovations in government generally, are difficult to resolve. The question of who would control these entities and the data base created, parochialism, and the perennial "rice bowl" problem seem unavoidable. Other questions might include the following: who shares in the information, how is operational data protected and compartmentalization maintained, how will dissemination be handled, what are the legal ramifications associated with the CI data base, and how will this DOD CI agency interface with the CIA, FBI and other intelligence agencies in terms of policy, operations, and resources?

A different approach might be taken in the effort to enhance US CI that would involve institutional changes at a higher level than

DOD. It is general knowledge that within the intelligence community there are committee structures to address various intelligence disciplines and functions. Serious thought should be given to creating such a structure with a national CI jurisdiction. This would bring the necessary focus to the complex and diverse realm of CI, and at the same time elevate it to a truly coordinate status with other intelligence disciplines.

An attractive spinoff from efforts to establish a national CI perspective is the development of a training program of common interest to the entire CI community. This would be an important means for unifying CI doctrine and procedures as well as imparting multidisciplinary, all-source capability to CI personnel.

A final recommendation is to satisfy the longstanding requirement for clear statutory authority for the conduct of CI activities in all their variants. Furthermore, clear guidelines are needed to facilitate and encourage the development of an all-source, multidisciplinary data base, along with the strictest safeguards for operational data.

These measures are recommended both as real solutions to real problems in the current US CI community and as stimuli for further discussion. They are limited in scope and address only a small part of the issues surrounding the question of US CI requirements for the future. If one theme is to emerge, however, that should cause little controversy, it is the immediate need to consolidate the US CI effort and to upgrade its role and standing in the intelligence community.

Notes

1. Sherman Kent, *Strategic Intelligence For American World Policy* (Princeton: Princeton University Press, 1949 and 1966), pp. 209-210.
2. Harry Howe Ransome, *The Intelligence Establishment* (Cambridge: Harvard University Press, 1970), p. 14.
3. Ibid.
4. Allen Dulles, *The Craft of Intelligence* (New York: Harper and Row, 1963), p. 121.
5. Miles Copeland, *Without Cloak or Dagger* (New York: Simon and Schuster, 1974), p. 161.
6. Christopher Felix, *A Short Course in the Secret War* (New York: Dutton, 1963), p. 143.
7. *Ibid.*, p. 150.
8. Department of Defense, *Dictionary of Military and Associated Terms,* JCS Pub. 1 (Washington, 1974), p. 90.
9. Alexander Orlov, *Handbook of Intelligence and Guerrilla Warfare* (Ann Arbor: University of Michigan Press, 1963), p. 5.

10. Executive Order 12036, ''United States Intelligence Activities,'' (24 January 1978). Emphasis added.
11. *Ibid.*
12. See Chapter 1, pp. 17-33, and Chapter 3, p. 58 in Sir John C. Masterman, *The Double-Cross System in the War of 1939 to 1945* (New Haven: Yale University Press, 1972), and Ewen E. S. Montagu, *Beyond Top Secret Ultra* (New York: Coward, McCann and Geoghegan, 1978), Chapter 4, pp. 36-45.
13. See Zwy Aldouby and Jerrold Ballinger, *The Shattered Silence: The Eli Cohen Affair* (New York: Coward, McCann and Geoghegan, 1971) for an account of the Isreali agent, Eli Cohen, who successfully penetrated the Syrian defense establishment prior to his arrest and execution.
14. See Robert H. Kupperman, *Facing Tomorrow's Terrorist Incident Today* (Washington: Department of Justice, 1977) for an excellent argument illustrating the importance of intelligence in the effort to counter international terrorism. In Kupperman's words, ''intelligence is the first line of defense.''

Discussants

Mr. Newton S. Miler: It is not easy, nor can one feel very confident, to reenter this world where, it has been said, the tortuous logic of counterintelligence prevails. I do take some heart, however, from the fact that there are a great many here who have been able to avoid the label of "counterintelligence professionals." For at least these next two days, straight logic may pervail.

If we are to answer the question, "What is counterintelligence?," we certainly need to think straight and logically. We also need to consider answering the question in two ways: First, we need to consider an answer that will tell the people and the government what counterintelligence is. Any government that produces proposed legislation such as the early spring versions of the National Intelligence Act of 1980 (S. 2284), needs all the help it can get in clearing up the misunderstandings, misrepresentations and confusions about intelligence and counterintelligence.

Then we need to consider answering the question more elaborately, along the lines of pre-1973 CIA CI definitions, Executive Order 12036, S. 2284, Mr. Zuehlke's essay, the definitions promulgated by the Joint Chiefs of Staff, or a combination of these.

Unfortunately, there seems to be no easy way to explain counterintelligence. Because effective counterintelligence is a combination of so many aspects of the intelligence business and other political, military, economic and societal factors, just trying to list them would take more time than I have been allotted.

Explaining counterintelligence is a lot like trying to explain how to understand art. As Mr. Zuehlke has illustrated, there are many schools and movements. There may be a Leonardo da Vinci or a Grandma Moses. There are expressionists and illustrators. There is fluidity and an interrelationship between the "useful arts" and the "fine arts." But underlying it all there are fundamental disciplines: color, composition, drawing, form, perspective. It is the way these fundamentals are used that distinguishes good art.

And so it is with good counterintelligence. Underlying every good counterintelligence system are disciplines of:

1. Knowledge of the enemy, foreign intelligence and security services;

2. A secure, properly compartmented counterintelligence and intelligence system;

3. The ability to research and analyze centralized counterintelligence information;
4. The resources to conduct investigations and operations; and
5. A comprehensive training program in which selected personnel learn the fundamentals and subsequently acquire or reacquire additional disciplinary skills.

Now, let us consider how to answer the question for the public and even for the intelligence community itself. Let us try to return to square one. Let us temporarily set aside all the definitions we have so laboriously considered. Let's start with this basic statement: Counterintelligence is detailed knowledge about all the activities of foreign intelligence and security services, and it is the development of resources to advance our national interest by countering those activities.

Oversimplified? Maybe. But does not that statement tell us what counterintelligence is and what we want counterintelligence to do? And is it not clear enough to permit the government and the people to understand the purpose of a counterintelligence system? Probably not.

I say "probably not" because we have gone beyond the point in our society where we can accept simple statements, simple principles, such as the first ten Amendments to the Constitution. We have to define and redefine them and explain them. The consideration then becomes one of answering the question: What is counterintelligence expected to *do* for us? This really should be an internal executive, governmental decision, but now we have to think about it in much larger terms, in terms intelligible to a broader public.

If we are to understand counterintelligence fully, we must recognize and keep in mind at all times that it is the KGB that directs all the Soviet Bloc services, that underpins the Soviet system and carries Soviet strategy throughout the world; and we must remember that the only function that directly counters these KGB activities is counterintelligence.

Therefore, counterintelligence is the art of examining the entire spectrum of enemy intelligence activities in the light of enemy intelligence strategy, our own national objectives and the performance of our own and allied intelligence and counterintelligence services, for the purpose of devising better means of advancing our policies and protecting our nation from espionage, subversion, disinformation and deception and adverse military and political and economic actions. The government must regard counterintelligence as the essential tempering ingredient that will harden the weapons to dull the Soviet strategic sword—the KGB.

The methodology to cope with the KGB is to build a counterintelligence capability based on three objectives and one condition. These objectives are:

1. To continually gather from every available source, overt and covert, detailed knowledge about every enemy service activity;
2. To centrally research, analyze and disseminate this knowledge, including estimates of future activities; and
3. To develop the investigative intelligence collection, operational, and security resources to exploit the enemy's vulnerabilities and neutralize its activites against us.

The condition is that our focus on the fundamentals of counterintelligence objectives must remain constant over a long period of time.

Counterintelligence is a discipline that must concentrate always on its basic responsibilities; be monolithically centralized; be apolitical and provide balanced, objective, appraisals; be based on long-term goals, although quick to seize an immediate advantage; and be guided by national, not by individual, agency policy direction.

But even as I list these objectives, I realize there is no readily accessible summary of CI functions for us to refer to; and, despite my simplified statement, most of us are conditioned to think of and to define counterintelligence functionally.

Therefore, I offer for your consideration a list of what I consider the eleven basic counterintelligence functions that any centralized intelligence organization must perform:

1. It must conduct research and analysis based on hundreds of case histories, on information from sensitive sources and defectors, on current and past CI and intelligence collection operations, on overt information and information from foreign services.

2. CI must review and provide advice about the operational security of human, scientific and technical intelligence collection and covert action operations.

3. It must initiate and conduct counterintelligence operations and investigations overseas to protect the US from foreign penetration.

4. It must support the CI activities of other US agencies and the military services.
5. It must run double agent operations.
6. It must participate in support of and undertake directed deception operations.
7. This centralized intelligence organization must conduct CI liaison with foreign services.
8. It must provide counterintelligence analysis and estimates about foreign intelligence and security service functions and activities, including those supporting political, economic, military and disinformation objectives.
9. It must participate directly in the establishment of CI operational assets and intelligence collection assets overseas.
10. It must conduct sensitive CI operations and exploit foreign intelligence service defectors who have knowledge of penetration. And lastly;
11. It must establish good counterintelligence reporting and information dissemination systems.

Finally, let me make two additonal points. First, with reference to Mr. Zuehlke's paper, we might want to discuss his thesis that Executive Order 12036 represents "an important step towards meeting the world-wide, all-source, multidisciplinary, CI threat."

From a certain perspective, perhaps a view grounded in military counterintelligence experience, the Order may appear to do this. But from the perspective of the attempt to establish a centralized counterintelligence program, such as the CI effort from 1955 to 1973, it is inadequate. In fact, as far as I can understand it, the Order contains only two substantial provisions to enhance counterintelligence: that the National Security Council/SCC is to develop standards and doctrine for counterintelligence *and* that it resolve interagency differences concerning implementation of CI policy.

My second point is to commend to your attention two recent articles which are significant to any counterintelligence practitioner and which dovetail to support what I have been saying, and, indeed, all of the papers we will be considering.

The first article, entitled "Soviet Global Strategy," is by your esteemed Consortium colleague, Dr. Richard Pipes, and appeared in the April 1980 edition of *Commentary*. I only wish that Dr. Pipes had

had the opportunity to include some mention of the role of Soviet intelligence in advancing Soviet grand strategy, Dr. Pipes' term, beginning perhaps with Lenin's use of the OGPU to implement the New Economic Policy. Later we may want to ask Dr. Pipes to address this subject.

The second article is an extract from a forthcoming book, *High Treason,* by Vladimir Sakharov and Umberto Tosi, which appeared in the April 12, 1980 *Saturday Review* under the caption, "Revelations of a Soviet Diplomat." I do not know Sakharov, and some of you may question my reference to him because I am in no position to assess his *bona fides*. But what he details about the KGB's role in Soviet diplomacy and strategy is exactly what has been known and what has been of great concern to many of us involved in counterintelligence for twenty-years—and this is why we continue to advocate a comprehensive, monolithic, methodical, centralized counterintelligence program.

Unfortunately, to date our government never has acknowledged that the KGB is a political action force to be reckoned with, nor have we developed political or even effective intelligence strategies to counter it. Some even have thought that we could simply evade the KGB. Others of us still wave the tattered *"Vox Clamantis in Deserto"* banners.

Finally, I would like to suggest we may find that in counterintelligence, as in art, as in life, the whole is always greater than the sum of its parts.

Major General Edmund R. Thompson, USA: Before commenting on Mr. Zuehlke's remarks I would like to note that I am especially pleased to participate in these discussions of one of the most important aspects of our national intelligence and security effort. In Army intelligence we have been encouraged by the growing awareness in recent years on the part of national leaders that our US counterintelligence effort had to be given greater attention, and that US counterintelligence policies and programs had to be updated.

Mr. Zuehlke's assessment reflects what has already been done to improve our approach to this extremely important intelligence and security task. He has done an excellent job of laying out the overall structure of the problem. Much of what he has said about current policies and new programs reflects my own as well as the Army's approach to current counterintelligence activities. While I generally agree with Mr. Zuehlke's description of what counterintelligence is all about, I believe I can extend some of the ideas he presented, and there are some of his points with which I do not completely agree.

My own view of counterintelligence, to use the Army's historic-vintage 1917 terminology, is as "negative intelligence," but not in a derogatory sense or in the sense of limiting CI to its defensive aspect. The negative is negative in the sense of encompassing all that positive intelligence entails, of being the reverse side of the intelligence coin. In that sense, I agree with Mr. Zuehlke's multidiscipline views of CI and with his recognition of its aggressive, preventive and defensive aspects. Although I recognize the definition in EO 12036 (presumably for bureaucratic, regulatory and oversight reasons) as excluding personnel, physical, document or communications security, I do not share his enthusiasm for their exclusion from the "true function" of CI, but rather believe they are essential ingredients of any systems approach to looking at the total CI system.

With that kind of a view of CI, it probably is not surprising that I do not see the "four broad perspectives on the nature and purpose of CI" as necessarily being "ambiguous and fragmented." The various practitioners of CI may emphasize one or more of these perspectives (of law enforcement, adjunct to collection, neutralization of hostile activity, or operations security) because the missions of our parent organizations differ. But if we lose sight of the need to consider all of these perspectives, we are allowing the press of daily events to cause us to be remiss in remembering the big picture.

I recognize that in the Army we emphasize the OPSEC perspective. As such, we believe that one of the dominant purposes of counterintelligence is to contribute to security. I do not believe it fruitful to try to separate CI from this or any of the other perspectives.

Conceptually, the Army considers CI in the broad perspective I have just outlined, as an integral part of the Army Intelligence System. CI is one of the five functional subsystems, viz: C^2, Production, Collection, Counterintelligence, and Support. Organizationally, unlike the Navy and Air Force, we do not incorporate CI with law enforcement, while respecting their license to organize as best suits their needs. I subscribe to former Deputy Secretary of Defense Duncan's statement to Senator Nunn that: "I think it would be a mistake to try to achieve identical management structures in each military department, when it is their essential dissimilarity that accounts for their being separately organized and administered in the first place." In the Army, CI units are manned both by traditional CI Special Agents and by SIGSEC specialists, both of whom are trained across-the-board in multidiscipline CI. And these CI units are part of larger multidiscipline intelligence organizations: the INSCOM (Intelligence and Security Command) that operates at echelons above the corps and CEWI (Combat Electronic Warfare and Intelligence) groups and battalions at corps and division respectively.

I am particularly glad to find in this paper the kind of recognition of multidiscipline CI that I believe is the clear imperative of modern CI. The Soviets mount a multidiscipline collection effort which we must counter in all its facets, and they certainly recognize the concomitant requirement for their own multidiscipline CI. I am proud of the fact that in this country the Army has been a pioneer in multidiscipline CI. We have been about it for six or seven years now and I believe the Army has benefited from that approach.

I enjoyed and generally agree with Mr. Zuehlke's comments on Aggressive CI Operations. We in the Army believe they are a very essential part of any successful CI effort. I applaud his addressal of the need for and necessary scope of CI analysis; it is an area frequently forgotten in discussions of CI. Likewise, I agree with and support his views on deception operations. I would add to his statement that use of the HUMINT channel in such operations needs to be reinforced by SIGINT and PHOTINT channels, to say that most successful deception operations in this day and age should be planned from the outset as multidisciplinary. And, although in the military, deception is a responsibility of operations rather than intelligence, I too have long believed that successful deception or counterdeception efforts require the kind of outlook, skills and especially operational mind that intelligence and counterintelligence people have—or as Eric Ambler has described us: "the most suspicious, unbelieving, unreasonable, petty, inhuman, sadistic, doublecrossing set of bastards in any language."

Finally, I will comment on Mr. Zuehlke's proposal for a DOD CI agency. I am opposed to the idea. I have mentioned the differences among the Services. I believe we get all the policy and program direction we need from the already existing Office of the Secretary of Defense for Policy.

It has been the fashion in DOD since World War II to see greater organizational centralization as the answer to all sorts of problems. So we now have a DCA, DIA, DIS, DMA, DNA, DSA—but please not a DCIA. A number of conglomerates in the private sector, on the other hand, have gone in the direction of centralization of policy, standards-setting, and inspection in a central headquarters, while decentralizing execution to subordinate profit centers. Modern organizational theory, I believe, supports the latter approach.

General Discussion

Two major questions recurred throughout the discussion—and, as most participants agreed, they represented complementary aspects of essentially the same question: what *is* counterintelligence (in all of its various dimensions), and by what criteria can we measure CI performance?

Various answers were put forward. A former senior intelligence officer suggested, not wholly in jest, that the best measure might be "how many spies are you catching"? Another preferred to focus on the success of collection operations—on the accuracy of the information collected and its utility for sound estimates and policy. A congressional staff member felt that a more objective perspective might be that of foreign policy in general: that is, if we are having reasonable success in meeting our foreign policy objectives, our CI efforts (as a key component of our total intelligence system) are probably effective—and *vice versa*. At the same time, several participants warned that overreliance on quantitative measures, e.g., on the number of double-agent operations mounted in a particular time span, would never provide a fine enough test of CI quality. Another suggested criterion was "knowing what you are up against and knowing the dimensions of the threat." There was general agreement that CI deals (as one former intelligence professional expressed it) with "knowable details about a knowable adversary" and that knowing too little defines the "CI gap". This gap can be narrowed, in the main, by the use of sophisticated social science indicators and by a multidisciplinary approach.

Many participants maintained that, since mid-1973, US CI capabilities have deteriorated drastically, and especially in CIA.

A senior military CI specialist agreed with this evaluation. He gave good marks, however, to military CI overall, particularly since 1973 when, with the establishment of the Defense Investigative Service, CI resources were freed from routine personnel security, were able to focus on major targets, and even began to develop multidisciplinary approaches within military CI components. A former senior intelligence officer demurred in part: we are still relying on 35-year-old concepts, he pointed out, developed by men like Kent and Copeland who had no CI experience and knew virtually nothing about it. He went on to say that the critical need is for basic definitions (with an emphasis on the plural) to comprehend the multifaceted nature of CI, modern deception techniques (both human and technical), and organizational imperatives which must involve some departmental and some national components as well as some "super-coordinating mechanism". Otherwise, he concluded, we will not have begun to address the problems of the eighties.

A congressional staff member continued this line of analysis: does not the nature of the threat and of deception techniques, he asked, require a new multidisciplinary CI organizational structure? The senior military officer disagreed. As long as accurate information is being fed into the system, into reports and analysis, a new organizational structure will solve no problems and may even create needless complexities. He felt this conclusion was valid for Defense Department CI components and for the CI community as a whole.

Another congressional aide wondered whether the US or any open society could successfully engage in deception and misinformation techniques. He asked specifically who or what is responsible today in the US for trying to read how the Soviets are reading us? Several participants offered partial answers. It is not easy for an open society to engage in successful deception, one agreed, but it can be done. Another felt that the US is not now making net threat analyses, much less reading how they are reading us; intelligence analysts do this to some extent, but they do it without a specifically CI mentality. He concluded that such analysis can be done with a high degree of coordinated effort. A former intelligence officer noted in passing that deception operations are traditionally the weapons of the "weak" and that, up to now, the US has not been in such a posture.

An academic participant suggested looking closely at the Boyce-Lee case (two TRW employees who sold highly classified information on technical systems to the Soviets) and asking the question, was this a CI failure? What could or should have been done to prevent it?

A former senior intelligence officer said that this case represented a breakdown of the usual, classical ingredients of effective CI, personnel and installation security, failure to recognize that new weapon systems would logically be major Soviet intelligence targets, as well as sloppiness in routine checks on the Mexico City Soviet Embassy, known for years as a major Soviet operations base. He also observed that this case made an implicit argument for *not* separating normal security functions from CI as an integral whole. As to the further question, would multidisciplinary CI have helped to prevent this breakdown, there was disagreement. A senior military specialist felt it would not: all that was needed was good, aggressive, coordinated CI, nothing essentially new. A congressional staff member observed, however, that at just the critical juncture in the evolution of this case, the Soviets began using coded telemetry, they changed their behavior in other words, and this should have been seen as a tip-off that they were acting on information derived from Boyce-Lee; in all likelihood, a multidisciplinary central CI organization would have been alert to such a tip.

Another congressional staff member argued that the Boyce-Lee case demonstrates that no one is responsible, no one is really in charge and that this, in turn, does argue in favor of some new coordinating mechanism. A number of former senior intelligence officers disagreed: it was a failure to be sure, but there could be no question that CI was responsible and that the lead agency should have coordinated its efforts with the FBI, the Air Force, and others. There is no need, they maintained, for a super-entity, simply for a clear focal point and for "traditional" coordination. The ancillary point was also developed by several participants that new laws and guidelines, as exemplified in Executive Order 12036, positively inhibit effective CI coordination and render liaison with indigenous police/security forces "from difficult-to-impossible."

The great problem, in the judgment of one former senior intelligence officer, is not so much "compartmentation" as it is "departmentation," both of which a new coordinating mechanism would seek to overcome. But, in any event, such a department-by-department CI orientation will continue to be a fact of US practice in CI and in intelligence generally. There was, however, no question about responsibility: where reading the Soviet disinformation thrust, from 1959 onwards was concerned, for example, CIA/CI clearly had the action. Confronting an integrated, monolithic adversary is never easy; but it can and indeed has been done through intensive case studies, the accumulation of basic files, and then "suppression" and "manipulation" of adversary agents and principals, through basic CI tradecraft, in other words, with effective coordination throughout the process.

Mr. Zuehlke agreed, in summing up, that CI definitions do depend on the particular needs and missions of particular agencies and departments. He stressed the broad consensus that, insofar as the KGB is emerging as the principal agent of Soviet strategy, within the CPSU and in domestic affairs as well as worldwide, so the mission of US CI is much more than just combatting hostile actions against US targets. In the eighties, in his view, CI must receive greater emphasis, perhaps even more than basic analysis and what has traditionally been meant by positive foreign intelligence.

CHAPTER THREE

Counterintelligence Jurisdiction and the Double-Cross System by National Technical Means

---

Paper:

William R. Harris

Discussants:

Rear Admiral Donald P. Harvey
USN (Ret.)

Dr. Roland Herbst

The focus of this paper is a traditional one for lawyers: subject-matter jurisdiction. What difference does it make if counterintelligence jurisdiction is confined on the one hand, to the human sector or if it is extended to all sources of foreign intelligence—to evaluate, correlate, protect and counter threats to all sources of foreign intelligence?

I. The Double-Cross System by National Technical Means

In a postwar report, John C. Masterman reviewed the origins and significance of a "double-cross system" of manipulated human intelligence in World War II. Published a quarter century later, as *The Double-Cross System in the War of 1939 to 1945,* this study indicated the importance of controlled agent networks in the defeat of Germany.[1] The Masterman study did not purport to encompass the entire allied strategic deception program.

At least by 1939, the technological revolution in intelligence had established a new domain for deception and its detection: technical collection, in the SALT era recognized in international agreements as *national technical means* of verification.

In World War I, aerial reconnaissance provided a means of technical documentation of positional changes. Signals intelligence bureaus provided recurring access to enemy communications. By the end of the war, the manipulation of intelligence was based in field deception planning staffs.

Nevertheless, it was World War II, not World War I, that laid the institutional foundation for the modern double-cross system by national technical means. The principal innovation was the location of deception planning staffs within the high command responsible for overall strategy. German deception staffs played a role in German preparations for war, in contrast to *ad hoc* efforts to exaggerate German air power in the mid-1930's.[2] Soviet deception planners supported the *Stavka,* at least as early as the battle of Leningrad, and at least on an *ad hoc* basis in the defense of Moscow in 1941. At General Wavell's suggestion, British deception planning shifted from field commands to predominantly central staffing by about 1941. American deception planning followed the British model, once it was understood.

Once deception planning was part of the strategic planning process, the systematic targeting of an adversary's technical means of collection was inevitable. Unlike their counterparts in the field, the planners at the political centers had access to the most sensitive counterintelligence resources. These resources included access, through decryption of enemy ciphers, to key intelligence and decisionmaking channels of communication. This feedback respecting the preconceptions of adversaries and the channels upon which they relied for assessments led deception planners to the targeting of technical indicators, and especially those that were most credible to an adversary.

Systematic application of aerial reconnaissance, radar, and computer technology provided predictable and reliable sources of collection at great distance, at great speed, in foul weather, and at night. The combination of predictability and feedback aided deception planners. Whereas only 48 percent of land battles in World War I resulted in surprise, fully 68 percent of those in World War II resulted in surprise respecting key elements of the attack: the intention to attack, the time, place, relative strength, or style of operations. Barton Whaley, who reported on 20th century wartime deception in 1969, identified a trend to utilize a larger number of channels, including technical channels, to assure the misdirection of enemy resources:

> From this it could seem that surprise has become "easier" to achieve. In fact, the table [of deception cases] also shows that this could be entirely accounted for by the parallel rise in the use of deception.[3]

Whaley demonstrates that high-intensity deception, measured by the number of modes for communicating deceptive indicators, is virtually assured of success. In at least 27 of 28 cases of high-intensity deception, the intended victim is indeed surprised, and the tactical surprise achieved at Luzon qualifies, in some minds, as a case of enemy paralysis and misdirection. The feasibility of monitoring the status of enemy preparations has resulted in a uniform practice since at least 1939: the decision to initiate a war or open a new front is itself conditional upon the attainment of surprise. Thus, surprise is the norm, not the exception. When the Pakistanis, caught by surprise when the Indians attacked in 1971, flew aerial sorties directly into Indian radar networks, this hasty counterattack was a noteworthy exception in a 40 year traditon of surprise-dependent attacks.

The test of surprise pertains to the proposed victim, not the bystander. So, if the British expected Operation BARBAROSSA in June 1941, or if the Americans expected the Soviet invasion of Afghanistan in December 1979, such knowledge does not offset the late mobilization of Soviet forces in 1941, nor the Afghani removal of tank batteries—suggested by Soviet advisers—in 1979.

Modern intelligence systems may be credited with the occasional postponement of attacks or recurring successes in estimative battles with nature—a confusing but not generally a deceptive adversary. Yet, the strategic warning that is the reason for their existence is not the warning that can be expected when it is most needed.

The technological revolution in intelligence since the era of Sputnik encourages investments in the sensing of physical indicators. Redoubling collection efforts or supplementing these efforts with novel methods of sensing is a bureaucratic imperative. The revolution in collection merely guarantees that the "double-cross system" will emphasize not human channels but mainly the national technical means of collection:

> . . . Intelligence gathering is the problem, not the cure as so many of us have felt. It is the act of seeking information and of turning this information into finished intelligence and the credible presentation of this intelligence to decision-makers that enables the deceiver to succeed. For if we did not seek and react to information about the external world, the deceiver would have little bait with which to lead us astray.[4]

In assessing the significance of international deception, can we derive any clues from the evolution of other species? The literature on *interspecific mimicry,* or the imitation by one species of the behavior or other characteristics of another species, has its origins in the Darwinian exploration of natural selection. The mimicking of the warning coloration or other characteristics of a model that is inedible, poisonous, dangerous, or otherwise unappealing to a potential predator is known at *Batesian mimicry.* Batesian mimicry utilizes indicators to enhance deterrence and aids species survival. A second form of mimicry, known as *Müllerian mimicry,* involves the clustering of species in biosystems that accentuate the visibility of warning indicators of effective defenses. While each species has its own defenses, the grouping of species decreases the risk of unwitting attack. Müllerian mimicry educates potential predators regarding risks of attack and also aids species survival.

Regarding the literature on *intraspecific* deception, akin to the deception of man against man, one finds fragmentary evidence supporting the view that intraspecific deception for purposes of attack is both uncommon and unsupportive of species preservation. Intraspecific deception is generally observed in connection with the reproduction process. Intraspecific deception running counter to the preservation imperative is a great rarity. While there may be advantage *within* our species in favor of those who practice deception, there does not appear to be advantage *for* the species adopting intraspecific deception.[5]

In a provocative study, *Lying: Moral Choice in Public and Private Life,* Sissela Bok concludes:

> . . . Trust and integrity are precious resources, easily squandered, hard to regain. They can thrive only on a foundation of respect for veracity.[6]

Expections respecting the veracity of individuals are frequently disappointed. Expectations respecting governmental standards of veracity are not high, and should not be so regarding communications or indicators of governments in a competitive or adversarial relationship. Reducing the expectation of success or the incentives for deceit can, however, affect behavior:

> Throughout society, then, all would benefit if the incentive structure associated with deceit were changed: if the gains from deception were lowered, and honesty made more worthwhile even in the short run . . . . It ought not to be beyond human ingenuity to increase the incentives for honesty even in such circumstances.[7]

II. Why Is Counterintelligence Pertinent?

Is there a role for counterintelligence in reducing opportunities for strategic deception among nations? At the outset it should be noted that counterintelligence is much more than:

> Information gathered and activities conducted to protect against espionage and other clandestine intelligence activities, sabotage, international terrorist activities or assassinations conducted for or on behalf of foreign powers, organizations or persons, but not including personnel, physical, document, or communications security programs.

This is the definition of counterintelligence in Executive Order 12036 of February 28, 1978. This concept of what might be called the "old counterintelligence" emphasizes protection against human mischief. It protects against human penetrations, guards against unreliable or deceptive information through human sources, and protects against acts of malevolence through human hands.

Both the proposed National Intelligence Act of 1980 (S. 2284) and the Intelligence Activities Act of 1980 (H.R. 6820) adopt a more contemporary definition of counterintelligence, a "to counter or protect" standard:

> The term "counterintelligence activity" means
> (A) the collection, retention, processing, analysis, and dissemination of counteringelligence; and
> (B) any other activity, except for personnel, document, physical and communications security programs, undertaken to counter or protect against the espionage, other clandestine intelligence activity, covert action, assassination, or sabotage, or similar activities of a foreign government.[8]

To counter or protect against foreign deception activities is within the counterintelligence mission. Why, then, has the counterintelligence jurisdiction been limited to human reliability issues? The limited role of counterintelligence is not occasioned by any exclusivity of compromises or any undue concentration of deceptive efforts in the human sector. The technical means of collection have also been the technical means of deception. As summarized by Dr. Robert Cockburn of the Telecommunications Research Establishment, "A shilling's worth of radio counter-measure will mess up a pound's worth of radio equipment."[9]

Traditional limitations on the jurisdiction of counterintelligence are predicated on the assumption that the methodology of counterintelligence is irrelevant to the "scientific revolution" in intelligence collection. Otherwise, the counterintelligence jurisdiction in World War II and thereafter would have encompassed the new technical means of collection. At least through most of the 1970's, counterintelligence jurisdiction has concentrated on the human sector. Three recent studies of counterintelligence reflect this preoccupation: Edward Jay Epstein's *Legend: The Secret World of Lee Harvey Oswald* (1978), John T. Elliff's *The Reform of FBI Intelligence Operations* (1979), and William C. Sullivan's *The Bureau: My Thirty Years in Hoover's FBI* (1979).

Concurrently, the timely identification of deception has been seen as within the responsibility of the positive intelligence process and sometimes as exclusively within that domain:

> . . . It would be my hope that existing mechanisms could be used . . . and that one effect of the existence of such a [deception analysis] group would be pressure on the larger community to do its duty by the problem of deception without creating a special interest group.
>
> Above all, this small group should not attempt to dominate the analytic work itself. Deception is not a narrow problem that should be delegated to a few good men for resolution. The working level analyst can and should accept that deception is basically his problem and that no one has a better base of information and expertise to do the analyses suggested here.[10]

The premises of counterintelligence are different than those of the scientific tradition. This does not mean that the methodologies of each should not complement the other's. Scientific education involves an immersion in literature and laboratory experiments designed to uncover nature's secrets. Errors of measurement of variations in observed phenomena are assumed to be random or, if systematic in bias, then at least not designed to mislead the scientific observer.

The premises of counterintelligence conflict with the scientific training and expectations of openness nurtured in the scientific community. The adversary is not nature, but man. Indicators are intentionally withheld or manipulated to produce systematic biases favorable to an adversary. Thus, the tradecraft of counterintelligence includes a recurring attention to field experimentation, designed to identify which side is controlling the "laboratory" under investigation.

The methods of counterintelligence are, however, appropriate for "scientific" inquiry through channels of observation that are vulnerable to deception. The monitoring of channels, to identify indicators of manipulation, is a legitimate and necessary activity. The design and operation of experiments that trace effects of compromises upon data collected is a legitimate and necessary activity. The assistance of counterintelligence staffs in designing the procurement of technical intelligence is needed, if an increased proportion of technical collection is to be derived from unexpected sources or analyzed by unexpected methods. Without such unexpected sources and methods, quality assurance programs will fail to limit deception vulnerabilities, and the timely detection of strategic deception programs in the future is likely to occur about as often as in the past.

There is one particular strength of counterintelligence methodology that is essential in the timely detection of deception. Counterintelligence monitors channels of feedback: collection priorities of foreign intelligence services, patterns of reporting through such channels as may be sampled, and channels of our own collection that may be manipulated by such foreign services. Through the monitoring of feedback, counterintelligence staffs have at least the potential to identify links between self-deception and deception by adversaries.

Studies by Klaus Knorr, Roberta Wohlstetter, Barton Whaley, and others emphasize the centrality of self-deception in predictive failures. Michael Handel emphasizes the importance of self-deception in limiting the acceptance of intelligence warnings by decision-makers. Preconceptions are a critical resource for deception planners, if they understand them, and if they have the ability to monitor their efforts to reinforce or alter these preconceptions.[11] By monitoring feedback channels, counterintelligence staffs may contribute both hypotheses and channels of data that will assist in positive intelligence warning.

Thus there are practical reasons of great importance not to limit a definition of "counterintelligence" to espionage or other clandestine or covert actions of humans. The technological revolution in intelligence has established a new domain for deception and its detection. Technical collection diminishes the relative role of humans in the strategic deception of US intelligence and those whose decisions rely upon it. If intelligence charters are to anticipate future needs rather than codify outmoded concepts of the past, there must be room for all-source counterintelligence. Otherwise, predictable and partially-compromised intelligence systems will be increasingly vulnerable to a double-cross system by national technical means.

III. Coping with Deception Under Limited Counterintelligence Jurisdiction: A Retrospective on Assessments of Soviet ICBM Missions and Numbers

Technological collection has in some respects bounded the feasibility of some deception techniques. Even without the application of counterintelligence methods, it was possible to discredit Soviet claims in 1954-1962 that projected long-range bomber and intercontinental missile capabilities beyond those that now appear to have been deployed.

Efforts by the Soviet government to facilitate US overestimates of Soviet bomber production in the 1950's were defeated by the U-2 collection program. That program was both swift and unexpected in capability, so that countermeasures were not available before vital intelligence was in hand. Later collection by technical means allowed Deputy Secretary of Defense Gilpatric to indicate firm US knowledge that the number of deployed Soviet ICBMs was substantially lower than suggested by Soviet leaders. Once again, the technical capabilities of the United States were not adequately anticipated.

> Nevertheless, during the 1960's, just as U.S. intelligence analysts were growing confident that the Soviets overrepresented capabilities, and that we could catch them every time, just the opposite happened. With an understanding of the technical indicators and methods of U.S. estimation of ballistic missile accuracy, the Soviets managed to underrepresent the accuracy of intercontinental ballistic missiles. The earlier bluffing upward corresponded to decisions not to invest in nuclear-armed rockets early, while seeking silo-killing capabilities. U.S. Defense Secretary Harold Brown has recently indicated that the Soviet SS-9 ICBM was always aimed at the launch control centers of the Minuteman missile complexes. Only systematic biasing of technical indicators would produce the apparently large errors in guidance and the actually quite limited errors needed to justify attack on so hardened a set of military targets.[12]

Former Air Force Intelligence chief, Major General George J. Keegan, Jr., attributes a decline in predictive analysis to the immersion in physical indicators of force structure deployments:

> . . . with the advent of space surveillance technologies, the community became immersed in the process of verification, in which the bulk of the community's analysts were largely employed in the repetitive counting of ICBM's, submarines, and other major artifacts of war. Predictive analysis has declined markedly since the advent of the new collection technologies.[13]

Moreover, a long-term underestimation of Soviet defense investments also corresponded with a recurring underestimation of Soviet technological capabilities:

> By and large, our scientists erred seriously in their advice about Soviet capabilities to develop the atomic bomb, heavy jet bombers, intercontinental ballistic missiles, high yield thermonuclear weapons and sophisticated naval weapons systems . . .[14]

Kenneth Adelman, formerly in the Office of the Secretary of Defense, has observed that the underestimation of Soviet intercontinental missile deployments corresponded with an underestimation of the accuracies and independent targeting capabilities (MIRV), as well. Ernest Conine concludes:

> The answer does not seem to lie in the lack of raw intelligence—from satellites, electronic eavesdropping and material published in the Soviet military press—but in a mind-set that rejected the evidence that was there.[15]

Former CIA analyst David Sullivan has reviewed evidence of silo construction starts, arguing that US intelligence should have recognized a commitment to steady ICBM buildup in the 7-year Soviet Defense Plan for 1963-1970. With hindsight, it appears that Soviet defense planners procured sufficient ICBMs for a preemptive counterforce attack on the 1000 Minuteman ICBMs and 54 Titan II ICBMs housed in protective silos. Sullivan's chart (reproduced here) indicates what might have been predicted. Albert Wohlstetter's tables I-1 and IV-1, (also reproduced here) from his *Legends of the Strategic Arms Race* indicate what was predicted by US intelligence and the systematic underestimation that occurred.

But neither Sullivan nor Wohlstetter provides a coherent explanation of why the predictors went astray, systemically and for the entire period 1962-1969.

What overwhelmed evidence of silo start rates and Soviet military doctrine was the confidence of Western intelligence services that the accuracy of Soviet ballistic missiles was insufficient to threaten silo-protected Minuteman and Titan II missiles.[16] As former Assistant Secretary of Defense for Intelligence Albert C. Hall observed in 1977:

> Since the USSR deploys more than 1400 missiles, its nuclear arm has almost inconceivable destructive ability. It is difficult to see why the Soviet Union requires a force of this magnitude, since less than one-fifth the force could destroy the economic structure of the US and there are no defenses to penetrate.
>
> One must conclude that some fraction of the Soviet ballistic missile force is planned to attack the Minuteman force. Major changes now underway in the Soviet land-based force support this view . . . .[17]

As long ago as 1960, at the Summer Study on Arms Control of the American Academy of Arts and Sciences, a team of experts warned: "Improvements in missile accuracy appear to be the most destabilizing of all possible improvements."[18] Apparently incontrovertible "scientific" evidence confirmed the guidance failures of Soviet missile and electronic instruments in the early 1960's. Thus, it is too facile to blame US predictive failures regarding the Soviet ICBM force upon ideology or wishful thinking alone. If the Soviets were incapable of mass-producing intercontinental rockets that were

Chart I

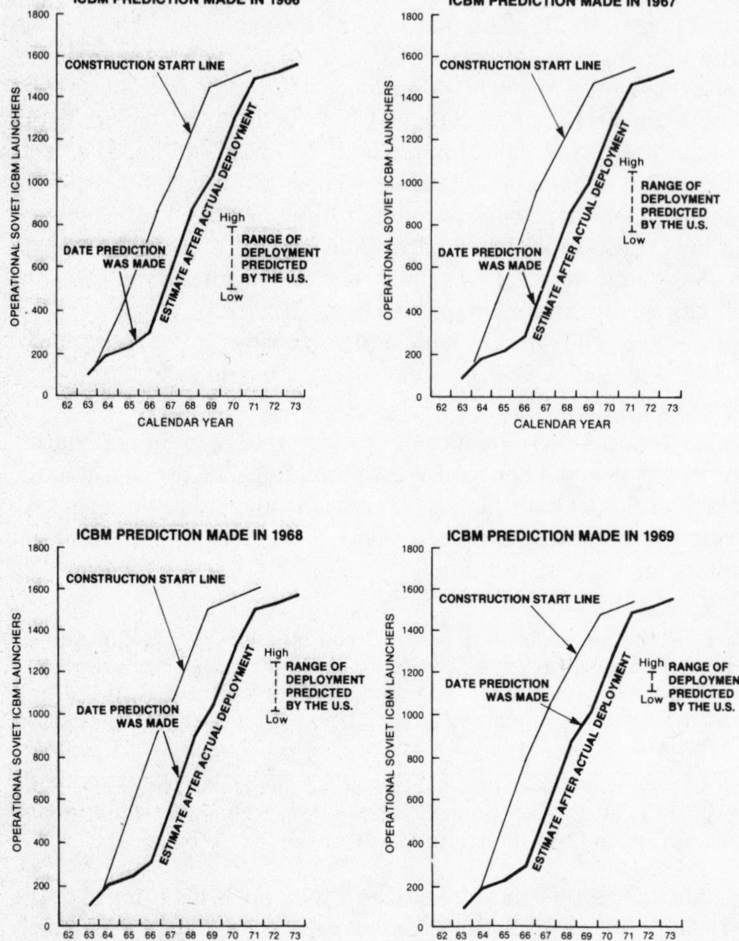

Source: David S. Sullivan, "Evaluating U.S. Intelligence Estimates," in Roy Godson [ed.], *Intelligence Requirements for the 1980's: Analysis and Estimates,* Washington, D.C. National Strategy Information Center, 1980, p. 56.

Table I-1

ICBM LAUNCHER PREDICTIONS THAT GO BEYOND OBSERVABLES
Predicted Operational Soviet ICBM Launchers Compared to the Actual Number

	Predicted and Estimated Actual Inventory			*Ratio: Predicted to Estimated Actual*		
Date Prediction Was Made (First quarter of year)	*Date Referred to in the Prediction (mid-year)*	*Predicted Number*	*Estimated Actual Inventory*	*Low*	*High*	*Mid-Range*
1962	1967	350-650	570	0.61	1.14	0.88
1963	1967	300-600	570	0.53	1.05	0.79
	1968	475-700	858	0.55	0.82	0.68
1964	1967	325-525	570	0.57	0.92	0.75
	1969	400-700	1028	0.39	0.68	0.54
1965	1967	330-395	570	0.58	0.69	0.64
	1970	410-700	1299	0.32	0.54	0.43
1966	1970	505-795	1299	0.39	0.61	0.50
1967	1971	805-1080	1513	0.53	0.71	0.62
1968	1972	1020-1251	1527	0.67	0.82	0.74
1969	1972	1158-1276	1527	0.76	0.84	0.80
			Average:	0.54	0.80	0.67

By "predictions that go beyond observables" we mean those extending far enough into the future to include in the cumulative estimate (besides estimates of launchers already completed and those started but not yet completed at the time when the prediction was made) those that were expected to be newly started after the time when the prediction was made and completed by the future date referred to in the prediction. For ICBM launchers these are the predictions for more than 18 months into the future. (Since these predictions, short and long-range, were presented in January or February and always referred to mid-years, they are for 4 or 5 months ahead, or for that plus some whole multiple of twelve, i.e., 16-17 months, 28-29 months and so forth.)

Only predictions referring to mid-1972 or before are included in the Table since data on estimated actual inventories beyond mid-1972 were not available at the time of the analysis.

All formal ICBM predictions of the Secretaries of Defense from 1962 through 1972 satisfying the above conditions are included in the Table.

Source: Albert Wohlstetter, *Legends of the Strategic Arms Race* Washington, D.C.: United States Strategic Institute, 1975.

Table IV-1

OPERATIONAL SOVIET ICBM LAUNCHERS, SLM LAUNCH TUBES, AND BOMBERS ESTIMATED AFTER ACTUAL DEPLOYMENT

	ICBMs	*SLBMs and SLCMs*					*BOMBERS*				
			SLBM Launchers					*Heavy*			
Mid-Year	*Total Launchers**	*SLCM Launchers*	*Diesel*	*Nuclear*	*Total*	*Total SLBM and SLCM Launchers*	*Medium Bombers*	*Tankers*	*Bombers*	*Sub-Total*	*Total Heavy and Medium (inc. tankers)*
1963	91	—	80	27	107	—	925-950			195-215	1120-1165
1964	188-191	152-160	80	27	107	259-267	800-875	40-45	160-175	200-220	1000-1095
1965	224	208-216	80	27	107	315-323	770-820	45-55	160	205-215	975-1035
1966	250	264-292	80	27	107	371-399	745-785	45-55	155	200-210	945-995
1967	570	320	80	27	107	427	750	50	160	210	960
1968	858	348	78	43	121	469	730	50	155	205	935
1969	1028	368	76	120	196	564	725	50	145	195	920
1970	1299	370	72	232	304	674	730	50	145	195	925
1971	1513	404-406	72	376	448	852-854	710	50	145	195	905
1972	1527	420-422	60	440	500	920-922	635-690	50	145	195	830-885

*Excluding test-site and training launchers.

Source: Albert Wohlstetter, *Legends of the Strategic Arms Race* Washington, D.C.: United States Strategic Institute, 1975.

sufficiently accurate and reliable to destroy US land-based communications and retaliatory forces, what reason was there to expect that the Soviet leadership would continue its puzzling rate of investments?

At the 1960 Summer Study on Arms Control, John Mullen warned that the stability of silo-based missile forces might not last. But US policymakers had confidence that the scientific revolution in intelligence collection would provide timely warning of future vulnerabilities:

> . . . it would appear that from a hardened force of missiles on both sides, we may expect to receive only a *temporary* stability; the length of the stable period being purely a function of technology. We are committed to the concept of the hardened missile force; for the time it is clearly a good one, possibly the best one, and probably will remain so for five or ten years. It only remains for us to observe the lesson of history and put our faith in a dynamic rather than a stagnant posture.[19]

The temporary stability of which Mullen warned appears to have lasted closer to five than ten years. By 1965-1966 the recently tested SS-9 and SS-11 ICBMs were in process of emplacement in silos of the Strategic Rocket Forces, their mission the preemptive destruction of Minuteman and Titan II missile systems before retaliatory launch. It is fair to state that this conclusion about the SS-9 was not widely shared partly because the numbers deployed were insufficient to target Minuteman launch silos. And it is fair to state that this conclusion about the SS-11 is not widely shared even today, mainly because of "lessons learned" about SS-11 accuracy, from scientific knowledge about contemporaneous Soviet missile systems, and secondarily because the SS-11 and SS-7 missiles together would have been required to cover the Minuteman system before multiple warheads were available in the 1970's.

It has not been easy for US analysts to rethink the possibility of Khrushchev as a pioneer of counterforce missile strategy. Those expecting a "missile gap" favorable to the Soviets were perplexed that he did not authorize the deployment of larger numbers of SS-7s and SS-8s. These ICBMs could be emplaced in hardened launchers, but they could not be expected to destroy Minuteman launch communication centers and pin down Minuteman missiles in silos until an attempt to destroy them could be made.

The infatuation with the scientific revolution in collection carried with it a faith in powers of induction from technical indicators. While counterintelligence officers in the 1960's worried about the *bona fides* of human agents who asserted that the Soviets lagged significantly in missile guidance and reliability,[20] counterintelligence officers were simply not positioned to advise on methods of monitoring for a "double-cross system by national technical means."

Did the Soviet leadership see in nuclear rocket technology an opportunity to insure against damage to the homeland by decisive pre-emption in the initial phase of war? Strategic deception was not essential to success, so long as the command and control system of the main enemy could be destroyed before a decision to respond could be executed.

However, at the beginning of December 1959, Secretary of Defense McElroy indicated publicly that the Minuteman ICBM system would obtain priority over the Atlas system, and the Minutemen ICBM system included both plans for silo-protected command and control and an alternate Airborne Command Post, known as LOOKING GLASS, initiated on a trial basis in July 1960 and in continuous operation from February 1961 onwards.[21]

Once the United States was committed to the Minuteman system, strategic deception would be required to acquire a capability to destroy the command and control system, then the missile silos. Without a mismatch between Soviet perceptions of their preemptive capabilities and US perceptions of Minuteman survivability, the economics of strategic competition would have favored the US defense of survivability. Additional hardening and insulating of silos, redundant communications, and potentially a commitment to launch on warning or to a hard-point anti-ballistic missile (ABM) systems were available to the defense.

The origins of a Soviet commitment to missiles for counterforce attack appear to have preceded the commitment to deceptive indicators by at least a couple years. A conference on military science in May 1957 "opened the way for significant improvement in the study of military science and scientific research," and "especially" the problems of "military art" and "strategy."[22] As one analyst expressed it:

> There was a real prospect of preemptive capability against soft, slow bomber forces deployed on a small number of airfields, particularly if they were in Europe or elsewhere on the Soviet periphery . . . . It is likely that the early Soviet deployment of medium and intermediate-range ballistic missiles targeted against the NATO bases on which U.S. strategic forces were only recently deployed was the outgrowth of this kind of perspective. Unfortunately, the American strategic forces were in the process of being withdrawn to the continental United States, as increasing range in follow-on aircraft permitted. This, in turn, helped to stimulate increased Soviet

efforts to deploy intercontinental-range ballistic missiles. The deployment of MRBMs and IRBMs proceeded, since NATO bases continued to deploy nuclear capable aircraft.[23]

Efforts by the US to reduce vulnerabilities to and incentives for preemptive attack were reflected in the April 1954 "Basing Study"[24] and in Albert Wohlstetter's January 1959 article in *Foreign Affairs*, "The Delicate Balance of Terror." Such efforts to achieve strategic force survivability constituted an intellectual challenge.

Discussions in 1958 within the Soviet General Staff led to important sponsored research in 1959. Particularly noteworthy was the analysis of Lieutenant General A. I. Gastilovich, since February 1958 Deputy Commandant of the Academy of the General Staff for Scientific Research. In September 1961, Gastilovich and others received the Order of Lenin for "great service in preparing specialists and the development of science." Gastilovich had commanded the World War II 18th Army, whose political adviser, Leonid Brezhnev, had assumed primary jurisdiction for ballistic missile management even while Khrushchev served as First Secretary of the Party.[25]

The principal Soviet military debate in 1958-1959 was not over the question of whether to design a missile force to strike the nuclear rockets of the main enemy, but whether to count on that accomplishment. If the preemptive destruction of the enemy's missile force was not assured, then the initial phase of war might not be as decisive as some claimed. Back in 1955, Marshal Rotmistrov had asserted that surprise attack in the nuclear era could:

> . . . cause the rapid collapse of a government whose capacity to resist is low as a consequence of radical faults in its social and economic structure and also as a consequence of an unfavorable geographic position.[26]

M. V. Frunze had stressed the significance of boldness in the offensive:

> The victor will be the one who finds within himself the resolution to attack: the side with only defense is inevitably doomed to defeat.[27]

The SS-6 ICBM, though the first available ballistic rocket of intercontinental range, was a reminder to First Secretary Khrushchev that, "First and foremost we had to develop an electronic guidance system. The *Semyorka* (SS-6) was reliable neither as a defensive nor as an offensive weapon."[28]

The designer of the SS-6 ICBM worked principally with fuels requiring extensive preparation before launch, thus missiles more suitable for space launches than for salvo firing of nuclear-armed missiles.[29] So, while Sergei Korolyov reportedly held the title of chief designer of rocket-cosmic systems, the principal task of producing counterforce ballistic missiles fell to rival design bureaus. M. K. Yangel, with a design bureau at Dnepropetrovsk, is credited with developing the SS-7, then the SS-9 ICBM system, and later the SS-17 and SS-18. V. N. Chelomey, heading another design bureau, is credited with the SS-11 and SS-19 ICBMs. Khrushchev's son, Sergei, worked as an engineer under V. N. Chelomey, whose SS-11 ICBM became the most widely deployed ICBM of all Soviet systems, and surpassing the number of deployed Minuteman ICBMs before SS-19 substitutions in the mid-1970's.[30]

By 1959-1960, when a special collection of articles on strategy was prepared for general staff readership, it was acknowledged that the operational targeting of Soviet ballistic rockets was unfit for discussion at a Top Secret level.[31] By this juncture, concerns about the potential for a US launch-on-warning policy were real. Moreover, by 1959 Khrushchev had not only established his control over the state security apparatus but also Shelepin, as KGB Chairman, had centralized strategic deception planning under a special Department of the KGB, just as the primacy of the Strategic Rocket Forces was established.

The hypothesis that the Soviet commitment to a counterforce ICBM capability followed the Cuban missile crisis, or even that it followed the ouster of Khruschchev as First Secretary in October 1964 lingers on. However, by April 1957 there were reports that the Soviet Union had established a separate but secret rocket force.[32] In early 1958 the Soviet Union embarked on a new nuclear test program, before announcing a test moratorium on March 31, 1958.[33] In 1960 Khrushchev revealed that since December 1959 the Strategic Rocket Force was the pre-eminent branch of the Soviet military services. D. F. Ustinov and L. I. Brezhnev played key supervisory roles in the development and production of the Soviet missile program.[34] An American analyst concluded:

> From the end of the Korean War to the beginning of the SALT era in 1970, the most rapid growth in Soviet military expenditures occurred in the years 1959-1963 and 1966-1970. In the former period, Soviet military expenditures increased from about 13 to about 23 billion rubles (in 1955 prices), or nearly 75 per cent; in the latter period Soviet outlays nearly doubled from about 25 to about 49 billion rubles.[35]

The period 1959-1963, during which the Soviet military expenditures rose nearly 75 percent, included many of the key decisions resulting in the Soviet acquisition of a counterforce ICBM capability.

Decisions on strategy appear to have been made in 1958-1959, before decision on rocket force reorganization. By March 1961, changed Soviet negotiating positions on a nuclear test ban signaled a commitment to test nuclear weapon designs that would optimize attack by the SS-7, and later the SS-9 ICBMs on the Minuteman command, control, and communication systems. The SS-7 flight tests proceeded in that year. The nuclear test moratorium ended with Soviet weapon tests in September 1961. In October 1961 the XXIInd Party Congress ratified decisions on the 5-Year Defense Plan through the year 1965.[36]

If ICBMs without counterforce accuracy had no place in Khrushchev's view of defense strategy, then the procurement of inaccurate missiles was unacceptable. Particularly in light of the heavy diversion of resources to the defense sector, Khrushchev sought savings in conventional manpower and strategic systems that would soon be obsolete.

If this was the "hare-brained scheming and superficiality" within Marshal Zakharov's experience as Chief of the General Staff under Khruschchev in 1960-1963,[37] it was the unexpected American ability to identify a dearth of SS-6 deployments that made it so. While Khruschchev had reason to wait for the counterforce ICBMs—particularly after the successful nuclear weapons tests of September 1961—he also had reason to hope that short-term economies would not be noticed by the Americans.

The announcement by Deputy Secretary of Defense Gilpatric in October 1961 that the ICBM balance was favorable to the United States encouraged Khruschchev to negotiate for MRBM and IRBM basing rights in Cuba.[38] These new bases could shore up the strategic balance, and allow attacks on SAC bomber bases even before the SLBMs on Yankee-Class submarines, and land-based ICBMs in the Soviet Union would be installed for a pre-emptive defense of the homeland.

David Sullivan independently reached a similar set of conclusions regarding Khruschev's commitment to the SS-9 and SS-11 ICBMs *before* the Cuban missile crisis of October 1962:[39]

> . . . Missile designer V. N. Chelomey, who, according to Nicholas Daniloff had been associated with the development of third generation ICBMs,[40] was promoted in June 1962 to the Soviet Academy of Sciences. Khrushchev's son, Sergei, worked for Chelomey and brought him into close contact with the senior Khrushchev. We can infer that this promotion signified approval of Chelomey's work on missilery—all of which suggests that Khrushchev was committed to deploying the SS-9 and SS-11 as early as June 1962, even before the Cuban missile crisis.

Sullivan's writings on the SALT I negotiations suggest that the substitution of SS-19s for the SS-11s, both reportedly built at Chelomey's design bureau,[41] constituted a critical deception of the SALT I bargaining.[42] But the extraordinary and recurring underestimation of SS-11 deployments is ascribed by Sullivan to US estimative incompetence, not Soviet deception: ". . . this debacle in estimation occurred in the absence of large-scale Soviet efforts at deception."[43]

A contrary view is at least as strongly supported by the available evidence: the central deception respecting Soviet ICBM capabilities and intentions occurred in the 1959-1964 period of Khrushchev's leadership. If deception programs were continued into the Brezhnev-Kosygin era, they were constrained by Brezhnev's concern that American overconfidence about the strategic balance be corrected before a war engulfed the superpowers. The replacement of SS-19s in SS-11 silos merely allowed the Soviet Ministry of Defense to continue in its commitment to pre-emptive attack on land-based strategic assets of the United States upon warning of impending war—nothing more than had been sought and perhaps achieved in the 1960's. Soviet negotiators at SALT I indicated their unwillingness to agree to a freeze on missile replacements, and indicated that there would be a new missile that was closer to the characteristics of the SS-11 than the SS-9. If both attacked the Minuteman launchers, why should intelligence analysts claim deception respecting the *replacement* missile, if the fundamental misunderstanding occurred respecting the *replaced* missile, constituting two-thirds of the Soviet ICBM force at the outset of SALT I? Is it realistic to expect that the Soviets should have sacrificed the SALT I agreement merely to educate the Americans about Minuteman vulnerability, or so as to make a full disclosure of the SS-19's throw weight?

What were the indicators of Soviet ballistic missile performance that led US intelligence analysts to recurringly underestimate the numbers and deployment rate that the Soviets actually chose? There was not a fundamental disagreement on the parameters of performance in missile duels. The Soviet Academy of Sciences published in 1959 unclassified studies on the relationships between missile accuracy, yield, target hardness, and target survivability. There was general agreement on the key parameters of counterforce exchange. If there was a disagreement about projected outcomes, that disagreement was premised upon inconsistent perceptions of the actual values of the parameters involved: missile accuracy, warhead yield, target hardness, and perhaps also missile force reliability and replenishment capability. If the Soviet leadership authorized a program to create a gap between US perceptions of key parameters and Soviet perceptions of those same parameters, that program was not established without substantial knowledge of the key parameters and their use by US intelligence in evaluation of ICBM capabilities.

In the first five years of centralized deception operations within the KGB's Department "D" (1959-1964), the Soviets tested a variety of missiles. Three ballistic missiles designed at one missile design bureau, the SS-5, SS-7, and SS-9,[44] are of particular interest to historians of deception, because they are ideally suited for a "scientific" display of performance parameters respecting the apparent accuracy of each system.[45] These missile systems may be characterized as the "peacock systems" of the Soviet ballistic missile arsenal of the 1960's. It is not every system of technology that affords a deception planning staff the opportunity to provide credible, scientific evidence to a skeptical adversary. The "peacock" missile systems are an exception, and can provide a different display to different audiences.

These three ballistic missiles, a single-stage SS-5, a two-stage SS-7, and a much larger two-stage SS-9, have the advantages and disadvantages of redundant measurement of physical events. When two or more instruments report on the same event, they provide an opportunity to measure instrumentation error, and if data is transmitted in a form that might be intercepted by an adversary, that data is a source of security concern. The principle of using two or more instruments to measure the same experiment, thus to determine instrumentation error, is known to every high school physics student. To obtain the high confidence in nuclear rocket performance needed to allow politicians choice among strategies that affect millions of lives requires an effort to understand the reliability of one's own instrumentation. It is simply unacceptable to manipulate data to deceive an adversary if the field experiments concurrently undermine confidence of the test's sponsors.[46]

Those systematic errors that are known and controllable are of lesser concern than random errors that may be studied but not controlled, and systematic errors that are unknown, or known but beyond control. Following operational deployment of the SS-9 and SS-11 ICBMs, Engineering Lieutenant Colonel M. Dullin discussed the "Measure of Accuracy" for readers of the Soviet Defense Ministry's journal, *Technology and Armament:*[47]

Errors in measurements are subdivided into three main categories: systematic, accidental, and large (blunders). Systematic errors also include errors the value and sign of which on making measurements either remain constant or change in accordance with a certain law. These errors in their turn are subdivided into four groups: instrument (caused by design shortcomings in the instruments, incorrect graduating of their scales, eccentricity in the rotating parts of the instruments); errors in methods (which occur because of imperfection in the method used for measuring or incorrect selection of it); personnel (depend on the individual traits of the operator and mainly on his level of training); adjusting (occur as a result of incorrect location of the measuring instruments and other attachments).

In the process of making measurements an attempt is always made to compensate for systematic errors. For this purpose use is made of the methods of displacement, compensation according to sign, or method of repeated measurements. The first method makes it possible to replace a value being measured with the value obtained by a calibrating instrument. . . . While systematic errors can be taken into account relatively easily, and compensated for, it is much more difficult to deal with random errors. The latter are found only as a result of repeated measurements of one and the same value under one and the same conditions. It is impossible to eliminate random errors completley. However, an effort must be made to reduce them to a minimum.

If a systematic error is intentionally incorporated into a system for precision guidance, a means must be found to remove the effective error without alerting an observing adversary to the fact of compensation for the known systematic error. There may be a need, from time to time, for the temporary removal of systematic biasing or the removal of telemetry systems to assure a test of the adequacy of the weapon system without simultaneously alerting the adversary.

Even if recurring statistical tests ultimately disclose the systematic biasing of instrumentation data so as to make ICBMs appear less accurate than they are in fact, the beauty of a technical biasing program involves the *time advantage* accruing to the sponsor of the systematically skewed test program. Particularly when intelligence analysts have strong biases in favor of the random distribution of errors, a high confidence level will be required to convince analysts even to *consider* that they might be the victims of a double-cross system by national technical means. Thus, sample size is increased, along with the time to acquire it. If a statistician helps to design a statistical deception effort, additional time may be required to unravel the mystery. Thus, even if with hindsight it appears that some countermeasure would have been appropriate, a continuing time lag in perceptions and decisions to reduce vulnerabilities provides a payoff that is hard to beat.

If a technical deception program is centered around the "peacock systems'' of instrumentation display, other ballistic missile programs can ride along on the security coat tails of the deception program. Once it is part of the conventional wisdom that some Soviet guidance components are inferior to comparable US instruments by a determined proportion, then other Soviet ballistic missiles which use the same guidance components will be guaranteed a similar perception of inferiority, unless some other slip-up in a test program occurs.

Feedback through technical and human sources of intelligence provided Soviet strategic planners insights into the vulnerabilities of land-based US missiles and US assessments of the Soviet ballistic missile threat. Based solely on that element of Soviet knowledge to be found in the open literature on US defectors and the trial records of convicted criminal defendants, Soviet insights of the period 1959-1964 were substantial. Assessments by the US of the SS-4 (MRBM), SS-6 (ICBM), and early SS-5 (IRBM) tests preceded the defections of employees Mitchell and Martin from the National Security Agency to Moscow on June 25, 1960.[48] Between December 1959 and February 1961 a Lieutenant Colonel of the US Army on the staff of the Joint Chiefs of Staff, transmitted information on ''atomic weaponry, missiles, military plans for the defense of Europe, [SAC] retaliatory plans'' and military intelligence reports.[49] In the late 1950's a KGB agent in German counterintelligence was positioned to evaluate favorably KGB disinformation reports, and to identify for the KGB which West German collection assets were considered reliable and which were not.[50] By mid-1960 a chauffeur and courier for the Assistant Director and Chief of Staff of the National Security Agency was selling documents to Soviet intelligence, apparently until his death in 1963.[51] A communications operator assigned to HQ USAF communications center comprised cryptosystems in the period 1965-1966.[52] An employee of a principal contractor for design of the command and control system of the US Strategic Air Command (system 465L) transferred documentation to Soviet intelligence at least through April 1963.[53] Monitoring of the Anglo-American agent, Colonel Oleg Penkovsky in 1961-1962, other known US agents, and any false defectors in contact with the US intelligence agencies would round out the picture that deception planners would require.

In sum, a potentially critical difference of perceptions about US ICBM survivability may be involved in estimations of USSR guidance component accuracy. A second difference, at least between Soviet nuclear effects tests of 1961-1962 and later US nuclear tests, may have involved perceptions about whether US silo designs were adequate to meet survivability specifications. By 1970, officials in the Office of the Secretary of Defense indicated their determination to mandate improvements in silo hardening. By 1975 a variety of improvements in the Minuteman basing system were completed.[54] A third difference in perceptions may have involved the yields and principal effects of Soviet nuclear weapons against US strategic assets within hardened silos. But accuracy was the most important parameter in assessing the survivability of US land-based strategic assets.

Two additional considerations deserve brief attention. The first is the potential effects of systematic errors that are not identified on the outcome of counterforce missile duels. As Professor and Rear Admiral N. Pavlovich has noted:

> A certain theoretical overestimation of accuracy led to a reduction in the norms for the means of destruction necessary for the achievement of decisive results.[55]

The larger yield of Soviet nuclear weapons makes the effect of modest but unknown systematic errors less significant than for US nuclear weapons. Moreover, as a hedge against systematic downrange error, Multiple warheads—for example those of the SS-11 Mod 3—can be offset up or downrange.[56] Still, Soviet confidence in the 1960's may have been based, in part, on Soviet analytic errors, and not merely on those of the United States.

A second consideration has the effect of reducing error, should the Soviets have adopted a space-based Doppler-aided guidance system for the SS-11 missiles. If this development occurred and US intelligence neglected it, the cause would appear to have been self-deception that the Soviets were careful not to upset, rather than a deception program originating in Moscow.

For US intercontinental ballistic missiles, the debate about whether to utilize mid-course correction systems was resolved in favor of all-inertial systems that worked better than initially expected. Externally-aided guidance systems were at least theoretically vulnerable to counter-measures, and complicated system planning. On the other hand, they might reduce crossrange or downrange errors in guidance. By the time that the Soviet SS-9 and SS-11 missiles were tested in 1963 and 1965, the US government had opted for all-inertial guidance.

However, in 1960 and afterwards, the US Navy tested a Doppler-transmitting satellite system that resulted in precise location of a moving or stationary object, if the location of the satellite were precisely known. This so-called *TRANSIT* system was the subject of an extraordinary quantity of descriptive and analytical material, all in the US open literature in the early 1960's.

Soviet guidance principles for ballistic missiles were derived in large part from thrust control and correction techniques adopted by the Germans in World War II.[57] Soviet ballistic missiles were well suited to accept guidance corrections that could improve the timing of vernier engine cutoff, or reset inertial guidance systems to reduce net guidance errors.

> In the postwar period . . . Soviet military radioelectronics began a period of accelerated development with radar and communications . . . Remote radio control which had played an exceptionally important role in the development of rocket weapons entered into the arena of practical application.
>
> The characteristic feature of the rocket weapons which differentiates them from the preceding varieties of weapons such as artillery is that the rockets may be controlled in flight, thus permitting precision-destruction of targets since errors in initial sighting of deviations . . . may be corrected by control of the rocket in flight.[58]

Did the Soviets activate a Doppler-aided missile guidance program in the early 1960's, or were they content to follow the American lead in utilizing all-inertial guidance systems? During the SS-9 missile tests of 1964, the Soviets experimented with Doppler communications from satellites. By the time of the SS-11 missile tests in the spring of 1965, the Molniya I satellite communications system was on station over the northern latitudes of the Soviet Union. Throughout the period of SS-11 operational deployments, the Molniya I satellite system provided multiple frequencies for military and other uses. If the evidence of Doppler-aided correction of ICBMs in powered flight is inconclusive, US analysts should not reject this possibility for improving the accuracy of Soviet ICBMs merely because the United States chose another course of action.[59]

On June 30, 1965, the US Strategic Air Command accepted its 800th Minuteman I missile. Orders for improved Minuteman II missile had been announced on May 19th of that year. The prowess of the United States in intercontinental missile technology was recognized in speeches indicating the importance and invulnerability of these silo-hardened missiles.

By this date in mid-1965, launcher silos of the USSR's Strategic Rocket Forces were in preparation to accept SS-9 and SS-11 missiles. SS-7 and SS-8 missiles were operational. Soviet deployments of

SS-7s, 8s and 11s were behind, but racing to catch up with Minuteman deployment, while SS-9s covered the Titan II missiles and the command and control silos for the Minuteman system. The Molniya I military communications satellites had been tested and declared operational.

On July 3, 1965 First Secretary Brezhnev responded to American assessments of the strategic balance, during an address to military academy graduates:

> While we do not want to threaten anybody, it is necessary to note that the figures and calculations quoted in the West concerning our rocket and nuclear might are far from accurate and lead one to question the information possessed by their compilers, particularly the intelligence services of the imperialist states. We wish to declare quite positively that any attempt at aggressive acts against our country on the basis of such evaluation of our military potential will be fatal for its initiators.[60]

The extension of counterintelligence jurisdiction to all sources of US intelligence collection would not have *guaranteed* a more timely recognition of the vulnerability of land-based strategic assets. Admiral Godfrey, Director of British Naval Intelligence in World War II emphasizes three lessons for intelligence that are pertinent today:

1. The unwillingness of authority to believe information that has awkward political implications.
2. The tendency of naval officers, and others who have taken part in negotiations, to become advocates of the integrity of the persons with whom they secured agreement, and to lose the skepticism which is part of vigilance.
3. Our technicians may not be the best judges of enemy intentions and achievement. They find it hard sometimes to believe that what they cannot do or have not thought of doing has been done by the other side.[61]

But all-source counterintelligence can challenge the conventional wisdom, identify channels of active deception, and protect the precious margin of unexpected collection that is needed for quality control of other sources. While positive intelligence missions cannot be delegated to counterintelligence staffs, neither can the mind-set of the traditional intelligence analyst cope with the double-cross system by national technical means.

A divergence of assumptions and perspectives should be encouraged, not only among competing sources of positive intelligence analysis but also between the staffs and working methods of counterintelligence and those who are trained to uncover the secrets of nature.

IV. All-Source Counterintelligence and National Intelligence Charters

If all-source counterintelligence is to be undertaken, it will require at least some coordination among the various agencies. Under the existing National Security Act of 1947, the Director of Central Intelligence has the flexibility to coordinate analysis, training, and resource allocations for counterintelligence relating to foreign intelligence.

Legislation under consideration by Congress would vest the principal coordinating authority for counterintelligence in the Director of the Federal Bureau of Investigation. Section 503(a)(1) of the proposed National Intelligence Act of 1980 (S. 2284) would designate the Director of the FBI as:

> . . . The principal officer of the Government for the conduct and coordination of counterintelligence activities and counterterrorism intelligence activities within the United States.[62]

The principal legislative purpose behind this section appears to be to assure that CIA's counterintelligence jurisdiction will not, without FBI and Department of Justice review, result in encroachments upon the personal privacy of Americans. There is also an interest in assuring proper coordination and liaison among the various counterintelligence entities of the intelligence community.

It is doubtful, though, whether the concept of all-source counterintelligence was even contemplated when this section was drafted. This is not to claim that all-source counterintelligence jurisdiction does not now exist, but rather to suggest that the traditional performance of FBI counterintelligence functions has resulted in little contact with the national technical means of deception, and only limited familiarity with US programs for technical collection abroad.

Moreover, the traditional FBI focus on the human counterintelligence problem has perhaps even contributed to US deception vulnerabilities. If all an agency has for assets are human sources, then that agency is likely to have a powerful bias in favor of the acknowledgement of the reliability of the best-placed sources under apparent control. What if some of the key sources are under control of foreign deception officers? Any agency that is unduly reliant upon a single type of information collection should not be entrusted with coordinating all-source counterintelligence relating to foreign intelligence.

The same Achilles' heel is exposed when an agency of technical collection has primary responsibility to evaluate the reliability of a source on which that agency principally relies. If, for example, a unique channel of signals intelligence is tentatively identified as compromised to an adversary, the proprietor of that channel is perhaps the last to be interested in the veracity of this counterintelligence insight. If there is any possibility of intellectual escape, the proprietor of the channel that cannot be replaced will cling to the illusion that the compromised channel is not really compromised, or that even if compromised, it is impractical to target the channel in deception activities.

If the coordination of all-source counterintelligence is to succeed, the coordinating function should be vested in an entity of the intelligence community that is knowledgeable about all of the principal activities of the intelligence community but independent from them. Thus, the coordination of counterintelligence relating to foreign intelligence should be a duty of the Director of Central Intelligence, or the Director of National Intelligence, if the framework of the National Intelligence Act of 1980 is adopted or reconsidered in 1981.

As simplified and streamlined intelligence charters come before Congress and the American public, those who are intent on improving them should anticipate challenges and provide the flexibility to meet them.

All-source counterintelligence can play a key role in transforming the national means of self-deception into the national means of detection. Legislative charters can provide a positive mandate to protect even our scientific genius from human folly.

Notes

1. Yale University Press, 1972.
2. See Michael Mihalka, *German Deception in the 1930s, forthcoming, and* D. Maxim, M. Walsh, and B. Whaley, *Covert Rearmament in Germany, 1919-1939: Deception and Misperception,* Mathtech, Inc. and the Office of Research and Development, Central Intelligence Agency, March 1979.
3. Barton S. Whaley, *Strategem: Deception and Surprise in War,* Cambridge, Massachusetts, Center of International Studies, Massachusetts Institute of Technology, 1969.
4. Frederic S. Feer, "Incorporating Analysis of Foreign Governments' Deception into the US Analytical System," in Roy Godson (ed.), *Intelligence Requirements for the 1980's: Analysis and Estimates,* Washington, D.C. National Strategy Information Center, p. 141.
5. See, for example, H. B. Cott, *Adaptive Coloration in Animals,* London, 1940; Wolfgang Wickler, *Mimicry in Plants and Animals,* London, 1968, especially chapter 16, "Intraspecific Mimicry," pp. 221-227.

6. New York, Random House, 1978; Vintage Books ed., 1979, p. 263.
7. *Ibid.*, pp. 260, 261.
8. Definition in S. 2284, Feb. 1980, §103(3). H.R. 6820, Mar. 17, 1980, §401 has minor variants in language.
9. Quoted in Barton Whaley, Mary Walsh, and Dan Maxim, *Thoughts on the Cost-Effectiveness of Deception and Related Tactics in the Air War, 1939 to 1945,* Deception Research Program Staff, Mathtech, Inc. and the Office of Research and Development, Central Intelligence Agency, March, 1979.
10. Frederic S. Feer. "Coping with Deception," *op.cit.,* p. 150.
11. See Amrom H. Katz, *Verification and SALT: The State of the Art and the Art of the State,* Washington, D.C.: Heritage Foundation, 1979, on symbiosis between observer and observed.
12. William R. Harris, "The Effectiveness of U.S. Counterintelligence and Its Congressional Oversight under the National Intelligence Act of 1980," Testimony, U.S. Senate Select Committee on Intelligence, April 2, 1980.
13. George J. Keegan, Jr., "Is Russia Really Stronger than the U.S.?" *The Baltimore Sun,* February 13, 1977, p. Kl.
14. *Ibid.*
15. "The CIA Bumbles its Way into Yet More Criticism," *Los Angeles Times,* April 14, 1980, p. II-5.
16. Reviewing doctrinal indicators of 1955-1957, Herbert S. Dinerstein projected a Soviet commitment to pre-emptive counterforce capabilities in a *Foreign Affairs* article published in January 1958. In an April 1958 reply, Deputy Chief of the General Staff, General Kurosov, dismissed these indicators as "theoretical statements of individual authors" in "On the Question of the Pre-emptive Blow," *Krasnaya Zvezda* [Red Star], April 27, 1958. Defense Minister Malinovsky reiterated, "Our peaceloving policy does not permit any kind of 'preventive war,' 'pre-emptive blows,' or 'surprise attack' about which some foreign slanderers are trumpeting." *Pravda,* May 9, 1958. See also the earlier, less authoritative claim by Major General N. Talenskiy, carried by TASS on March 6, 1958, that in the Soviet Union "no one speaks or thinks about the necessity of . . . a preventive war and surprise attack. . . ." and the assertion by Lieutenant General S. Krasilnikov, carried by Radio Moscow on March 9, 1958, that "The Soviet Union will never be the first to take up arms."
17. Albert C. Hall, "The Case for an Improved ICBM," *Astronautics & Aeronautics,* Vol. 15, No. 2, February 1977.
18. Raymond Foye, Thomas Brewer, and John Phelps, "The 'Destabilizing Effects' of Changes in Missile Performance Parameters," Paper ACS-W2, August 17, 1960, in AAAS, *Summer Study on Arms Control 1960, Collected Papers,* I, p. 132.
19. John Mullen, "Nuclear Exchange Ratios," in AAAS, *Summer Study on Arms Control 1960, Collected Papers,* I, p. 139.
20. Robert Moss reports in the *London Daily Telegraph,* November 12, 1979, on "The Intelligence War: New Challenge to CIA" of:
"acute concern . . . that . . . the KGB may have succeeded over many years in systematically deceiving United States intelligence about Moscow's military capacities and intentions. Prior to the sacking of the key members of the CIA staff at the end of 1974 they were engaged (with the help of the CIA's Directorate of Science and Technology) in . . . assessments of military intelligence culled from Soviet agents recruited by the FBI in New York . . . . The tentative conclusion reached was that much of the information from these suspect sources—for example, exaggerated accounts of problems faced by the Russians in constructing missile guidance system[s]—was part of a strategic deception programme which

was at least partly responsible for the CIA's notorious undervaluation of the Soviet defence effort in the mid-1970s."

21. J. C. Hopkins, *Development of Strategic Air Command, 1946-1976,* Omaha, U.S. Air Force Strategic Air Command, Office of the Historian, March 21, 1976, p. 93.
22. See *50 Years of Armed Forces of the USSR* [in Russian], Moscow, Voyenizdat, 1968, p. 521.
23. Stanley Sienkiewicz, "SALT and Soviet Nuclear Doctrine," *International Security,* Spring 1978.
24. Rand Report R-266, Santa Monica, California, April 1954.
25. See Stanford Research Institute, *Soviet Military Strategy,* 3rd ed. introduction.
26. "On the Role of Surprise in Contemporary War," *Voennaia Mysl',* February 1955.
27. Quoted in Col. A. A. Sidorenko, *The Offensive,* Moscow, 1970.
28. See *Khrushchev Remembers: The Last Testament,* Boston: Little, Brown, 1974, pp. 45-50.
29. Khrushchev contrasts Korolyov's *Semyorka* with the work of Academician Yangel, who developed "a quick-firing rocket engine." *Khrushchev Remembers: The Last Testament,* Boston: Little, Brown, 1974, p. 51.
30. *Ibid.,* and see Nicholas Daniloff, "How We Spy on the Russians," *Washington Post Magazine,* December 9, 1979, p. 33.
31. See *The Penkovsky Papers,* Garden City, N.Y.: Doubleday, 1965.
32. Edmund Beard, *Developing the ICBM: A Study in Bureaucratic Politics,* New York: Columbia University Press, 1976, p. 203.
33. On the date that the Supreme Soviet announced its nuclear test moratorium, March 31, 1958, the U.S. State Department announced: "The Soviet statement comes on the heels of an intensive series of secret Soviet tests." State Department Press Release No. 158, March 31, 1958.
34. General V. Tolubko, *Voenno Istorischeskii Zhurnal,* No. 4, 1975, and No. 10, 1976. Brezhnev became a Candidate Member of the Politburo and returned to the Central Committee Secretariat on February 27, 1956. He became a Full Member of the Politburo in June 1957, and remained in the CC Secretariat until July 16, 1960. See *The Soviet Leadership Since Stalin: CPSU Politburo and Secretariat, 1952-1979,* CIA/NFAC/CR Document CR79-14399, August 1979.
35. William T. Lee, *Soviet Defense Expenditures in an Era of SALT,* Washington, D.C.: United States Strategic Institute, USSI Report 79-1, 1980.
36. *Ibid.*
37. *Krasnaya Zvezda* [Red Star], February 4, 1965, p. 2. For an overview of the role of the so-called Manchurian generals and their World War II experience with lightning strikes and deception, see John Despres, Lilita Dzirkals, and Barton Whaley, *Timely Lessons of History: The Manchurian Model for Soviet Strategy,* Santa Monica, Cal., The Rand Corporation, Report R-1825-NA, July 1976. Marshals Vasilevskii, Malinovsky, and Zakharov were among the key Manchurian campaign participants or involved General Staff officers.
38. "And the Gilpatric speech was followed by a round of briefings for our allies—deliberately including some whom we know were penetrated, so as to reinforce and confirm through Soviet intelligence channels the message carried openly through the Gilpatric speech." Roger Hilsman, *To Move a Nation: The Politics of Foreign Policy in the Administration of John F. Kennedy,* Garden City, N.Y.: Doubleday, 1967, pp. 163-164.
39. "Evaluating U.S. Estimative Intelligence," *op.cit.,* 1980. V. N. Chelomey is further identified as Chief of an Aviation Design Bureau since 1960. See CIA/

NFAC/CR, *Reference Aid: Membership, USSR Academy of Sciences,* March 1977, CR-77-11360, p. 7.

40. See Nicholas Daniloff, "How We Spy on the Russians," *Washington Post Magazine,* December 9, 1979, p. 33.
41. *Ibid.*
42. "The Legacy of SALT I: Soviet Deception and U.S. Retreat," *Strategic Review,* Fall 1979, and *Congressional Record,* Vol. 125, November 6, 1979.
43. Sullivan, "U.S. Estimative Intelligence . . .," *op.cit.,* p. 33.
44. See Nicholas Daniloff, *loc. cit.*
45. See William R. Harris, *A SALT Safeguards Program,* Santa Monica, California: The Rand Corporation, Paper P-6388, September 1979, pp. 13-16.
46. See, for example, Part III, "Experimental Development and Testing of Missiles," in V. I. Varfolomeyev and M. I. Kopytov, eds., *Proyktirovaniye i Ispytaniya Ballisticheskikh Raket* [Design and Testing of Ballistic Missiles], Moscow: Military Publishing House of the Ministry of Defense, signed to press October 8, 1969, translated in JPRS No. 51810, November 9, 1970.
47. *Tekhnika i Vooruzheniye,* No. 1, January 1967, pp. 43-50, translated by U.S. Army Intelligence, April 1967, Series J1863.
48. David Kahn, *The Codebreakers,* New York: Macmillan, 1967, pp. 693-694.
49. F. W. Kenworthy, "Officials Say F.B.I. Agents Shadowed Spying Suspect from 1959 to 1961," *The New York Times,* July 14, 1966; "Retired Colonel Pleads Guilty in Soviet Agent Plot," *The New York Times,* December 17, 1966, p. 14; Fred P. Graham, "Retired Pentagon Officer Is Seized as Spy for Soviet," *The New York Times,* July 13, 1966; U.S. Dept. of Justice, "Prosecutions for Violations of Espionage Statutes," in *The Use of Classified Information in Litigation,* 95th Cong., 1978, pp. 227-235.
50. Soviet utilization of German scientists in ballistic missile programs is reported by Clarence G. Lasby, *Project Paperclip: German Scientists and the Cold War,* New York: Atheneum, 1971, pp. 178-184, 269. KGB agent Heinze Felfe worked in the Counterintelligence Section of the German Federal Intelligence Service (BND) at its Püllach headquarters. He came under suspicion in 1960, but was not arrested until 1963. See Reinhard Gehlen, *The Service: The Memoirs of General Reinhard Gehlen,* New York: Popular Library, 1972, pp. 245-246.
51. David Kahn, *The Codebreakers,* New York: Macmillan, 1967, pp. 696-697.
52. *Ibid.,* and *Facts on File 1966,* p. 501E3.
53. *New York Times,* October 28, 1964, p. 48; conviction, December 3, 1964, p. 1. See e.g., *The SACCS (465L) Study Project: A Report,* 27 October 1958, declassified.
54. *The New York Times,* December 6, 1970, p. 1; December 7, 1970, p. 37; J. C. Hopkins, *Development of Strategic Air Command, 1946-1976,* p. 182.
55. *Voenno Istorischeskii Zhurnal,* No. 12, December 1974, "Basic Factors in the Development of the Art of Naval Warfare."
56. See testimony of Lt. Gen. Glenn A. Kent, House Armed Services Committee, February 7, 1978, and H. Kruger, *Monte Carlo Calculations of Cumulative Target Survival Probability in the Presence of Warhead Fratricide,* Lawrence Livermore Laboratory, Report UCID-16880, September 18, 1975, 167 pp.
57. See W. Oppelt, "An Historical Review of Autopilot Development, Research and Theory in Germany," *Am. Soc. Mech. Engr. Series G,* Vol. 98, No. 3, pp. 215-223; "Radio Direction-finding and Navigation Aids; Some Reports on German Work Issued in 1944-45," *Dep. Sc. Industr. Res. Radio Res. Rep.,* No. 21, 1951, 92 pp.; P. T. Astashenkov, *Radioelectronics in Guided Missiles* [in Russian], Moscow,

1960; V. G. Vlasov and V. G. Svechnikov, *Fundamentals of Radio Engineering and Electronic Navigation Devices* [in Russian], Moscow, 1960; G. I. Tuzov, *Isolation and Processing of Information in Doppler Systems,* Moscow, 1967; Y. E. Belen'kii, et al., "Errors in the Velocity Vector Measurement of Moving Objects in Two-Point Ranging Using Doppler Effect," *Otbor Peredacha Inform.,* No. 24, 1970, pp. 130-135.

58. A. V. Gorasimov, "Progress in Radioelectronics," *Krasnaya Zvezda* [Red Star], May 6, 1962, p. 4, in JPRS 14, 560, July 23, 1962. In January 1958 Major General G. I. Pokrovsky of the Moscow-based Air Force Academy Emeni Zhukovskiy wrote favorably about velocity correction using the Doppler principle with missile-based transponders. See *Technika Molodezhy,* Jan. 1958, and Radio Moscow, February 5, 1958, at 1500 GMT.

59. Premier Kosygin refers to "wide possibilities" for "use of satellites and rockets for . . . navigation," in September 1965. See Radio Moscow, September 28, 1965, 0600 GMT. See also the January 1966 *Five Year Plan* and Academician Keldysh on April 3, 1966. A June 1966 article claims navigation accuracy for ships and aircraft of 200 meters. *Sovetskiy Patriot,* June 22, 1966, p. 4. Because the capability is acknowledged in 1966 but no navigation satellite is identified, it is assumed that "such flights serve military purposes." Barbara M. DeVoe, chapter 8 in *Soviet Space Programs, 1966-1970,* U.S. Senate Comm. on Aeronautical and Space Sciences Doc. No. 92-51, Washington, D.C., GPO, 1971, p. 314. "Even with Soviet reticence in discussing more than optical tracking, there were Western reports of a network consisting of a master station and 12 others eqipped with receivers to measure Doppler shifts . . . transmitting data to [a] central computation center." *Ibid.,* p. 149.

60. Foreign Broadcast Information Service, USSR, July 6, 1965, and Peter Grose, "Soviet Says Missile Power Exceeds West's Estimates," *The New York Times,* July 4, 1965, § 1, pp. 1, 2.

61. Quoted in Donald McLachlan, *Room 39—A Study in Naval Intelligence,* New York: Atheneum, 1968, and Amrom H. Katz, *Verification and SALT: The State of the Art and the Art of the State,* Washington, D.C.: Heritage Foundation, 1979.

62. A revised draft of April 1980 would merge the definition of counterintelligence and counterterrorism intelligence, but retain the overall mandate.

Discussants

Admiral Donald Harvey: It is probably fair to identify my biases. One is that I have served as the head of a counterintelligence organization. And I have been involved with counterintelligence before Executive Order 12036 and subsequently. That probably gives a certain cast to my approach to the subject that otherwise it might not have.

Another bias is that I probably could be categorized as belonging to the Roberta Wohlstetter school of thought which, if I understand that very splendid lady correctly, is that the United States, not uniquely but specially has a capability of self-deception far exceeding the capability of others to deceive us. I have scars of some 28 years in the business to prove it, and as a consequence I find myself identifying with her school of thought rather strongly.

One other bias, and that is in the explanation of strange phenomena, whether induced by deception or not: more often than not, the ultimate explanation turns out to be infinitely more prosaic and understandable than any of the 57 varieties of explanations that analysts, scientists, and academicians ascribe to that phenomenon prior to its being understood. If there is a slight degree of cynicism noted there, that is probably a correct perception.

I agree with many of Dr. Harris' major points. He makes the point that surprise, and consequently deception, is as important now in 1980 as it has ever been in national struggles in the past. I certainly can agree with that. Another point that he makes rather strongly is that National Technical Means (NTM) of verification and the technological successes with which intelligence in the United States has been increasingly associated do not rule out the possibility of successful deception. Once again I am in total accord. I cannot exclude the possibility that long-term deception is possible. That may be the long-term intelligence officer's normal bureaucratic caution. We always can hide behind at least one weasel word, so we would not exclude the possibility of a long-term deception.

And with Dr. Harris' minor premise that all-source counterintelligence is necessary and desirable, I think anyone who has worked with NTM and with counterintelligence would certainly agree.

Points where we may not be in total accord would be the definition of counterintelligence as exemplified in Executive Order 12036, which Dr. Harris believes is outdated. I am not totally convinced that, in the sense that there is an implication that the functions in that definition are themselves outdated. Certainly from a military standpoint I would not agree—and I may be reading more into it than Dr. Harris means. He perceives what I would call counterdeception in the proposed definition of counterintelligence, and I don't quite see that in there.

With regard to systematic underbiasing of ICBM accuracy, I must here defer to my colleagues who may be in a better position to judge. Failing a definitive verification of the hypothesis, I would fall back on the bias I have already identified, which is that the explanation may be considerably less exotic than as postulated. And I do not exclude the possibility of a considerable amount of American self-deception on an number of these things.

Dr. Harris' paper advocates the importance of all-source counterintelligence and the expansion of counterintelligence to encompass, I gather, all-source analysis under a counterintelligence organization or subset of an organization. He does not explore the alternative, which would be to emphasize, inculcate, and require counterintelligence or—and here I am using Dr. Harris' terminology—counterdeception awareness in our regular positive intelligence analysts. In fact, in at least one instance I know of, that has been done from an organizational standpoint on a continuing basis. It is at least a feasible alternative.

Dr. Harris makes a considerable point that positive intelligence analysts are not trained in the methodology, mysticism, or what you will, of the counterintelligence world, and consequently may miss deception. And I don't mean in any way to derogate the danger of deception. We are dealing with the world's most ardent believers in deception, and certainly on a broad, longterm basis I think we would have to say the prime practitioners of deception.

On the other hand, some of the finest reasonings I have ever seen, absolutely brilliant deductions, have been made by positive intelligence analysts, especially if they are involved in internecine warfare with their peers. As an alternative—and one which probably wouldn't be any more expensive in terms of people or money—I believe one should explore the possibilities of what the current situation really is: namely, a nice, healthy, almost bitter rivalry between positive intelligence analysts in assessing data from particular sensor or in correlating data from a number of systems. Nothing whets the mind of the little old ladies in tennis shoes in the back room more than the possibility of one-upping a peer analyst, preferably in another organization.

With regard to the proposed legislation, S. 2284, Dr. Harris says one of its failures is that it splits positive and counterintelligence—and I certainly could agree with him that there needs to be a better definition of "foreign intelligence." We have lots of them, premised on the FBI coordinating counterintelligence domestically and the DCI coordinating counterintelligence outside the United States. That happens to be the current situation, to the best of my knowledge. In an organization with which I was associated, we thought we had some successes in counterintelligence, both domestically and overseas, and we had no great problem coordinating domestically with the FBI and with the DCI's representative, the CIA, overseas. A common problem with both, which can be worked out and usually is, is that if it looks good, they always want to take it from you. I found no great problem and no great dichotomy in working with the existing situation.

Naval Intelligence is very small—ancient, but small. Our counterintelligence organization was headed by a man who had spent over 20 years in positive intelligence—it has been for at least the last four incumbents of the position—and he reported directly and daily to a man with some 25 to 30 years experience in positive intelligence. We didn't have too much trouble in a small organization, and it may be a special case—in the crossover between positive and counterintelligence.

I am well aware of Langley's problems between the intelligence people and those who did things other than pure and substantive intelligence. We did not have that problem. So I submit there is an alternative.

One thing that would be interesting to address at some point would be counterintelligence in the field as contrasted to counterintelligence at the national level. Here, again, the military brings a particular bias to the question, which is not addressed in this paper at all. But it might be well worthwhile to address it if one is going to cover counterintelligence thoroughly, because a division commander in West Germany, surrounded by almost as many East German and Soviet agents as he has sergeants, tends to think that counterintelligence is a common function which he needs to preserve the security and efficiency of his organization. This gives rise to a very distinctive view about counterintelligence.

Dr. Roland Herbst: I am going to comment from a narrow point of view, that of a relatively well-informed bystander for many years in the area of technical intelligence, but with no ability to make judgments in the HUMINT areas.

Dr. Harris has presented the proposition that for about a decade there was a fairly well-determined Soviet deception program in the area of ICBM accuracy. Because he has only presented it as a proposition, I might just let it go at that. But I think it would be worthwhile to give my opinion on that subject; it may illustrate something that I would like to pursue a little further.

If I were asked, "Are you confident that there is a Soviet deception program in this area?" I'd say "No," at least at the level of acquitting somebody in a criminal trial. On the other hand, if I were asked whether we were vulnerable to deception in this area, and again I am limiting myself to technical intelligence, I would say, "I'm sure." And so I am stuck with a situation where I have no strong opinion that we have been deceived, but I have a strong opinion that we were, during the period in question, *vulnerable* to deception in this area.

Is that important in this discussion? I think it is because, in the subtle properties of modern weapons system, there is a large class of those properties that are both critical to the operation of the system and judgments about its effectiveness and, I believe, subject to deceptive procedures relative to the testing of those systems.

Counter to some of the things Admiral Harvey implied, at least, but agreeing with Dr. Harris, I think from my observation that the technical analysts not only do not take that as a very serious threat but indeed tend at least in some cases to regard it as a joke. But they are in the bad position that many of their most important techniques will disappear as useful tools if this possibility is admitted. Therefore, they are psychologically unable to take it seriously.

For that reason, while I agree that there is often strong competition within the community, I believe there is also a strong drive to finally to come to an agreement on something or other. The intelligence community is pressured by the fact that their bosses, the customers, want an answer, not "I don't know." And so they've got to get an answer. And that applies more often than not.

I really do believe that the idea of the B Team, for example, was a good one, that is, we need competitive procedures. But the introduction of counterintelligence into this confuses the issue. It is a necessary confusion but a confusion nonetheless, because there are a lot of different aspects of counterintelligence. Even sticking with the ferreting out of deception procedures concerning your positive intelligence, there are still nuances of differences here. I am somewhat concerned about what we might mean.

First, one might mean a counterintelligence point of view when looking at technical intelligence. That is, one looks at the technical intelligence in its own limited context, but applies the cynicism of counterintelligence in doing so. I believe the technical community is capable of this if there aren't other constraints stopping them, such as "Last year we said something so we can't reverse ourselves," or "You are not allowed to do it," or "I don't want to ask that because I don't know how to live if I ask that question."

The other issue is the all-source issue, that is, ferreting out the deception not by technical intelligence but by collateral evidence in other areas. I don't feel at all competent to comment on that, except I would hope that process would be separated in your mind from the first one. Because I believe we can get the advantage of other technical people in the first process, while it is very difficult to bring in temporaries and outsiders into the second process.

(Prior to the general discussion, **Dr. Harris** *made these additional observations.)*

I don't mean to imply that self-deception isn't the fundamental precondition of deception. Take, for example, the hypothesis on missile accuracy and missions; the idea that mutually assured destruction was something the Soviets would be willing to accept after Malenkov had said so, and we hoped others would; the idea that the Soviets had low missile reliability; the idea that we thought the objective of crisis stability was so important that, if you delayed buying an SS-6 and bought an SS-7 and an SS-9 and an SS-11, you would be putting them in silos so they could ride out an attack.

I am saying that, first of all, we can have deception with self-deception; the two often go together and reinforce each other. But we should assume that self-deception is a resource of the planners. And that relates to whether there is a roll for counterintelligence with regard to our self-deceptions. Part of counterintelligence involves monitoring channels of feedback. Our channels of feedback are from a closed society, and theirs are from an open society. What are they targeting? What are the themes they are getting? What do they think we are concerned about? Through counterintelligence, it is possible to identify where the Soviets have themselves identified some of our key self-deceptions. At least it's another source of competition.

Second, on the organization of counterdeception analysis, I do not in any respect dispute the view that analysis is important. I do not dispute the view that positive intelligence analysts should from time to time spot deception and be capable of doing so. I do dispute the view that they are particularly good at it on balance. Whaley shows, for example, ten cases of battle plans provided to analysts in advance of the battle in 68 cases of wartime surprise. Five of the plans were good; five of the plans were false. They were basically analyzed by the positive intelligence analysts; there may be one or two exceptions, but most of the analysis was really centered there. Four of the five true plans were determined to be false, and all of the five false plans were determined to be true.

I am saying that there is an important link to the positive intelligence process, that the counterintelligence process being linked to it will encourage competitive analysis. They will find the people in the positive community who will be willing to accept deception hypotheses, who will be willing to accept hard evidence of a compromised channel when others would say that if there is no way to reproduce that data, the channel cannot be compromised despite the evidence or, if compromised, cannot be targeted by deception planners because there is no way to replace the work they are doing.

I am saying that we should not exclude the counterintelligence process. When some of us see the reactions of the positive analysts, I think there is no reason *ab initio* to exclude the counterintelligence analysts from at least identifying hypotheses that come from controlled assets that have been identified, and to pass those on to the positive analysts; to look for relationships between a style of deception in one program and a style of deception in another; to give some indications of the kinds of systems we think involve unexpected collection vs. those we think are compromised. It will help the positive analysts to do quality control checks, to help design experiments, to do collection across systems when we already know the answer, to see whether we get that answer through a system that is in doubt as to whether it has been played back against us.

They do it with humans. There is no reason we can't do it with technical systems. And if you think the positive analysts are going to design those, you have an illusion.

Finally, I'd like to turn to one of Dr. Herbst's comments on the role of the counterintelligence community as it relates to the production of positive intelligence. Two issues were raised.

One involved the issue of all-source counterintelligence, whether the technical analyst could be brought into the human sector. Historically, we have brought in people like Dr. Herbst, from outside the community on *ad hoc* panels, Scientific Advisory Boards, and the like. They have made major contributions in testing deception hypotheses and a lot of other unconventional hypotheses. It is true they have not generally been given access to human source data, which often gets in there first and forms the preconceptions that can cut across technical systems. That is another argument, for having the counterintelligence jurisdiction extending to all of our sources, so that we build an in-house capability to do analysis and to experiment across the technical systems, including some people who have access to human sources who may in the past have supported some of the deceptions that we may have encountered across the technical systems.

If we look at the record of prediction of intelligence agencies, they do very well in combat with nature—even there, however, there is trouble—that is, how much oil or grain or whatever. And they do well with the humans where the payoffs aren't so high, where there isn't so much payoff to organized deception programs. But where the payoffs are the highest, such as strategic warning of war, or perhaps—this is an hypothesis—as to the forces to accomplish a strategy, there they don't do well. If we have any hope at all of their doing well, it is getting the warnings that will come through counterintelligence channels—the key warnings we are trying to get.

General Discussion

A participant wondered whether systematic US underestimation of Soviet strategic capabilities in the 1960's and 1970's was the result of deliberate Soviet deception (reinforced by self-deception)—or simply of faulty methods of analysis and, ultimately, ignorance. Dr. Harris reiterated that only systematic biasing of technical indicators could account for these recurring estimative errors. He agreed that the Soviets had not deceived us as to doctrine; that is as to their broad strategic intentions, but rather as to indicators of accuracy and thus as to their missile capabilities: neither ignorance alone nor self-deception alone seemed to him a sufficient explanation.

On another point Dr. Harris explained how he would attempt to test his hypothesis. First, he would force re-examination of the primary data. Then, after correcting for biases that might be expected for tactical security, he would determine whether the biases seemed clearly to point always in the same direction—and beyond the bounds of random bias. He would look also for parallel indicators such as Soviet strategic force procurement, for example, that provided collateral; and he would review critically the confidence level in those human sources whose information tended to substantiate the deception by technical means. In the end, he said, it is a matter of judging the weight of all the available evidence. As the discussion later developed, a participant with extensive experience in the operations of foreign intelligence services strongly underscored the importance of collateral information and sources—even, for example, in so successful a deception as the "double-cross system" in World War II. A congressional staff member observed that, far from self-deception and deliberate Soviet deception being contradictory, they feed on one another: all too often we *want* to be deceived. He suggested that the necessary starting point should be reverse role-playing—"these are the deceptions that I would like to run against them, now let's see if they are not doing them to us."

A scholar engaged in intensive research on deception noted that, as he recalled press reports, the B Team composed of outside analysts was about three times more accurate than the A Team of insiders in estimating Soviet strategic capabilities: he wondered whether a deception hypothesis could accommodate such a discrepancy. There seemed to be no unambiguous answer to that question. In the course of the discussion, however, it was pointed out that critically important deceptions by technical means more typically involve much narrower discrepancies. A relatively small degree of misinformation concerning missile accuracy, for example, could lead to decisive errors as to the "destructability" of hardened silos compared to urban/industrial targets, and thus to errors in judging Soviet strategic capabilities. The deceptions turn on quite subtle differences, not on such gross considerations as the range of the Backfire bomber or the operational reliability of a certain generation of tanks in the forests of East Germany. It was also pointed out that deceptions might involve slight manipulations of only a few key indicators—even when, after the Mitchell and Martin defections, the Soviets may have been put on warning as to US technical and analytic capabilities.

A former senior CI intelligence officer strongly objected to the implication in Dr. Harris's paper that many US intelligence failures could be traced to the lack of coordination within and among the various agencies and to the absence of clear lines of jurisdiction. He felt these points were greatly exaggerated and did a serious disservice to the counterintelligence community: coordination efforts were not always successful, to be sure, but these efforts were made—in the case of CI and technical analysis, as early as 1965. He also expressed the view that CI and deception-analysis derived from national technical means *should* in great measure be kept separate—that "mixing disciplines" might mean a foot in both camps and a firm foundation in neither. There was very substantial disagreement among the participants about the latter point in particular; a number of them cited personal experiences where coordination, or even effective communication, was conspicuous only by its absence and where jurisdictional lines became insuperable barriers.

A participant experienced in military CI questioned whether technical analysts who work with "sensor-collected information" are sufficiently aware that these sources, too, could be deceived. A former senior military officer judged that most such analysts are woefully inadequate in detecting sophisticated deceptions; he extended this judgment to analysts generally, most of whom were reluctant to lose those sources of data with which they are comfortable.

CHAPTER FOUR

Soviet Intelligence and Security Services In the 1980's: The Paramilitary Dimension

Paper:

John J. Dziak

Discussants:

Lt. Colonel John Guenther

Lt. General William Odom

Introduction

Western discussions of the Soviet threat to US and Western European security have, until recently, tended to focus on its purely military aspects. Our fixation with quantitative military indices, whether conventional or nuclear, is underscored by the seemingly perpetual MBFR and SALT processes. Lately, however, the threat posed by Soviet and satellite intelligence and security services appears to have been rediscovered, and concern over the plethora of activities of the KGB, GRU, DGI, and the rest is now spreading beyond the confines of Western security services. This recognition that the problem transcends a strictly military dimension is tardy but most welcome.

Moreover, determination of our counterintelligence requirements to meet this threat in the 1980's should not be bounded by the espionage activities of the KGB's First Chief Directorate and its subcontractors alone. There is a category of the Soviet problem that falls between the military threat and the intelligence/security threat, yet partakes of both. For want of a better term I have labeled this the "paramilitary dimension." It is an area of activity closely related to or conjoint with military operations but which, because of the political sensitivity of the objectives and the methods employed, is either controlled or monitored by the Soviet intelligence and security services. At issue here is a facet of Soviet "active measures" beyond the periodic kidnappings or assassinations by the First Chief Directorate's "Wet Affairs" Department or the deception operations of the Disinformation Directorate. My concern in this survey is with the role and operations of Soviet special purpose troops which during crises or wartime, would be deployed under the control of the intelligence and security organs of the USSR on highly sensitive missions.

"Active Measures" and Military Operations

"Active measures" (aktivnoye meropriyatye) have been a feature of aggressive Soviet security operations from the earliest years of the Soviet state. Western counterintelligence possesses numerous case studies of assassinations, kidnappings, fabrications, deceptions, and disinformation ploys employed in the pursuit of Soviet political objectives. This unusual category of extralegal activities is complemented in military affairs by "special designation" (*spetsnaznacheniya* or *spetsnaz*) units charged by the Party with missions too sensitive for the regular military.

It is useful to recall that the Party, from its earliest years in power, saw fit to create special categories of military forces subordinate not to the line military but rather to the various state security and interior organs. Collectivization and the breaking of the peasantry were enforced by OGPU troops. Leadership security was and still is provided by the elite blue-tabbed troops of the KGB's Kremlin Kommendatura. NKVD, NKGB, and "SMERSH" forces not only penetrated the Soviet military during World War II to ensure loyalty but also deployed in the Red Army's rear to prevent "unauthorized" retreats. As the war progressed in Moscow's favor, these same forces served as the Party's instrument for reimposing Soviet control in the reconquered territories and for introducing Soviet-style socialism to Eastern Europe.

In addition, after the Nazi invasion of 1941, the Party's Central Committee created a "Central Staff of the Partisan Movement" which conducted guerrilla, espionage, sabotage, and assassination operations behind German lines.[1] Apparently three groups exercised strong influence over the partisan movement: the General Staff's Chief Intelligence Directorate (GRU), the Fourth Directorate of the NKGB, and the Armed Forces Counterintelligence Directorate (GUKR NKO, or SMERSH) headed by General Abakumov, an NKGB officer. The two former of these three were part of the state security apparatus. SMERSH, though nominally subordinate to the Commissariat for Defense, was in fact directly answerable to Stalin.[2] Central political control was an operative reality. Actual day-to-day operations of the Partisan movement were controlled by NKVD Major General Pavel Sudoplatov, known as the "master of special detachments" in the German rear.[3] After the war he became a senior official in the Ministry of State Security (MGB).

The Partisan experience had a profound impact on subsequent Soviet planning and organization for special operations against the newly designated enemy—the US—following Germany's defeat. The MGB drew on the talents of officers who had served in Sudoplatov's "special detachments" to help build an underground infrastructure "to establish combat operations for weakening the network of military bases of the American command in Europe."[4]

There were other uses for special security troop units during World War II. State communications were too important to be entrusted solely to the Communications Commissariat or to the General Staff's GRU. Special signal units subordinate to the security organs provided redundant and secure communications nets for Party wartime leadership echelons—for the Politburo, State Committee of Defense (GKO), and the STAVKA. These units also provided intercept functions, providing the General Staff with tactical and strategic intelligence derived from German military communications. According to General G. K. Tsinev, Deputy KGB Chairman, state security agencies (including military counterintelligence) performed yeoman services in this regard:

> More than 4,000 communications on the enemy and his plans were received during the war from operative groups of military counterintelligence agencies and the NKVD operating in the enemy's rear. Around 1,500 of these were transmitted to the General Staff, more than 600 to the long-range air command, and more than 400 to the commanders and military councils of the fronts.[5]

Tsinev points out that these special units served even more exotic missions, such as deception and disinformation:

> Operating in close contact with the Red Army General Staff and taking advantage of various opportunities of the moment, military counterintelligence agencies systematically misled the fascist command and its intelligence services relative to the plans and intentions of the Soviet Command and to the situation on various sectors of the front. From the end of 1941 until March of 1943 alone, 80 radio stations captured by Soviet Cheka agents from German secret agents were used to transmit false information to the enemy.[6]

He might have added that the radio deception operations of these special security units played a major role in crushing Hitler's "Operation Citadel" at Kursk in the Summer of 1943, the true strategic turning point of the war on the Eastern front. They also supported the subsequent major Soviet offensives that culminated in the Battle of Berlin and the collapse of Germany.

These were not the only missions of Soviet *spetsnaz* units during World War II. Crack, fanatical NKVD units made the German capture of Rostov a costly one, turning that city into a death trap.[7] Around the same time (Summer 1942) and in the same frontal area, Stalin let loose Beria and his NKVD troops where they soon set up a parallel NKVD Staff for the "defense" of the North Caucasus, rivaling the military's, and even threatened General Malinovskiy (later Minister of Defense) with close arrest.[8] Beria and his troops then set about, on Stalin's personal orders, deporting and murdering the various minority peoples of the region (Chechens, Crimean Tatars, Ingushi, Balkars, Volga Germans, etc.).

Other *spetsnaz* groups were reported to be in control of advanced weapons systems, such as the *Katyusha* multiple rocket launchers. The tradition of special weapons being put under the control of the security forces and *not* the regular military was reported to have carried over into the postwar years, especially with regard to nuclear weapons. Some sources believe that KGB troops still control nuclear stockpiles and other highly sensitive installations.[9] Brezhnev appears to have continued the practice of retaining the services of military forces other than those of the Ministry of Defense.

The Soviet leadership is not one to fret over cost-effectiveness or problems of duplication or redundancy when it comes to Party security and the expansion of Party power. Nor has it ever shown any concern over the unhappiness of the regular military with the presence of rival military units whose political clout is underwritten by Party fiat. As early as 1924, a fusion of two CHEKA units resulted in a Division of Special Designation, later renamed (in 1926) the Dzerzhinskiy Detached Motorized Infantry Division of Special Designation, or OMSDON (Imeni Dzerzhinskogo).[10] Still later it was renamed the First Dzerzhinskiy Motorized Infantry Division and continues, to this day, to serve as the security police's own special, or punitive, troops charged with suppressing uprisings against the Party leadership.[11] It probably is subordinated to the 9th Directorate of the KGB, known also as the Bodyguards, Government Guards, and Kremlin Kommendatura.[12] A fairly recent Soviet book on the Dzerzhinskiy Division has it subordinated to the Ministry of Internal Affairs (MVD).[13] This writer believes that the unit most likely is a KGB one; at the very least, it would remand to KGB authority at Andropov's will, as is the case with other MVD Internal Security Divisions and GULAG and prison operations. Emigrés and defectors have reported that this unit, or others like it, have special sensitive external missions beyond that of leadership protection. These would occur in periods of international tension and crises, or in actual war.

An insight into the internal use of such forces was provided in early 1953 during Beria's attempted *putsch* following Stalin's death. After fusing the MVD and MGB into one massive security organ, Beria had at his disposal not only the traditional secret political police and regular militia (civil police) but also several hundred thousand internal security troops, border guards, and elite elements like the Dzerzhinskiy Division. Not hesitating to play such aces, he deployed the Dzerzhinskiy Division and a sister unit, the Second Motorized Infantry Division, to Moscow in an attempt to control the seat of all power.[14] At the same time he "arranged" for the Army troops of the Moscow Military District to be sent to Byelorussia for exercises. However, he made the supreme error of sending his divisions back to their barracks before he could outmaneuver his rivals. In a counterconspiracy, Beria's Politburo peers arranged for the showcase unit of the Moscow Military District, the Kantemirovskaya Armored Division, to deploy its tanks and troops in Moscow.[15] With no *spetsnaz* forces to oppose them, Khrushchev, Bulganin, Voroshilov, and others confronted Beria and arrested him on June 26, 1953. He was executed six months later. The leadership had gone to great lengths to involve the regular military in the Beria affair, not merely by the use of the Kantemirovskaya Division but by using Marshal Konev as one of Beria's interrogators. Here was a case where the Party used the military against the security forces, rather than the reverse—which was, and is, the norm.

Deriabin believes that something equally weighty may have occurred in 1967 when the Supreme Soviet announced a special award for the Kantemirovskaya Armored Division but declined to give any reason.[16] The award followed the terse announcements of the sudden and unexpected deaths of at least 15 senior KGB, MVD, and military officers, including two KGB generals (one of whom was the Chief of the Third Directorate—military counterintelligence). Was the Kantemirovskaya used against KGB *spetsnaz* troops? If so, the Party has developed more than one Praetorian Guard. More recent developments, however, suggest that the KGB/MVD axis still maintains a virtual monopoly in these matters with the full confidence of the Party leadership.

In sum, the Party apparently has seen fit to create elite military formations under direct Party control, through the security services, for special sensitive missions. Until World War II, these missions had a primarily internal security focus. With the extension of Soviet power into Central Europe after the defeat of Germany, *spetsnaz* units gradually took on external tasks. But it was not until the massive expansion and modernization of Soviet military power following the so-called "revolution in military affairs" in the post-Stalin period that Western observers began to appreciate the extent and direction of these tasks.

Military Buildup, Power Projection, and the Security Services

The strategic significance of the Soviet military buildup of the 1960's and 1970's is underscored by the break in the US strategic nuclear monopoly as well as in the continental bonds and traditions of the Soviet armed forces. In retrospect, the Soviets had to achieve the former—i.e., acquire strategic parity (at a minimum)—before they could proceed with the latter: the projection of Soviet conventional power.

In Soviet perceptions, the political strategy of the Party is determined by an assessment of the "correlation of forces," which Moscow claimed shifted significantly in its favor in the late 1960's and early 1970's when it achieved strategic parity with the United States.[17] This shift in the strategic balance was hastened by what the Soviets perceive as a "general crisis of capitalism" referred to by Brezhnev at the 25th CPSU Congress in 1976.[18] The political strategy of the Party is to continue to exploit both the shift and the crisis, in which their military power is claimed to have played a significant role. Furthermore, senior political-military figures assert that as a result of all this a much greater "external" role for the Soviet armed forces is demanded.[19]

The projection of Soviet conventional power under an umbrella of strategic strength was not the result of first purchasing a capability and then searching for a mission to justify it. Soviet military doctrine and the Party's military equipment policy never work that way. In a political system that prides itself on central planning, a command economy, and centralized hierarchical political control, little happens in the realm of power accretion by accident.[20] Within the limits of economic, technological, and institutional constraints, the purposeful pursuit of specific goals characterizes Soviet leadership style. In the perceptions of this leadership, there are connections among everything, a sense of order, and a chain of authority that invariably results in a plan to be worked out in the real world. Plan and doctrine determine and precede capability.

In the early 1960's, Khrushchev did not yet have the military capability to capitalize on the "wars of liberation" aspect of his peaceful coexistence policy. His inability to underwrite his 1962 Cuban adventure militarily underscored Soviet strategic weakness as well as power projection inadequacies. The correctives to these weaknesses were actually under way before the 1962 missile crisis and gained impetus under the Brezhnev regime following the coup against Khrushchev in 1964.

That the Soviets fully intended to address the expansion of their power projection capability once the strategic nuclear equation was corrected can be seen in a major Soviet work on military doctrine and strategy. Marshal Sokolovskiy's seminal work, *Voyennaya Strategiya* (Military Strategy), was the unclassified version of the famous "special collection" of military-scientific writings published in the classified General Staff journal, *Voyennaya mysl'* (Military Thought). The "special collection" reflected a Party-initiated "ordered" ferment in military thinking which presaged the new stage of military doctrine.[21] In 1968 the third edition of Sokolovskiy's *Military Strategy* was issued. As in the previous two editions (1962, 1963), a major section was devoted to the nature of modern war, especially to such "just" wars as wars of national liberation. In the earlier editions it was declared that the Soviet Union had the ". . . duty to support the sacred struggle of oppressed peoples and their just wars of liberation against imperialism." This included not only ideological and political help but also material aid.[22] However, the third edition added: "The USSR will render, when it is necessary, *military support as well* to people subject to imperialist aggression."[23]

This was the first instance of a prominent Soviet strategist writing in an authoritative work clearly stating that Moscow intended to become *militarily* involved in wars of national liberation. If this statement had been made in the earlier editions, its credibility would have been automatically blunted by lack of forces and mobility. But by the late 1960's, the expansion in both strategic strike forces and general purpose forces was already under way, lending ominous substance to Sokolovskiy's declaration. By 1972 when General Yepishev confidently proclaimed "external missions" for the Soviet military, the USSR was at least the strategic nuclear equal of the United States, and its new conventional power projection forces were appearing in increasing numbers beyond the continental confines of Eurasia. Under its new nuclear umbrella, the General Staff could deploy its projection forces in a highly visible manner with none of the qualms of 1962.

But the General Staff does not exercise exclusive, plenary authority in projecting Soviet power and influence abroad. Party political strategy determines everything, including military affairs. Sokolovskiy himself stressed this Soviet reality when he quoted Lenin: ". . . politics is the reason and war is only the tool, not the other way around. Consequently, it remains only to subordinate the military point of view to the political."[24] In Soviet experience, the principal instrument of the Party, and hence of politics, is the KGB. Whether known as the "Action Arm," "Sword and Shield," or "Most Trusted Cadre" of the Party, it has an exclusive charter as the cutting edge for projecting Soviet power. For this charter, it draws not only on the traditional instruments of "active measures" in its First Chief Directorate but also on those "special purpose" formations honed in World War II.

What are the forces available to the KGB for military and quasi-military missions in the 1980's? Not necessarily in priority order, the following components comprise its capabilities:

- There are the KGB's own armed forces, the Border Troops of between 200,000 to 300,000 men.[25] They are organized as a Chief Directorate, unnumbered, of the all-union KGB and are equipped with tanks, self-propelled guns, armored personnel carriers, aircraft, and ships. They are considered an elite force, receiving the more politically reliable conscripts in the semiannual callup. Answerable directly to KGB headquarters in Moscow, the Border Troops are in no way subordinate to the Ministry of Defense and its General Staff. Along with hermetically sealing the Soviet frontier, their uses in World War II suggest something of their other current and projected missions: absorbing and holding an invasion until the regular ground forces deploy; preventing "unauthorized" retreats by the regular military; providing rear-area security; fighting guerrillas/partisans/rebels; deporting "unreliable" and "traitorous" elements of the population; imposing Party control in reconquered and newly conquered territories, and helping to weed out and execute or deport anti-communist elites in the latter. They were and would again be assisted in these missions by MVD Internal Security Troops. The bulk of the fighting along the Sino-Soviet frontiers since the late 1960's has been borne by KGB Border Troops. A hint about another external mission is provided by Barron: Border Troops' officers served as advisors to Hanoi during the Vietnam War.[26] As noted earlier, the Chief of the Border Troops, V. A. Matrosov, was promoted to four-star rank in December 1978, along with Brezhnev cronies

KGB First Deputy Tsvigun and Deputy KGB Chairman Tsinev. One source claims that Matrosov, too, is a member of Brezhnev's *banda*.

• Among KGB controlled elements, the troops of the Ninth or Guards Directorate must also be included. They are charged with the physical protection of critical Party and state leaders and their families and also guard the Kremlin and other key government offices and facilities throughout the country. Defectors and emigrés generally report that the Guards Directorate includes elite troop formations of regimental size and higher. Deriabin (who was a KGB Guards officer) identifies specifically the First Dzerzhinskiy Motorized Infantry Division as one such organization whose job is the suppression of rebellions against the Party.[27] The Soviets publicly have identified the Red Banner Dzerzhinskiy Division as MVD-subordinated, but as noted earlier this would not prevent it from "chopping" to the KGB in crises.[28] They devote considerable attention to the combat role this Division played in World War II as a "special unit". Rumors have persisted for years that Guards Directorate *spetsnaz* units have sensitive external missions, and the Dzerzhinskiy Division appears to be one such unit.

• Troops of the KGB's Eighth or Communications Directorate may fall into the category of *spetsnaz* units (also sometimes called *Osnaz* for *Otryad Osobogo Naznacheniya,* Detachments of Special Designation). However, their missions are exclusively those of communications security, communications intelligence, and the maintenance of special state communications. Other than supporting special overseas operations of other *spetsnaz* units, they apparently would have no direct political action or combat role.

• The KGB's Third Directorate (Armed Forces Counterintelligence) is charged with penetrating the Soviet military from highest to lowest levels to ensure loyalty and to prevent the armed forces from being subverted or from turning on the Party. Its World War II predecessor, SMERSH, performed similar security tasks and carried out special combat missions of particular sensitivity. Will it do so again? General Tsinev, Deputy KGB Chairman, suggests in a tantalizing hint that it will: ". . . military counterintelligence agents will continue to apply every effort to reliably protect the Soviet Armed Forces against the subversive activities of intelligence agents of the imperialist nations, various kinds of foreign anti-Soviet centers, and hostile elements."[29] His statement carries a projective quality about it.

• The Ministry of Internal Affairs (MVD) deploys approximately 260,000 Internal Security Troops organized into Motorized Rifle Divisions equipped with tanks, artillery, armored personnel carriers, etc.[30] As with the KGB's own troops, these forces are *not* subordinate to the regular military. Something akin to a praetorian guard, MVD divisions have the primary mission of ensuring the continuation of CPSU control (the Dzerzhinskiy Division allegedly is one of these units). They are known to have been used to quell internal uprisings that strained the capacity of the civil police (Militia). In World War II they worked closely with NKVD units in the rear of the Red Army, participated in imposing Soviet rule in reconquered and newly conquered territories, and waged counter-guerrilla operations against anti-Soviet partisans in the Baltic area and Galicia (the latter continuing into the late 1940's). Refugees reported that MVD troops participated in crushing the Hungarian revolt in 1956. An intriguing recent case of MVD foreign involvement is that of First Deputy Minister of the MVD, Lt. General V. S. Paputin. Paputin is reported either (1) to have died during the coup against Afghan strongman Amin in December 1979 or (2) to have committed suicide after botching the affair.[31] His death was announced by Moscow as occurring on 28 December, one day after Amin's execution. Paputin earlier was reported to have been in Kabul immediately before the coup as part of an official Soviet delegation meeting with Amin. Was the No. 2 MVD man a principal in the affair? (More on this later.) Equally interesting were Paputin's links to Brezhnev. Both Paputin and his boss, MVD Chief General N. Shchelokov, were identified as members of Brezhnev's *banda,* dating back to the Dnepropetrovsk days.[32] Still another MVD official, Lt. Gen. Churbanov, recently promoted to First Deputy Minister after Paputin's death, also belongs to the *banda*.[33] Gen. Shchelokov received his 4-star rank along with Andropov in 1976 and is a voting member of the Central Committee. Paputin was a candidate member of that body. So a leader of a security organ that controls nearly a quarter million elite troops, who was a candidate member of the Central Committee, and who was an insider in Brezhnev's ruling clique died in circumstances possibly related to Soviet "active measures" in Kabul. An interesting event!

• Both the KGB and GRU maintain links with and training facilities for Third World liberation groups and foreign terrorists.[34] The links between these activities and the operations of Soviet *spetsnaz* forces are murky and difficult to define. The most instructive precedent available here is the case of Partisan chief, NKVD General Sudoplatov, who after World War II was ordered to transform his operations into "active measures" against the West, employing sabotage, assassination, and terrorism.

• The regular Soviet military also maintains *spetsnaz* forces with sensitive strategic missions beyond the USSR's frontiers, especially in Western Europe. Principal among these are the eight divisions of airborne troops under the direct command of the General Staff in Moscow.[35] Either full airborne divisions or units of them are designated as Special Purpose Airborne Troops (*Spetsnaznacheniya Vozdushno-Desantnykh Voysk*) and are targeted against key political, military, command and control, transportation, and industrial targets in the enemy's rear. It is generally believed that, depending on the sensitivity of the operation, such units may well be under KGB control. Indeed, in Czechoslovakia in 1968, the seizure of the Prague airport and of Prague itself was carried out by *spetsnaz* airborne units under KGB orders.[36] They not only secured vital points until relieved by the slower-moving ground forces but also arrested Dubcek and dispatched him, as a prisoner, to Moscow. Similar missions were carried out against other "enemies" on the KGB lists. Practically the same tactics were repeated in Kabul in December 1979. *Spetsnaz* units from airborne, and probably from other special purpose elements, were already in Kabul and Bagram airfield at the time of the coup (27 December). Working with Soviet military advisors to the Afghan Army, they employed a number of deceptions to neutralize real or potential opposition from the Afghanis.[37] One respected Soviet specialist, Professor John Erickson of Edinburgh University, believes the Soviets did exactly the same things as in Prague, 1968. He feels a "special assignment" brigade of the 105th Airborne Division "under the direction of the KGB" spearheaded the Kabul operation.[38] Most observers generally agree that special Soviet units went to Amin's palace (where the Soviets had urged him to go for "protection") and that Amin died in an assault by his Soviet "protectors" on the night of 27 December. One source insists that "far from being executed after a summary trial" by the new regime, "Amin was killed in cold blood by the Russians" along with "at least 40 members of his family, staff and friends."[39] Here is where the mystery of General Paputin begins. Was he involved in the operation against Amin and did he die in the ensuing fire-fight?

What was an MVD First Deputy Minister, Central Committee candidate member, and crony of Brezhnev doing there anyway? Was that operation an example of something so politically sensitive that the leadership required such high-ranking personalities on the scene and in action? How did he relate to the KGB and the military, or were the "military" forces involved (MVD troops?) under his control? One British source claims that Paputin was sent to Kabul—under cover to "modernize" the Afghan security forces—to help set the stage for the Soviet invasion.[40] With a team of 80-90 Soviet intelligence and military personnel (*spetsnaz* forces?), he proceeded to secure key Afghan government posts without consulting Amin. On the night of December 26, 1979, General Paputin was killed in a wild shootout in or near Amin's palace when the latter balked at Paputin's maneuverings.[41] One thing we can be sure of is that the Soviets were far gentler with the Czechs and Dubcek in 1968!

• Fewer in number than the airborne units are *spetsnaz* units of regimental size or less, known as "diversionary brigades" and subordinate to the General Staff's GRU.[42] Their main tasks include preparing for the landing of airborne units behind enemy lines, reconnaissance and real-time intelligence reporting on particularly critical targets, sabotage, disruption, and even the use of nuclear, chemical, and bacteriological weapons.[43] They would work in conjunction with "sleeper" agents long since placed in the target areas. Myagkov puts it this way:

> Shortly before the outbreak of war the KGB would activate its agents in Western political and military circles in an attempt to conceal Soviet intentions of launching an attack. Soviet diplomats would likewise use disinformation and other methods of dulling the awareness of the target countries. Some of the saboteurs would begin operations a few days before the outbreak of war but in such a way that enemy activity will not be suspected. In the first hours of war the special sabotage groups and paratroops would be added to the agents already operating in the target area.[44]

A number of former Soviet military and intelligence officers have argued that even the GRU "diversionary brigades" would come under KGB control in actual operations. World War II experience would seem to bear this out. Again, recent events in Afghanistan may prove instructive. Were "diversionary" units involved in the coup against Amin? Answers to this and previous questions about that affair could prove to be extremely helpful in gauging future Soviet actions.

• To the Soviet airborne and diversionary formations must be added similar units of the Warsaw Pact countries. At least 20,000 of these troops are available for behind-the-lines operations and come mainly from Poland, East Germany and Czechoslovakia.[45] Additionally, Naval Infantry of the USSR, Poland, and East Germany would be used in special missions such as seizing beachheads, or in commando raids using tactics similar to those of *spetsnaz* units.

• Finally, a category of forces that has a "special purpose" mission involving high political sensitivity (and payoff) is that of military and security aid personnel. Little if anything ever appears about them. Their presence in large numbers throughout the Third World is accepted as a fact of international life. Included are Soviet, East European (specifically East German), and Cuban cadres, plus a smattering of other nationalities. USSR military aid personnel apparently are controlled directly by the General Staff through its Military Assistance Directorate.[46] Additionally, GRU cadres complement aid personnel by providing guerrilla, diversionary, and intelligence training. The GRU, in turn, is complemented by KGB officers who, in addition to subverting and destabilizing even friendly governments (e.g., Afghanistan), provide the expertise for structuring internal security replicas of the USSR in the host country or movement. Like the GRU, the KGB also is heavily involved in sabotage and guerrilla training and is believed to enjoy higher rank than its sister service. The First Chief Directorate (foreign operations) is the organizational focal point for these activities. Cuban, East European, and other surrogate security services perform similar tasks under the guidance of the KGB.[47] Especially in Third World countries, the Soviets have found it critical to win over control, or weaken the indigenous military because of their political power. Politburo candidate member Boris Panomarev went to the heart of the matter when he stated:

> Experience confirms that the position adopted by the army largely determines whether a particular regime can remain in power or not.[48]

Control the military and you control the government! It is this writer's suspicion that because of the political focus and sensitivity of such operations, Soviet military aid and GRU personnel may very well be under some type of KGB oversight or control. In a very real sense they, too, are *spetsnaz* forces when deployed out of the USSR in places like Angola, Ethiopia, and without doubt, in Afghanistan.

The Soviet Union, its satellites, and clients have invested in large numbers of elite military or quasi-military forces whose missions clearly are of a *political*-military nature. The critical nature of these missions make it imperative that the control of such forces be linked in some special way to the political leadership. Traditionally, this has been via the security services, principally the KGB and its predecessors. That linkage continues to this day.

In Soviet political strategy and military doctrine, state objectives ultimately are political objectives. Military force is one of several means for achieving them. In the Third World, the Soviets have employed, generally adroitly, a mix of military and security aid, military presence, subversion, and other "active measures" and more traditional political techniques to promote their goals. *Spetsnaz* forces and operations are used to greater or lesser degrees, depending on the importance of the target country and Moscow's assessment of the situation.

In the case of Afghanistan, the Soviets had a test bed for employing "active measures" and *spetsnaz* forces in a mode and intensity not seen since World War II. From April 1978 when their Afghan clients were first installed, through the coup against Amin in December 1979, the Soviet security services appeared to be in the forefront of Soviet involvement. KGB officers were widely reported by press and diplomatic sources to be in control of the operation that resulted in the gunfight in which US Ambassador Dubbs was killed. Special purpose airborne troops from the 105th Guards Airborne Division in Central Asia began arriving at Bagram airbase north of Kabul in early December 1978, and probably sooner.[49] Already in place before that were several thousand military advisors and an unknown number of KGB officers. There may also have been other *spetsnaz* units, such as diversionary elements, deployed in-country around the same time. Thus, when the Soviets began their massive regular military infusion after Christmas, they already had their KGB and *spetsnaz* assets in place for the operation against Amin.

Outlook

The military equation between the United States and the USSR has changed significantly since the Cuban missile crisis in 1962. Few analysts at that time would have conjured up a strategic situation in the 1980's in which US defense planners would be agonizing over the vulnerability of our land-based nuclear deterrent. Still fewer would have guessed that Moscow's strategic strides would be followed so quickly by across-the-board improvements in general purpose forces or that Soviet and surrogate forces in considerable numbers would be deployed to the likes of Ethiopia, or South Yemen, or Angola. For the first time in Soviet history, Moscow has the capability militarily to propel the "historical process' in regions well beyond its continental confines. Marshal Tukhachevskiy may have dreamed of employing Soviet arms as a revolutionizing force in foreign territories; Brezhnev gave the dream substance. At the leading edge of this new capability is an older tradition: special purpose forces linked to the security services.

Should we continue to treat such special units either as just another element of the total Soviet military picture or lump them together with the overall problem of Soviet intelligence—to be dealt with by traditional counterintelligence means? On this question I share the misgivings of Myagkov in urging that the *spetsnaz* problem requires a greater level of scrutiny, analysis, and programmatic response:

> In discussing future wars attention tends to focus on two major aspects—thermonuclear weapons and conventional forces. But a third aspect is no less important—that of saboteurs, secret agents and special forces. They are not easily counteracted and can destroy objectives which are immune to other forms of attack. Armed with atomic, bacteriological, and chemical weapons these special forces can cause untold damage to the enemy. Use of such forces would change the whole character of a future war. . . . [50]

The future use of these forces appears to be along two major axes. One is the Third World where the precedents of Soviet intervention, as in Africa or Afghanistan, portend either more or a greater intensity of Soviet involvement. The second is NATO Europe, the great political-strategic prize. In a major crisis or war, the ultimate Soviet objective would be the total political collapse of key NATO governments or their destruction or neutralization.[51] Frontal military assaults may not accomplish this, which is why Soviet military strategy devotes almost as much attention to operations in the "rear"—the realm of *spetsnaz* forces. Their operations are intended to sow the disruption designed to hasten the enemy's political-military collapse.

Notes

1. Intelligence Division, Department of the Army, *Survey of Soviet Intelligence and Counterintelligence* (Washington, 1947), Record Group 319, 350.05, FW259, National Archives. Declassified from Secret. pp. 33, 163. It is interesting to note that the current KGB Chief, Yuriy Andropov, served with the Partisans during part of WW II.
2. Office of Naval Intelligence, *Espionage, Sabotage, Conspiracy: German and Russian Operations, 1940 to 1945.* Excerpts from the Files of the German Naval Staff and from other captured German Documents. (Washington, April 1947.) D498.1, 12236-a. Declassified from Confidential. Appendix I, p. 18.
3. Nikolai Khokhlov, *In the Name of Conscience* (New York: David McKay Co., Inc., 1959), p. 31.
4. *Ibid.,* p. 127. Khokhlov was a member of Sudoplatov's Partisans during the war and later moved into MGB "wet affairs" activities.
5. General G. K. Tsinev, "Guarding the Interests of the Armed Forces of the USSR: Soviet Military Counterintelligence is Sixty Years Old," *Kommunist Vooruzhennykh Sil,* No. 24 (December 1978), pp. 26-31. Tsinev was promoted to the rank of General of the Army shortly after his article went to press. Two other KGB senior officials received promotion to 4-star rank at that time (13 December 1978): General V. A. Matrosov, KGB Border Guard Chief and General S. K. Tsvigun, KGB First Deputy Chairman. There are now four officials with the rank General of the Army in the KGB, Andropov having received his 4-star rank in 1976. Similarly, the Minister of Internal Affairs (MVD), Nikolai Shchelokov, was promoted to General of the Army in 1976. All appear to be members of Brezhnev's *banda* (or "mafia"), intimates dating back to Brezhnev's days as Party boss of Dnepropetrovsk. Tsvigun has the added link of being Brezhnev's brother-in-law.
6. *Ibid.* Tsinev gives no operational specifics in this regard. David Kahn, however, seems to have identified one of these principals as the doubled Abwehr agent, MAX, who fed endless streams of misleading data on behalf of the Soviets to the endlessly gullible Germans. See David Kahn, *Hitler's Spies* (New York: Macmillan, 1978), pp. 313-317, 368-369.
7. John Erickson, *The Road to Stalingrad* (New York: Harper and Row, 1975), pp. 370-371.
8. *Ibid,* pp. 378-379.
9. Harriet F. and William F. Scott, *The Armed Forces of the USSR* (Boulder, Colorado: Westview Press, 1979), p. 221.
10. Peter Deriabin, *Watchdogs of Terror: Russian Bodyguards from the Tsars to the Commissars* (New Rochelle, New York: Arlington House, 1972), pp. 258, 265.
11. *Ibid.*
12. *Ibid.* See also, Deriabin, *The Secret World* (New York: Doubleday, 1959) and John Barron, *KGB* (New York: Reader's Digest Press, 1974).
13. I. G. Belikov (*et al.*). *Imeni Dzerzhinskogo* (Moscow: Voyenizdat, 1976).
14. Deriabin, *Watchdogs of Terror,* pp. 328-329.
15. *Ibid.,* pp. 332-333. This Division still serves as a showcase unit for parades and visiting dignitaries. It was used by the Party leadership in the late 1970's to show off the T-72 main battle tank to Western observers.
16. *Ibid.,* p. 346.
17. See G. Arbatov in *Izvestiya,* 22 June 1972; N. V. Podgorniy in *Izvestiya,* 13 February 1975; and M. A. Suslov in *Pravda,* 23 April 1975.
18. *Pravda,* 25 February 1976.

19. General A. A. Yepishev, "This Historic Mission of the Army of the Socialist State," *Kommunist* No. 7 (May 1972), p. 62; Marshal A. A. Grechko, "The Leading Role of the CPSU in Building the Army of a Developed Socialist Society," *Voprosy Istorii KPSS,* No. 5 (May 1974), pp. 30-47.
20. For an expansion of this theme, see the author's "The Institutional Foundations of Soviet Military Doctrine," *International Security Review* (Winter 1980), and *Soviet Perceptions of Military Doctrine and Military Power,* unpublished manuscript (Washington, D.C.: National Defense University, 1979).
21. Oleg Penkovskiy, *The Penkovskiy Papers* (New York: Doubleday, 1965), pp. 223-225.
22. For the three editions in one volume see Harriet F. Scott's translation with commentary: *Soviet Military Strategy* (New York: Crane Russak, 1975).
23. V. D. Sokolovskiy (ed.), *Military Strategy,* 3rd ed. (Moscow: Voyenizdat, 1968), p. 222. (Emphasis added.)
24. *Ibid.,* p. 24.
25. *The Military Balance, 1979-1980,* p. 11, lists 200,000 KGB Border Troops. John Barron gives a figure of 300,000. See Barron, *KGB,* p. 85. The former figure appears too low, especially in view of the steady buildup of forces on the lengthy Sino-Soviet frontier.
26. Barron, *Ibid.*
27. Deriabin, *Watchdogs . . .,* p. 265.
28. Belikov, *Imeni Dzerzhinskogo.*
29. Tsinev, "Guarding the Interests of the Armed Forces of the USSR . . .," *Kommunist Vooruzhennykh Sil,* p. 31. (Emphasis added.) As an aside, the current head of the General Staff's Chief Intelligence Directorate (GRU), General Ivashutin, is a former Third Directorate Chief, SMERSH officer, and Deputy KGB Chairman.
30. *The Military Balance,* 1979-1980, p. 11.
31. *The Washington Post,* 4 January 1980; 18 February 1980; 14 March 1980.
32. *Daily Telegraph* (London), 30 April 1979.
33. *Ibid.*
34. Barron, *KGB; Daily Telegraph,* 20 November 1979; 16 July 1979; Leonard Schapiro, "The Soviet Union and the PLO," *Survey* (Summer 1977-78), pp. 193-207.
35. Aleksei Myagkov, "Soviet Sabotage Training for World War III," *Soviet Analyst* (20 December 1979), pp. 2-6.
36. *Ibid.*
37. *Los Angeles Times,* 10 January 1980.
38. Quoted in *The Sunday Times* (London), 13 July 1980.
39. *The Sunday Times* (London), 20 January 1980.
40. *Foreign Report* (The Economist), 9 January 1980.
41. *Ibid.* This source lists three reported versions of Paputin's death. All three involved firefights at or near the Palace between Afghan units and Paputin's bodyguards.
42. Mayagkov, *Soviet Analyst,* 20 December 1979, 9 January 1980; C. N. Donnelly, "Operations in the Enemy Rear," *International Defense Review,* No. 1 (1980), p. 37.
43. Mayagkov, *op. cit.*
44. *Ibid.,* 9 January 1980, p. 5.
45. Donnelly, "Operations in the Enemy Rear," p. 37.

46. Scott, *The Armed Forces of the USSR,* p. 110.
47. Brian Crozier, *The Surrogate Forces of the Soviet Union,* Conflict Studies No. 92 (London: Institute for the Study of Conflict, 1978), pp. 7-12.
48. *Kommunist* (October 1971), quoted in Crozier, *ibid.,* p. 3.
49. *The Sunday Times,* (London) 20 January 1980.
50. Myagkov, *Soviet Analyst,* 9 January 1980, p. 5.
51. Donnelly, "Operations in the Enemy Rear," p. 35. See also Joseph D. Douglass, Jr. *Soviet Military Strategy in Europe* (New York: Pergamon Press, 1980).

Discussants

Lt. Col. John Guenther: I want to acknowledge Dr. Dziak's contributions to a subject that in our estimation has not received due attention in the past, but one which I believe will receive much more attention in the immediate future.

My interest and comments today on this subject are not theoretical but rather real-world, immediate, and critical to the US military's contributions to national security.

The threat described by Dr. Dziak is a current capability—and one, which judged by recent events in Afghanistan, the Soviets are not hesitant to apply—ruthlessly and effectively. It is a capability currently posed against US and NATO troops in Europe and forward deployed Marine Corps units in the Indian Ocean and other areas.

If the situation in the Indian Ocean would deteriorate and require the deployment of the recently commissioned Rapid Deployment Force, I think we could anticipate that the KGB's paramilitary threat would be manifested and somehow exercised against US forces in that part of the world.

In an earlier discussion, Admiral Harvey referred to the Counterintelligence concerns of the division commander. I'll go further and express my concern for the lower tactical levels, for it is at these levels in the Marine Corps where capabilities of the Soviet paramilitary or other intelligence threats would be manifested.

I strongly support the multidisciplinary concept of counterintelligence. Command responsibility for counterintelligence in the military dictates the different types of organizational responses to the counterintelligence threat that are seen in the four military services.

Now to turn to the CI threat as it affects our military services in the 1980's. From the military counterintelligence point of view, I see several matters of serious concern.

Dr. Dziak's statement that Soviet Special Force Troops in wartime or crisis would be deployed under control of Soviet security and intelligence services on highly sensitive missions concerns us because we know very little about the threat. There is a disturbing paucity of information concerning the subject.

I am concerned with the history, tradition, and successes of the *spetsnaz* troops. These are not the amateurs who caused considerable confusion in the Ardennes in 1944, but rather the troops who are trained in considerable depth and scope for very special types of operations.

I am concerned with the *Spetsnaz* and *Osnaz* units of the KGB's Eighth Directorate, whose COMINT capability adds another dimension to the threat, particularly since US forces are now known for their outstanding communication security.

I am concerned also with the capabilities of the Soviet's Special Purpose Airborne Troops, the diversionary brigade subordinate to the GRU and perhaps in a parochial vein reflecting my Marine Corps background the Soviet naval infantry, because of their special capabilities, although not documented as well as the airborne troops.

Like Dr. Dziak, I am also concerned that the term "diversionary" troops is a misnomer and doesn't do justice to the realm of their activities that comprise threats to the United States military forces.

I am also very much concerned about the vulnerabilities of our forces, particularly since Soviet *Spetsnaz* activities are focused in the rear areas. It is in the rear areas that security and procedures frequently do not receive the degree of emphasis found close to the shooting.

Moving from Dr. Dziak's paper and looking at some of the comments of former KGB Captain Myagkov who Dr. Dziak mentioned, I find them also of considerable concern to the CI community. He emphasizes the following:

1. Great attention to operations behind the enemy lines and ". . . large units of special forces for conducting subversive activities which in size, training, and equipment are virtually without equal."
2. Emphasis on disrupting LOC's. (Lines of Communications).
3. The role of the airborne troops in the Czech events of 1968, in which he documents how a Special Reconnaissance Sabotage Unit took a very active part.
4. Reconnaissance and sabotage teams with qualified linguist and other specific sabotage and espionage skills.
5. The detailed plans for Western Europe against NATO military.
6. And last, but certainly not least, training in the use of atomic and bacteriological weapons which, after various stories concerning Afghanistan, is not as far-fetched as some people thought in the recent past.

I would also refer the audience to a recent article in *Commentary* by Edward Luttwak. The following quote amplifies the capabilities discussed by Dr. Dziak: "The airborne descent on Kabul, the special operation for the use of deception and sabotage to paralyze the Afghanistan forces that might have been hostile, the willingness to rely on the swift follow-up of follow-up forces with narrow roads with tunnels and bridges, all represent a familiar aspect. The Kremlin leaders who sent such forces into action to use such high-risk methods obviously had acquired an operational competence in them and the leaders they had lacked as recently as 1968."

And finally, going on further: "The Russians apparently relied on surprise, deception, and special-purpose covert action to immobilize the Afghan armor. They certainly could not count on being able to defeat the armor with the small number of light armor flown in. It denotes self-confidence of a high order matched by trust on the part of the leaders who sent in these troops."

With that background, it is obvious that the counterintelligence analyst and counterintelligence manager are confronted with a multidisciplinary CI threat with a dimension not thoroughly analyzed nor appreciated at this time. I believe we need a corresponding multidisciplinary counterintelligence response to that threat. We cannot focus on one hostile capability to the exclusion of the others. However, from the comments made earlier, it appears that one doesn't always get this multidisciplinary approach to the counterintelligence problems.

Because it is quite obvious that future military operations will be at joint service in nature, and very possibly combined service with our allies, the multidisciplinary CI response poses problems, both organizationally and doctrinewise. By definition, the Rapid Deployment Joint Task Force denotes joint operations. But, as General Thompson mentioned, military service counterintelligence doctrines and perspectives differ; and these differences, although founded on unique service needs, pose problems for a joint counterintelligence coordinator.

The service organizations were developed to provide command and counterintelligence support for that service. They were not organized with the ultimate objective of facilitating effective joint or combined counterintelligence operations against the multidisciplinary threats.

I experienced this problem in Vietnam in 1968 and 1969. As the Third Marine Amphibious Force staff counterintelligence officer responsible for coordinating all CI activities in the five northern provinces of Vietnam, I worked with Army, Navy, Air Force, and Marine Corps counterintelligence units. The Navy and Air Force units traditionally not organized for tactical counterintelligence operations, adapted quickly and worked quite well with the Army and Marine counterintelligence units. However, to operate effectively against today's more sophisticated CI threat, we must formulate doctrine that incorporates a multidisciplinary approach.

I will comment on the Rapid Deployment Force, although acknowledging that it is still in its very early stages. Without getting into some of the sensitive aspects, I think we all can visualize that a rapid deployment operation in the Middle East, for instance, would have significant CI vulnerabilities.

The lines of communications would be extremely vulnerable. The limited port/airfield facilities comprise very significant sabotage targets, and something as basic and simple as the water supply would constitute a very lucrative sabotage target.

The more one conjectures this type of operation and juxtaposes it next to the Soviet KGB paramilitary threat, one can see awesome counterintelligence problems facing us in that part of the world.

Must we not suppose that the Soviets and/or their surrogates have intelligence coverage in these Third World areas where US forces may be deployed in future years? Can we sit back and apply traditional passive CI and defensive measures, or should we mount some offensive CI measures?

We would be well served to conduct some type of offensive CI measures to prepare for deployment to such area, but that is not within the capability of US military forces in that area. I submit that this will require in the future a closer degree of cooperation between the military counterintelligence services and the civilian services in the CI response to this paramilitary threat.

Looking further at the Soviet paramilitary threat discussed by Dr. Dziak, it is obvious they place a great credence on disrupting command, control, and communications (C^3). C^3 and counter-C^3 (CC^3) are receiving a great deal of attention in current military thinking. What we have here is a Soviet paramilitary effort HUMINT to disrupt our command and control operations through these means, focusing on the military-political command and control of forces opposing them. This subject is worth further consideration.

In response to a question posed earlier, "How do you determine if counterintelligence activities are successful?" you do so in military operations by reviewing the results. Was your mission successfully achieved? Did it fail? What were the costs in time, casualties, and material? These indicators permit a clearer evaluation of the CI effort than in the classic CI/counterespionage field. I believe as a result of papers such as Dr. Dziak's, the military counterintelligence community will have an improved understanding of the role of the KGB.

While we have always considered that the GRU would be the primary CI threat to our military forces, the increased role of the KGB is one we will appreciate more in the future.

What must we do to prepare for the counterintelligence threat in the 1980s?

First, we must appreciate the hostile SIGINT and HUMINT threat, not in isolation, but rather as interactive components of the multidisciplinary counterintelligence threat. We must increase collection, analysis, training, education, and programmatic emphasis on this particular problem. I see no need for organizational changes, certainly not a new DOD counterintelligence operation. However, I think we must look at our joint counterintelligence doctrine, including means to improve coordination between the military and the civilian agencies.

Lt. General William Odom: I think the paper itself is provocative in its choice of subject and scope; it raises a number of implications for counterintelligence activities; and it provides a survey of a large number of Soviet capabilities that are not widely known or understood. In other respects, however, I find the paper frustrating. Let me explain why.

There seems to be no unifying overall theme. There is an effort, toward the end, to ask the question: Should we lump this paramilitary capability into the overall military balance or treat it separately? That is a key question. But what is the answer and how would one subfactor military balance categories so that they would give us a better appreciation of where to fit these things?

The paper has lots of raw material, some of it not possible so to classify properly under its general topic area. To talk about the "paramilitary dimension" without creating confusion is impossible if you are going to lump together in that category as broad a group of forces as border troops, SIGINT, MVD units, partisan activities, and other *spetsnaz*. I think the missions and activities are simply too diverse to put into that category and say no more about it.

Nonetheless, I think scattered through the paper are some concepts that might be rearranged and put together to give a bit more coherence. And let me suggest a couple of them.

I like the historical allusions, particularly the one that Professor Pipes made, about the origins of "special forces" and their relation to the Soviet intelligence capability and the informer network in their own forces.

In his introductory comments, Dr. Richard Pipes observed that Imperial Russia did not have such special forces. Indeed the separation between the military and the intelligence services was complete. What brought about the demise of the Imperial Government was the refusal of the ordinary troops at the end of February 1917 to fire on crowds. The Bolsheviks learned that if you are going to use military force to suppress the civilian population, you have to have special forces which are not under ordinary army command.

I think this goes back, however, a little earlier than 1918—to 1917. The late Professor Henry Roberts always used to be fascinated by the Lettish rifle battalions in 1917. And I sometimes think Lenin would never have made it in November and December without the Lettish rifle units that were brought into Petrograd from Riga. They were reliable for rounding people up, and they could be counted on to shoot people, or whatever Dzerzhinskiy thought was essential to carry the day.

In the same light, it is useful in my view to remember that revolution itself is a military activity. We tend to lose sight of that. It is a form of civil war, one that tends to blur the boundary between civil and military relationships. One senses from both Dr. Dziak's paper and Colonel Guenther's discussion of it, this desire to integrate the two—"multidisciplinary" is the word we have heard several times here. It does call for a fusion and integration, and much Bolshevik writing and thought on this subject is an effort to achieve those things.

My next point is related to external versus internal missions for Soviet forces. I remember being in Moscow in 1973 and coming across Marshal Kulikov's pre-February Armed Forces Day article. I was very struck by his point that heretofore the emphasis had been on the internal political role for the military; henceforth there would be a larger role for the Soviet Armed Forces in external policy matters. It was a highly suggestive statement of a policy shift. How that would be operationalized, of course, was hardly clear, and I think Dziak's paper suggests some ways in which it now is occurring.

The next point I would make, which I think flows from the previous one, concerns the concept of power projection as opposed to force projection, with which we in the military are familiar. Force projection—the Marines and Navy talk a lot about it—includes such things as amphibious operations, the ability to project sea power onto land.

But that is a somewhat narrow conventional notion of military operations. I know in the early days of the administration in 1977 when we were trying to draw a net assessment of how the Soviet Union and the United States were doing vis-a-vis one another in the world, we came across the notion of the broader concept of power projection in which we would lump very disparate things like political and diplomatic activities, economic activities—not just trade and commercial relationships but also noticing things like Soviet commercial ships designed so they are convertible for military sealift on a rapid basis, the "Ro/Ro" ships that are fairly broadly used in the Soviet merchant fleet. The close coordination between the civil and military air fleet suggests potential missions for Aeroflot that may not often be thought of frequently. We had already begun to see in the use of surrogate armed forces in Angola. All of these capabilities together with espionage and other sorts of activities—military assistance programs, advisory efforts, larger numbers and amounts of arms transfers—add up to Soviet "power projection."

If you take note of where the Soviets were using those capabilities in a coordinated fashion, you will see some strategic areas of the globe that are quite interesting. You see very advanced developments in Southeast Asia, vigorous but less-advanced efforts in the Persian Gulf, a mixed development in the Caribbean. I think many of the Soviet units and capabilities mentioned in the paper do have roles and missions in this power projection area.

Where does one go from here in the analysis? I leave that for discussion. The material before us is sufficient for a rich number of comments and future studies.

General Discussion

A former senior intelligence official, with a breadth of military as well as international experience, opened the discussion by designating himself as "devil's advocate." He observed that the success of the paramilitary threat can be measured, in major part, by overreaction to its seriousness and by the draining away of always limited resources into defensive, protective measures. He commented on the pervasive myth concerning paramilitary or partisan activity in World War II which greatly exaggerated its contribution to "actually winning the war" and still lends a special cachet to nonconventional force capabilities. CI must of course be cognizant of and counter this threat—it is CI's mission alone to do so—but he argued that the only really effective countermeasures are total control of penetration and/

or "hitting the terrorists" before they can strike. Finally, he advocated taking advantage of the Soviets' own vulnerabilities by threatening (whether by actual intent or deliberate deception) to undermine satellite regimes with our own "special forces". The Soviets are vulnerable, in his view, and we should play on their fears.

A congressional staff member carried this line of argument further: accepting the premise that we should not waste our resources on passive defense, the key questions become, what do we need to know about our adversaries and their plans (in quasi-peace and eventually in wartime) *and* what kinds of counterintelligence efforts on our part will best meet the threat? Another former senior intelligence officer suggested that the necessary beginning of an answer to these questions is to "know the adversary"—to know the KGB as an organization and as a "multifaceted operational threat". He defined this imperative in terms of both words and deeds—of what the Soviet leaders say about the use of special forces (doctrine), and what they in fact have done (in-depth case histories, "counterintelligence research"). An academic participant added that we should indeed take the Soviets at their word, but not to accept their "threats of success" at full value.

Another participant asked about current Soviet doctrine on the interface between special forces and theatre forces: is there such doctrine and, if so, what is it? It was pointed out, in partial answer, that Myagkov has systematically articulated Soviet training requirements for "Third Directorate" and airborne forces, primarily in conjunction with operations in Europe, but that very little is yet known in this area either from a CI or a positive intelligence perspective. This is a serious gap in our knowledge, and much more work needs to be done on Soviet doctrine and tactics—on how special forces would actually link up with regular-line military units.

The question of "what we do about this threat" was further amplified by a scientific/technical specialist who expressed serious concern about our vulnerabilities—especially in light of our diminished CI capabilities, technological and budgetary problems, the "learning gap", and the probable swiftness and decisiveness of future warfare. A senior military officer responded by reiterating the critical need, first, to develop a "total mosaic" of force projections and Soviet doctrinal intentions into which specific threats can be fitted (as, for example, the "training battalion" in Cuba). He went on to say that the Soviet view of general war is not that of "one quick exchange", but rather of an extended series of campaigns, albeit with weapons systems of tremendous potency; he expressed the view that such a war would involve "some rather primitive approaches"—even though spotter-commands to longrange patrols might be via satellite rather than binoculars.

The former intelligence official who began the discussion then continued his argument by suggesting that if we know less than we would like to know about specific Soviet intentions and operational plans for special forces, in all likelihood the Soviets don't know either—not much beyond the broad threat of employing a multiplicity of special and regular forces. He offered a four-part prescription for targeting our own CI resources to meet this potential threat: (1) pinpoint and neutralize internal threats—an FBI mission in the main—posed by violence-prone radical movements and by foreign agents and clandestine organizations preparing for sabotage within the US; (2) learn all we can about Soviet, Bloc, and surrogate paramilitary forces designed to operate behind western lines—their capabilities, operational plans, and weapons; (3) learn all we can about the bases from which these forces are likely to operate—and hit them before they start; and (4) if we cross over into enemy territory, what kinds of paramilitary units might we expect to encounter? And most importantly: don't overrate their capabilities.

In answer to a final question about the role of nonconventional forces in Soviet power projections, Dr. Dziak summarized his presentation by noting that in Ethiopia, for example, virtually every category of special-purpose forces described in his paper have been utilized, whereas in other parts of Africa and the Third World, there has been particular reliance on surrogate forces. The Afghan operation, he suggested, has been a virtual textbook illustration of how special-purpose units, political action, and regular forces were fused together to achieve very clear political objectives—all under the operational control of agents on the ground, both KGB and military aid personnel from the General Staff. He noted also that we drew precisely the wrong conclusions from the absence in Afghanistan of the traditional signals of a military build-up. This experience, he concluded, might serve as a guide for our CI and positive intelligence efforts in the future.

CHAPTER FIVE

Insurgency, Terrorism, and Intelligence

Paper:

Schlomo Gazit

and

Michael Handel

Discussants:

Mr. Robert Chapman

Dr. Abram Shulsky

"The history of failure in war can be summed up in two words: ***Too late.*** *Too late in comprehending the deadly purpose of a potential enemy; too late in realizing the mortal danger; too late in preparedness; too late in uniting all possible forces for resistance; too late in standing with one's friends."*

General Douglas MacArthur

Definitions

We believe that a brief introduction concerning the general nature of insurgency and terrorism is necessary before we can approach the analysis of the responsibilities, problems, and possibilities of intelligence in fighting terrorist organizations.

First, then, a brief definition of insurgency:

> *Insurgency* is a type of warfare intended to compensate the relative weakness of the initiating party. The insurgent does not aim at a military victory, but wants to undermine the morale, the will to resist, and the self-confidence of its adversary. Insurgency strives to make its opponent abandon the fight irrespective of his military superiority.

A variety of different organizations with different goals, different operational tactics (or techniques) with different objectives for attack is covered by the term "insurgency warfare." We would therefore like to *classify* the organizations according to their different characteristics. Planning countermeasures should be adapted to each insurgent organization according to its particular characteristics.

The Enemy: The first criterion to classify different insurgency and terror organizations is based on the enemy against which they direct their campaign. We can distinguish between two types of enemies:

• *A foreign enemy:* War against a foreign enemy can be a war of liberation against an occupying foreign enemy or war by a national or ethnic group against the majority rule of a different national or ethnic group (e.g., occupied Europe in World War II, IRA, PLO).

- *Replacing a regime or an internal system:* Insurgency aimed at changing the person or party in power and the system of government and ideology may be of the same national or ethnic identity (e.g., Castro in Cuba, The Red Brigades in Italy).

Political versus Violent Struggle: According to this criterion we suggest that not every underground movement will necessarily choose a violent struggle. We distinguish between the following types of struggle:

- Non-violent underground political activity. In some countries a political party or movement may be outlawed. Thus, for example, the communist party is outlawed in a large number of states. In almost all cases the communist party will continue to operate and proselytize underground. The dissident movement in the Soviet Union operates under similar conditions.
- Passive resistance can be characterized by non-cooperation, strikes, non-violent demonstrations, or even massive scale popular demonstrations (such as Ghandi's struggle against the British in India or, more recently, the demonstrations that led to the collapse of the Shah's regime in Iran). This type of struggle, despite its essentially non-violent character, is conducted in most cases by a leadership that operates in underground conditions or semicovert conditions. This is dictated above all by the wish to continue the struggle even if the government arrests the known active leaders.
- The violent struggle.
- A combination of two or all of the above-mentioned possibilities.

Bases, Sanctuaries, and Hideouts: The bases for covert underground activities are determined by a variety of factors among which are support from the population, the physical characteristics of the terrain, the relative military strength of the opponents, tactical considerations, modes of operation, and the reactions of the opponent.

The support of the local population is of great importance to insurgents when they seek cover for underground activity. The more brutal the reprisals of the opponent against the population supporting terrorist or insurgent activities, the less inclined the population will be to support their operations. On the other hand, terrorist organizations that have to resort to coercion and terror in order to get support from the local population endanger their own long-range interests. This may superficially increase its support, but it also presents the intelligence organization with opportunities to recruit agents and penetrate insurgent and terrorist operations.

A similar interrelationship exists between topography and physical environment and the forces and weapon systems used by counter-insurgent forces. The sheer size of an area of operation and hideout can be of great importance. Jungles, mountainous areas, and rugged terrain will give the subversive force a better cover than open, flat terrain or an open desert in a clear weather environment. Conversely, the weapons and other material devices may reduce the advantages of the insurgents. Helicopters and a variety of techniques may be used to clear a jungle area, for example.

We can distinguish among three types of sanctuaries:

- The "Human Jungle"—when terrorists take cover within the dense urban population, often in small compartmentalized cells and complete secrecy. In some cases they may be supported by a small number of civilians (e.g., the IRA, Baader-Meinhoff).
- Sanctuaries in rural areas—jungles, mountains, caves, marshes, etc.—may offer cover and partial security against enemy operations (e.g., Russian partisans in World War II, the Viet Cong in South Vietnam).
- Protected sanctuaries—relatively large areas under the complete and open control of the insurgents based on a locally favorable balance of power (Chinese Communists in Yenan, Tito's partisans in Yugoslavia, Greek positions in Crete and Northern Greece).

Types of Targets: Four types of targets may characterize insurgency warfare:

- Unprotected infrastructure targets such as roads, bridges, power stations and power lines, telephone cables, etc.
- Civilian unprotected targets of opportunity (occasional targets) mainly intended to cause the highest possible material damage and/or casualties.
- Selective operations against specific political leaders, local dignitaries, military men, security personnel, and the like.
- Protected government and/or military targets.

Adherence to the Mission: The degree to which insurgent or terrorist units adhere to their assigned mission is of particular interest from the intelligence and defender's point of view. The degree to which these units will attempt to carry out their orders and plans of operations with precision may determine the intelligence and defense agencies' capability for taking effective countermeasures. Some clandestine organizations will try to carry out their attack explicitly according to orders given to them; others may assign only little importance to exactness in carrying out their instruction. There is a correlation between an organization that will maintain ethical and moral standards while attacking government or military targets and, on the other hand, precise fulfillment of its tasks. Similarly, there is a correlation between an organization that has no moral scruples or ethical standards and will indiscriminately attack defenseless civilians and unprotected civilian installations and, on the other hand, loose adherence to the assigned operational goals.

Moral Distinctions: Any moral distinction between insurgent organizations must be based on the targets chosen for attack.

- "Moral warfare" drives at attacking only government officials, armed forces, and the police. It tries, as best it can, not to inflict casualties and damages among noncombattants.
- "Immoral or unethical warfare" does not hesitate to take action against innocent civilians, women, and children. Often action is deliberately concentrated almost entirely against such "soft" noncombattant targets.

Terrorism: Any regime will view insurgent operations against it as illegal and will view the participants as criminals, accrediting no legitimacy to their struggle. It is not surprising, therefore, that all insurgent warfare is defined by its opponents as terrorism and the active participants as terrorists.

Nevertheless, there is a type of insurgency that deserves to be branded as terrorism from an *objective point of view*. Insurgency that targets innocent civilians must be considered as terrorism. Bombing crowded public facilities, planting bombs in civilian airplanes that are scheduled to explode in mid-flight, firing rockets and missiles at civilian aircraft, holding and executing innocent hostages—any group that does not hesitate to adopt such measures must (or can only) be defined as terrorist and the organization as terroristic.

As we have suggested above, insurgency is defined as the weapon of the weak. Generally speaking, this definition is valid. Nevertheless, there is a tendency, particularly in Western liberal society, to identify the "weaker side" also with the "just side." Certainly such an identification cannot be accepted as axiomatic. Quite to the contrary, many organizations representing anti-democratic anarchist or even reactionary religious ideologies, acting against the majority public opinion, against the will of the people, take advantage of this tendency, and use and abuse the mass media in a highly selective and distorted form to increase the support of their cause.

Frequently insurgent organizations employ terroristic methods because they cannot secure any popular support from the population they are pretending to represent. A terrorist organization will try to impose by terror (i.e., target civilians) a political ideology that contradicts the expressed democratic will of the majority of the society, thus trying to change the rules of the game.

In order deliberately to confuse concepts and deceive public opinion, terrorist organizations compare their operations to conventional warfare in which many innocent people also are wounded or killed. This is a completely distorted presentation. In conventional warfare targets are military objectives, and civilian casualties are the unavoidable price of the military confrontation. In terrorist activities innocent civilians are the main target and not a regrettable by-product of war.

The terrorist organizations themselves are sensitive to this criticism and frequently claim to have attacked "military targets" when in fact it is clear that they have attacked civilian targets and had no intention of attacking a military one.

Secrecy and Compartmentalization: An organization that is operating with the balance of power in favor of its opponent must maintain a high degree of secrecy and compartmentalization concerning its leaders, active members, weapons, installations, principal funding sources, and the like. The maintenance of such secrecy is a necessary condition that enables it to compensate for its relative inferiority. In this context we must expand our discussion in two additional directions.

Taking Advantage of the Law by Terrorist Organizations: The first is the degree to which the terrorist opponent will adhere to the principles of law while combatting the terrorist organization. Paradoxically, terrorist organizations whose sole essence is fighting existing law and order of their society are often aided and covered by the very law it tries so hard to destroy. This is obviously the case if and when its opponent adheres to the accepted legal norms of democratic society. (Laws that determine the rights of the individual and prevent the government from penetrating the individual's privacy do not allow preventive arrests and strictly forbid the use of any pressure during interrogation, and adhere strictly to the legal procedure. Such laws serve as an important device in the protection of clandestine and terrorist organizations.) Against such an opponent, the terrorists can operate more freely and more openly as long as they are careful not to have their people caught in action. Moreover, the organization can often afford overt operations to organize, recruit new members, publish newspapers, pamphlets, and such—which the law does not forbid—and thus considerably facilitates solving problems of its own organization as well as reducing the extent of the illegal and dangerous dimension of its operations.

Sanctuaries Across the Border: The second aspect is the degree to which neighboring and other countries are ready to support the activities of a terrorist organization. In cases in which an insurgent organization finds it difficult to establish a minimal infrastructure within its target territory, it may find such support across the border—provided that the host country is ready to give it reasonable protection against the opponent's forces. Such sanctuaries across the border are essential if and when the insurgent organization is incapable of recruiting the necessary support from within its target area. But even if such domestic support is available, there is still great importance to the outside sanctuary since it helps the terrorists organize, train, and prepare for action undisturbed—which will be more difficult domestically in any case.

Defining the Strategic Goals of the War Against Terrorists

It is essential for any intelligence organization operating against any type of adversary to have the strategic goals it has to serve clearly defined from above. The strategic goals of fighting terrorist organizations must be similarly defined. The strategic goals of counter-terrorist warfare may be different according to the following categories:

- *A Defensive-Passive Strategy.* The primary goal of an intelligence organization under such a strategy is to give a warning on the appearance of an underground terrorist threat even before it has started to operate. What are its operational goals, its targets? Who is supporting it, who are its members? What measures can be taken to prevent it from resorting to its planned terrorist operations? How to make it more difficult for it to operate, and how to reduce possible damage?

• *An Active Counter-Strategy*. While the defensive goals of intelligence work are the automatic result of the existence of an insurgent threat, this is not the case concerning goals for active counter-terrorist operations. Without having it defined explicitly as a strategy for war, the intelligence organization will not automatically cover such strategic goals:

1. Active actions within your *own* territory for the denial of infrastructure for training, organization, recruiting efforts, confiscation of weapons and equipment, preventive arrests, and so forth.

2. Active operations *outside* your own controlled territory, operations across the border against the terrorist organizations which can be covert or overt, as well as military operations to bring pressure on the neighboring government supporting the terrorists in order to force it to stop supporting the terrorist organization or give it a sanctuary within its territory.

3. A variety of deception and disinformation operations.

4. Operations intended to create intrigues, friction, and intra-organizational conflicts or conflicts between competing terrorist organizations.

Terrorist Organizations as Targets for Intelligence

It should perhaps be emphasized that in counterterrorist warfare more than any other type of war, the intelligence organization itself is in the forefront of military operations; frequently the border between intelligence work and combat activity is blurred.

1. The first area that constitutes a target for intelligence operations is the *ideological* and *political* system of the organization. Even if such an ideology seems to be strange, unintelligible, or even repulsive, it exists and, therefore, it has to be carefully studied. The ideology may consist of religious, political, or social goals. Understanding the ideology, closely monitoring its evolution and change as well as its growing or decreasing influence are essential for the understanding of the organization and hence for the war against it. This is also of importance on the personal level, because in many cases it is difficult to make a distinction between the ideological leadership and its

operational command. There are cases when the ideological and/or political leadership is operating more in the open and is thus easier to identify and reach than the operational elements. The subjects that require careful knowledge and need to be followed closely are:

(a) Leaders of the political-ideological hierarchy.

(b) Publications of the organization (as well as the place of publication).

(c) Favorite arenas and meeting places in which ideologies are developed and new recruits are mobilized—where they are taking place, who participates, and what is said.

(d) Public protest movements that reflect and support the terrorist organization's goals.

(e) Ideological and operational affiliations with other organizations and movements both domestically and abroad.

2. The *organizational-operational infrastructure* of the terrorist is, of course, one of the central targets. It is this infrastructure that would make the violent operations of the organization possible and hence also increase the importance of learning as much as possible about it. Moreover, the organizational infrastructure is closely related to the operational system itself; therefore, the more we know about the former, the more also we may learn of the latter, which is naturally much more compartmentalized and difficult to penetrate. The following are some of the organizational facets that will merit attention by intelligence:

(a) Following the recruitment process to the organization—where are candidates recruited, from what social strata and groups, in what regions, by what methods? etc.

(b) What are the financial sources of the organization, what is its budget, and how is it divided?

(c) Training and instruction installations, including those in foreign countries.

(d) Workshops for the development and production of weapons and other items of special equipment.

(e) Weapons and ammunition depots.

(f) The logistical infrastructure including communication networks, medical services, printing shops, secure houses, welfare services for families of dead members, and the like.

3. *Operational activities of the organization.* This is obviously the most difficult and also the most important task for our intelligence efforts. In the first place, as we have already mentioned above, operations are always the most compartmentalized. Only a very

small number of participants share knowledge of forthcoming operations. Perhaps even more problematical from our point of view is that terrorist organizations frequently do not plan their operations in great detail in advance but rather leave a good deal of the details to the discretion of the operating units. Targets for terrorist operations are set only in general terms and the way to accomplish the agreed goals are left for improvised tactics as dictated by circumstances. Thus, for example, a general goal would be to "ambush civilian vehicles in order to cause casualties"—while the timing, place, and methods for the ambush are chosen by the unit according to its possibilities and the prevailing circumstances. Moreover, it frequently occurs that even in those cases in which clear and well-defined targets are selected for attack that the standard of execution—as well as difficulties encountered during the operation itself—cause considerable deviations from original plans. Terrorist units do not on the whole assign great importance to precision in carrying out the exact objectives assigned to them.

A typical case is that of the so-called "country club unit" as it later came to be known. This was a PLO unit that was sent by sea from a base in southern Lebanon and was supposed to hold a large number of hostages in a hotel in southern Tel Aviv. Technical problems with the ship carrying the unit caused a delay in the operation of two weeks. (The unit departed twice and returned before it finally got on its way.) Later its rubber dinghies were launched on the high sea in the wrong place. The unit finally reached the shore some 50 miles north of its planned landing site and, again, instead of capturing hostages in a hotel south of Tel Aviv, it stopped a bus on the highway between Haifa and Tel Aviv and killed some of its passengers as well as others in passing cars while driving toward Tel Aviv. The unit was finally stopped near a country club north of Tel Aviv. In the ensuing exchange of fire most of the bus passengers and most of the terrorists were killed. This episode implies that even perfect knowledge concerning the operational plans would not necessarily have helped in the interception of this unit or in taking effective precautionary measures—given the considerable deviation from its original plans.

It goes without saying that it is desirable for intelligence to penetrate the various operational headquarters, although this may not be enough; in addition, we must sometimes aspire to penetrate into the operational groups themselves. In such cases, there are immediate ethical and legal problems. Are we allowed to permit our agents to participate in actions that may cause casualties and damages? Who should be authorized to make such decisions? How does one control and supervise such activity?

A subject that requires considerable attention is the establishment of a reliable and fast communication system between the sources planted inside the terrorist organization and our intelligence headquarters, to enable immediate warning and alert for preventive or security operations.

4. *The support infrastructure.* Very few organizations can operate in complete or full compartmentalization and do not depend on networks of local supporters. Such supporters help the terrorist organization, either because of ideological motivation or through fear and blackmail, without being directly involved in terrorist operations. The importance of penetrating the sympathizers' or supporters' system lies in the fact that it is easier to penetrate it than the more highly closed terrorist organization. By penetrating this supportive system it may be possible to penetrate the organization itself or obtain indirect information about it. Also, it is much easier to deter such supporters from continuing their assistance than to deter the members of the organization itself. By reducing or eliminating this supportive system, we can undermine the capacity for action of the terrorist organization. This infrastructure is composed of:

(a) *Political and ideological elements* close to the subversive organization but, for reasons of age, health, economic considerations, and frequently also fear, they are reluctant to join the terrorist organization itself.

(b) *Professional support* by ideologists and politicians who will be busy recruiting new members for the underground, lawyers who defend terrorists in court, doctors who administer medical help in secret, and others who help by supplying information, shelter, or any other form of support.

5. *International connections* are usually of great importance for terrorist organizations. They are important in providing mutual support in the following areas:

(a) Common ideological background is of great importance although most often pragmatic considerations dominate such connections.

(b) Furnishing shelter and sanctuaries. It is very common among terrorist organizations when members of one have to hide or disappear across the border that a friendly organization will provide the necessary hideouts.

(c) Support in the acquisition of weapons, ammunition, and other necessary equipment.

(d) Operational collaboration—starting with help in collecting information (it is always easier for members of a different nationality, race, or culture to appear as innocent tourists in target countries without drawing much attention) and ending with active participation in terrorist teams or even by having a foreign terrorist team in the service of another terrorist organization. Israel's war against PLO terrorist activity provided encounters with a large variety of types of foreign participation in PLO operations against it. These included collection of intelligence, communication services, smuggling weapons and ammunition, as well as involvement in direct attacks and the taking of hostages. A Japanese team in service of the PLO attacked passengers at Ben-Gurion Airport, and two Germans participated in the kidnapping of an Air France Airbus to Entebbe.

(e) Indirect participants support terrorist operations with transportation, communications, etc.

(f) It must be emphasized, however, that the direct aid given by other governments is often the most important. Thus, for example, the government identified more often than any other in support of terrorist activity (such as that in Italy, for example) is the USSR, either directly or through one of its client states—Czechoslovakia, East Germany, Cuba, Libya, Syria, South Yemen, and others. Radical Arab states, such as Libya, Iraq, Algeria, and South Yemen also are well known for their support of the terrorists. Some other moderate but weak Arab states, such as Lebanon, Kuwait today, or even Jordan several years ago, cannot afford direct confrontation and prefer to support the terrorist organizations.

6. *Targets for counteraction.* These obviously depend on the definition of strategic targets but, if penetration is seriously considered, then the collection of information on the following subjects is of great importance:

(a) political leaders, operational and planning personnel;

(b) installations—workshops, offices, headquarters, ammunition depots, training and instruction centers, etc.;

(c) support systems—medical support, communications networks, shelters, financial support, etc.

Collection Sources on Terrorist Organizations

Almost all intelligence agencies can participate in collecting information on the terrorist organizations. There are, however, some characteristics that reflect the particular nature of terrorist organizations as a target for intelligence work:

1. Overt collection is the least important. In the first place, there are very few terrorist organizations (the PLO is a notable exception) that publish newspapers, journals, and control other mass media. Also, such publications would not be likely to disclose or expose anything concerning their subversive action or operational plans. Nevertheless, occasionally they may publish names or photographs that may help to identify people, installations, or locations. Overt intelligence collection is very important, however, in studying the ideology of an insurgent organization.

2. Aerial photography can be of value only against terrorist and insurgent organizations with relatively large operations. Reconnaissance photography may help in identifying training and instruction facilities and even, on rare occasions, preparations for terrorist attacks. Air photos also can be useful in debriefing agents returning from certain targets or in the interrogation of captured terrorists.

3. Technical intelligence is of great importance. There is a need to know what weapons are used by the enemy, what are his methods for hiding or camouflaging these weapons, what is his *modus operandi* with these weapons, etc. An immediate investigation following every terrorist operation is very important in order to develop appropriate countermeasures and to take the necessary precautions.

4. The interception of radio, telephone, and other types of communications is, of course, an important source for intelligence. The problem with clandestine organizations is that, unlike governments or conventional military, they very rarely have an organized operational communications network.

5. The most important source of information on terrorist activities is what is normally referred to as human intelligence (HUMINT). This is the area in which imagination and creativity of the intelligence organization in recruiting and manipulating sources is of the greatest importance:

(a) Agents recruited among the terrorist organizations themselves (on all levels—support as well as those on operational teams). In some cases, it may prove to be difficult for the intelligence service to recruit agents directly by its own name. It may find it easier to recruit agents by approaching them with some false cover, pretending to represent another terrorist organization or a differing ideology.

(b) If it is difficult to recruit agents, it may prove easier to plant into the terrorist organizations new members who, from the very beginning, are in the service of your intelligence. The character of terrorist organizations is such that it may be relatively easy for planted agents to rise quickly to key positions and supply excellent information.

(c) The "cheapest" and easiest source of information available is an immediate, thorough, and systematic interrogation of a captured terrorist. In such cases, there is always a race against time between the capacity to gain an immediate advantage from the information obtained by interrogation and the precautionary measures taken by the terrorist organization immediately receiving the news that one of its members has been captured. An obvious conclusion is, of course, to delay as long as possible the publication of the capture or detention of a terrorist member.

The Collection of Information for Operations Against Terrorists

In general, we can see four types of operations against insurgent and terrorist organizations that require precise and up-to-date intelligence:

1. *Anti-terrorist police-type operations*. This type of operation does not differ substantially from any police action against organized and armed criminals. In such operations emphasis must be put on three particular elements:

(a) To carry out the operation in such fashion that members of the organization cannot escape once the operation has started.

(b) To capture them *alive,* because their interrogation may yield more vital information. It is of the greatest importance to issue strict orders to the force involved in the operations not to kill the terrorists during the operation. (There are practical considerations that may encourage this, like the desire to avoid casualties and unnecessary risk, often also feelings of revenge and hate among members of the police force.)

(c) It is necessary to cover and protect intelligence informers and sources that helped to prepare the operation.

2. *A conventional military-type operation*. It does not matter in this context whether it is a ground operation, an attack by aircraft from the air, or a naval operation (i.e., shelling from a ship or landing troops by sea). The intelligence required will differ greatly according to the type of operation.

In general, the essential elements of information may be divided into three relevant areas:

(a) *The designated target:* Description of the target, its site, protection and defenses, natural obstacles, weapons and forces available to the defender, level of alert, etc.

(b) *Other enemy forces that may intervene from the outside:* Whether they be other terrorist units in the neighborhood or military units of the host country (assuming, of course, that this operation is across border).

(c) *Civilian elements present in the target area:* Terrorists will often deliberately station in an area densely populated by civilians in order to find cover and hideout, as well as to make it more difficult to hit them. This will require up-to-date information necessary to permit a decision whether or not to attack the target at all—and if to attack, *how* to attack it, using means and tactics that will minimize civilian casualties. It must be borne in mind that the political damage caused by unintentionally inflicting civilian casualties may outweigh the direct benefit of attacking the terrorists.

Again, in this type of land operation, it is important to bring back documents, samples of equipment captured at the target area, as well as live prisoners for interrogation. This may be viewed by the unit in action as a real nuisance to be bothered with in the midst of fighting. It is important, therefore, to impress on such forces the necessity of these requirements. One possible way to help solve this problem could be to *attach intelligence experts to the attacking units*. The presence of intelligence experts during such operations may prove to be useful by:

- Immediate on-the-spot interrogation of the captured terrorists that may lead to additional hideouts, installations, and equipment in the target area that were not known to exist to the attacking force and may remain otherwise undetected. An interrogation on the scene may also up-date the attacking force as to possible reinforcements arriving on the scene of attack.
- An on-the-spot screening may help to determine which of the prisoners should be taken back with the force for further interrogation (usually logistical problems will limit the number of prisoners that can be taken by the attacking force to two or three). The same holds for an early analysis of documents, weapons, equipment, etc. After all, the collection of intelligence on-the-spot is the best way to obtain information on the enemy.

3. *Counter operations by covert violent means.* The emphasis here is on the technique of operations that is covert and limited in scale compared to unrestricted conventional operations. Such operations

are supposed to be designed in a way as to avoid leaving any marks and evidence as to the attacking force. They will not be formally acknowledged even after the operation has already taken place, even if the evidence left leaves little doubt as to the identity and origins of its performers.

The great advantage of such covert operations is that they may permit a disguised approach to the targets and achieve results that cannot be obtained by conventional operations. Such operations will involve the highest level of sophistication, precision, and effective results—utilizing relatively limited resources.

Such operations can be of a large variety:

(a) Operations against key leaders of the terrorist organization. These may include sabotage, the use of weapons, and they may even be performed in such a way as to leave doubt whether they were performed by the opponent or by another competing group, or whether they may have been the result of an accident.

(b) Operations designed to hit installations such as offices, training bases, meeting places, private apartments, and the like—these can be either violent operations including the use of weapons and explosives, or operations that look like accidents—the result of a fire, for example.

(c) Operations against equipment, ammunition, and weapons depots of the organization.

All of these types of operations require first-rate, up-to-date, and detailed intelligence above and beyond the intelligence required for normal military operations. In order to attack a specific building that serves as a hideout for terrorists, different levels of intelligence are required for an attack from the air, or for a secret unit that must reach that building on the ground, penetrate the building, and hit a specific object in one of the rooms. In such a case, a direct contact will be necessary between the intelligence officer serving at the operational level and the general intelligence system. Normally an intelligence organization will not be seeking such information on its own.

Moreover, despite all the secrecy required for such operations, it is very important to expose the detailed plan of operations before a limited number of senior members of the intelligence system—provided they serve in key positions. It can never be known in advance what a specific officer or expert may contribute to the planning and coordination necessary for a specific operation. It is very important, therefore, to consult officers who have a broader perspective on the intelligence work and whose attention may be alerted to a seemingly innocent piece of information that may have important implications for the operation. For example, unexpected causes may lead to the closure of certain roads or approaches to the target that may force changes or delays in the operation. Only on a higher level in the intelligence organization may there be officers who are aware of both the planned operation and the fact that on a certain date some VIPs are coming for a visit to the target area, which may lead to temporary changes in traffic and security arrangements.

The great advantage of operations of this kind is that they employ the very tactics used by the terrorists in the fight against them. No absolute defense can be devised against such operations. Such operations will, therefore, force the terrorist organizations to divert considerable attention and resources to self-defense, make life more difficult, force them to be continuously on the move, frequently seek new hideouts, and the like. Such measures, if taken by the terrorists, can be considered as an achievement on our part, in some cases even without having to resort to action.

All the collection sources mentioned above will contribute their share to the success of such operations. Above all, such operations will require the presence of our men in the target area *before* the operation takes place. It is essential that they be familiar with all alternative approaches to the target, the structures and facilities in the target area (at least from the outside); that they follow closely members of the terrorist organization in order to identify them; and that they are acquainted with them well enough to predict some of their likely reactions. The most important source of information for the preparation of such an operation is human intelligence (HUMINT) in all its shapes and forms.

Intelligence Warfare Against Terrorists

The variety of actions that can be taken by intelligence against insurgent and terrorist organizations is very great. Intelligence operations can be divided into two major categories—deception operations and psychological warfare. The responsibility for both operations should lie with an intelligence organization.

1. *Deception Operations*. It is not necessary to elaborate in this context on possible directions for deception. Clearly, every organization will have to choose those deception plans that would best suit

its methods and goals. We can nevertheless point to three different targets that can be served by deception:

(a) Misleading information concerning the security and defensive arrangements for possible terrorist targets.

(b) Misleading information concerning weapon systems and other equipment available, and used in combatting the guerrillas.

(c) Deterring terrorists by spreading rumors and stories concerning the fate of those captured and detained. (Such rumors must be tailored to fit the national character, the religion and culture of the terrorists—what they hate and what scares them.)

2. *Psychological Warfare.* Psychological warfare is a powerful weapon in the war against terrorism. Its aim is to hit the terrorist organization at its most vulnerable spot—the motivation of its members and the readiness of others to join its ranks or to remain and operate within its framework. Again, the variety of possible initiatives is unlimited. There is no one dominant recipe for action, but some possible targets and directions for action may be mentioned:

- Undermine internal cohesion by stories of traitors/spies/or informers from within.
- Undermine the credibility of the leadership and command.
- Create friction and internal rivalry among top leaders of the organization.
- Promote conflicts between different terrorist organizations.
- Draw a wedge between the organization and its supportive civilian infrastructure.

The Vulnerabilities of Insurgency and Terrorism

The Ideological Base: Ideology is the most important basis for recruiting members of terrorist organizations. Initially almost all members join the organization out of ideological motivation, although many remain out of the fear of the consequences if they withdraw.

Vulnerabilities: (a) Political: The development of a different plan or ideology which is tempting to some members of the organization but is *less* than the initial goals sought by the organization. Raising such proposals will reduce popular support ("see what you can get without violence!") and open a debate and a schism within the organization(s).

(b) The mobilization of opposition and withdrawal of popular support for the formal ideology or at least for violent terror operations. Divisons between terrorist organizations and their popular supporters should be encouraged—if necessary even by carefully planned provocations.

(c) Support for ideological competition between rival organizations or within the organization. This is not too difficult and may be intensified by provocations. The goal should be to intensify intraorganizational fighting that will transfer energy from fighting against an external enemy into internal conflicts.

The Small Size Factor: The clandestine character, the narrow ideological base—both dictate an organization based on a small command staff and rank and file structure. The organization does not grow or expand naturally from the bottom up (i.e., advancing through a routine career). As a result there is a very small number of specialists for staff work, operations, explosives, communications, and the like. It follows that, unlike in a regular army, the loss of any key member of the terrorist organization is extremely difficult to replace. Often the loss of a key member may temporarily terminate or delay operations, assist in the disintegration and weakening of the organization, result in the desertion of its members, etc. (e.g., the death of the head of Lechi, Yair, Stern, or Wadia Haddad of the PFLP).

Soft Spots: (a) Heavy dependence on a small number of key leaders.

(b) Personal corruption of key members—whether they are corrupted in reality or whether they are perceived to be corrupt by fabricated "framing." Key members can be accused of taking money for their own personal use. As no terrorist organization keeps orderly accounts it is difficult to prove or disprove such accusations.

(c) Clandestine organizations have only weak supportive services. This supportive system is easy to interfere with and to confuse.

(i) Even if the organization is effective in collecting the information necessary for its terror operations it will be relatively weak in other aspects of intelligence work and will therefore be vulnerable to deception, disinformation, and the like.

(ii) Logistically it will have a relatively limited base and only few alternative and back-up systems—ammunition, communications, etc. Any disruption of the logistical support will cause severe damage to the organization's activities.

Clandestine Activity: Whether operating on the ememy's territory or outside it, clandestine activities impose serious limitations on the organization and create vulnerable points.

Problems of defense and security: The best way to defend themselves and obtain better security is by compartmentalization:

- Extensive security and defensive burdens divert important resources and impose heavy burdens on members of the organization.
- Extensive protective measures paradoxically reduce the security of clandestine organizations. They allow their adversary to collect information about them more easily.
- Obversely, any initiative to deepen compartmentalization further decreses operational flexibility.
- Compartmentalization provides us with opportunties to penetrate, deceive, and disinform the terrorists.
- Finally, no clandestine operations can function without external supporters. However, external supporters increase the vulnerability of the organization.

In addition to the prepared paper, General Gazit added some informal remarks.

We began our paper with a quotation from General MacArthur summing up the history of failure in war with two words, *"Too late."* In fighting insurgency and terrorism I think these two words also are pertinent and very, very important.

First of all, we have to realize that fighting insurgency and terrorism *is* war. Perhaps we don't like it, maybe we'd prefer different sorts of war, but it is a war we have to fight. The second point is that, unfortunately, as far as the Western democracies are concerned, this war has been a failure on our side so far. We have not been successful. And the third point, with a question mark: Is it going to be too late before we reorganize ourselves, before we really start considering terrorism within our own borders or international terrorism as threats that we really must treat in the right way?

We originally entitled our paper "Intelligence *Warfare Against* Insurgency and Terrorism." And I think that these two words, "warfare against", are very important. To begin with, I am translating here a Hebrew term. We call it "intelligence warfare," and "warfare" makes it an active and dynamic action. But there is something else. I believe that intelligence can be very effective, very important, in the overall war against terrorism, and not only in the obvious sense of collection and analysis.

I am a great believer in the importance of intelligence in any sort of warfare, and in any military campaign. Intelligence is, or can be, a very important instrument to change the balance of forces in such a way that the side that uses intelligence correctly will do the job better, cheaper, and quicker.

The correct use, the precise use, of intelligence against insurgency is mostly important from two points of view. The first is that when we talk about insurgency and terrorist, clandestine organizations, they can only be really hurt by a direct hit. This isn't at all like covering an area with artillery or air bombardment. Let me provide an illustration.

If one scored a direct hit on the Pentagon in Washington it doesn't really matter who might be in the Pentagon at the time. The very fact that you hit the site, that you destroyed part of the building and part of the facilities, maybe the communications system—is already an achievement. But if you want to hit the command post of the Baader-Meinhoff in Germany, and if you know that they are just then in a certain room, in a certain apartment, on Unterdenlindenstrasse in Berlin, unless you can hit the exact room, with the people inside at that moment, you haven't achieved anything. This can be done only with the most accurate, precise, up-to-date intelligence. It is rather like medicine, the difference between fine surgery and a butcher. Both deal with so-called "meat," but there is all the difference in the world.

And there is the other aspect. In your endeavors to fight insurgency, anything that doesn't hit the right man, that makes the wrong man suffer, the innocent man, the noninvolved man suffer, not only does it not *hurt* insurgency, it *serves* insurgency. This is one of the most important ways of mobilizing public support to the insurgent cause. They say, "Look what those so-and-so's are doing. They are killing innocent people." So that, again, makes it much more important to have precise, up-to-date information.

I would like to emphasize one point about our paper. We started with a rather long preamble that defined insurgency and terrorism in general, the different characteristics, the different classifications of organizations, and we concluded with a description of the vulnerabilities of insurgency. Unless we understand these classifications and definitions and vulnerabilities of insurgency, we will never be capable of fighting it effectively.

I want to emphasize a point of very great importance in our view—defining war aims and war strategy. You cannot do anything in intelligence unless you have been tasked to do it. Intelligence has great capabilities. But somebody has to tell me, "I want this, and I want that. I plan to do this, and unless you give it to me I won't be able to do it." But if I am not told, it will be very, very seldom that I will supply the kind of information that might be helpful to a strategy which hasn't even been planned yet.

Whoever adopts a defensive, passive strategy against insurgency, I would say, is almost doomed to failure. You cannot fight and win any war by defensive means only. And technically, from many points of view, I think that intelligence can be more effective in the effort against insurgency targets from an active, offensive point of view than from a defensive, passive point of view.

What is the defensive problem? Defensive intelligence can be successful only if you can tell me that a group of three men or one man on the seventeenth day of May at exactly 04:31 is planning to plant a bomb at a certain crossroads. Then I might be able to prevent it. But if you just tell me that somebody is planning to plant a bomb in Washington, D.C., or if you say, "it is going to be in May," or even, "on the seventeenth of May," this is insufficient. Yet that precise kind of information is almost impossible to get.

There are in any case limits to the capabilities of intelligence. Even with all resources put in, we can't delude ourselves that a little extra will produce superior results. One of the major problems is that terrorists don't care if it is five or six o'clock, or at this corner or another corner. How can we get intelligence about it—just because someone decided to do it one hour earlier? On the other hand, if you want to hit targets offensively, the terrorists also have static targets, and they have to put *them* on the defensive. Make them waste their defenses in hiding, in moving, and in changing places.

This is perhaps, from my point of view, the most important message I want to convey: we should never concentrate our resources only on defensive measures.

Now, if this is true about our overall strategy in dealing with insurgency and terrorist organizations, it is definitely true when it comes to intelligence. Intelligence, as I've said already, should not be limited only to collection and analytical efforts.

First of all, in planning any military operation or any operation against insurgency, there is a constant problem, a constant competition, between the needs of compartmentation on the one hand, and the best possible coordination on the other. Normally we in the intelligence community have the so-called compartmentation phobia—about secrecy and leaks. Unfortunately, we worry so much about it that we forget our problem is not secrecy: our problem is to succeed in our operation. And the success of an operation should always be more important than secrecy, than this compartmentation.

Of course, one shouldn't go too far in either extreme. Any operation against insurgency, against a terrorist target, is very, very complex. It has to be very accurate in its execution. We can never really tell what kind of intelligence might be needed in order to succeed. And the more people within the intelligence community who know about the plan and who might contribute just one single item of information may change the whole thing from failure to success. From my personal experience, I was able to contribute information on intelligence operations I had nothing to do with; but knowing that something was going to be done, I could contribute all sorts of pieces of information and say, "Listen, are you aware of this or of that?" And this *did* change the results.

Surprise is of major importance in fighting insurgency, not only in the active but also in the defensive. You can always be successful in making the other side guess wrong as to when, where, and how. And it can make a lot of difference.

We all know the story of Entebbe. The problem was we knew that we couldn't do that kind of an operation in a small country like Israel by calling in Air Force pilots from a civilian air company without its being known immediately. We were worried much less by the Ugandans or the PLO than we were by the media present in Israel, who were trying to cover us—and incidentally by your military attaches. So we developed a deception plan. Our plan was that we were going to attack targets in Lebanon, and to hold hostages there to counter the Entebbe hostages. Your American military attaches in Israel were all running to the northern border—I enjoyed it!

My next point is: incorporate your intelligence officers and analysts in the operation itself. Let them be on the spot. This is another aspect of what I call "fine surgery." Only your capability of immediate exploitation of whatever you see on the spot, of an immediate interrogation of the people who are on the spot, may permit quick action or reaction before the other side has time to change places, to change hideouts, to adjust its plans. Unless you have an expert on the spot you will never be capable of doing this exploitation.

The last point on the use of intelligence—and we did enter into it quite at length in the paper—is how to use intelligence for covert violent operations against insurgency, for all different sorts of deceptions in fighting insurgency and terrorism, and for psychological warfare. These are very, very important vulnerabilities of the other side. Use them.

One point on the collection problem. With insurgency, HUMINT and not any of the technical means is perhaps the most important agency. You have problems, even legal problems. First of all, you don't really know which twelve youngsters in this or that university will turn out to be a potential threat to your system. If you don't penetrate them today and you wait until they start planting bombs, it will be too late. Remember the motto, those two words, *Too late*. Do it earlier and not later.

A second point. With insurgency there isn't a key position that you penetrate and say, "If I'm there, I'm secure; I will know everything." This isn't the way a terrorist clandestine insurgency works. Unfortunately, you need a very wide penetration.

And my last point is, I really am glad that the problem of fighting insurgency has been incorporated into this conference. Unfortuantely, the problem of fighting insurgency is sort of an unwanted child that has been falling between the different stools. Is it a police action? Is it an FBI action? Is it a counterintelligence action? Is it a positive intelligence possibility?

If you want to succeed, most important are:

- to define terrorism as an enemy par excellence.
- to define terrorism as a target for your intelligence.
- to decide exactly who is responsible for this function within the intelligence community.

Discussants

Mr. Robert Chapman: This paper is a much-needed text on the insurgent's tactical use of terror, and it should become, I believe, a reference work for all military and all intelligence organizations in this country. I will try to add to its content. First, I will discuss a kind of terrorism that in the 1980's destroys the United States' political base abroad and closes our foreign markets and our supply of raw materials. And it now reaches inside our own country.

General Gazit described an insurgent's use of terror to win a military victory. I will discuss the use of terrorism by urban guerrillas, not as a tactic of revolution, but terrorism as a *form* of revolution to *create* an insurgency.

The difference between terror as a revolutionary tactic and terrorism as a form of revolution is that in the latter the government under attack is mortally wounded by terrorism *before* the insurgency results. An example today is El Salvador. Through the use of terrorism, people lose faith in the government's ability to govern. The army and the police are demoralized and unwilling to fight, and there is little left with which the government can fight once the insurgency comes.

This concept of insurgency is based on the assumption that the masses are no longer willing to start a revolution. This was the thesis of Herbert Marcuse and his revolutionary proponents—they believed that to wait for the conditions of revolution is to wait forever. It is the duty of the revolutionary, they maintain, to make the conditions for revolution, and thus to make the revolution itself.

With this rationale, minuscule groups of revolutionaries rob banks, assassinate, kidnap, bomb, hijack, and commit other terrorist acts to obtain publicity for their cause. This in their jargon is called "armed propaganda." Their intent is to terrorize people, damage the economy, force the government to suspend constitutional guarantees, and, above all, make the military respond with roadblocks, searches and seizures, and military operations. And when these factors occur, a revolution exists where non existed before and where none was wanted. A peaceful political situation is turned into a revolutionary one. It is sometimes called the "foco" concept of urban terrorism.

The Weathermen, trained in Cuba, returned to the United States and wrote: "It is not necessary to organize the population as a whole to accomplish a revolution. A small group of insurgents can act as a voice for the discontented elements to channel all their energy into the defeat of the government—it is the duty of the revolutionary to make the revolution."

Today foco-type urban terrorism is being fought in Northern Ireland, Spain, Italy, West Germany, Greece, Turkey, all of Latin America, the United States, and it is now beginning in the Arabian Peninsula.

The *modus operandi* of adherents of the foco concept is similar to the techniques described in General Gazit's paper. There are minor modifications because of the small number of urban guerrillas who comprise the foco.

They operate from clandestine cell structures like the insurgents described in the paper. But Abraham Guillen, a Tupamaro strategist, concluded that because of the terrorists' operational command structure, the compromise of one cell led to the compromise of another, and still another until the entire organization was destroyed. He urged urban terrorists to replace cells by organizing along the lines of the Chinese guerrilla armies. He proposed that urban terrorists be native to the city, that they lead normal lives, and then rise together to attack the enemy and after the attack to fall back into their normalcy only to rise and attack again.

But the demands of clandestine security prevented most urban terrorists from implementing Guillen's advice. Only the Weathermen in the United States were successful. They achieved this by organizing independent cells, not linked by a command structure, with each cell capable of self-support and independent action.

All urban terrorists who practice the foco concept are Marxist-Leninist and Communist. All can be traced and linked together internationally. In the international links of these groups, the magnitude of counterintelligence needs in the 1980's becomes very, very apparent.

General Gazit's paper accurately states that the Japanese Red Army assisted in the Soviet-supported and financed Popular Front for the Liberation of Palestine (PFLP) by committing the Lod Airport massacre. He also stated accurately that the Baader-Meinhoff gang took part in the Entebbe operation.

The Vienna OPEC seizure was staged by three separate terrorist organizations acting together: the PFLP, the 2 June Movement, the Revolutionary Cells, under the leadership of Carlos Ramirez Sanchez. The PFLP subsidized the Revolutionary Cells, the 2 June Movement, and the Baader-Meinhoff gang. Luduina Janssen of the Dutch Red Help was recruited by the PFLP to case the Lod Airport.

The Irish Republican Army is linked to the Palestine Liberation Organization (PLO), the PFLP, Algeria, and Libya. The Frente Sandinista de Liberacion Nacional, the FSLN, was trained, guided, and supported by Castro's Cuba for 20 years. As early as 1970 the FSLN participated in hijackings with the Palestinians. In return, the PLO ferried arms into Nicaragua. The links between the Puerto Rican Frente Armada de Liberacion and Cuba are also very well documented.

Each foco group is linked with the others. The Baader-Meinhoff gang received arms from the Petras Krause organization in Switzerland, and both gave explosives to Spanish terrorists. The IRA is allied with the Brittany Separatists and the Basque Separatists ETA-Military. And on and on the connections grow. It is a worldwide web of terror, and each strand can be traced back to the Soviet Union.

Urban guerrillas target superior manpower and firepower against a weaker enemy. The principal targets are civilians and isolated military posts. Terrorists take no chances. For this reason, indiscriminate bombings account for about 70 percent of all terrorist acts, because bombing obviates dangerous frontal confrontations with the enemy.

I would differ slightly from the paper by saying that about one year ago the targeting of urban guerrillas changed. Groups that I classify as "homeland liberation" guerrillas, including the IRA in Ireland, the Frente Revolutionaria Antifascista y Patriotica in Spain, the Ejercito Guerrillero del Probre, the EGP, in Guatemala, and the FALN in the United States, underwent this change. Their target selections are now members of the government, the military, and the police. And the reason for the change in targeting is Protocol II.

Protocol II is the supplement to the Geneva Convention of 1949. The Geneva Convention of 1949 provides prisoner-of-war status to combattants between two countries. Protocol II grants prisoner-of-war status to combattants of one country—to insurgents. Captured insurgents, including urban terrorists, are to be confined in POW camps rather than prisons. They are eligible for prisoner exchange, and their treatment is overseen by international representatives of neutral states. The conditions for such treatment are that the insurgents be identified by uniform, distinctive clothing, an armband, a beret, or by the open display of weaponry, and, lastly, that they attack government, not civilian, targets.

When caught red-handed, members of the IRA and the FRAP have thrown their hands in the air, dropped their guns, and shouted "prisoner of war," "freedom fighter." In April 1980, when police surrounded armed FALN terrorists in Chicago, they, too, demanded treatment as prisoners of war. Word of Protocol II is reaching all terrorists worldwide.

Protocol II was initialed by the Department of State in the summer of 1977 and is now somewhere before the Senate Foreign Relations Committee. Protocol II is part of the counterintelligence dilemma that we face in the 1980's. If not ratified here, it will be ratified elsewhere.

I will now briefly describe how urban guerrillas in the foco mold have been combatted. Urban terrorism can be fought only by military means. Urban terrorists are satisfied only by political victory and they cannot be otherwise mollified. Social reforms in El Salvador simply intensified terrorism. So, too, did political concessions in Spain.

Only Uruguay defeated a full-bloom urban terrorist insurgency. The primary weapon was intelligence obtained through interrogation. This is in agreement with General Gazit's paper, that interrogation is one of the easiest forms of intelligence gathering. However, on instruction, the captured insurgents resisted interrogation to gain time for their compatriots to flee; but this tactic only intensified the interrogation.

Formerly, the United States aided such friendly countries under attack by internal insurgency. Aid was not given because of terrorism *per se,* because we were opposed to terrorism in principle. It was political. It was to prevent a friendly country from falling into hostile hands. The United States gave such besieged governments money, logistics, and the services of counterinsurgency experts. And above all, the United States gave such countries moral support.

The counterinsurgency assistance that was given was intended first, to obtain intelligence on the insurgents; second, to use as intelligence to apprehend the insurgents; and third, after their apprehension, to publicize the fact so that others would be deterred from repeating the performance.

In 1980, however, the United States no longer gives beleaguered friendly countries any such help, even though the internal adversaries of these countries are trained, guided, and supported from abroad by the Soviet Union and Cuba. Instead, US policy has changed and now is aimed at "moderating" the insurgents to positions more compatible with US interests. This was the policy in Iran; this is the policy in Nicaragua.

The Soviet Union, however, has a very different policy toward urban terrorism. Overtly, the Soviets oppose terrorism which disrupts diplomatic activities, transportation, and communications, and I should add international meetings as well—that will take care of OPEC.

But since November 1979, the Soviets have encouraged the terrorists holding American diplomats captive in Iran. The Soviets emphatically refuse, even in public, to extend the concept of terrorism to wars of national liberation, to resistance against an oppressor, and to working people's demonstrations against oppression by exploiters. Thus, the Soviets support terrorism directed against democratic states. It is no secret; one can read it in the press.

A change in attitude of the United States Government and the American people is needed. The primary intelligence tool against insurgency, interrogation, is a tool we hold in the lowest repute; we deny ourselves its use.

General Gazit spoke of the intelligence technique of planting agents in a terrorist movement. But under US laws, regulations, and procedures, an agent cannot participate even marginally in a felony act. He must be withdrawn from the operation before he can achieve a position where he will obtain quality information.

If an agent obtains information that will save the life of another, the information must be used to save that life, and the agent's future utility is lost. It is the just and civilized approach, but we weaken ourselves before a barbaric and unrelenting foe.

With these and other restrictions too numerous to mention, in the past four years or so, much-needed human intelligence, the core of counterintelligence against insurgency, is perhaps irreparably damaged in this country and can no longer serve us in the 1980's.

Counterintelligence is a challenge of the eighties; but we are so inadequately prepared. The question today is, as General Gazit says: What can be done, and is there time to do it?

Dr. Abram Shulsky: We in the United States have been very fortunate with respect to terrorism. While we have had our problems, they have been minor compared to those of many other countries, including the major Western democracies.

We would be foolhardy, however, if this fact were to deter us from examining how well prepared we are to combat terrorism of a serious sort; we do not clearly understand why we have been lucky so far. One suggestion has been that there is something in the character of the US that has prevented the rise of a serious terrorist threat here.

Perhaps, but we don't know what it is, and we cannot rely on it. It may be that previously acceptable FBI activities of the COINTEL-PRO type prevented the various radical groups the FBI harrassed from developing into full-fledged terrorist cadres. If so, then we must be prepared for terrorism in the future. Similarly, it may be that, until recently, Europe represented a more attractive arena for international terrorism because of the smaller size of the countries and the easy accessibility of havens across international borders. If so, recent cooperative measures in Europe may take away this relative advantage, and direct the attentions of international terrorist groups to our shores.

If we recognize in the paper a concise "textbook" of counterterrorism, backed by much difficult and tragic experience, and validated by the relative success of the efforts it summarizes and categorizes, then we have a standard by which to judge how well prepared the US is to combat terrorism. Weighed against this standard, we are found wanting.

General Gazit distinguishes between two types of counterterrorist strategies, a "defensive-passive" strategy and an "active counter" strategy. I believe the United States is not in a position to implement either.

The passive strategy, in a sense, automatically recommends itself to any intelligence agency, whose mission it is to give advanced warning of any threat to the nation's security or tranquility. Unlike foreign countries, however, terrorist groups do not typically announce ahead of time their hostile intentions or even their existence. Hence, if intelligence is to give advanced warning of their actions, it must be directed not only against known, active groups, but against the social and political milieux from which terrorist groups arise. A meteorological analogy might be helpful here: once a tornado is sighted, it is often too late to give its potential victims much warning. Tornado watches and warnings are announced not only when tornadoes are sighted, but also when general meteorological conditions exist that are known to spawn them.

From the civil liberties perspective which has informed the legal framework within which our intelligence agencies operate, it is precisely this surveillance of suspect social and political milieux which is to be prohibited. Indeed, it is argued that no exercise of First Amendment rights, including the announcement of an intention (as long as it is stated in general terms) to engage in terrorism, should trigger surveillance of an individual or group.

Furthermore, it is unclear to what extent "support" or

"front" groups may be subject to surveillance as a means of learning about the general characteristics of the terrorist group. (Although it may be taken for granted that, in the case of a sophisticated terrorist group, the "support" or "front" group members will have no knowledge of operational details of plans, surveillance of them might well enable the intelligence agencies to understand the logistical and other support mechanisms.) From the civil liberties perspective, members of these groups are to be shielded from any government surveillance unless they have some direct involvement in the criminal nature of the terrorist enterprise; in many cases, (e.g. lawyers who represent the terrorists in court, doctors who provide medical care, those who raise funds for propaganda activities, etc.) there will be no such direct criminal involvement; in many others, there will be, but it will be extremely difficult to detect.

With respect to the active strategy, the civil liberties problems are even greater. While no attempt has been made in recent draft legislation to promulgate standards for the conduct of active measures, the tendency has been to place the ultimate authority in the hands of the Attorney General, rather than in the hands of an intelligence or security agency. This implies a primacy of the rule of law, and suggests that active measures will be severely limited in scope; strictly defensive measures would presumably be permitted (such as covertly replacing the terrorists' store of dynamite with harmless material), but measures which harmed the terrorists, even indirectly (such as stirring up feuds and rivalries among the members of a terrorist group or between different groups) would be forbidden.

As General Gazit's paper makes clear to anyone familiar with recent debates concerning intelligence charters, the US lacks a clear sense of what standards of conduct ought to apply in the fight against terrorism. From the legal point of view, our society recognizes two kinds of threats: crime and war. With respect to crime, the model is the individual criminal who is very much weaker than the state, and is hence entitled to all sorts of procedural due process to make sure that the state doesn't simply crush him. Because the criminal is ultimately much weaker than the state, we can afford to be guided by the principle that it is better for 100 guilty men to go free than for one innocent man to be convicted, and its corollary in the field of intelligence, that it is better for 100 guilty men to escape surveillance than for one innocent man to be subjected to it.

At the other extreme is war, where, except for a few rules such as the prohibition against the use of poison gas, the general sense is that anything goes.

Terrorist actions are indeed crimes, but they are committed not by generally isolated individuals interested in pecuniary gain, but by well-organized groups interested in conducting political and psychological warfare against liberal democratic states. The absence of a proper legal regime to govern the conduct of the fight against terrorism may be the most important deficiency in our counterterrorist capabilities.

General Discussion

(Dr. Richard Pipes, the session Chairman, then added a brief comment to the presentations prior to opening the general discussion.)

As a Russian historian, as I listened to these remarks, I had the overwhelming feeling of déja vu. Everything described about the structure of terrorist cells today, about their programs, was initiated in Russia in 1879 and 1880 when modern political terrorism had its beginning. Indeed, the whole war against the Imperial regime which began late in the reign of Alexander II was led by 30 people organized in different cells that had no common command structure, and they kept the whole Imperial police hopping.

The tactic of breaking the government down by striking at officials, by destroying the respect that people normally have for government, was developed by Russian terrorists in those years.

I would also add that after 1906, the *agent provocateurs* as they were called in the Russian police were not allowed to engage in felony acts. The Prime Minister made a strong point about this. He said, "They can gather information but they cannot involve themselves in political action."

Nevertheless, despite this constraint, the Russian police managed to destroy the terrorist movement completely by World War I, by the use of extraordinary measures. They introduced field court-martials by which the terrorists could be executed immediately.

I am struck by the extent to which Russian history and the overthrow of the Imperial regime are now being repeated on a worldwide scale. This in itself is not surprising, because the people who are today running the Soviet government are essentially the ideological heirs of the people who brought down the Imperial government. And we ought to learn from these lessons. Unfortuantely, we are not.

(Dr. Handel, Gen. Gazit's co-author then added a brief comment.)

When we wrote this paper, it obviously reflected Israeli conditions, but perhaps we can say in some ways British conditions as well. Both countries are democracies, but nevertheless a democracy doesn't tie its hands if it has to take action. But it strikes me as background for this colloquium: A democracy that binds itself by excessive legalism can invite paralysis and self-destruction. The point is, I believe, to find ways to change that and lead to operations that can be done in a situation like the one in the United States today.

I believe it is a major problem. Unless we can rid ourselves of this excessive legalism, it will lead to self-destruction.

•

A participant with long professional experience in domestic security and counterintelligence opened the discussion with an expression of deep concern about the possible, even probable chilling effects on countermeasures against urban guerrillas and terrorists of the Attorney General's guidelines now in force, and other restrictive regulations and legislation under consideration. In addition several of the senior CI officials who were beginning to make substantial inroads on these terrorists, are themselves under indictment for employing the previously accepted techniques of aggressive, effective CI. And various restrictions threaten to strip us of the tools we must have to meet the threats of the 1980's.

Another participant, continuing this line of thought, asked why terrorists—who typically operate indiscriminately against the civilian population and "carry on warfare against society"—should not be treated as, in effect, "spies behind the lines . . . engaged in sabotage" and dealt with accordingly. A former senior military officer agreed. He referred to a pending Protocol II to the Geneva Conventions. Only Libya, it was pointed out, has yet ratified this Protocol. But the thrust it represents is already being used in this country—if only as a diversionary propaganda tactic.

Several participants with professional expereince in counterterrorism pointed to the extreme difficulty in combatting these groups. One used an illustration drawn from Cyprus, where entire villages were terrorized into shielding murderers; another cited a recent case in Iran where the Mujahadin killed one of their own who was simply suspected of being an informer and then literally obliterated the corpse with explosives and grenades—a grim but effective warning about what happened to those who might be tempted to reveal information about this organization. A third participant with personal experience in the international roots of terrorist and insurgency groups then addressed the role of the KGB and of satellite intelligence services in their activities. It was his view that although the KGB had penetrated these groups earlier, the Russians were themselves surprised by the "revolutionary wave of the 1960's" and thus exploited but did not control it. He felt that the situation changed in the late 1960's when the satellite services' terrorist, sabotage and disinformation units were reorganized and integrated under one central control. He judged that this more integrated system, with effective links to terrorist groups around the world, pertains today.

A congressional staff member accepted the proposition that terrorist movements are strong, effective, and ruthless, and constitute a serious threat—yet wondered if the discussion should not focus as well on their inherent weaknesses and vulnerabilities and that of their "friends" and support groups. An academic participant added to this the question of whether effective countermeasures might require some "extralegal" techniques to deal with them. General Gazit responded in part—while disclaiming any expertise in American values or the US legal system—that it did not seem possible to fight this kind of a war (and he viewed it as war and not a criminal problem) within the traditional framework of "legalisms" and due process. He reiterated the basis of his previous presentation that terrorists have many and quite specific vulnerabilities: their political/ideological base is shaky; they are usually very small groups and, once on the defensive, their capability for the initiative is restricted; and they are both vulnerable to psychological warfare and open to various forms of corruption. What is required, he stressed, is aggressive action against them—precisely to put them on the defensive.

The balance of the discussion turned on the question of the effects of the Attorney General's guidelines (with particular reference to the FBI), including such restrictive legislation as the Foreign Intelligence Surveillance Act (FISA), which imposes the "criminal standard" as a control on what may and may not be done in CI surveillances). One participant observed that, almost more important than the laws and guidelines themselves, is a prevailing "state of mind" within the "political and operational leadership" in our country: this must change first.

Finally, a former CI official returned to the earlier point that our political leadership—both in Congress and in the executive branch—has simply never recognized that terrorism is supported and possibly even controlled by the Soviets. He pointed out that we were never able from a counterintelligence standpoint to take a photograph of a KGB officer passing money to a Weatherman. Therefore, it has been the conclusion of this Congress and this administration that there is no Soviet support to the terrorists. Insofar as present and proposed laws and guidelines make it more difficult to obtain knowledge of these ties it is reasonable to ask whether we are prepared to meet present and future challenges.

CHAPTER SIX

Soviet Intelligence in the United States

Paper:

Herbert Romerstein

Discussants:

Mr. William A. Branigan

Dr. Allen Weinstein

In attempting to identify the specific strengths and weaknesses of Soviet collection and covert operations targeted against the United States, this paper implicitly addresses the challenges to US counterintelligence in the 1980's, and beyond. It is this writer's contention that the Soviets (currently the KGB) always have drawn on three pools of assets for their US operations: on the ideological spy under tight organizational control (now largely denied them), on the ideological spy with no or very loose ties to communist groups (useful to them for some collection but mostly for covert operations), and on mercenaries (their principal reliance for collection). These three categories are not neatly isolated; there are areas of overlap, and there are muddy boundary areas. But as a general proposition, the three categories can be distinguished, and it will be useful in the following pages to keep the distinctions in mind.

No intelligence service in the world has had opportunities comparable to those of the Soviet Union. At the same time, no intelligence service in the world has had its problems. Only the Soviets have available an organized reservoir of people ideologically oriented to providing them with espionage agents. In addition, only they have the machinery in place, in most countries of the world, to contact and make use of these people. On the other hand, the ideologically committed may become alienated from the apparatus because of political deviations, and the machinery (i.e., the local Communist Party) may be penetrated by hostile police and intelligence services.

The United States always has been an important intelligence target of the Soviet Union. Certainly since World War II, it has become the "main enemy." The United States, therefore, is targeted both for collection and covert action. While clandestine collection is conducted by the Soviet intelligence service, overt collection is conducted both by covert operatives and by "friends of the Soviet Union" who are often unwitting and in contact with the intelligence service only through "cutouts." And while some covert action, particularly propaganda, is conducted by the local Communist parties, parallel but coordinated activities are conducted by the intelligence service through media placements and agent-of-influence operations.

Soviet intelligence has had its most striking successes during periods of "American-Soviet friendship," "peaceful coexistence," and "detente." Soviet espionage has been more difficult during periods of "cold war" and militant anti-communism in the United States. So, although ideological supporters often are more useful as spies than are mercenaries, during the difficult periods the Soviets must rely on mercenaries. They have from time to time used dissident communists in espionage, and in recent years they have been able to use the Cuban intelligence service as a conduit to New Left and "radical chic" circles in which an avowed Soviet presence might be unacceptable. Coping with Soviet intelligence operations thus requires both an active internal security apparatus and a continuous campaign of public education among potential targets of Soviet or Soviet surrogate recruitment.

The Early Years

In Soviet practice there is no sharp demarcation between overt diplomacy, on the one hand, and propaganda and covert operations of the Soviet intelligence service on the other. Both overt and covert operations are coordinated to achieve strategic and tactical goals. While Soviet diplomatic establishments serve as cover for intelligence officers, any Soviet diplomat or other Soviet citizen abroad can be co-opted for intelligence purposes. So, too, with members of local Communist parties and support groups. While the parties themselves are under the control of the Communist Party of the Soviet Union (from 1919 to 1943 through the Communist International—the Comintern—and since that time through a variety of other vehicles, including at present the International Department of the CPSU), individual members are available for recruitment by the Soviet intelligence service—which also has gone through numerous identities (from the CHEKA to the OGPU, GPU, NKVD, MVD, and the present KGB) but all in one line of unbroken descent. The 4th Department of the Red Army and GRU are designations for Soviet Military Intelligence.

A description of this phenomenon was provided by Leon Trotsky in a letter to the Attorney General of Mexico, dated June 1, 1940, written shortly after an unsuccessful attempt on his life. Trotsky wrote in part:

> The general scheme of the GPU organization abroad is the following: in the Central Committee of each section of the Comintern there is placed a responsible director of the GPU for that country. His status is known only to the secretary of the party and one or two trustworthy members. The other members of the Central Committee have but a slight inkling of the special status of this member.
>
> As a member of the Central Committee the country's GPU representative has the possibility of approaching with full legality all members of the party, study their characters, entrust them with commissions, and little by little draw them into the work of espionage and terrorism, appealing to their sense of party loyalty as much as to bribery.[1]

The first Soviet "diplomatic" representative appeared in the United States in 1919, long before formal US recognition of the Soviet Union. Ludwig Martens was in fact a Communist residing in the United States who was given a mandate by the Soviet Union to operate as the unofficial ambassador.[2]

In testimony before the Senate Foreign Relations Committee in 1920, Martens presented a list of employees of his unofficial Soviet Embassy, including Santeri Nuorteva and Arthur Adams.[3] In September 1918, Nuorteva had identified himself as a representative of the Finnish Workers Republic, a short-lived Communist regime that had operated in Finland for only a few months.[4] Adams, who was to be a very important Soviet intelligence agent in the United States in the 1940's, was described in Martens' list as follows: "Arthur Adams, director (Technical Department). Born in Russia. Citizenship: British. Graduate of School of Science, Kronstadt, and of University of Toronto, Canada (NE). Appointed June 22, 1919."[5] Martens said of Adams, "he belongs to the Socialist Party." In another part of his testimony, however, he indicated that when he said "Socialist Party" he meant it in a generic sense—as a term that embraced not only the Socialist Party but also the Communist Party and the Communist Labor Party. Martens explained, "Because we have a Socialist government . . . we prefer to employ socialists."[6]

The role of Adams and his technical department was to promote what we now call technology transfer. Adams was deported with

Martens in 1920, but was to return to the United States on a number of later occasions to organize such technology transfers. In 1927, he came to the United States in connection with the building of the first automobile plant in the Soviet Union and, in 1932, to purchase airplanes from Curtiss Wright. In 1938, he returned again and then again in 1942. In the middle of World War II he was involved in the theft of atomic secrets.[7]

Shortly after his return to Russia, Martens participated in what appears to be the first Soviet agent-of-influence operation directed against the United States. A young American who was visiting the Soviet Union was developed into the Soviet "path" to the American business community. On October 14, 1921, after meeting with Boris Reinstein, an American Communist living in the Soviet Union, Lenin wrote the following note to all members of the Central Committee of the CPSU:

> Reinstein informed me yesterday that the American millionaire Hammer, who is Russian-born (is in prison on a charge of illegally procuring an abortion; actually, it is said, in revenge for his communism), is prepared to give the Urals workers 1,000,000 poods of grain on very easy terms (5 percent) and to take Urals valuables on commission for sale in America.
>
> This Hammer's son (and partner), a doctor, is in Russia and has brought Semashko $60,000 worth of surgical instruments as gifts. The son has visited the Urals with Martens and has decided to help rehabilitate the Urals industry.
>
> An official report will soon be made by Martens.[8]

Doctor Julius Hammer, who was in fact in prison for bungling an abortion, was one of the founders and financial angels of the Communist Labor Party. Benjamin Gitlow reported collecting Communist Party USA dues from him as late as 1929 when they both were in Russia.[9]

On October 19, 1921, Lenin wrote to Martens about Hammer's plan to supply grain to the Urals and suggested that it should be in the form of a contract or concession.[10]

On May 24, 1922, Lenin wrote an urgent and secret message to Stalin with a request that it be circulated to all politburo members, "being sure to include comrade Zinoviev":

> On the strength of this information from comrade Reinstein, I am giving both Armand Hammer and B. Mishell [a director of Hammer's company] a special recommendation on my own behalf and request all CC (Central Committee) members to give these persons and their enterprise particular support. *This is a small path leading to the American 'business' world, and this path should be made use of in every way.*[11] (Emphasis added.)

The extraordinary measures taken by Lenin to cultivate the young Armand Hammer and use him to convince American capitalists that it was profitable and useful to invest in Soviet concessions paid substantial returns to the Soviet Union. The relationship between the Soviet Union and Armand Hammer continues to this day.

When Hammer returned to the United States, he painted a somewhat different picture of his relationship with the Soviet Communists. Hammer was quoted in the *New York Times* of June 14, 1922, as saying:

> When I conferred with officials of the Government I told them I was a capitalist; that I was out to make money but entertained no idea of grabbing their land or their empire. They said in effect, 'we understand you did not come here for love. As long as you do not mix in our politics we will give you our help.' And that is the basis on which I conducted negotiations.[12]

Wherever possible, Soviet intelligence used Communist Party members and sympathizers. These were people who could be trusted. A classic example is the case of Richard Sorge, a German Communist who became the Soviet Union's masterspy in pre-World War II Japan. Sorge was captured by the Japanese in 1941 and signed a lengthy confession. He had joined a Communist group in Germany in 1918 that soon became part of the German Communist Party. In 1925, he went to the Soviet Union where his party membership was switched from the German to the Soviet Communist Party. He was assigned to work in Comintern intelligence collection until 1929 when he was switched to Soviet military intelligence. Sorge identified five Soviet government departments or agencies engaged in intelligence collection: the Tass news agency, the Comintern, the Foreign Commissariat, the GPU, and the Fourth Bureau of the Red Army.[13] This pattern of recruitment through a Communist Party, the development of the agent, and eventual transfer to military intelligence was repeated time and again in later years.

One problem that Soviet intelligence had in the United States, unlike any other country, was that their major recruiting ground did not consist of Americans. The bulk of CPUSA membership during the 1920's was uneducated foreign-born workers. For example, in 1922, out of a party membership of 12,058, only 1,269 were assigned to English-speaking branches, and not very many of them spoke English particularly well. By 1925, party membership had risen to 16,325 but still only 2,282 were in English-speaking branches.[14] Such people had no access to classified information. They had practically no access to the American working class. It was only a decade later that any substantial number of American intellectuals would be recruited into the Communist Party.

Because the United States did not recognize the Soviet Union, diplomatic cover was not available for Soviet intelligence officers. Some operated as illegals, but many used the semi-official cover of the Soviet trading organization, Amtorg. On November 25, 1930, Vasil W. Delgass, a former vice president of the Amtorg Trading Corporation told a congressional committee that Amtorg was being used for intelligence collection, for example, to obtain samples of military equipment and diagrams. Delgass testified that he saw secret war department drawings in Amtorg in 1927. In addition, Soviet intelligence personnel, sometimes using Amtorg as a cover, purchased airplane engines and weapons and secretly shipped them to the Soviet Union.[15]

Michael Handler, a former Soviet intelligence officer, testified before the same committee on July 24, 1930, and later sent the committee a letter with substantial information about Soviet intelligence activities in the United States. He said that one Trillisser was the Chief of the Foreign Division of the OGPU—an apparent reference to Mikhail Abramovich Trillisser, a longtime Soviet intelligence official who died in the Moscow purges of 1938 and was rehabilitated by the Soviets in 1962. According to Handler:

> Paying daily visits to the Foreign Department of the OGPU, before leaving Moscow, I was once requested by Trillisser to recommend to him an experienced trustworthy man, to whom he could entrust the organization of undercover connections between Amtorg in New York and Hamburg Nuclei of Berlin branch of OGPU.
>
> I have presented to him a man, whom I knew under the name Mikhail. This man received instruction and departed to New York, where he arrived illegally.
>
> Before my last departure from Moscow in November 1926, I attend a secret meeting of the officials of Foreign Department of OGPU, where it was decided to send to Amtorg three employees—Checkists, (sic) who would fill official posts in Amtorg, but who would actually work under orders of OGPU, military espionage division of the Red Army and Comintern.
>
> I have been employed for several years as responsible agent of military espionage division and also of foreign division of OGPU and therefore I have a thorough knowledge of their organization work and methods.
>
> I can swear that nuclei of OGPU, military espionage and Comintern exist without exception in all Soviet organizations abroad, including all embassies, commercial organizations, and red cross missions.[16]

The close relationship between Soviet Military Intelligence and the Comintern intelligence apparatus continued for many years, for the simultaneous collection of military, economic, and political intelligence. In spite of all shortcomings and the lack of available assets, the Soviets did substantial work during the 1920's in meeting their intelligence requirements.

American Communists served wherever possible to aid Soviet intelligence in its activities. An interesting phenomenon began during the 1920's that was to have substantial significance in later years. This was the use of dissident Communists or radicals not under discipline for Soviet intelligence purposes.

Ludwig Lore was one of the founders of the American Communist Party. He was expelled in 1925 as a "deviationist." According to Benjamin Gitlow, a charter member of the American Communist Party and until 1929 one of its top officials, "Lore, when a Communist, did what was expected of him, he collaborated with the OGPU and served them in whatever capacity possible . . . Lore, the split personality, became so involved with the OGPU that in spite of his expulsion from the Communist Party and the Comintern, he could not extricate himself from their clutches. The transformation of Lore who was basically honest in his convictions, did not come on the moment of his expulsion. It took a long time, many years, during which he considered it an honor to serve the Soviet government with the result that, when he wanted to tear himself loose from the OGPU, he could not do so."[17]

Whittaker Chambers has described how, during his service with Soviet intelligence in the early 1930's, he was instructed by his Soviet control officer to make contact with Lore. According to the Soviet officer, Lore had been connected with the apparatus but "something stupid had happened" and they had lost contact. Chambers re-established the contact and knew Lore for many years. Eventually, in 1941, Lore denounced Chambers to the FBI as a Soviet intelligence agent.[18] Chambers did not describe in detail what services Lore performed for the Soviets, but he did indicate that they were interested in Lore because of his good contacts as a journalist.

One of the most interesting uses of a dissident communist group by Soviet intelligence relates to an organization led by one of the most remarkable men in the history of American radicalism. Jay Lovestone began his political activity in 1912 and remains active today. A founder of the American Communist Party, Lovestone was its secretary in the late 1920's. He made frequent trips to Moscow in his capacity as an official of the Comintern. In 1929, Lovestone lost a faction fight within the Comintern. At a series of meetings in Moscow guided by Joseph Stalin, Lovestone was denounced and removed from the leadership of the American Communist Party.

The expectation was that Lovestone would quietly surrender and do Stalin's bidding. Instead, he denounced Stalin to his face and refused to remain under Soviet control. In a speech to the American commission of the Presidium of the Executive Committee of the Comintern, on May 6, 1929, Stalin ordered Lovestone to remain in Moscow "at the disposal of the Comintern."[19] Later that month, in response to a cable from the Comintern Secretariat regarding Lovestone's desire to return to the US for two weeks on "personal business," the CPUSA answered that they would prefer that he be kept in Moscow for the time being.[20]

Lovestone was in a most precarious position. As he later told the Dies Committee, "I might say that I have received or been subjected to the highest honors of the Communist Party in my time, save one, and that is liquidation by a firing squad."[21] Lovestone and hundreds of his followers were expelled from the CPUSA. Lovestone's eventual exit from Russia is still mysterious, but it was probably facilitated by Nicholas Dozenberg, a former member of the CPUSA who had dropped out of the Party when he was recruited by Alfred Tilton for Soviet military intelligence in 1927.[22] Tilton was then head of Soviet military intelligence in the United States. He returned to Moscow in early 1929 and was replaced by Mark Zilbert.

In the fall of 1929, Tilton requested that Dozenberg transfer to Moscow where General Berzin, the head of the Soviet military intelligence, instructed him to help set up cover identities for Soviet military intelligence personnel for operations in various parts of the world. They would be supplied with false American identities and passports.[23]

Dozenberg had been a member of Lovestone's faction in the CPUSA. When he returned to the United States in 1932, he met with Lovestone and was assisted in making contact with US government agencies to obtain information needed for the creation of proprietaries for his espionage work.[24]

At about this same time, Dozenberg involved an active Lovestoneite in his espionage activity. This was Dr. William Gregory Burtan, who helped Dozenberg organize the American Rumanian Film Corporation as a cover for Soviet intelligence in Rumania. In 1933, Dr. Burtan was arrested by the US Secret Service on charges of possession and passing of counterfeit bills—money manufactured in Moscow and smuggled by Dozenberg into the United States. After serving ten years in jail, Burtan testified to the Dies Committee in 1949 that the Lovestone group would use some of the money for their expenses and the rest would be used by Dozenberg to finance Soviet espionage operations in Rumania.[25]

In 1929, Mark Zilbert replaced Alfred Tilton as head of Soviet military intelligence in the United States. His real name was Moische Stern.[26] As "General Kleber," Stern (Zilbert) led the International Brigades during the Spanish Civil War in the defense of Madrid. This service was noted in a recent Soviet book on the Spanish Civil War which identified Kleber as "Manfred" Stern. No mention was made, however, of his execution in the Soviet Union during the purges of 1937-38. General Kleber apparently has been posthumously rehabilitated.[27]

Lovestone testified to the Dies Committee that he had met with General Kleber to discuss the possible reunification of the Lovestoneites with the CPUSA and the Comintern. He indicated that Kleber agreed with the views of the Lovestoneites, which might explain why Kleber was later executed in the Soviet Union. Lovestone gave no date for this meeting, but it apparently took place before 1932, while Kleber was working for Soviet military intelligence in the United States.[28]

As late as November 1935, the Lovestoneites were still writing letters to the Comintern seeking re-admission for their "International Communist Opposition" to the World Movement.[29] By 1940, however, they had dissolved their organization and, as Theodore Draper reported, "All its principal leaders became intransigent enemies of Communism. Since they were still relatively young men, they were able to spend far more of their lives opposing Communism than they had spent espousing it."[30]

Although Soviet intelligence made a considerable effort in the United States during the late 1920's and early 1930's, the returns were limited. We know, for example, that in 1931 Zilbert (Kleber) contacted an American engineer and offered to pay a substantial amount of money for confidential plans of US Navy equipment. The engineer immediately reported this contact to the government, and the plan to steal the documents was aborted. Zilbert's apparatus also attempted to obtain classified US Army documents from Cpl. Robert Osman, who was stationed in the Panama Canal zone. Osman was apprehended attempting to transmit the documents.[31]

During the late 1920's a number of American Communists were

assigned to the international operations of the Comintern and related intelligence organizations. These included Eugene Dennis, who operated in China in the late 1920's as Paul Walsh,[32] and Earl Browder, James Dolsen, and Margaret Undjus, all of whom worked for the Pan Pacific Trade Union Secretariat, an apparatus of the Red International Labor Unions. The RILU was a Comintern front in the international labor movement. Its personnel were Comintern functionaries and had both intelligence and operational responsibilities.[33]

Browder served as General Secretary of the CPUSA from 1930 until his removal by the Soviet leadership in 1945. Dennis succeeded him. Margaret Undjus, under the names Cowl and Krumbein, served for many years as a party functionary as did Dolsen. Although Soviet intelligence in the United States during these early days had access to limited assets, patterns were set that were to have an important influence on Soviet intelligence in the 1930's and 1940's—and still do. These included the use of American Communists, dissident communists, and other radicals for espionage activity, and the combination of political work and intelligence.

The People's Front: Heyday for Espionage

The first significant breakthrough for Soviet intelligence in the United States took place in November 1933, when the US government officially recognized the Soviet Union. This provided the opportunity for the Soviets to use official cover and diplomatic immunity for their intelligence officers, in addition to those serving with semi-official cover (Amtorg, etc.) and the illegals.

A secret memorandum from the Central Committee of the CPUSA to all districts and sections, dated December 12, 1933, gave instructions to be discussed in the party units. The memorandum termed recognition a victory for the Soviet Union. It described the reciprocal pledges given by the two governments at the time of recognition and explained how these were to be viewed by the Communists.

The agreements included pledges:

> To refrain from interfering in the internal affairs of the other country. Not to permit the formation, or the residence on its territory, of any group or organization, or of a representative of such a group or organization, that aims to overthrow by force the political or social system of the other.

According to the CPUSA memorandum:

> The CI (Comintern) and the Soviet Government are not one and the same thing, and they have different functions to perform. The function of . . . the CI on the international scale is to lead in the struggle of the masses and to organize them for the overthrow of capitalism . . . The function of the Soviet Government, which is the organ of the dictatorship of the proletariat, is to consolidate its power within the country.[34]

In other words, the Soviet government would continue to use the Comintern to organize the overthrow of other governments—and so much for pledges of "noninterference."

A second phenomenon that created major opportunities for Soviet intelligence was the Comintern's new line of a "united front against fascism." This, of course, was in response to Hitler's victory in Germany. The new line was ratified in August 1935 at the Seventh World Congress of the Communist International in Moscow. It led to the rapid expansion of Communist parties around the world, including the CPUSA, and respectability for Communist front organizations. In the late 1920's and early 1930's, the front organizations consisted only of Communists and their closest sympathizers; after 1935, in contrast, the fronts became vast "sucker traps" attracting many people who were not Communists and would not knowingly join Communist organizations.

From a membership in 1921 of approximately 7,000, the CPUSA grew by 1938 to a membership of 66,000.[35] Of this number, over 40,000 were American born. Writing in 1960 about the CPUSA in the 1930's, Earl Browder boasted:

> It became a practical power in organized labour, its influence became strong in some state organizations of the Democratic Party (even dominant in a few for some years) and even some Republicans solicited its support. It guided the anti-Hitler movement of the American League for Peace and Democracy that united a cross-section of some five million organized Americans (a list of its sponsors and speakers would include almost a majority of Roosevelt's Cabinet, and most prominent intellectuals, judges of all grades up to State Supreme Courts, church leaders, labour leaders, etc.). Right-wing intellectuals complained that it exercised an effective veto in almost all publishing houses against their books, and it is at least certain that those right-wingers had extreme difficulty getting published.[36]

Browder stated publicly on a number of occasions during that period that if Moscow ever sent him a message, he would tear it up and throw it in the wastepaper basket. But his friend Philip J. Jaffe has published the text of two coded messages radioed to Browder from Moscow in September and October 1939. Those messages were given to him by Browder.[37]

Anti-Nazism and anti-Fascism were strong recruiting cards for both the Communist Party and the Soviet intelligence apparatus. Elizabeth Bentley has described how, after a trip to Italy, she came back to the United States in 1934 and joined the American League Against War and Fascism, a Communist front. By March of 1935 she had been drawn into the Communist Party. In October 1938 she got a job with the Italian Library of Information, an Italian government front, through the placement office at Columbia University. She reported this to the Communist Party and was put in touch with the Communist underground apparatus. She was soon collecting information from her employer. Her contact in the underground was Jacob Golos, who got her deeply involved in Soviet espionage.[38]

By the mid-1930's, the CPUSA had succeeded in recruiting not only intellectuals but also some who had already assumed positions with the government. In 1934, Whittaker Chambers was assigned the job of liaison between the Communist underground apparatus in Washington and J. Peters, who was head of the underground and also the contact with Soviet intelligence. Chambers found an apparatus already in place. It consisted of a leader, Nathan Witt, and a committee of seven members, each of who led his own cell of government employees. Chambers knew the leaders of the cells and only a few of the individual members. The committee comprised Lee Pressman, Alger Hiss, Donald Hiss, Victor Perlo, Charles Kramer, John Abt, and Henry Collins.[39] Members had been recruited into "Marxist study groups" and later into the Communist Party.

During the 1930's and 1940's these eight held important government posts. Nathan Witt was with the Department of Agriculture and the National Labor Relations Board; Lee Pressman, with the Department of Agriculture and Works Progress Administration; Alger Hiss, with the Department of Agriculture, the Senate Special Committee investigating the munitions industry, the Justice Department, and the State Department; Donald Hiss, with the State Department and the Labor Department; Victor Perlo, with the Treasury Department, the Office of Price Administration, and the War Production Board; Charles Kramer, with the National Labor Relations Board, Office of Price Administration, and the Senate Subcommittee on War Mobilization; John Abt, with the Department of Agriculture, Works Progress Administration, Senate Committee on Education and Labor, and the Justice Department; and Henry Collins was with the Department of Agriculture and the National Recovery Administration.[40]

In a relatively short time, some members of the Communist underground found themselves working for Soviet intelligence. One of them, Alger Hiss, rose to a high position in the State Department. The story of Hiss and Chambers has been told many times, most recently and in the greatest detail by Allen Weinstein in his book, *Perjury*. There is no reason to repeat that story here, except to emphasize that the CPUSA was used as a recruiting ground by the Soviet espionage network.

Whittaker Chambers broke with the party in 1938 and lost contact with the espionage groups. But in mid-1941, when Elizabeth Bentley was assigned by Jacob Golos to take over contact with the espionage groups in the US government, she found some of the same people Whittaker Chambers had known. These included Victor Perlo, John Abt, and Charles Kramer. They were in a cell known as the Perlo group. Another group, headed by Nathan Gregory Silvermaster, had among its members Laughlin Currie, an administrative assistant to President Roosevelt. Bentley remained in the Soviet apparatus until 1944.[41]

Harry Dexter White was identified by both Chambers and Bentley as a member of a Soviet spy ring. When he testified before the House Committee on UnAmerican Activities, on August 13, 1948, he categorically denied that he had ever supplied information to the Soviet Union or that he even knew Whittaker Chambers and Elizabeth Bentley.

However, when Chambers turned over to the government the documents he had secreted away as a member of the Communist underground, some of them were in White's handwriting. Chambers told the FBI that he had received them from White.[42] White died of a heart attack a few days after appearing before the committee and was unaware that Chambers was able to produce actual handwritten documents, thus proving that White had turned classified information over to Soviet agents.

Both White and Alger Hiss served the Soviets in two ways: they collected classified information for transmission to the Soviet Union, and they served as agents-of-influence within the US government. Hiss of course played an important role at Yalta as an advisor to President Roosevelt, and for many years he was an important policymaking official of the State Department. White was Assistant to Secretary of the Treasury Henry Morgenthau. In that capacity he not only provided valuable information to the Soviets and influenced US policy but also played a part in one of the most outrageous Soviet operations in all of World War II.

In 1943, the US government decided to begin printing currency for the future occupation of Germany. These notes would be available to the Allied military authorities in each of the four zones of occupation. The Soviets, however, insisted on having the plates, the ink, and a sample of the paper so that they could print their own notes. The Director of the Bureau of Printing and Engraving, A. W. Hall, protested vociferously against giving the Soviets the plates but he was overruled at the highest levels in the Treasury Department. He pointed out that, "to permit the Russian government to print a currency identical to that being printed in this country would make accountability impossible." But a memorandum of a meeting held at the Treasury Department on March 7, 1944, shows that Harry Dexter White did not appreciate Hall's position: "Mr. White said that he had read with considerable interest the memorandum of March 3 from Mr. Hall . . . on this subject but that he was somewhat troubled with the views expressed therein, which indicated that we could not make these plates available to the Russians. Mr. White said that, in all probability, such an answer would be construed by the Russians as expressing a lack of trust and confidence in their handling of the plates." Moreover, "Mr. White reiterated . . . that Russia was one of the allies who must be trusted to the same degree and to the same extent as the other allies." On April 14, 1944, Secretary Morgenthau personally advised the Soviet ambassador that the decision had been made to provide the plates, and specimens of the plates were turned over at that time.[43]

To make Soviet accountability for the occupation plates even more difficult, they were given a numbering system that hopelessly confused replacements for damaged notes with the Soviet printed notes.[44] As a representative of the Department of the Army testified before the Senate Government Operations Committee, on October 20, 1953, ". . . there is no way of determining just to what extent the Russians did use these plates."[45]

Throughout these years there were many cases of CPUSA members serving as sources for Soviet intelligence or lending operational assistance to Soviet espionage. Three of these cases involved atomic secrets.

One was that of Clarence Hiskey. Paul Crouch, a former party functionary, identified Hiskey before the House Committee on Un-American Activities as having been a Party member in Tennessee in 1939-1941.[46] John Chapin testified before the same committee that Clarence Hiskey had arranged for him to meet Arthur Adams, the same Arthur Adams who engaged in Soviet espionage in the United

States in the '20s. Adams asked Chapin to provide him with information concerning Chapin's work at the University of Chicago on the atom bomb project.[47]

Another case was that of Steve Nelson, a longtime CPUSA functionary and graduate of the Lenin School in Moscow, who had served in numerous Comintern assignments abroad. During the Spanish Civil War, he rose to the rank of Lt. Colonel in the International Brigades. In March of 1943, a man identifying himself as "Joe" told Nelson that the nuclear experiments then in progress at the radiation laboratories at the University of California, Berkeley, had reached the experimental stage in the production of an atom bomb. "Joe" was identified by the FBI as Joseph W. Weinberg, a scientist working on the atom bomb project. A few days later, Nelson met with Peter Ivanov, a Soviet vice counsel in San Francisco, in the "usual [safe] place"—in the middle of a park—where FBI agents observed Nelson passing an envelope or package to Ivanov. Soon after, Vassili Zubilin was assigned to the Soviet Consulate in San Francisco and began meeting with Nelson. Both Ivanov and Zubilin were identified as Soviet intelligence officers, under official cover.[48]

The third and most notable case was that of Julius and Ethel Rosenberg and Morton Sobell. Overwhelming trial evidence, including the testimony of Ethel's brother, David Greenglass, showed that they had been involved in stealing atomic secrets and passing them to Soviet intelligence officers. The trial judge concluded that the Rosenbergs' "betrayal" was "worse than murder" and had "altered the course of history to the disadvantage of our country." He sentenced them to death. Their co-defendent Morton Sobell, who was the recruiter for the spy ring but was not shown to have passed atomic secrets, was sentenced to 30 years in prison.[49]

As soon as the trial ended, a massive Communist propaganda campaign got under way, insisting that the Rosenbergs were innocent and that they had been convicted only because they were Jewish. In answering these charges, Rabbi S. Andhil Feinberg (in his book, *The Rosenberg Case, Fact and Fiction*) demolished the arguments of Rosenbergs' defenders and provided some interesting insights into Communist espionage activities. In May 1953, two years after the conviction, the American Committee to Secure Justice in the Rosenberg Case, the Communist front set up to defend them, revealed that it had obtained new documentary evidence proving the Rosenbergs' innocence. The evidence consisted of memoranda stolen from the files of O. John Rogge, the attorney for David Greenglass. The documents showed only that Greenglass, in talking to the FBI, had attempted to shield his wife. The bulk of his testimony was unshaken. Of particular significance is that the Communists had burglarized the lawyer's office and shipped the stolen documents to Paris, where the French Rosenberg Committee produced them at a press conference. They were then sent back for use at a press conference in the United States.[50]

Just as Communist regimes have their purges, so too do Communist intelligence services. The two most significant purges were those of 1936-38 in the Soviet Union and 1949-53 in Eastern Europe. One of the Americans working for Soviet intelligence who got caught up in the Eastern European purges was Noel Field, who had been a Communist since the late 1920's. He was employed in the State Department when he was recruited for Soviet intelligence.[51] After many years of such service, including operations in Europe under the cover of the Unitarian Service Committee, a refugee relief organization, Field was arrested in Hungary. Although very badly treated in prison, he remained a loyal Communist and after his release wrote an article describing his thinking as a prisoner of his own comrades:

> Many an inner conflict had to be fought out and overcome before the pacifist idealist—a typical middle-class intellectual and son of a middle-class intellectual—could become the militant communist of later years and of the present. Yes, of the present, too, though I am called an imperialist spy and treated as a traitor . . . My accusers essentially have the same convictions that I do, they hate the same things and the same people I hate—the conscious enemies of socialism, the fascists, the renegades, the traitors. Given their belief in my guilt, I cannot blame them, I cannot but approve their detestation.

Field was released from prison in 1956 at the time of the Hungarian uprising; he then supported the suppression of the Hungarians by Soviet troops.[52] By 1963, Field was back working for the Hungarian intelligence service. He assisted them in preparing forgeries of Time Magazine that were used for propaganda around the world.[53]

The Soviet purges of 1936-38 were designed to liquidate any opposition within the CPSU—principally the followers of Leon Trotsky, who had been exiled from the Soviet Union in 1929. At the height of the purge, in 1937, Stalin addressed the Party Central Committee and published the speech under the incredibly frank title, "Defects in Party Work and Measures for Liquidating Trotskyite and Other Double-Dealers." The purges in the Soviet Union were reflected in purges in the worldwide Soviet intelligence apparatus.

The blood bath extended not only to Trotskyites in the Soviet Union but also to Trotskyites abroad, and finally to Trotsky himself.

On October 12, 1939, in response to a telegram from J. B. Matthews, the Chief Investigator for the Dies Committee, Leon Trotsky (then living in Mexico City) agreed to testify before the committee. But the State Department prevented his entry into the United States.[54]

On May 24, 1940, an assassination squad organized by the GPU with the cooperation of the Mexican Communist Party machine-gunned the house in which Trotsky was staying. They also kidnapped one of his guards; his body was later found in a limepit. Finally, on August 20, 1940, a GPU assassin succeeded in murdering Trotsky.[55]

The Classic Spy Ring

An important role in the blood purge of the Trotskyites and the murder of Trotsky was played by a spy ring that later operated in the US for a number of years. This ring was headed by Jack Soble, a Soviet intelligence agent since 1931. He was a leading supporter of Trotsky and had been recruited by the GPU under threats of harm to his wife, who was then in the Soviet Union. Soble's brother, Robert Soblen, also worked against Trotsky for the GPU. Trotsky became suspicious of them and broke off relations. Soble came to the United States in 1941 and established a spy ring here. Some of the people in that ring had previously worked for Soviet intelligence in other capacities. The ring had a variety of functions, ranging from stealing classified US government documents to penetrating political organizations, including the Trotskyites and the Zionists. All of the Americans in the ring were recruited through the CPUSA. The foreigners had GPU experience abroad before coming into the United States.[56]

Some of the Americans had helped prepare for the murder of Trotsky before the ring itself was established. These preparations began in 1934, when the American Trotskyites merged with a group called the Conference for Progressive Labor Action headed by A. J. Muste, an incredible eccentric even by American radical standards. Two of the leading members of the Muste group refused to merge with the Trotskyites and instead joined the CPUSA. They were Arnold Johnson, who is still in the Party hierarchy, and Louis Budenz, who finally broke with the Party in 1945. Shortly after joining the CPUSA, Budenz was put in touch with Soviet intelligence by

Jack Stachel, an official of the CPUSA, and Jacob Golos, who ran a Soviet espionage net. In 1936, Budenz was introduced to an intelligence officer he knew only as "Roberts"—in reality, Dr. Gregory Rabinowitz, whose cover was representative of the Russian Red Cross in the United States. Rabinowitz told Budenz it was necessary to penetrate the Trotskyite movement to learn what plots were being hatched there against Stalin. Budenz in turn introduced Rabinowitz to Rudy Weil, a former Muste supporter, who had secretly become a member of the Communist Party. She was still in touch with some of the Trotskyites whom she had met at the time of the merger. One of them, Sylvia Ageloff, was working as a courier for the Trotskyites. Weil contrived to introduce Ageloff to a GPU agent using the name Jacques Mornard. It was Ageloff who brought Mornard into the Trotsky household where, on August 20, 1940, he murdered Trotsky.[57] After release from a Mexican jail in 1962, Mornard lived in Eastern Europe. He died in Cuba in 1979.

Budenz also introduced Rabinowitz to Sylvia Franklin, also known as Sylvia Caldwell. According to Budenz, "By first volunteering to do secretarial work in the national Trotskyite office in New York, Sylvia Franklin under the direction of Roberts-Rabinowitz gradually made herself indispensable to James Cannon, then head of the American Trotskyite movement. She became his secretary and served in that capacity for some time. Roberts-Rabinowitz advised me that she proved to be invaluable in bringing copies of all Trotsky's mail and other Trotskyite communications to him for his information."[58]

In 1960, Dr. Robert Soblen was arrested by the FBI. He had taken over the spy ring from his brother. The *New York Times* of November 30, 1960, listed as an unindicted co-conspirator one Sylvia Callen. This is the maiden name of Sylvia Caldwell-Franklin. The *Times* reported that she was one of the couriers for Soblen's spy ring. But the American Trotskyites still refuse to believe that she was a Stalinist agent.[59]

Also listed as a courier was Esther Rand, long a Party member. She was one of the ring's agents within the Zionist movement. Soble revealed after his conviction that he had been assigned by his Soviet control officer, Zubilin (also involved with Steve Nelson), to penetrate the Zionist movement: "A man and woman, dedicated Communists, were planted in the offices of the United Jewish Appeal. Through them I obtained secret correspondence between Zionist leaders and the State Department as well as reports of conversations. I received minute details of the activities of other Zionist organizations."[60] Jane Foster Zlatovski was another member of the ring; she had penetrated the OSS, the early CIA, and US Army Intelligence and was obviously a valuable source of intelligence information. Zlatovski was indicted for espionage in 1957 but has never returned to the United States to face the charges.[61]

The member of the spy ring with the most to answer for was Mark Zborowski. He was born in 1908 in Russia and brought to Poland in 1921; in 1928 he went to France to attend school. Zborowski has told contradictory stories about his activities in Poland. To some he said he had been a Communist, to others he denied it. In 1933, he made his first contact with Soviet intelligence and was recruited as an agent. Initially ordered to spy on Russian monarchists, he was reassigned to penetrate the French Trotskyite group. He was soon involved in international Trotskyite activity and became a close collaborator of Leon Sedov, Trotsky's son. After an abortive attempt to organize Sedov's kidnapping, Zborowski was able to set up his murder. Sedov had complained of abdominal pains, and Zborowski rushed him to the hospital where they operated for appendicitis. Zborowski informed the GPU of the address of the hospital. The operation was a success but the patient soon died.

Zborowski also was able to organize the theft of Trotsky's archives in Paris. As a close collaborator of Trotsky's son, Zborowski read all the mail coming into the Trotskyite international headquarters in Paris; thus he helped arrange for the assassination of an important defecting GPU agent, Ignace Reiss, who had written to Sedov of his intentions. After the murder of Reiss, his close friend in the GPU, General Walter Krivitsky, decided that he too wished to defect. His letter to Sedov also was intercepted by Zborowski, but it was signed with a code name that only Reiss's widow could identify. Krivitsky saw his own letter in the hands of a fellow GPU agent shortly before his defection. But the GPU could not identify the code name. Krivitsky came to the United States, testified before the Dies Committee, and wrote a book about his experiences in the GPU. The CPUSA's cultural magazine *New Masses* in its issue of May 9, 1939, carried an attack on Krivitsky in which his real name, Schmelka Ginsberg, was revealed—information that could have come to the American Communists only from the GPU. Krivitsky took this article to be a threat against his life. On February 10, 1941, he was found shot to death in a Washington, D.C. hotel room. Although the room had been cleaned before the police arrived, the official version was suicide. But there is every good reason to believe that this was another GPU murder.

Zborowski used the pen name "Etienne" in the Trotskyite movement. His control officer was one Alexeev. General Alexander Orlov, who had been the head of GPU operations in Spain during the Civil War, met with this CPU officer, Alexeev, on a visit to France. Orlov later testified: "Once when I came out of the Embassy together with Alexeev he told me 'I have a man who was planted on Trotsky's son' . . . Well, I became very interested. I put a couple of questions and learned that his first name was Mark, but I didn't inquire about his last name. He worked at the Institute of Boris Nikolayevsky." On another occasion, according to Orlov, he was actually taken by Alexeev to a meeting with this agent, Mark. Later, Alexeev told Orlov that Mark wrote in Trotsky's "Bulletin of the Opposition" which was published in France and had used the pen name "Etienne."

The next year Orlov broke with the GPU. He came to the United States with his wife and child and attempted to establish a new identity. But he felt he had to warn Trotsky of the agent in his organization. He wrote Trotsky under a pseudonym advising him that Mark also known as Etienne was a GPU agent in the Trotskyite movement. When the letter arrived in Mexico, Lola Estrine was visiting Trotsky. She too had been a close collaborator of Trotsky's son, Leon Sedov, and a friend of Zborowski. She convinced Trotsky that the letter must be a GPU provocation and that Zborowski was a trusted comrade. Trotsky disregarded the warning.

Lola Estrine then married the anti-communist writer David Dallin and is now known as Lilia Dallin. In 1941, David and Lilia Dallin sponsored Mark Zborowski's entry into the United States, befriended him and found him an apartment and a job. Zborowski learned from the Dallins in 1949 that a high ranking Soviet official was defecting. He reported this information to his superiors in Soviet intelligence, but they could not identify the man. He was Victor Kravchenko. Zborowski thus almost succeeded in preventing that significant defection. But, through the Dallins, he became a friend of Kravchenko and actually helped him with the manuscript *I Chose Freedom*. He reported all of these contacts with Kravchenko to his Soviet control officer and developed the friendship on their instructions.

By 1955, Zborowski was a member of the Soblen spy ring. In a conversation with David Dallin, Orlov learned Zborowski's full name, and that he was alive and in the United States. Orlov immediately reported this information to the Justice Department, and FBI agents interviewed Zborowski. Zborowski told the FBI the truth about his activities in Europe but denied any activities in the United States. Others in the ring were concerned that if he told the whole truth, he could identify them. Soble wrote a letter to Moscow explaining the Zborowsky problem and entrusted it to the courier for the spy ring, Boris Morros.

Morros was a popular Hollywood producer-director. He was able to use his travel between the United States and Europe to carry messages for the spy ring. But he had in fact been "turned" by the FBI years earlier, and every message sent to Moscow was read first in Washington. The FBI thus knew they had been lied to by Zborowski. He was subsequently tried and convicted of perjury and served a jail sentence. He now lives in California and is a lecturer on sociology at the University of California, Berkeley. In 1969 his book, *People in Pain*, was published with an introduction by Margaret Mead.[62]

Jack Soble was convicted and sentenced to seven years in prison after pleading guilty to spying for the Soviet Union. Robert Soblen, his brother, was convicted in 1961 of spying for the Soviet Union and committed suicide after an escape attempt. Many members of the ring escaped to Europe to avoid prosecution. Some testified at the Soblen trial and at Zborowski's perjury trials. This was apparently the last major ring consisting of a substantial number of CPUSA members operating on behalf of Soviet intelligence.

The Lean Years

By the early 1950's, the Soviets were having serious problems using members of local Communist parties in intelligence operations. In the United States, for example, as a result of the Smith Act trials, it became clear that the FBI had substantially penetrated the CPUSA and might very well have identified those members of the Party assigned to Soviet intelligence activity. A similar situation had developed in other countries. In about 1952, a directive went out to the Soviet and satellite intelligence services advising them that they could no longer use local Communist Party members for intelligence operations except in extraordinary circumstances and with great attention paid to security. Some longterm agents were retained.[63]

With the loss of the local parties as an important recruiting ground for espionage, the Soviets have had to rely on mercenaries or persons they could terrorize into spying. The major effort to collect technical and scientific information has continued since the early 1950's. But without the American Communists whose ideological purity and loyalty could be reasonably assured, the Soviets have had many difficulties. In a number of cases, agents they had recruited and paid for information were subsequently revealed to be under the control of the FBI. Even in some cases where the subject had not come to them, but had been carefully targeted, they found themselves with double agents on their hands. Restrictions on travel by Soviet diplomats also severely impeded intelligence operations. An FBI report entitled *Exposé of Soviet Espionage*, released in May 1960, documented case after case of Soviet "diplomats" in contact with sources controlled by the FBI. After playing them for some time, the FBI finally exposed them—with the result that they were declared *persona non grata* and expelled from the United States.

Other Soviet intelligence officers operate here as "illegals." One was the man we know as Colonel Rudolf Abel. He was exposed because another Soviet officer, Reino Hayhanen, defected in 1957 to the United States. Hayhanen revealed that for five years he had worked as an illegal for Soviet intelligence in the United States. His first control officer, in 1952-53, was Mikhail Svirin, the First Secretary of the Soviet Delegation to the United Nations, who later became an assistant to the Assistant Secretary General of the UN. From 1954 to 1957, Hayhanen's control officer was a man he knew only as "Mark." An FBI investigation of Mark identified him as Abel. On June 21, 1957, Abel was apprehended by the Immigration and Naturalization Service. He was using the names Emil Goldfus and Martin Collins. He then claimed his true name to be Rudolf Abel and admitted that he was a Soviet citizen. He was tried, found guilty of conspiracy to commit espionage, and sentenced to jail. He was subsequently exchanged for the pilot of the U2 plane shot down over the Soviet Union in 1960.

If the CPUSA could no longer serve as a recruiting ground for espionage agents, it still could serve a useful Soviet purpose as a propaganda mill. The Party of course distributes open or white propaganda on behalf of the Soviet Union. Party members in front organizations serve the gray propaganda role as well. And there have been some instances of black propaganda. One such took place in 1963. In that year, a scurrilous pamphlet appeared, entitled *Birch Putsch Plans for 1964*. It was purportedly by a "John Smith" "as told to Stanhope T. McReady." Neither was ever identified. The pamphlet reported that John Smith, a member of the John Birch Society, had learned the plans of the American right wing to organize a coup. Part of this coup was the election of Barry Goldwater as President in 1964. Among the plotters identified by "Mr. Smith" were every conceivable conservative organization, various "rightwingers," and even some "liberals" such as Sen. Thomas Dodd, who had made anti-communist statements. The pamphlet was published by Domino Publications and gave no address. However, on April 25, 1963, the pro-communist National Guardian carried an advertisement for the book, which listed the publisher at Suite 900, 22 West Madison Street, Chicago, Illinois—the headquarters of Translation World Publishers, which had published a number of official Soviet propaganda tracts. It had registered as an agent of the Soviet government in 1961 and revealed that it had received funds from the Soviet government for the publication of books and pamphlets. The officers of the company were Leroy Wolins and David S. Canter, both of whom had been identified as members of the Communist Party in sworn testimony before the House Committee on UnAmerican Activities. Both took the Fifth Amendment when asked about their Party membership.[64] In 1965, Domino Publications reappeared with a pamphlet entitled *MLF—Force or Farce*, an attack on NATO. This pamphlet was signed by David S. Canter.

A New Era and New Opportunities

The United States today is a happy hunting ground for hostile intelligence services. The CPUSA and its fronts still serve as propaganda conduits, and the supply of mercenaries shows no signs of drying up. Far more important, however, various new opportunities have become available to the Soviets and their surrogate services. The New Left and those who accept "radical chic" as a way of life constitute potential supporters and assets, directly or indirectly, witting or not. Anti-Vietnam War activists also are prime targets. And, reinforcing these "positive" opportunities, in the wake of Vietnam and Watergate there are key "negatives" at work. US intelligence capabilities have been severely undercut, and nowhere more deeply than in counterintelligence. Statutory and executive regulations and guidelines have made hostile operations easier and effective counter-operations more difficult.

In the remaining pages of this paper, a number of specific cases will be described to throw light on this new atmosphere and these new opportunities—and an important *caveat* is in order. As noted at the very outset, the various categories tend to blur. The lines of demarcation are not easy to define. But, if anything, this will make the challenges of the '80s more rather than less rigorous. US counterintelligence indeed has its work cut out for it.

As one illustration of the role of the antiwar activists, consider the case of Robert Greenblatt. In 1967-68 he was coordinator of the National Mobilization Committee to End the War in Vietnam. On October 3 and 4, 1968, he was a reluctant witness before the House Committee on UnAmerican Activities. Under persistent questioning he admitted that he had traveled to Paris in June of that year (in the company of David Dellinger of "Chicago Six" fame) to meet representatives of the North Vietnamese government. He brought with him a letter of introduction from Tom Hayden, dated June 4, 1968, which in the end he did not need.

On June 16, Greenblatt and Dellinger met with two Viet Cong officials and five Czechs. Greenblatt conceded that he had agreed to supply the Viet Cong with "reports on the following subjects: the work of the anti-draft movement, special emphasis on activities since the Tet offensive and President Johnson's decision not to run, and also reports on the anti-war agitation or experience of organizations at work among the members of the armed forces." He further admitted that he had agreed to make available to the Prague office of the Viet Cong recordings on tapes or discs that could then be transmitted to North Vietnam.[65]

None of this necessarily violated the law. Nonetheless, it is obviously valuable for a hostile government to have access to people in the United States willing to report on political and military developments in this country, and to make recordings that can be broadcast as part of the propaganda campaign against the United States.

On another aspect of the "new opportunities," some Soviet operations are now conducted through surrogate intelligence services. The Cuban DGI, for example, sometimes can reach people who might be "turned off" by the Soviets themselves. A number of American journalists have been captivated by the charm of the First Secretary of the Cuban Intra Section in Washington, Teofilo Acosta, even though they know he is high in the ranks of the DGI. Acosta also has many friends and contacts on Capitol Hill.[66]

In the Humphrey-Truong espionage case, the Communist Bloc was represented by the Vietnamese Intelligence Service. Ronald Humphrey was recruited by offers of help to his Vietnamese wife and family. David Truong, the son of a leading Vietnamese antagonist of the Thieu government, had been involved in US antiwar activities for many years; and, even after being convicted of espionage, he still speaks for Communist groups in this country. On June 8, 1980, for example, Truong was a featured speaker at a testimonial meeting in New York City for Charlene Mitchell, a member of the CPUSA Central Committee. The meeting was sponsored by the National Alliance Against Racist and Political Repression, a CPUSA front run by Mitchell.[67] On April 11, 1980, the New York chapter of the Alliance had Truong as a speaker, along with an ex-GI who was jailed for refusing to fight in Vietnam, a left-leaning member of the New York City Council, and a radical clergyman.[68]

Or consider the case of Wilfred Burchett. He has been identified as a KGB agent and has wide acceptance in New Left circles. Yuri Krotkov, a defector from the KGB, testified before the Senate Subcommittee on Internal Security that he had been Burchett's control officer for many years.[69] In the course of a libel suit brought by Burchett against a member of the Australian Senate, former US POWs in Korea testified that Burchett "was actually a Communist agent who participated in the brainwashing of Americans captured in North Korea."[70]

For 22 years, from 1957 to 1979, Burchett had served as a foreign correspondent for the *Guardian*, a major New Left newspaper in the United States. He resigned from that post in 1979 when the paper supported Cambodia against Vietnam. Burchett's support for the Soviet position in that dispute—pro-Vietnam—might have damaged his credibility with the New Left.

The value of a well-placed journalist to Soviet intelligence cannot be underestimated. One such contact, as recently described by Robert Moss, was the French newsman, Pierre-Charles Pathe—who was arrested by the French government during a meeting with his KGB control officer, Igor Kuznetsov. According to Moss:

> Pathe was never in a position to supply the KGB with top secret government documents, although the social entree he enjoyed allowed him to transmit a fair amount of titillating personal gossip about leading politicians and journalists, who the Russians wished to compromise or manipulate. After he became an organizer of the anti-American Movement for an Independent Europe, he was in contact with many leading Gaullists as well as socialists. He was also able to supply personnel background on a member of the French secret police, SDECE, with whom he had become familiar. But Pathe's importance to the KGB was not as a conventional cloak-and-dagger spy but as a disinformer and an agent of influence, someone in a position to deceive the media and Western public opinion about the real nature of Soviet designs.

Moss went on to say, "By putting Pathe behind bars the French court of state security publicly recognized that this form of Soviet covert action—which has attracted astonishingly little attention in the Western press—may represent a danger equal to traditional espionage."[71]

The Soviets' interests in "the main enemy," the United States, continue to be much the same as before. The collection of scientific, technical, and military information is paramount. They have been able to get this kind of information from a range of sources—from mercenaries like William Kampiles, a former CIA employee, who sold them the technical manual for one of our satellites, which he had stolen "on the job"; and from such people as Christopher Boyce and Andrew Lee, heavily into the drug culture, who also sold them highly classified information that they had stolen from a corporate contractor, TRW, with the US government.

Information on American technology, largely open-source, is a prime Soviet target. It is collected by visiting Soviet Bloc engineers and technicians and by Soviet students in American universities. An examination of a list of hundreds of Soviet students in the US in 1977 shows that their areas of concentration are most intensive in the physical sciences. Ironically, the same list shows that Americans in the Soviet Union tend to study such topics as "marriage patterns in Russia and the USSR, 1887-1975" and "the prose fiction of A.S. Pushkin."[72]

Penetration of Capitol Hill, among other agencies of the US government, has long been a Soviet target. Soviet diplomats and newsmen, for example, attend congressional hearings, acquire printed transcripts, and engage in discussions with congressional staff. And there have been outright attempts to recruit congressional staff by Soviet intelligence. Three such cases are in the public record.

Two of the staff members, James Kappus and Keith R. Tolliver, were "turned" by the FBI and served as double agents in their relations with the Soviets. Kappus worked for Representative O'Konski, who was at that time (1966-70) a member of the House Armed Services Committee. The Soviets gave Kappus the assignment of stealing confidential material from the congressman's files. Tolliver was on Senator James Eastland's staff; he claims that between 1968 and 1974 he was paid nearly $20,000 by the Soviets for information that the FBI cleared and allowed him to pass.[73]

The third case involved a person who was not doubled. He was James Frederick Sattler, who was almost hired as a minority staff consultant to a subcommittee of the House International Relations Committee. He had been recommended for the job by Congressman Paul Findley. Findley was warned by the FBI that Sattler was an East German agent. He did not get the job but somehow learned of the FBI's interest. He filed a foreign agents' registration statement with the Department of Justice, hoping that this would insulate him from any criminal charges. In this statement, filed March 23, 1976, Sattler admitted that in 1967 he had been recruited by an individual named Rolf, who he later learned was an East German agent. Sattler also admitted that he had received $15,000 for his services and an honor decoration from the Ministry of State Security of the German Democratic Republic. He stated: "Since 1967, I have transmitted to my principals in Berlin, GDR, information and documents which I received from the North Atlantic Treaty Organization and from individuals in institutions and government agencies in the Federal Republic of Germany, United States, Great Britain, Canada, and France. I photographed a portion of this information with a microdisc camera and placed the microdiscs in packages which I mailed to West Germany which I know were subsequently received by my principals in Berlin, GDR. Other documents and information I photographed with a Minox camera and personally carried the film to my principals in Berlin or handed them to a courier." After filing his registration statement, Sattler disappeared.

Soviet needs on Capitol Hill range from military and scientific to political information. The collection of political information may not be illegal, of course, and Americans who cooperate with the Soviets in that regard without pay may not be breaking the law. One example of a Soviet attempt to collect political information from an American was revealed in 1975 by a young reporter who cooperated with the FBI during the time of his contact with Soviet intelligence. Paul Jay Browne was attending classes in journalism at Columbia University when he met Alex Yakovlev, a Russian employed by the United Nations to broadcast news to Eastern Europe. Yakovlev wined and dined the young American and subsequently asked him to write freelance articles for the Soviet press. He would be paid $30 to $50 each. It bothered Browne that the Russian kept asking questions about Jewish professors and students at Columbia University; he was also put off by Yakovlev's clandestine attitude. The FBI advised Browne that he would soon be introduced to another Russian—that Yakovlev was merely the recruiter. They were right. Yakovlev introduced Browne to Boris Mikhailov, a translator at the UN. During a meeting with Mikhailov, he was asked to write a report on the Jewish Defense League. After discussions with the FBI, Browne broke his contact with the Soviet agents.[74] In another case, an FBI-controlled source in the Chicago area was given the task by the Polish Intelligence Service of gathering information on Congressman Daniel Rostenkowski. This source also was asked to try to develop derogatory information on eight Chicago attorneys who handled cases for Polish defectors.[75]

The Soviet UN Mission, like the Soviet Embassy in Washington, is a major Soviet espionage base. Soviet defector Arkady Shevchenko, who was Under Secretary General of the United Nations before his defection, revealed in a BBC broadcast on September 24, 1979, that Soviet intelligence has made a substantial penetration into the UN Secretariat. He referred to the United Nations in New York as "the most important base of all Soviet intelligence operations in the world." He said that as many as 300 KGB officers are stationed in New York, among them a Special Assistant to Secretary General Kurt Waldheim. It was clear that the individual he had in mind is Special Assistant Victor Lesiovsky.[76]

KGB officers under diplomatic cover are a problem, but with proper surveillance they are identifiable. More difficult problems are created by the illegal Soviet agents operating in this country. On March 3, 1980, the FBI surfaced Colonel Rudolf Herrmann, a KGB officer who was doubled by the FBI. Before coming to the United States, Colonel Herrmann had worked as an Illegal in both West Germany and Canada. He had returned periodically to the Soviet Union for training. He wife and son were also cooptees of the KGB. From 1962 to 1968, Colonel Herrmann operated in Canada. He then illegally entered the United States with his family. He received intelligence assignments by coded radio messages which ordered him to service other Soviet agents and locate dead drops or hiding places. In carrying out these assignments, Herrmann visited various cities in the United States. Although he participated in a number of KGB-directed activities, his main function was as a "sleeper agent" to take control of Soviet espionage in the United States in the event that US-Soviet relations so deteriorated that KGB agents under official cover would have to be withdrawn. Herrmann's son was instructed to enroll in an American college with the understanding that some day he would seek employment with the US government. A Georgetown University newspaper, *The Georgetown Voice*, on April 1, 1980, identified Colonel Herrmann's son Peter as a former

Georgetown student and a photographer for the *Voice*. As a result of turning Herrmann, the FBI was able to identify numerous KGB operators and contacts in the United States and Canada. One of them was Hugh Hambleton, a professor at Laval University in Quebec, Canada.[77]

This Canadian economics professor, who had worked for the KGB for fully 30 years, was interviewed by the *Toronto Sunday Sun* on January 13, 1980. He described in great detail his KGB assignments—which took him as far afield as Latin America and the Middle East—and the elaborate tradecraft involved.

As noted before, the recruiting ground for Soviet intelligence is no longer the CPUSA. In addition to mercenary spies, the Soviets have concentrated on recruiting New Leftists and others in "radical chic" circles. These people are basically anti-American, not necessarily pro-Soviet. They can be recruited in major part because they are convinced that what they are doing opposes "narrow" US interests and supports the "progressive forces" of the Third World. This is very different than the recruitment in the 1920's and '30s of dissident Communists who hoped thereby to get back in the good graces of the Soviet Union. The current crop really does not much care about the Soviet Union. They are, however, enamored of Cuba. The Cubans often serve as a "cutout" between such people and Soviet intelligence.

The Cubans have come a long way since the early 1960's when young American Communists visiting the island were asked to do background checks on other Americans who had applied for visas. Now the Cubans have a sophisticated intelligence service. The DGI collects information and coordinates its work with the KGB. The Americas Department of the Central Committee of the Communist Party of Cuba similarly coordinates its work with the International Department of the CPSU. Its function is primarily "covert action," such as propaganda and support for insurgencies. A number of DGI officers have turned up as officials of the Americas Department, and a number of Americas Department officials have turned up as Cuban ambassadors in Latin America.

A potential talent pool of great interest to Cuban intelligence is the Venceremos Brigade, which consists of young Americans—many of them New Left—who have visited Cuba over the past ten years ostensibly to cut sugar cane. According to a top secret FBI report that has been sanitized and publicly released, the Weather Underground terrorist organization formed the Venceremos Brigade on the

Cuban's behalf. According to the FBI:

> The DGI interest in the VB is an extension of its overall policy relating to the collection of intelligence on the US, its primary target. The DGI considers recruitment of VB members selected after detailed assessment, as one of the primary means through which intelligence can be collected on the US.
>
> The DGI believes that it is to their advantage to establish and maintain contact with organizations, groups, and individuals who are sympathetic to the Cuban Revolution and who are disenchanted with the present conditions in the US, and sees the VB as such a group.
>
> The ultimate objective in the DGI participation with the VB is the recruitment of individuals who are politically oriented and who someday may obtain a position, elected or appointed, somewhere in the US government, which would provide the Cuban government with access to political, economic, or military intelligence. In addition, the DGI attempts to select individuals who can legitimately apply for membership in various political or student-type organizations to report on the activities, personalities, and political orientation of the group. The DGI also seeks individuals among the VB who can fulfill operational support roles; that is, who wittingly or unwittingly would serve as an accommodation address or serve in some other intelligence support capacity.

The FBI also reported: "A very limited number of VB members have been trained in guerrilla warfare techniques including use of arms and explosives. This type of training is given only to individuals who specifically request it and only then to persons who the Cubans feel sure are not penetration agents for American intelligence."[78]

Cuban support for terrorist activities in the United States goes back to as early as 1962, when three Cubans attached to the UN Mission were arrested in a bomb plot. Explosive devices were found in their possession.[79] The Puerto Rican terrorist group, FALN, which has been responsible for five murders in New York City, issued a communique on October 27, 1975, stating in part: "We especially acknowledge the moral support given to our organization by the Cuban people and government in a speech made by Prime Minister Fidel Castro in August in which he said that the Cuban government would do all it could to support the FALN."

How radicals are chosen to visit Cuba was revealed in a letter that the Communist-front National Lawyers Guild sent to its members in Washington, D.C., in 1974. According to the letter:

> The process used to select the delegates and the alternates was difficult, and of course, subjective to some degree. The first criterion was determined by the Cubans themselves. They asked that the Guild send men and women who would be able to serve them as contact and resource

people in Washington during the upcoming period of transition in Cuban-US relations; they desired a delegation which would have a broad background in governmental, professional and legal work.[80]

The Cubans also have encouraged visits by congressional staff members.

The DGI has shown a great deal of interest as well in Cuban refugees in the United States. But recently the emphasis has tended more to influencing American attitudes toward Cuba. Members of the Americas Department have visited here recently to propagandize among those who might be most susceptible—as, for example, one high ranking official who met with American dissidents and explained to them which candidates would be most beneficial to Cuba if they were elected in 1980.

Moreover, Cuban intelligence is engaged in the recruitment of agents-of-influence regarding the US political situation. Orlando Letelier, the former Chilean diplomat who was murdered in a Washington bombing a few years ago, was such a Cuban agent. He received money and instructions through the Cuban UN diplomatic pouch. His contact was Julian Rizo, who has been widely identified in the press as a DGI officer. Rizo is now the Cuban ambassador to Granada. Letelier spent a great deal of time on Capitol Hill making contacts and propagandizing for the anti-Chile, pro-Cuba cause. A collection of letters and other documents was found by the D.C. police in his briefcase at the time of his death—and soon leaked to the press. The documents showed that the money used by Letelier was sent to him from Cuba by Beatriz Allende Fernandez, the daughter of the late Marxist President of Chile and the wife of a DGI official. In a letter to her, dated March 29, 1976, Letelier wrote about an anti-Chile propaganda group that his wife directed and that was financed from Cuba. He said in this letter: "I think that given the nature of its 'sponsors' . . . it is preferable that information about it not be spread from Havana, because you know how these 'liberals' are. It is possible that congressmen serving as patrons could be afraid that they could be linked with Cuba and eventually drop their support of the Committee . . ." Letelier also used some of the Cuban money to reimburse a US Congressman for a trip to Mexico to participate in an anti-Chile conference organized by the World Peace Council.[81]

The Cubans also have played a role in promoting one of the two magazines published in the United States for the purpose of undermining or even destroying the CIA. These are *Covert Action Information Bulletin*, the first issue of which was released in Cuba in 1978, and *Counterspy*. Both of these publications have been used by Soviet propagandists to disseminate false anti-CIA material.

On February 6, 1980, CIA presented an unclassified report on Soviet covert action and propaganda to the House Permanent Select Committee on Intelligence. One aspect of that report was the Soviet forgery campaign. The CIA exposed 16 recent forgeries as being of Soviet origin. One of them, supposedly a US Army field manual, identified as FM 30-31B, purported to show that the United States was organizing violent groups on the territory of allied countries. The CIA identified this document as a total forgery disseminated by "a Spanish Communist and a Cuban intelligence officer." The January 1979 issue of *Covert Action Information Bulletin* contained the full text of the forgery and claimed of course that it was authentic. The next issue of the *Bulletin*, dated April/May 1979, contained the text of a truly authentic secret document prepared by a member of the US military liaison office in Rome. That document, dated January 31, 1979, was a frank discussion of the Italian intelligence services with comments on specific individuals. A copy of this secret cable had been stolen from the State Department and sent to Italy where it appeared in the newspaper "La Republica" on February 13, 1979. Publication of the cable resulted in the author being declared *persona non grata*. The thief has never been identified. Not only did *Covert Action Information Bulletin* publish the full text in English but also it provided the Italian newspaper with a commentary on the document which appeared in the same issue as the document itself—indicating that the stolen document was in its possession prior to the time it was printed in Italy. In an introduction to the document in the *Bulletin*, former CIA agent Phillip Agee argued that this genuine document authenticated the forgery he had published in the previous issue.

The Soviets have developed a major propaganda campaign in defense of their aggression in Afghanistan. It serves a useful purpose for the Soviets to be able to pretend that their invasion was to counter some American activities. For example, a Tass transmission in English on February 25, 1980, claimed that the Soviets would not be in Afghanistan at all if the Americans had not been there stirring up trouble. A rumor was floated that the Soviets would agree to neutralize Afghanistan if the Americans would pull out. This was revealed in the London *Daily Telegraph* of February 28, 1980, as the product of Victor Louis—a well-known KGB conduit to the media who frequently floats Soviet propaganda themes.

As part of the propaganda campaign, Radio Moscow on February

27, 1980, broadcast an interview with Armand Hammer who had just met with Brezhnev. According to Hammer, "If the United States and the neighbors of Iran [sic, Afghanistan] would guarantee there would be no interference in the internal affairs of Afghanistan and the people of Afghanistan, Russia would remove her troops, since the cause for which they went there would be removed." Armand Hammer, after all these years, is still serving as a propaganda tool for the Soviet Union.

Counterspy, the sister publication to *Covert Action Information Bulletin*, published an article in its issue Vol. 4, No. 1, undated but distributed in December 1979, entitled "US Intervention in Afghanistan" by Konrad Ege. He claimed that there was evidence in the press that the US was training and supporting Afghan rebels. His sources for the allegation were Soviet radio broadcasts and *Pravda*. The next use of the story was in the CPUSA newspaper, *Daily World*, on February 22, 1980, where Ege is quoted and *Counterspy* is identified as "a prominent Washington magazine that specializes in information on the spy organization." The same theme appeared in the Soviet newspaper, *Sovetskaya Rossiya*, March 18, 1980, which ran an interview by their correspondent V. Gan with Konrad Ege. The interview had taken place in Washington, and Ege told the Soviet reporter the same story he had originally picked up from the Soviet press. This was then played back by world wide Soviet propaganda to indicate that the story was authentic because it was coming from an American source.[82]

The State of Our Counterintelligence Defenses

As a result of Attorney General Levi's domestic security guidelines promulgated in 1976, the FBI is no longer able to investigate groups or individuals that are not committing or about to commit a crime. Nor can the FBI investigate groups that are only directed, but are not directed and *controlled*, by a foreign power. As a result, FBI counterintelligence has been severely limited: it cannot monitor the very groups that the Soviets intend to recruit. Because many intelligence activities, other than collection of classified information, are not necessarily in violation of US law, it is all but impossible to keep track of those who are engaged in Soviet-directed covert action against the United States. And the Justice Department carefully monitors FBI compliance with the guidelines—strict and even nitpicking compliance. It has reached the point, according to some FBI officials who have testified before the House Intelligence Committee, that agents are not even permitted to read the publications of organizations that are not under investigation—not at any rate on company time! They are thus cut off from publications of groups that advocate the overthrow of the US government by force and violence or that advocate the use of violence against other Americans to deny them their constitutional rights. It is the responsibility of the FBI to conduct background investigations under the federal loyalty program. But there is no way that they can provide authoritative information to the hiring agencies on the background of individuals who are "mere members" of subversive groups or are merely "planning" to commit violence in the future—but have not yet set the date! Because so many subversive groups are not now under investigation, the data base has atrophied alarmingly since 1976.

The FBI is capable of doing a very effective job in regard to the agents of hostile intelligence services operating in this country under official cover. With adequate manpower, it also has demonstrated an ability to penetrate the illegal apparatus of Soviet intelligence and even to identify "sleepers" as in the Herrmann case. But it cannot get the job done under wraps. The frightening possibility thus exists that the US government and the American people are now, and increasingly will be, defenseless before their enemies.

Conclusions

The most effective spy is the ideological one. The mercenary or the person terrorized into spying will be much easier to turn and double than the ideological spy. As we have learned from the past the Soviet Union is prepared to use, as agents, even those who have ideological disagreements but who are willing to collaborate. Today the Soviets are prepared to use the "New Left," the drug culture, the radical chic activists, who would not consciously collaborate with the Soviet Union, but would work with the Cubans. The Cubans working as cutouts for the Soviet Intelligence Service are extremely effective.

The FBI is hamstrung by the fact that collaborating with a hostile intelligence service may not be a crime in this country. It isn't even a crime to reveal classified information, if the person revealing it does not have authorized access in the first place. We have publications such as *Covert Action Information Bulletin* and *Counterspy* identifying real or alleged CIA officers. Ladislav Bittman in testimony before the House Intelligence Committee on February 19, 1980, revealed that when he was with the Czech Intelligence Service, he had helped produce the book *Who's Who in the CIA* which was a product of the Czech and East German Intelligence Services. The "author" Julius Mader is an East German Intelligence Officer. Bittman explained that many of the identifications of alleged CIA officers were inaccurate. The purpose of the false identification was that it would disrupt the State Department and other US government agencies just as much as a true identification would disrupt the CIA. Similar false information has shown up in *Counterspy* and *Covert Action Information Bulletin*.

The ease of travel in today's world has greatly facilitated the work of hostile intelligence agents. Illegals operating in the United States can fly out of the country in hours to meet their control officers. The simplicity involved in entering the United States allows tourists, "businessmen" and students easy access for the transfer of intelligence information.

It has been suggested that a more extensive counterintelligence apparatus be established in the United States. It should have input from the CIA, the FBI, and military intelligence. It should establish a data bank on worldwide activities of hostile intelligence services and be able to identify those officers and agents when they enter the United States. It has been further suggested that the FBI be permitted to investigate organizations and individuals that are collaborating with hostile intelligence services, even when they are not under total control, or are not violating American laws. Certainly the FBI should have the same facilities available to it in counterintelligence that a newsman would have when gathering a story. That is, the ability to penetrate an organization with an informant, the ability to surveil individuals both for purposes of identification and to determine their activities. And lastly, to be able to gather the publications of dissident groups, so that it is possible to know in advance if and when they intend to commit a crime.

Notes

1. *Socialist Appeal*, June 15, 1940.
2. Testimony of Ludwig C.A.K. Martens before the Senate Subcommittee on Foreign Relations, "Russian Propaganda," January 19, 1920, p. 14.
3. *Ibid.*, pp. 41-42.
4. Santeri Nuorteva, *An Open Letter to American Liberals* (New York: Socialist Publication Society, 1918).

5. "Russian Propaganda," *op. cit.*, p. 42.
6. *Ibid.*, pp. 125-127.
7. David Dallin, *Soviet Espionage* (New Haven, Connecticut: Yale University Press, 1955), p. 469.
8. V. I. Lenin, *Collected Works* (Moscow: Progress Publishers, 1979), vol. 45, p. 337.
9. Benjamin Gitlow, *I Confess* (New York: Dutton, 1940), pp. 118-119; 569.
10. Lenin, *op. cit.*, pp. 346-347.
11. *Ibid.*, p. 559.
12. For a more detailed account of the career of Armand Hammer and his relationship with Lenin, see "One Man's Soviet Trade" by Congressman John Ashbrook, *Congressional Record*, October 17, 1973, p. H9239f.
13. Translation of Statement by Richard Sorge (printed in Japan) by Gen. Charles A. Willoughby in *Sorge Espionage Case*, presented to the House Committee on Un-American Activities, 1950, Part 2, pp. 33 and 28.
14. *The Fourth National Convention of the Workers (Communist) Party* (Chicago: Daily Worker Publishing Co., 1925), pp. 27 and 37.
15. US, Congress, House, Special Committee to Investigate Communist Activities in the United States, "Investigation of Communist Propaganda," 1930, part I, Vol. 4, p. 2-1-213.
16. *Ibid.*, pp. 217-218.
17. Benjamin Gitlow, *The Whole of Their Lives* (New York: Scribers, 1948), pp. 336-337.
18. Whittaker Chambers, *Witness* (New York: Random House, 1952), pp. 353, 389-390, 392, 492.
19. *Stalin's Speeches on the American Communist Party* (New York: Central Committee, CPUSA, 1929), p. 19.
20. Benjamin Gitlow, Jay Lovestone, et al., *Appeal to the Comintern*, undated tabloid, p. 4.
21. Testimony of Jay Lovestone before the House Special Committee on UnAmerican Activities, vol. II, December 2, 1940, pp. 7097-7098.
22. Testimony of Nicholas Dozenberg before the Special House Committee on UnAmerican Activities and Dies Committee Executive Session, vol. 2, May 21, 1940.
23. Statement of Nicholas Dozenberg before the House Committee on UnAmerican Activities, "Hearing regarding Communist Espionage," November 8, 1949, pp. 3540-3542.
24. Dies Committee Executive Session, 1940, *op. cit.*, p. 566.
25. US, Congress, House, Committee on UnAmerican Activities, November 8, 1949, p. 3558.
26. US, Congress, House, *The Shameful Years* (Washington, D.C.: Government Printing Office, 1951), p. 11.
27. *International Solidarity with the Spanish Republic, 1936-1939* (Moscow: Progress Publishers, 1975), p. 46.
28. Dies Committee, vol. 11, 1940, pp. 7100-7101. Note: During Lovestone's testimony he referred to a pamphlet by Benjamin Gitlow saying, "To the best of my recollection the pamphlet essentially deals with the unity negotiations as conducted between General Klaber *(sic)* and myself" (R7101). The pamphlet entitled "Some Plain Words on Communist Unity" was published in 1932. A reference on pp. 10 and 11 indicates that the meeting between Lovestone and the Comintern

representative took place before January 15, 1932. Although Lovestone in his testimony says the meeting took place outside the United States, in 1931 Stern (Kleber/Zilbert) was still active with Soviet military intelligence in the United States.

29. *The International Class Struggle*, vol. 1, no. 1, Summer 1936, pp. 29-40.
30. Theodore Draper, *American Communism and Soviet Russia* (New York: Viking Press, 1960), p. 430.
31. *The Shameful Years*, op. cit., pp. 11-12.
32. *Sorge Espionage Case*, op. cit., pp. 34-35.
33. *Ibid.*, p. 40.
34. *Recognition, and the Tasks of the Communists*, Central Committee, CPUSA, mimeo., December 12, 1933.
35. *Material for the Organization Commission* (Tenth Convention, CPUSA, mimeo., May, 1938).
36. Earl Browder, *Socialism in America* (Yonkers, New York: Browder, 1960), p. 101.
37. Philip J. Jaffe, *The Rise and Fall of American Communism* (New York: Horizon Press, 1975), pp. 40, 44-47.
38. US, Congress, Senate, Committee on Expenditures, "Export Policy and Loyalty," testimony of Elizabeth Bentley, June 30, 1948, pp. 4-7; testimony of Elizabeth Bentley before the House Committee on UnAmerican Activities, July 31, 1948, pp. 504-505.
39. Testimony of Whittaker Chambers before the House Committee on UnAmerican Activities, Hearings Regarding Communist Espionage in the United States Government, August 3, 1948, p. 566.
40. US, Congress, House, Committee on UnAmerican Activities, Interim Report on Communist Espionage in the United States Government, August 28, 1948, p. 6.
41. *Ibid.*, p. 5 and House Committee on UnAmerican Activities, July 31, 1948, pp. 503-562.
42. Allen Weinstein, *Perjury: The Hiss-Chambers Case* (New York: Knopf, 1978), p. 173.
43. US, Congress, Senate, Committee on Government Operations, October 20, 23, 1953, pp. 45, 47, 48, 52, 53.
44. Raymond S. Toy, *World War II Allied Military Currency* (pamphlet), 1965, p. 20.
45. US, Congress, Senate Committee on Government Operations, 1954, *op. cit.*, p. 9.
46. Hearings Regarding Clarence Hiskey before the House Committee on UnAmerican Activities, May 24, 1949, p. 399.
47. Excerpts from Hearings Regarding Investigation of Communist Activities in Connection with Atom Bombs before the House Committee on UnAmerican Activities, September 16, 1948, pp. 52-56.
48. *The Shameful Years, op. cit.*, pp. 31-32.
49. US vs. Rosenberg, *et al.*, trial transcript (case on appeal), pp. 1614-1616 and 1620.
50. Dr. S. Andhil Fineberg, *The Rosenberg Case, Fact and Fiction* (Dobbs Ferry, New York: Oceana, 1953, pp. 37-90.
51. Testimony of Hede Massing before the Senate Subcommittee on Internal Security, "Institute of Pacific Relations," August 2, 1951, pp. 232-233.
52. Noel Field, *Hitching Our Wagon to a Star*, (Mainstream: January 1961), pp. 4-6; 13-14.
53. Statement of Laszlo Szabo before the House Committee on Armed Services, CIA Subcommittee, March 17, 1966, p. 5347.

54. Copies of the telegrams were given to the writer by Mrs. J.B. Matthews. J.B. Matthews told the writer about the role of the State Department in preventing the Trotsky testimony.
55. Albert Goldman, *The Assassination of Leon Trotsky* (New York: Pioneer Publishers, c. 1946), pp. 3; 65-66.
56. Jack Soble and Jack Lotto, *How I Spied on U.S. for the Reds*, N.Y. Journal-American, November 10-20, 1957 (series).
57. Affidavit of Louis Budenz before the House Committee on UnAmerican Activities, "American Aspects of Assassination of Leon Trotsky," November 11, 1951.
58. *Ibid*.
59. "Healy's Big Lie," *Education for Socialists Bulletin* (New York: Socialist Worker's Party, December 1976), p. 9.
60. Soble, *op. cit.*
61. *Exposé of Soviet Espionage*, FBI report printed by Senate Subcommittee on Internal Security (SISS), May 1960, pp. 25-26. For text of indictment see SISS Scope series, part 72, p. 4379f.
62. The facts in the Zborovsky case were compiled from a number of sources. The testimony of Orlov was compiled in a single volume by SISS, entitled *The Legacy of Alexander Orlov*, published in 1973 after his death. It contains testimony of September 28, 1955 and February 14-15, 1957. The testimony of Zborowski appears in SISS *Scope of Soviet Activities in the United States*, parts 4 and 5. Part 5 also contains the testimony of Mrs. Lilia Dallin. Other interesting details may be found in *Our Own People* by Elisabeth Portesky, the widow of Ignace Reiss (Ann Arbor: University of Michigan Press, 1969), and *The G.P.U. in the Trotskyist Movement* by George Vereeken (London: New Park Publishers, 1976). David Dallin provided additional information in the *New Leader* of March 19 and March 26, 1956.
63. Testimony of Wladislw Tykocinski before the House Committee on UnAmerican Activities, April 6, 1966, p. 873. (Tykocinski was a former Polish Intelligence Officer. His statement was confirmed to the writer by Ladislav Bittman, a former Czech Intelligence Officer.)
64. US, Congress, House, Committee on UnAmerican Activities, "Communist Outlets for the Distribution of Soviet Propaganda in the United States," Part 2, July 12, 1962.
65. US, Congress, House, Committee on UnAmerican Activities, "Subversive Involvement in Disruption of 1968 Democratic National Convention, Part 1, October 4, 1968.
66. *Daily Telegraph* (London), September 13, 1979.
67. Souvenir program, testimonial meeting for Charlene Mitchell, June 8, 1980, sponsored by the National Alliance Against Racist and Political Repression.
68. Pamphlet, meeting of the New York Chapter of the National Alliance Against Racist and Political Repression, April 11, 1980.
69. Testimony of George Karlin (Yuri Krotkov) before the Senate Subcommittee on Internal Security, November 3, 4, 5, 6, and 10, 1969.
70. *Washington Post*, October 26, 1974.
71. *Daily Telegraph* (London), July 14, 1980.
72. List of US and Soviet exchange students published October 13, 1977 by International Research and Exchange Board, New York.
73. *Time Magazine*, March 22, 1976.
74. *Washington Post*, February 9, 1975.

75. *Washington Post*, October 16, 1979.
76. *New York Times*, September 25, 1979.
77. Summary distributed at FBI press briefing, Washington, DC, March 3, 1980.
78. FBI report, *Foreign Influence—Weather Underground Organization*, August 20, 1976, pp. 125-126.
79. *New York Post*, November 18, 1962; *New York World Telegram*, November 17, 1962.
80. Undated letter signed Alan Dranitzke, Chairperson for the Executive Board on the letterhead of the Washington, DC Chapter of the National Lawyers Guild.
81. Congressman Larry McDonald printed the text of documents found in the Letelier briefcase by the police after the murder, which showed Letelier's involvement with Cuban operations, in the *Congressional Record*, June 23, 1977.
82. See Foreign Broadcast Information Service, March 25, 1980, Soviet Union section, P. A9-11, for translation from *Sovetskaya Rossiya*. Armand Hammer's Interview appears in FBIS, February 28, 1980, Soviet Union section, pp. A7-8.

Discussants

Mr. William Branigan: The thrust of Mr. Romerstein's paper is a recitation of the history of Soviet intelligence operations in the United States. And in this recitation he demonstrates the unique capability of the Soviets in this country, a capability that we can anticipate is going to continue into the 1980's.

Romerstein stresses the fact that the most effective spy is the ideological one, and I subscribe to that; the Rosenbergs, Judy Koplon—these were ideological spies. But it has been a long time, as is recognized in the paper, since the Soviets have had access to the reservoir of the CPUSA which was the prime recruiting ground in the thirties and forties for Soviet espionage.

So, at the same time they have been dealing with mercenaries. I submit that these mercenaries have done as great damage to our country and our national security as have the ideological spies. Take for example people like Cornelius Nelson Drummond, Sergeant Johnson, Colonel Whalen, Sergeant Dunlop, John William Potenko—these people have done inestimable damage to our country, in the millions and millions of dollars.

Romerstein places great stress on the early years of Soviet espionage in the United States, and I think he presents an excellent summary picture of Soviet intelligence during the years of the Comintern. He made mention of Nicholas Dozenberg and Dr. William Gregory Burtan—hardly household names these days. But there was one other that he didn't mention, and this was a man by the name of Yossep Garber. Garber was an old-time Communist who associated with Dozenberg and Burtan. He was convicted of passport fraud in the early thirties. What amazes me about Garber, with all the FBI's knowledge of him, was the fact that in the middle 1960's, when two illegal agents were sent to the United States by the KGB, they used the identification of Joy Ann Garber, the daughter of Yossep Garber, for their illegal agent Joy Ann Baltch. And this is one of the things that makes life in counterintelligence so interesting!

In the paper there is reference to "The People's Front: Heyday for Espionage." My first assignment in the Communist counterintelligence field was the East Bay section of the Communist Party headquartered in Oakland, California. This, of course, covered the elite campus section, or the professional section of the Party in Berkeley, California. The Joint Anti-Fascist League was the elementary school for recruitment into the Communist Party: people like Haakon Chevalier, George Elkington and even J. Robert Oppenheimer—great intellectuals who had a hearty hatred and aversion for fascism, but who had no idea of the politics of the Communists.

Romerstein refers also to the early cases of atomic espionage. He specifically refers to a man named "Joe," later identified as Joseph Woodrow Weinberg, who met Steve Nelson, then the Communist Party functionary in East Bay. The meeting occurred in March 1943. He also refers to a meeting between Vassili Zubilin and Steve Nelson a few days later.

I was the fortunate FBI agent who intercepted both of those meetings. I mention this not because of the personal satisfaction derived and not because it was those meetings that really changed my career in counterintelligence but for a very simple purpose: following those meetings, the FBI first learned of the Manhattan Project, the experiment to develop an atomic bomb.

Let's not repeat the mistakes of the 1940's in the 1980's. If we are going to have counterintelligence, and if counterintelligence is going to lend support to and attempt to protect the national security, then CI should at least know about those projects that would be logical, primary targets for the Soviets.

The paper has a section on the Classic Spy Ring. In this he details the activities of Jack Soble and his brother, Robert Soblen. What is not revealed is that this case originated with the meeting between Steve Nelson and Vassili Zubilin. The case was a snap because physical surveillance took Zubilin from San Francisco to Los Angeles, where he met Boris Morros, who later became an FBI double agent. Physical surveillance made this case. And as we in the operational side of counterintelligence know, physical surveillance is an important, indeed an essential, technique of counterintelligence. The physical surveillance of the early—and somewhat— sloppy years of the 1940's has vastly changed. In those days the countermeasures taken by the Soviets were faily simple. Today, they are highly complex. My question is: will the FBI in the 1980's be provided with the manpower and the technology to conduct very necessary physical surveillances?

There is another section in the paper about a new era and new opportunity. Romerstein says that new opportunities have opened up for contacts with the New Left and those of "radical chic" orientation and he is probably right. But I know that up until 1976—and we tried several dangle operations and enticement situations to get the Soviets interested in the New Left—the Soviets were simply not interested. They simply couldn't believe these new-left-type personalities and the new-left-type philosophy. Somehow, these people did not "belong" with the Soviets and they were not accepted.

The fact of the matter is, though, on reflection, up until the time I left the FBI in 1976—and this, too, has probably changed—many of the Soviet personnel in this country didn't believe the Watergate syndrome either. They did not credit the investigating committees that were operating on the Hill. They always felt that, sometime, someone was going to pull the rug out from under all that activity—and they weren't about to be left on the short end when that happened.

In the paper, finally, reference is made to the illegal or the deep-cover agent. He is the "stay-behind." There was a time in the Bureau's history when we had developed a self-capability for identifying illegal agents, without reference to a penetration agent who would tell us, "This is an illegal operation," or "Here is an illegal agent." This capability was very important to our development in those years.

There have been limitations, I'm sure, that have been placed on the FBI. My only hope is that those limitations are not such, in practical effect, as to make successful counterintelligence impossible in the 1980's.

Dr. Allen Weinstein: With Herb Romerstein's paper, the Consortium joins the Harvard Business School in practicing the case method—and it has its virtues. Romerstein's study is a fascinating one, a fascinating summary of much of the extraordinarily complex and elaborate processes of Soviet espionage in this country since the Russian Revolution.

As an historian I can't help but be somewhat pleased that a good deal of what David Dallin wrote a generation ago, and a good deal of what Earl Latham and others wrote, for they studied this subject before they had access to the range of materials presented in the paper, particularly for the earlier decades, that a good deal of what they wrote holds up today.

The paper, it seems to me, is strongest inevitably on those periods for which we have the greatest amount of information. Mr. Romerstein has said as much, and Mr. Branigan has confirmed it. Less than a third of the paper concerns the post-1950 period or the last thirty years, which is an imbalance that is perhaps inevitable given the paucity of recent materials, or the imbalance of materials.

The paper contains important, useful and evocative summaries of cases still relevant for intelligence analysis today. As Mr. Branigan points out, so much of what is significant in counterintelligence has to do with maintaining the most elaborate and finely-honed institutional memory of the sort that he described, which allows one to recognize the name of the daughter of a convicted former Soviet agent three decades later when her passport was used. That type of institutional memory cannot be reconstructed once it is lost.

But I think the paper also poses certain problems that I would like to raise today, some of which have to do with the fascinating dilemma for Soviet intelligence that Romerstein poses: the shift in the major sources of agents and assets from ideologically-committed ones in the period prior to the Second World War to mercenaries. The implications of this, for those of you who have either read Robert Lindsey's book, *The Falcon and the Snowman*, or read about the Boyce-Lee case, go well beyond mercenaries. And, I am not sure the paper says enough about the attempt to cultivate the alienated as sources of information in the last few decades.

One thing was fascinating to me as a sidelight in the paper, namely, the efforts made by Soviet intelligence agents to use dissident Communists like Jay Lovestone and the "Lovestoneites." And one point of fact I would like cleared up for my own benefit is that the paper implies that Jay Lovestone acted consciously as a Soviet agent as a way of negotiating his group back into the good graces of Mr. Stalin. Earl Browder is not mentioned. He also was utilized after his expulsion from the Party. He was given a number of commercial concessions and became a conduit for a lot of information in this country. It is still a largely untold story.

The Cuban connection, a crucial element in Romerstein's analysis, needs further explanation as well. I would like, for example, to have more material on the argument that the Cuban intelligence service is being used by the Russians—and I quote from the paper—"as a conduit to New Left and radical chic circles in which a Soviet presence might be unacceptable." These days I think a Cuban presence might be unacceptable, too, in those circles. Yet the question raised here about surrogate intelligence services being used by the Russians to gain ideological supporters whom they cannot gain in other ways, whether using Cubans or, in countries not under Soviet control, Mexicans coming into this country or Latin Americans generally, is an important issue.

I don't think Romerstein says enough about the Russian interest in the alienated—in the brooding, nondoctrinal, anti-Americans, who have no real ideological place but lack the firm moral or ethical moorings that will enable them to resist the approaches of foreign intelligence services.

I suspect, again on the basis of no more evidence than Romerstein has shown in his paper, that there is more recruiting for Soviet intelligence likely to be taking place at Seabrook than at the front tables of Elaine's. The Soviets may be more interested in the Arthur Bremers of our country than the Norman Mailers. So the whole notion of radical chic enrollment is one with which I have some problems.

I think we must ask ourselves what our perception of American reality is today, particularly as it concerns the intelligence community. I am refering to another paper at our meeting on recruiting for the intelligence community and the importance of establishing new perspectives on those who might contribute to intelligence work. But I will return to that later.

I want to limit my comments today to general observations on what in my opinion is a somewhat inadequate view of the context of Soviet espionage and its exposure and, also, to some specific caveats about the paper.

First, I think it is crucial to realize that not only is this paper based largely on public sources, as Romerstein pointed out, but also in this connection we know more about the failures of Soviet intelligence precisely because of the record established by defectors and those who have been caught. But I wonder whether, in fact, this does not impose a kind of documentary determinism on our overall view of the period that we might want to treat very carefully.

Do we, for example, know everything we want to know about the agents of influence in the period when Alger Hiss and Harry Dexter White, and others who were to some degree exposed, managed to fall into the net? Who else may have escaped. To what extent will we ever know? To what extent do we know as much as we want to know about Soviet operations even in the period that seems to be so well documented, the period prior to the Second World War?

Another point here is that much of our knowledge about the failures of Soviet intelligence in this country has come from the defectors, the internal defectors—the Whittaker Chambers, the Elizabeth Bentleys and Jay Lovestones—and from the external defectors, Igor Gouzenko and others. We are now in 1980, and there is an enormous amount of material Gouzenko gave to the Canadian Government in 1946 that was never passed to the US Government and never used by us.

So the defectors seem to me, particularly the internal ones, absolutely crucial in understanding what we did come to learn about Soviet intelligence—those who left Communist associations and espionage work of some kind or other on ideological grounds; perhaps disaffection with communism; flawed love affairs (and Miss Bentley is a good example of the convergence of motives); or fear for life (Chambers' fear when he was ordered to return to the Soviet Union).

And yet, what was their reception at the time? Well, for a time I am happy to say before Mr. Branigan and others were put in charge of this type of counterintelligence work at the FBI in the late 1930's and the early 1940's, in Chambers' case, for example, he was disbelieved for almost a decade until Elizabeth Bentley and Igor Gouzenko and other sources confirmed a lot of what he had been saying. Precious time was wasted in pursuit of leads he might well have provided the FBI in 1939 or 1940 or 1941 or 1942, had there been a disposition to accept even the slightest possibility that he was telling the truth.

The best card file on Soviet intelligence was certainly not in the FBI, by the way, or in Naval Intelligence, or at G-2. It was a card file kept by Herbert Solow, a dissident socialist who had the resources of the best anti-Stalinist underground going for him in the 1930's, namely, the network of New York political activists, socialists, Lovestoneites, Trotskyites and others who, apart from more exalted motives, were terrified of the activities of Stalinist agents in their midst. And with good reason, I might add, because the Soviets were able to kidnap Juliet Poyntz from the New York streets and nobody would believe the activists. Solow's card file, if you would care to consult it, is now at the Hoover Institution.

Those who did discuss the problem of Soviet espionage with government agencies were often disbelieved. Solow talked to Loy Henderson at the State Department, and he thought Solow was a bit "off." Chambers' initial interviews with the State Department and the FBI were to some extent marred by the fact that certain Bureau agents thought he was responsible for the death of Walter Krivitsky. There are a number of indications suggesting that at least in that era, prior to modern electronic counterintelligence, much of what we know about Soviet espionage came accidentally, almost fortuitously, and came not from the bowels of the government counterintelligence bureaucracy such as it was but from the disaffected amateurs, or from professionals like Chambers, who volunteered their information.

At that time, moreover, in the early 1940's, most government counterintelligence agencies displayed only the crudest understanding of Communist purposes, tactics and organization, at least well into the 1940's. Those who have problems with that point might well want to read some of the files and pick and choose any service at the time.

So now we are in 1980, forty years later. Has "coming in from the cold" been made any easier for the internal defectors? Is this process being pursued more effectively within the intelligence community for those of the disillusioned who have backgrounds as anti-American radicals? Is it easier for an ex-Weatherman, an ex-SDSer or an ex-member of the National Lawyers Guild, to come in and talk to anyone about experiences he may have had with Cuban or Soviet or East German or Czech or Hungarian intelligence? I wonder. And I certainly think we ought to talk about that.

It seems to me the political climate is crucial, that the climate is ripe, given the disillusionment with Cuba and with Castro that is growing daily both in Cuba and elsewhere, given the existence of dissident Castroites in this country and elsewhere, and given the number of Eastern Europeans who could be used in this connection. I see one of the most fruitful sources for potentially effective counterintelligence in precisely the members of what I suppose might be called the surrogate, or opponents of surrogate, intelligence networks.

I wonder if we have begun to use them effectively. In the same way, I wonder about the problems that may be presented by the existence of an increasing number of Chinese in this country because of the recognition of the People's Republic; and I wonder whether our intelligence services have even begun to try and utilize the Chinese Archives for whatever they may contain (I suspect it is quite valuable) on Soviets and Cubans and Eastern Europeans. This seems to me to be another crucial area but I am not in a position to say anything more about it than I hope that it is going on.

The links of all this to the problem of international terrorism are quite obvious and do not need any comment here on my part. But one can get too defensive. The time is ripe for an intelligence counteroffensive of a semi-public nature against the Soviets, against the Cubans, against other surrogates, putting *them* on notice that the measure of ideological disaffection from the various state fascist regimes that parade themselves as radical has reached the point where this country may be in a position, if it marshals its resources, to do something about it.

In that connection, I am not entirely certain that Romerstein's focus on alleged agents of influence—Armand Hammer, for example, whom he spends a good deal of time talking about—or on the allegedly subversive nature of or recruitment within the drug culture or the radical chic milieu (a term I have difficulty with because I'm not certain what it means) is the most effective way of approaching the matter—because it tends to polarize the world.

And it polarizes our view of the world to *our* disadvantage. It basically is an exclusionist view of recruiting for the intelligence process rather than an inclusionist one, if that isn't too bastardized a word or view of the process. In short, I think there are a variety of ways in which it is possible to regain the initiative here. Certainly the FBI must be given the ability to collect information to a degree that it could not in the last several years.

At the same time, I would hope to see a greater degree of discrimination than sometimes shown in the past in distinguishing among Soviet agents, agents of influence, fellow-travelers, and those who for a variety of reasons might oppose American policy, those who might not support every specific measure of that policy, and yet still be loyal, patriotic Americans from a variety of perspectives, ranging from radical to conservative and, therefore, capable of being involved in an intelligence effort.

And so, at the risk of being labeled a "soft-headed, radical chic symp," let me suggest what Midge Decter at a recent meeting on propaganda, on waging the battle of ideas, described as the "new wave of nationalism" now growing in this country, that this can best be harnessed to counterintelligence functions only if we learn whatever lessons of failure or inadequacy our earlier efforts may have displayed.

At this point, it seems to me we have to be much more inclusive than we were in recent decades. In short, a return to the days of Donovan and Dulles, not to be fearful of dissidents from newly-alienated groups but rather seeking recruits from such groups, not only penetrating from the FBI but trying with whatever halting measures of success to restablish the informal links between the intelligence community and other sectors of society, such as labor unions, press and the business community.

Let me return briefly to my point about defectors. The demoralization at the end of the 1930's on the radical left, on the Communist left, created an enormous opportunity for counterintelligence that was only taken advantage of partially. I sense a comparable climate today waiting to be taken advantage of in rebuilding American intelligence efforts, but one which can be taken advantage of only as long as the quarrels of the past do not become the basis of rebuilding and of new efforts.

And finally, my nonexistent hat is being tipped to Mr. Branigan. I am glad he used his Joy Garber story because it adds his name to those of the few individuals (and there are others in this room) who have maintained the institutional memory so crucial to counterintelligence which has become perilously weak with FBI and CIA retirements, the aging process, attacks from opponents, and the rest. I think it is not too much to say, for example, if Jay Lovestone and Sidney Hook were to defect to Cuba, we would have closed a chapter of personal knowledge on forty years of Soviet efforts on infiltration in the United States. Perhaps I am leaving out a few names but we are down to a hardy few in this regard. And that process needs a major rebuilding.

In conclusion, I would disagree on one final point with Romerstein's paper that otherwise I found very fine and provocative. If I asked for a show of hands, I don't know how many of you would concede that you were nine to five people. How many of us in this room are? Romerstein, you'll remember, was contrasting them with the 24-hour-a-day Soviet intelligence agent. Well, I think the Russians by this time may be seven-and-a-half-feet tall but I do not think they are ten feet tall in intelligence work. But, nor do I think that *we* are four feet tall in that regard.

I do think that we have the capacity as matters now stand to regain the intelligence initiative—and I would remind you of a story that comes out of the medieval Eastern European ghettos. A man was sitting on a bench and someone strolled into town and asked what he was doing there; he said he was waiting for the Messiah. It turned out that he waited there 24 hours a day, seven days a week, 52 weeks a year, received no pay and hardly any appreciation from the community. The stranger in town looked at him and said, "If all of this is true, why do you continue doing it?" And the man agreed that, yes indeed, everything he'd said was true, "But consider, the work is steady."

I think this is what has to be regained in US intelligence function.

General Discussion

Before general discussion began, Mr. Romerstein made two points of clarification. First, he noted that the ability of the FBI (in the

1930's) to conduct close, continuing physical surveillance of Boris Morros simply on the basis of his observed contact with a Soviet diplomat known to be an intelligence officer was essential. Turning Morros, whose freewheeling world-wide movements as a film impressario made him a uniquely effective courier, enabled the FBI to break a major Soviet spy ring. (The implication of this comment was that, under existing guidelines, the Bureau would probably not be able to maintain effective surveillance.) Second, as a follow-up to his description of some "Lovestonites'" cooperation with Soviet intelligence, even after their formal expulsion from the Comintern, Mr. Romerstein observed that this behavior represented no inconsistency: although outside the official Communist movement, the Lovestonites remained during the period in question fundamentally "Soviet patriots" and some performed liaison services for Soviet intelligence with that motivation.

The discussion then turned on the question posed initially by a congressional staff member of why the US government finds it so difficult to make a reasonable and prudent discrimination between those who are intellectually and culturally alienated from American society (one possible meaning of "radical chic" as used in Romerstein's paper) and those whose alienation leads them to become agents of foreign intelligence services and thus the legitimate and even essential subjects of attention by intelligence and counterintelligence officers. A number of themes then emerged.

One academic participant objected vigorously to the use of such broadbrush analytic categories as "radical chic" to denote susceptibility to recruitment by Soviet and/or Bloc intelligence services. Such a concept encompassed too many and too diverse individuals, groups, movements, and mindsets and may—if used to exclude—cut off US intelligence and counterintelligence from potentially valuable assets and sources. Any "ideological means test," this participant argued, poses the danger of a return to the worst and most self-defeating excesses of "McCarthyism."

On the other hand, as several participants responded, those "who have assaulted the very premises of civility and reason in this country" are indeed susceptible to recruitment at the very least, should be carefully monitored by US counterintelligence, and may well exert influence in our society far beyond their numbers or even their intent, simply through the power of ideas.

A second academic participant returned to the initial argument and urged adherence to the classical and fundamental distinction between intellectual dissent on the one hand and, on the other, disloyalty-bordering-on-treason the sharp line between ideas and action. For purposes of counterintelligence, ideas may be deemed "contributory" to suspect behavior but only contributory: "we should not concern ourselves with ideas *per se*."

On the subject of Communist parties as reservoirs for Soviet intelligence recruitment, another participant noted it is true that the Soviets no longer look to indigenous Communist parties as primary sources. But, he went on, they do seek to use them, just as they use a variety of radicals, along with the alienated and the disaffected, to manipulate public opinion in the free world on such issues, for example, as nuclear arms and the neutron "bomb". And the KGB is the "principal orchestrator" of these often effective covert intelligence operations.

A third academic participant strongly objected to any sharp and mutually-exclusive distinction between ideas and action: ideas are powerful weapons, he argued, and they do have profound consequences, as witness a Hiss or a Chambers, or so potent a force as the World League Against War and Fascism. Driving the ideas vs. action dichotomy too far, as we have so often been prone to do, can leave us defenseless before our avowed enemies. It can also, another participant suggested, undermine ideological commitment to an emerging "new American nationalism" and the affirmative thrust of American values.

Several participants, a number of them former intelligence officers, extended the focus of the discussion to another and parallel dichotomy, that between the ideological "amateurs" and the typically non-ideological "mercenaries" and "professionals," the Dunlops and Johnsons and Whalens. It is the latter, they argued, who pose the greater threat.

The discussion reached no general consensus, but ended as it began with suggestions that what is needed to rebuild an effective CI capability is a more rigorous and discriminating mindset that is able to identify potentially dangerous groups and individuals and distinguish them from those who merely spout outrageous ideas. It is a question of distinguishing between those who are genuinely *exercising* First Amendment freedoms (and who should not be targets of CI attention) and those who are *using* these freedoms as a cloak and cover for dangerous, destructive, and even illicit action. The latter are and must be legitmate CI targets.

CHAPTER SEVEN

Counterintelligence Organization and Operational Security in the 1980's

Papers:

I. Norman L. Smith

II. Donovan Pratt

Discussants:

Mr. Eugene Franz Burgstaller

Mr. David Ignatius

1. *Norman L. Smith*

Introduction

In his 1980 State of the Union message, President Carter devoted more prose to the intelligence community than perhaps any President of recent years. He stated: "We also need quick passage of a new charter to define clearly the legal authority and accountability of our intelligence agencies. While guaranteeing that abuses will not recur, we need to remove unwarranted restraints on our ability to collect intelligence and to tighten our controls on sensitive intelligence information. An effective intelligence capability is vital to our nation's security." President Carter's reference to tightening controls on sensitive intelligence information is basically a reference to counterintelligence.

Henry S. Bradsher, writing in the *Washington Star* on 3 February 1980, noted that: "The well publicized traumas of the CIA have left it weakened as it attempts to deal with the perils now facing the United States around the world . . . there is not as much at Langley to unleash as the government might now feel it needs."

One of the "traumas" of the CIA concerned counterintelligence which between 1973 and early 1976 was converted from what might have been described as a centralized line unit organization to a decentralized staff organization. This paper attempts to contrast the merits and effectiveness of the two types of counterintelligence organizations, the decentralized staff organization versus the centralized line unit. Then it goes on to describe the counterintelligence threat in the 1980's and the capabilities of each to meet this threat.

Definitions

The concepts discussed here are defined in great detail elsewhere in the intelligence literature. However, in order to put the discussion of prospects for counterintelligence in the 1980's into perspective, it seems useful to begin with a few short definitions so that the reader would be aware of the general context in which the terms are used here.

The core of intelligence throughout history and throughout the world today consists of the two matching halves of intelligence and counterintelligence. Intelligence, which is sometimes referred to as positive intelligence or foreign positive intelligence, is simply information needed by the officials of a government to carry out their tasks. This information ranges from that openly obtained to that obtained at great risk from those who go to elaborate measures to protect it.

Counterintelligence is the other half of the equation. Counterintelligence is concerned with the protection of information from those who are seeking to obtain it. Counterintelligence consists of three components: personnel security, physical security, and counterespionage. Personnel security is concerned with the protection of people with access to the protected information. Physical security is concerned with the protection of facilities containing the protected information from penetration by persons whose interests are inimical. This penetration can, of course, be technical or physical in nature.

Protection of personnel and facilities is essentially passive in nature. Experience has shown that these measures alone will ultimately be defeated by a determined and resourceful enemy. The third component of counterintelligence is concerned with the penetration of the intelligence organization of the enemy in order to ascertain what he is trying to accomplish, how he is doing it, and how successful he has become. Counterespionage operations range from the detection and arrest of foreign agents and their collaborators to a wide range of sophisticated techniques aimed at confusing, diverting, or deceiving the enemy's intelligence organization.

Intelligence organizations almost never are left alone to pursue these two matching core activities, intelligence and counterintelligence. Additional tasks are levied upon them by their masters, either because they are very effective in doing them or because they need to be done and no one else can be tasked to perform them. These satellite intelligence operations fall into four major categories: paramilitary operations, covert action, counterterrorist operations, and narcotics-related intelligence operations.

Paramilitary operations and covert action were heavily engaged in by US intelligence during the 1950's and 1960's. The successes and failures of these activities have been widely discussed elsewhere. The demand for personnel to perform these tasks and the career rewards for those who did so were sufficiently great that a case can be made that they came to overshadow and practically eclipse the intelligence/counterintelligence core activities. During the 1970's, the propriety of these activities came into serious question. As a result, the option to engage in them was effectively foreclosed and little or no capability to do so exists today. As the events in Iran and Afghanistan unfold, there is some groundswell once again for a United States Government capability somewhere between diplomacy and the Marines. It is likely that future administrations will demand, once again, the recreation of a capability in these areas of satellite intelligence operations.

With the demise of paramilitary operations and covert action, and with the rise of terrorism and narcotics traffic to epidemic proportions, the demand for intelligence operations to counter them in the administration and in Congress took on much the same proportions that the demand for the former had taken two decades before. These two have a negative effect on the core activities of intelligence and counterintelligence in terms of diversion of effort and personnel, but not nearly to the degree that paramilitary operations and covert action had during earlier times.

In summary, intelligence activities consist of two core items, intelligence and counterintelligence. To these are added various satellite or ancillary intelligence activities which reflect the international situation and the wishes of the administration and the Congress.

The Decentralized Staff

The staff, as opposed to line organization, is defined as those members of an organization serving only in an auxiliary or advisory capacity or a body of officers without command authority. A counterintelligence staff organization usually consists of a research unit and a coordination unit.

The research unit has a scholarly function. Its aim is to codify the methods of operation utilized by various foreign intelligence services, friendly as well as hostile. It maintains files on all known operations and the operators involved in each. The research unit performs analysis on the above so as to provide lessons learned to its consumers which include positive intelligence operators, counterintelligence operators, security personnel, and others.

The coordination unit carries out the classic staff function of coordinating counterintelligence-related operations between and among various clandestine service units. It provides professional counterintelligence advice and assistance when requested to do so by the operating units of the other components. It performs a limited liaison role in coordinating the activities of the operating units with domestic and foreign counterintelligence and security services.

Personnel Considerations: Counterintelligence is perhaps the most demanding intellectually of any of the intelligence functions. It requires a sophistication beyond that needed for most of the satellite intelligence operations and for all but a few of the intelligence collection operations. Therefore, the quality and expertise of the personnel assigned to counterintelligence is critical to the success of the function whether the organization is one of staff or of line.

For counterintelligence officers, lacking line authority by definition, the ability to sell counterintelligence to the operating units is most important. Frequent and routine rotation of personnel into counterintelligence and then out into operating units is a most important method of insuring that a wide body of counterintelligence understanding, awareness, and favorable recognition exists outside the counterintelligence organization itself. This exchange of personnel also allows personnel assigned to the counterintelligence staff organization to dovetail their careers with the general rapidly rotating career officer program which prevails in most intelligence organizations today without detriment due to their counterintelligence specialization and assignment.

Function: Within the intelligence agency, and within the clandestine portions of it, various units, usually organized on a geographic basis, conduct positive intelligence collection operations and to a greater or lesser degree, the various satellite intelligence operations discussed above. Within these geographic units, there is usually a focal point for counterintelligence in the form of a special officer who has the direct and continuing responsibility for interface between the operating units of his organization and the counterintelligence staff's coordination unit. Counterintelligence problems and doctrine flow back and forth through this channel, both in the form of general studies and in the form of specific assistance to operating units on specific cases. The command authority, with regard to these cases, rests with the operating unit with the counterintelligence unit providing staff support. Liaison with foreign counterintelligence units is performed by the operating unit, often through the same channel that all intelligence liaison is conducted. Liaison with domestic counterintelligence units is performed directly by the operating unit with the counterintelligence staff unit monitoring the liaison, either through an observer or by means of written communication from the operating unit to the counterintelligence coordination unit.

Advantages: Under this type of counterintelligence organization, the responsibility for success or failure is decentralized or delegated to the intelligence executive in charge of the lowest echelon operations conducting unit. Counterintelligence doctrine and tools are available to him through his own experience, that of his subordinates, and the assistance which can be obtained from the counterintelligence staff unit. The bottom line is that he is responsible for the basic integrity of the operations which he is conducting. With the decentralization of the responsibility for counterintelligence awareness to the lowest possible level, counterintelligence problems can be detected and countered early in the operation. Remedial measures can be initiated before substantial damange is done. Since these remedial measures will be initiated by the officer in charge of the operation, he is much more apt to do so that he would be if someone from the outside claimed that he had been duped by a foreign intelligence operation. Since he is directly responsible, he will tend to "think counterintelligence" more than he would if the responsibility lies with another and separate component.

This assumes that great emphasis is placed on counterintelligence at all levels of command, that counterintelligence staff participation is welcomed and appreciated, and that rotation of personnel through the counterintelligence staff produces a wide awareness and empathy for counterintelligence throughout the various geographic units conducting positive intelligence and other operations.

Disadvantages: This type of counterintelligence organization places a tremendous burden on the first line operational intelligence executive. For a typical positive intelligence operation, this executive is tasked to produce intelligence on a given subject or objective. Using his training and expertise, he recruits a source of such information. His superiors are pleased, and the intelligence and/or policy formulating consumers of his source's product are pleased. However, the source could have been under hostile control at the outset or he could be detected by the opposition and turned against us at any time during the operation. It must be borne in mind that even when the source is under hostile control, the information he supplies will be largely accurate and verifiable as the hostile service develops the credibility of their source in our eyes. When false or deceptive information is introduced into this channel, it is likely to be at a critical time; the information will be highly important and very hard to check.

To charge the first line intelligence executive with the primary and basic responsibility for his own counterintelligence protection is close to asking the impossible. For this executive, who is almost always a fairly junior and inexperienced officer, or his immediate colleagues to raise the red flag on a source they have been commended for recruiting in the first place is asking a great deal. To do so condemns him in the eyes of his superiors for having failed to detect hostile control in the first place. His superiors, in turn, are faced with the unhappy task of informing the consumers and policy makers that they have been deceived. All of this calls for a far greater degree of intellectual integrity than one can reasonably expect to find in this hard cruel world of today or any other time in history.

The counterintelligence staff organization acting in an advisory and staff role through a focal point within the organization involved is often too remote from the problem to detect trouble, and powerless to take action if they did. The operating unit can usually produce a hat full of case officers who have handled the source personally and have absolute confidence in his validity. Unless he has totally convincing evidence, the counterintelligence staff unit chief cannot raise very many of these issues with higher authority or he will find his staff no longer welcome within the geographic unit or privy to what it is doing. Without access to information volunteered by the geographic unit, the counterintelligence staff unit's function is seriously limited.

The Centralized Line Unit

The line unit is defined as that portion of an administrative organization consisting of persons actively engaged on a specific project or task, a body of officers with command authority. The counterintelligence line unit usually consists of a research unit and an operations unit.

As with the staff organization, the research unit has a scholarly function with the objective of codifying foreign methods of intelligence operations and providing the results of this analysis to its consumers who are involved both in collecting information and protecting the United States against hostile and friendly services seeking to collect against us.

The operations unit is a line unit with a charter to conduct counterintelligence and counterespionage operations. This mandate gives the operations unit preeminent authority in this field and allows it to review all operations being conducted by other components and preempt, direct, or otherwise control those operations it determines to have a counterintelligence connection. This is a continuing process. The operations being conducted by this unit may be unilateral or performed in conjunction with other domestic intelligence security units or foreign intelligence and security services. There is a distinct change in the nature of the liaison performed by this unit when compared with the staff-type counterintelligence organization. The line counterintelligence operations unit has the primary responsibility for carrying on this liaison. It is carried on directly with foreign counterintelligence or security forces. Any contact between the normal intelligence operating units and such organizations is through and under the control and direction of the counterintelligence operations unit. Note that this is in marked contrast with liaison practices in the typical staff counterintelligence organization where liaison is conducted through the same basic apparatus used for all liaison with any given foreign service. The counterintelligence liaison apparatus utilized by the line counterintelligence unit is distinct and separate.

Personnel Considerations: It should be reiterated that counterintelligence is the most intellectually demanding function of any intelligence function. The quality and expertise of personnel assigned to counterintelligence is critical. In the successful line unit, personnel assigned are counterintelligence specialists who serve for very long periods of time in the same unit. The research unit contains scholars specializing in the various fields of counterintelligence who, over an extended period of years, have acquired familiarity with the hundreds of counterintelligence cases and the intimate details of each. It takes years of experience to acquire such knowledge and while computers help, their output is only as good as their input. The recent flurry in the press about Anthony Blunt, fourth and fifth men, Kim Philby, etc., illustrates a counterintelligence case which began in the mid-1930's and is still front page news, and still an active counterintelligence case behind the scenes almost fifty years later. The fictionalized middle aged ladies with instant recall of the personal idiosyncrasies of some hostile official are, in fact, essential in real life. Few hostile services labor under a restriction imposed by their government that their official documents always bear their true name and identity. It is interesting to note that not only do the Soviet intelligence services place great emphasis on this sort of historical analysis but that a military historical unit is an integral part of the Soviet general staff at the various higher levels of command, and that the officers assigned to it are of the first quality.

The operational unit contains carefully selected, very mature, and experienced operations officers who have specialized in counterintelligence operations for many years. The author, Eric Ambler, categorized them thus:

> I'd think if asked to single out one specific group of men, one type, one category as being the most suspicious, unbelieving, unreasonable, petty, inhuman, sadistic, double crossing set of bastards in any language I would say without any hesitation the people who run counterespionage departments.

Function: In his book *The Double Cross System,* Sir John Masterman categorized the functions of a counterintelligence unit with a succinctness which is hard to improve upon. He cited seven specific objectives:

1. To control the enemy system, or as much of it as we could get our hands on.
2. To catch fresh spies when they appeared.
3. To gain knowledge of the personalities and methods of the German Secret Service.
4. To obtain information about the code and cypher work of the German Service.
5. To get evidence of enemy plans and intentions from the questions asked by them.
6. To influence enemy plans by the answers sent to them.
7. To deceive the enemy about our own plans and intentions.

The objectives of counterintelligence are the same today. Another conclusion reached by Sir John is equally applicable today. He noted:

> A spy who is prepared to take his time and observe all reasonable precautions is extraordinarily hard to catch and may obtain information of the highest value. On the other hand, counterespionage in peacetime is a matter of the utmost difficulty; it is immensely hard to secure proof; it is impossible to act on suspicion however strong; the whole tenor of our life

in this country is antagonistic to overregimentation and to rigid classification. It is better to let many spies run than to risk one mistake.
So we come to this provisional and admittedly theoretical conclusion: in peacetime espionage is easy and profitable, counterespionage is difficult and unrewarding; in wartime espionage is difficult and usually unprofitable, counterespionage is comparatively easy and yields the richest returns.

Advantages: At its best, the line counterintelligence unit concentrates the finest counterintelligence practitioners and researchers in one unit so that all of the sum total of the organization's experience can be brought to bear on the counterintelligence problems at hand in the most efficient manner. Since counterintelligence is the most demanding art in the intelligence field, it is probably no accident that the Soviet Union and all other professional intelligence services in the East and West utilize some version of the line unit, the centralized unit for counterintelligence.

Disadvantages: All of the foreign policy-related organizations of the United States government, including the intelligence community, utilize the rotational tour of duty, jack-of-all-trades personnel approach to career management. This policy is totally incompatible with the centralized counterintelligence line unit staffing with its long assignment specialists. This assembling of the best counterintelligence talent achieves two negatives. It effectively limits the career potential of personnel in counterintelligence if they remain there. Furthermore, it effectively isolates them from the operating geographic units. Under the staff-type of counterintelligence organization, the normal rotation of personnel from the field to geographic units at Headquarters to counterintelligence assignments, and back out to the field not only promotes a pervasive awareness of counterintelligence, it also promotes an old boy network which facilitates an awareness within the counterintelligence unit of problems related to counterintelligence through informal channels as well as through command channels. In the case of the centralized unit, this old boy network can quickly become united in denying information to the counterintelligence unit, particularly if the personnel in that unit acquire many of the personal characteristics described by Eric Ambler earlier. Thus, the centralized counterintelligence unit may have to organize penetrations of its own geographic units in order to obtain the information it requires about the attempts of hostile services against us. Without a widespread net of informants within the overall organization, the centralized unit management may become just as complacent about hostile successes against them as the staff unit whose high personnel turnover and requirement for cooperative geographic unit clients may render it indulgent on the other side of the coin. Finally, the centralized unit can profit from its highly experienced and specialized personnel for only so long before the organization becomes inbred (and its personnel over the hill) with a resultant isolation from the rest of the organization.

Summary: The preceding has attempted to describe the organization, function, personnel, and the merits and disadvantages of the staff organization versus the line organization in dealing with the problem of counterintelligence. As indicated at the outset, the discussion has been intended to portray each type of unit in its purest terms. In practice, neither exhibits the extremes to the degree portrayed, at least in this writer's experience. Both can and have functioned; the degree of success each has achieved is very hard to judge given the onionlike nature of this type of intelligence function. Both have, on occasion, peeled off various layers of the onion, just how many layers have remained is subject to partisan interpretation at any given point in time and positions change radically when new information is obtained.

On balance, the centralized type of counterintelligence unit seems to be the most efficient when positive steps are taken to obviate or otherwise rectify some of the disadvantages listed. The single factor with the most weight in leading to this conslusion would be the trust born of long-term association which develops between a centralized counterintelligence unit and its domestic and foreign associates. The United States cannot protect either itself or its allies by itself and without mutual trust among counterintelligence associates of the Western world, counterintelligence individually or collectively, is severely crippled. It takes a great deal of trust for a Western official to tell his counterintelligence counterpart in the United States, sometimes without authority from his government, that one of his ambassadors is working for a hostile service. He has to be confident that his American counterpart knows who to tell, when, and in what circumstances. This confidence is seldom bestowed upon the staff-type organization official rotated into a senior counterintelligence position just because he holds the assignment.

Finally, mention must be made of the role played by the director of the intelligence organization as a whole. By and large, it is he who dictates the success or failure of his counterintelligence, both by his basic understanding of its importance and by his judicious selection of and support for the chief of his counterintelligence organization, be it staff or line in organizational nature.

The Counterintelligence Threat in the 1980's

The foregoing discussion of staff or line organizational format as the most expeditious in handling counterintelligence pertains basically to the existing situation in most agencies of the intelligence community and their predecessor organizations dating back to World War II. Within these organizations, counterintelligence has been and is today a component of the larger unit handling clandestine positive intelligence collection operations. This organizational positioning of counterintelligence is based on the World War II premise that all the action takes place in the area of agent operations which now has the bureaucratic name HUMINT. The rest of the intelligence community, such as technical collection operations, and the analysis and production of intelligence as well as the four categories of satellite intelligence operations (paramilitary, covert action, terrorism, and narcotics), are judged by and large to be immune from counterintelligence situations and problems, and can and have largely been ignored from a counterintelligence point of view. The counterintelligence debate has been largely the staff versus line within the agent operations arena.

In this writer's view, this premise is demonstrably wrong. Counterintelligence operations today are taking place well outside of the clandestine services and the counterintelligence unit, be it staff or line, is very often not even in the ball game. In fact, for the most part, they lack the clearances to even know what game is being played.

This is the challenge for counterintelligence in the 1980's. How can the counterintelligence unit be positioned, trained, and integrated so as to effectively cope with the threat against the intelligence amalgam of agent operations, technical collection operation, and intelligence production of the American and allied intelligence community? Unless this can be done effectively it is a waste of time to worry about staff versus line organization in a counterintelligence environment divorced from a large part of reality.

According to the *Washington Post,* the United States spent roughly five billion dollars on direct intelligence activities during fiscal 1979. Roughly ninety percent of this amount went for hardware. Billions more are spent in the Defense Department for "intelligence related" activities and the integration of tactical collection efforts with "national means" where the emphasis is also on hardware and technical collection. In fact, the *Post* commented that one intelligence postmortem after another has noted that the National Reconnaissance Office and the National Security Agency collect far more intelligence than can be processed effectively. Undoubtedly, it was the product of these technical collection sources which led President Carter to assure the American Newspaper Publishers Association at their annual meeting in New York on 25 April, 1979 that he "is going to be able to verify a SALT agreement from the moment it is signed."

This vast national intelligence effort which with the accompanying analysis of the technically collected data consumes better than ninety percent of the manpower and the money expended by the United States for intelligence purposes is for all intents and purposes unprotected by counterintelligence, except in a very cursory and often postmortem fashion. There is no need here to retell the TRW-Boyce-Lee case or the Kampiles case, but they illustrate the point.

A year ago, three United States Senators replied to a *Wall Street Journal* editorial criticizing the Senate Select Committee on Intelligence for its legislative proposals pertaining to United States intelligence gathering. They noted:

> Most disturbing has been the intelligence community's gross underestimation of the Soviet buildup, and its dismissal of Soviet military strategy from the mid 1960's through the mid 1970's. If recent reports are to be believed, the new National Intelligence Estimate of Soviet strategic strength has finally yielded to massive evidence and has admitted the obvious, the Soviets are well on their way to achieving their goal of strategic nuclear superiorty.

Senators Bayh, Inouye, and Huddleston went on to speak of counterintelligence thus: The nation's capability for counterintelligence is a shadow of its former self, while the threat from hostile services has increased. The world is a more dangerous place for us than it was 20 years ago. Our counterintelligence is burdened by jurisdictional divisions between the FBI and CIA. For example, neither agency can have a comprehensive view of a terrorist group like the Puerto Rican FALN because its training and support comes from Cuba, which is in the CIA bailiwick while its members are United States persons who may be investigated only by the FBI. Moreover, the collapse of the CIA's own counterintelligence has been so drastic as to be the subject of newspaper headlines and books. The CIA's management, it seems, is unfriendly to counterintelligence. There are concrete problems abundant here which should be explored by vigorous hearings in closed session.

With regard to counterintelligence, the Senators are focused on its traditional role, the World War II premise as to its function. They fail to relate the counterintelligence problem to the gross underestimation of the Soviet buildup by the intelligence community for more than a decade. Is there a connection? It is unlikely that anyone is in a position to give any sort of authoritative answer to this question. Three of the seven salient functions formulated by Sir John Masterman, enunciated earlier in this paper, are very pertinent here:

- To get evidence of enemy plans and intentions from the questions asked by them.
- To influence enemy plans by the answer sent to them.
- To deceive the enemy about our own plans and intentions.

Because of the traditional focus of counterintelligence on operations within the clandestine services of which it had always been organizationally a part, the product of the intelligence production portions of the intelligence community has been for all intents and purposes neglected as a counterintelligence tool. This is regretable because in the few *ad hoc* instances where such relationships were established, the interchange proved quite profitable.

Given the vast resources devoted to technical collection for example, such simple information interchanges as verifying that an agent traveled to a destination he claims to have visited by matching his description against overhead photography have been useful. If he fails to mention an area of new construction that should have been obvious to him, a counterintelligence question is raised. The reader with a vivid imagination can raise this simple scenario to quite sophisticated levels. While some traditionalists might well question this exposure of operational information outside the operational unit, experience has shown that it can be done discretely and without exposing the information to a wide audience.

Another counterintelligence function defined by Masterman was the acquisition of information concerning the personalities and methods of a hostile service. This is the basic function of the counterintelligence research unit. Under traditional counterintelligence procedures, the information acquired along these lines stays within the research unit. Since hostile intelligence personalities are quite active in this country and in the lands of our allies, a great deal of information concerning their activities inevitably comes into the hands of the intelligence analysts on the other side of the house.

In this atmosphere, these hostile intelligence officers are seldom identified as such. They are specialists in aircraft design, researchers in microbiology, or members of the various institutes. Here, too, there has traditionally been a problem in integrating within the intelligence community all that is known about a certain individual who is a hostile intelligence professional. Because of this deficiency, an important indicator with regard to hostile intentions has been neglected. The Soviet invasions or interventions in Poland, East Germany, Hungary, Czechoslovakia, and now Afghanistan might have been forecast with far greater clarity had an order of battle of the Soviet intelligence and security forces been available in some form to the political analysts. Much of the Soviet military activity in connection with these incursions was camouflaged initially under the guise of manuevers. The movement of the KGB in that connection would have been much more revealing as to ultimate Soviet intentions.

The intelligence community today operates under the mandate of Executive Order 12036. A short review of its provisions with regard to counterintelligence makes the problem rather clear. The Order creates a Special Coordination Committee (SCC) of the National Security Council chaired by the Assistant to the President for National Security Affairs and tasks the SCC to formulate policy recommendations for the President in the areas of special activities, sensitive foreign intelligence collection operations, and counterintelligence.

In the area of counterintelligence, the SCC is asked to perform five tasks: counterintelligence standards and doctrine; central records maintenance; an annual counterintelligence threat assessment; dispute resolution; and the approval of specific counterintelligence activities. These are reasonable and bureaucratically correct objectives. They provide the vehicle for a sound overall counterintelligence community. The Order then tasks the various intelligence community organizations with regard to counterintelligence. The CIA is tasked to conduct counterintelligence activities outside the United States, and coordinate such activities abroad by other agencies. The FBI is tasked to conduct counterintelligence activities within the United States and coordinate the work of other agencies in this field in the United States. The Secretary of Defense is tasked to conduct counterintelligence activities, both at home and abroad, in support of the Department of Defense components, coordinating his overseas efforts with the CIA and his domestic activities with the FBI. This is basically business as usual. These guidelines differ little from those which have prevailed since World War II.

The Executive Order thus provides the mandate for the conduct of counterintelligence activities by the United States. It is, however, this writer's strong impression that the net result is a relatively ineffective, sterile counterintelligence operation overall. The machinery is there; what is lacking is a catalyst—a moving force, leadership.

This lack of leadership in the counterintelligence field is evident in the Executive Order itself. Section I-6 of the Order outlines the duties of the Director of Central Intelligence in some twenty-eight paragraphs. Nowhere in this bill of particulars for the Director of Central Intelligence is there any mention of counterintelligence. Even Section I-604, which deals with the protection of sources, methods, and procedures, is couched in language which makes it clear that the authors of this document viewed the task of source protection as an entirely different matter from that of counterintelligence.

Thus, counterintelligence is not considered to be a direct and important duty of the Director of Central Intelligence. It is a secondary and ancillary responsibility. The Directors of Central Intelligence have spent a great deal of time on positive intelligence production, covert action items, and paramilitary operations. Very little time and understanding have been vested in counterintelligence. The counterintelligence organizations within the CIA and the other intelligence community components are organizationally well subordinated and removed from the top. They are in large measure isolated from the other components of the organization to which they belong and in particular, those components engaged in the production of positive intelligence.

Throughout history, intelligence consisted of two matching halves, positive intelligence and counterintelligence. The current state of US counterintelligence is a faint shadow of what it should be, and must be if we are to survive in a world where we are no longer militarily dominant.

II. Donovan Pratt

Introduction

This paper argues that the time is at hand for the United States to create a new clandestine service which will conduct only clandestine missions. The non-clandestine functions assigned to the Central Intelligence Agency since the 1950's (covert action, paramilitary operations, counter-guerrilla activity, countering the traffic in drugs, and others) may continue to be conducted by an element still called CIA,[1] or some of them might be assigned elsewhere. The question of the allocation of these responsibilities, though important, is not paramount. The overriding need is to build a secret service which will engage solely in espionage and counterintelligence, undiverted to non-secret tasks and shielded from the security hazards inherent in the performance of non-secret tasks and in open association with those who carry them out.

Our country's problems may mount steeply, even ominously, in at least the first half of the 1980's. We can, and probably must, extemporize by such tactics as creating an anti-terrorist force and assigning it to CIA or elsewhere. For the long haul, however, we must be able to get from abroad information obtained, transmitted, and put to use under conditions of genuine secrecy.

If the US creates from the small sound nucleus still at our disposal a new and vigorous clandestine service, designed and managed to carry out espionage and counterintelligence under the cover of secrecy scrupulously maintained, the result will be a slowly expanding access to vital sources. If the future finds us without such a service, our nation will often be tossed by unexpected storms. We shall be compelled to react, defensively and somewhat precipitously, to unforseen hostile initiatives. The building of a clandestine service strong enough to withstand attacks from all quarters, is a laborious, inching, and irksome undertaking, but we have no choice. We cannot afford the weaknesses of the *status quo,* and we cannot afford drift.

The first part of this paper deals with certain definitions and with related topics that may be considered too elementary to be spelled out, as though those already versed in intelligence concerns needed a primer. This writer solicits patience. It is precisely our failure to reach shared understandings about the nature of intelligence functions and to shape our actions in careful conformity with our understanding that has led to some of the most damaging confusions and mishaps of the past.

I.

Operational security is that state of safety for intelligence installations, personnel, and activities created by procedures designed to protect secret operations and their products against unintended disclosure and covert operations against attributability. Conversely, operational security is the limiting of secret services and their assets to activity which does not, by its nature, make the maintenance of secrecy impossible.

Distinctions are often drawn among operational security, physical security, and security of personnel. Yet these disciplines are so intermeshed that a failure in one always jeopardizes the other two. A service that maintains rigorous standards of physical security can be devastated by a penetration agent. A service that cannot afford full protection to its records and reports, which cannot or does not make them inaccessible to hostile scrutiny, is also vulnerable even if all its members are dedicated people. And excellent physical security and trustworthy personnel cannot maintain security for an operation that was sophomorically planned at the beginning. In brief, the installations housing the headquarters and field personnel of a clandestine service, the people who comprise such a service (from the Director of Central Intelligence to a safe-housekeeper in Lower Slobbovia), and the operations themselves are one organism. A wound or site of infection in any part of this body endangers the whole. If the *corpus* is undamaged, and innately sound, it will be able to carry out those functions for which it was designed despite the acts of adversaries. It is this capability which is denoted by the term operational security.

The functions or operations which must be kept secure are of two kinds, clandestine and covert. Clandestine operations, in turn, consist of two types: espionage and counterintelligence. These are the only clandestine functions.

Espionage is conducted largely through human and technical agents. The former are usually spies. The spy who slips into the enemy's camp undetected, counts heads or guns, and steals away unnoticed has carried out a successful espionage operation, provided, of course, that his information arrives only at the "right" designation. At the heart of his undertaking, and crucial to its success, is secrecy. If detected and caught, he is no longer a spy. If detected but not caught, he may or may not spy again, but his operation has failed because the alerted enemy will make changes. The existence of the sound clandestine operation is unknown except to designated participants.

When we speak of counterintelligence, we mean two different, almost disparate, activities. The first of these is the security function: the guards at the doors, the classification system, the badges worn by authorized personnel, the safes carefully secured and checked, and all the other measures. These are safeguards maintained not against a known spy, a specific adversary, but against any and all who might obtain and misuse the country's secrets. Counterespionage, in contrast, consists of catching spies and either neutralizing them or compelling (or persuading) them to serve the captor's ends in ways unknown to those whom they first served. The agent may be caught and doubled back upon the dispatching service. Or he may be sent into the hands of the adversary to provoke recruitment, a tactic which the Soviets have used dexterously since the 1920's. Or an officer who wants to defect from an opposing service may be willing to defer the physical act and stay in place for a time. There are other variants. The aim, however, is unvarying: to penetrate the opposing service so thoroughly that in time American intelligence knows the entire gamut of the adversary's operations and therefore can control them, chiefly in the United States, but sometimes elsewhere as well. The security element of counterintelligence is defensive, whereas the counterespionage function is aggressive. Both espionage and counterespionage are pursuits requiring high levels of skill and secrecy.

Covert action, in sharp contrast, does not strive for invisibility and by its nature cannot be secret. The *raison d'etre* of covert action is to identify the common ground or areas of agreement between the USA and other countries and to further activity which will support and expand these shared interests. Attempts by other countries to persuade elected officials of the US Congress to adopt attitudes more favorable to their interests have been often exposed and have also frequently failed to achieve non-attributability. But it is improbable that very many of them have remained secret. At most, we can hope that the American hand has not been evident.

A vital question, almost never addressed, is whether paramilitary operations are in fact a genuine element of covert action. It is obvious that paramilitary operations cannot be kept secret, that is they cannot be clandestine. But recent history also suggests, if it does not in fact prove, that paramilitary operations sponsored by the United States are quickly attributed to us. No one doubted that the overflights of the U-2 were American in conception and execution. Long before the Bay of Pigs, the world press had reported CIA's role in that doomed undertaking. The Agency's extensive paramilitary role in Vietnam was known to all.

Others can certainly explain better why the responsibility for carrying out US paramilitary activity has not been allotted to the military, with its greater expertise in weaponry and tactics. It is true that CIA had achieved something of a reputation as a can-do service. The strongest CIA roots reached down into the OSS, into World War II. Whatever the varied reasons, we may not have examined with enough acuity whether paramilitary operations can best be conducted by a nonmilitary service as a part of a covert program (or can be conducted covertly at all).

Those with senior managerial responsibilities for US intelligence, including the President, might profitably ask:

- Can and should a proposed action be done clandestinely?
- If not, can and should it be done covertly?
- If not, can and should it be done openly?
- If not, can and should it be done at all?

The worst damage is inflicted when the first of these questions is answered wrongly. A clandestine service is a scalpel, not a meat cleaver. Compelling it to attempt what cannot be done secretly means more than a failed operation. It means the exposure and future uselessness of assets. The agent[2] employed by a secret service must be protected by a relationship which is, above all else, fiduciary. Whether this bond is breached through malevolence[3] or ineptitude is of little moment to the agent whose trust was violated. The CIA must seek to recruit precisely those foreigners whose access to important secret information sharply increases the penalty for detection. Such an agent must be shielded from exposure. The information provided by sources with access to especially important information is particularly likely to pinpoint or jeopardize the source. Our country's moral responsibility toward that source is shared by everyone made privy to his reports unless they have been so scrupulously sanitized that their contents cannot endanger him.

Similarly, the staff officer who has given years to the meticulous creation and living of cover, often with unpleasant consequences for his family and his private life, must not be wantonly pushed into the open. Exposure of both staff and agent assets does not result solely from direct involvement in failed operations. It ensues frequently from contamination. CIA assets used for the Bay of Pigs were blown, and their later roles in secret operations served not to decontaminate them but to alert adversary defenses.

We know that during the 1970's the KGB and the East European services subordinate to it have assiduously collected and collated all overt information about CIA personnel. Somewhere around 1968 the Bloc published the results in a book called *CIA From A-Z.* The security of Clandestine Service (CS) personnel going out on future foreign assignments requires that prior adversary knowledge of their service affiliation be given due weight.

The extent to which the persistent digging of the US press, congressional committees, and others contributed to this continuing adversary program is not known. But elementary prudence suggests that we stop feeding the Soviet kitty. One means of staunching this national wound is the far stricter observance of the need-to-know principle. Ever since Watergate, an element of the press has been performing as though its home were not America but Mount Olympus. As for congressmen and their staffs, the number of those who are now made privy to information about US intelligence operations is so large, and they constitute so heterogeneous a group, that the pre-conditions necessary for the keeping of secrets cannot be met.

If paramilitary and covert action programs cannot be kept secret, it follows that we should stop trying to make them seem secret. Information about paramilitary and CA operations can usually be entrusted to Congress not because it won't leak but because the leakage will not usually damage our national interests.

By the same token, however, sensitive information, gained from clandestine methods and sources, must be scrupulously shielded from all who cannot or will not place the protection of important and sensitive sources and methods above other concerns. Sensitive information should go from the procuring clandestine service only to the executive branch of the government and, within that branch, only to a small number of presidential designees who have a genuine need-to-know. The flow of information should be protected by stringent safeguards. For example, each copy of a sensitive paper should be numbered, and each recipient should sign a corresponding receipt. Each designee ought to sign personally and not be permitted to delegate this responsibility. Each numbered copy should contain differentiating variants. These variants should not be substantive; no recipient should be misled. Yet they should facilitate the identification of any illicitly published copy, by means of the earmarked information.

The National Security Act charges the Director of Central Intelligence with the protection of methods and sources. There is, however, no enabling legislation, no law that says what he can do in order to discharge this responsibility. The resultant dilemma was the cause of the Catch-22 predicament for which Mr. Richard Helms was made the scapegoat. That same time bomb is still ticking. Defusing it requires two steps. First, we need to define explicitly *which* methods and sources we mean. It is suggested that the Act was meant to apply to clandestine methods and sources only. If so, the Director's responsibility is more clearly delineated and much reduced. Within this smaller area, however, he must have the solid support of a law that will impose penalties upon those who willfully disclose sensitive information to the detriment of those who gave it to us and to our national interest. Perhaps no period in our history has been less propitious for advocating the passage of an American version of the British Official Secrets Act. Yet, if we pause for a moment and reflect dispassionately, we may conclude that we cannot afford the present ground rules. We do not want journalists to decide which of our secrets of state are to be declassified because they do not know the sources of secrets and probably do not lie awake nights worrying about how to protect them.

The outset of the 1980's is a fitting time to consider whether the damage done to American intelligence in the 1970's is reparable. Is the wound mortal? One is tempted to quote Mercutio: "No, 'tis not so deep as a well, nor so wide as a church door; but 'tis enough, 'twill serve." But so grim a view would be extreme. All the wounds combined, from Congressional probes and restrictions to books put into print by ex-CIA employees without prior review, to arbitrary reductions in personnel strength, are not enough to leave us blind and deaf. But they may prove mortal if we ignore them or reach for the Bandaid box. The wounds must be cleansed thoroughly and corrective surgery must be carried out. If anyone thinks that we can conduct business as usual, let him earnestly ask this question of himself: "If I were a citizen of a country other than the USA, and if I sympathized with the ideals of democracy, would I agree if tomorrow a United States intelligence officer tried to recruit me as a clandestine agent, and if I knew that divulgence of my role would quickly result in my imprisonment or death?" Today, only those profoundly ignorant of recent American history or wildly quixotic would be likely to assent. How likely are liaison services to share with us secrets considered vital by their own governments? Only a clandestine service, a group that potential agents and liaison services knows to be wholly able to keep their secrets, will benefit from geunine candor. Agents and services that have cause for doubt will not, as a rule, misinform us. They will simply withhold the most vital facts. (Because all intelligence services are instruments of nationalism, no liaison service confides wholly in another. This fact is mirrored in the counterintelligence dictum that there are no friendly services. But a good partner withholds openly, saying in effect, "Sorry, I can't tell you that." A worried partner does not. He creates the misleading impression that he has been unstintingly forthcoming. The difference is that between a misleading map and one bearing an area frankly labelled *terra incognita.*) Therefore, secret services and secret agents will mislead us, without intent to harm us, unless they are sure that they are dealing with an organization that has both the skill and the authority to prevent leaks.

II.

The old adage has it that it is always darkest just before the dawn. It is plain that CIA and FBI have been targets for the slings and arrows of outrageous fortune. Consequently, there has never been a more propitious time for a wise restructuring of US intelligence. The present weaknesses are not solely the result of recent events, and some of the present problems were seeded in the late 1950's and in the 1960's.

A logical starting point is the building in Langley. It cannot house the clandestine services, for reasons as obvious as it is.[4] But it is well designed for the needs of the non-secret elements of CIA. These are the entire NFAC complex (the editors who collate intelligence); the DDA complex (those who supervise the logistics of intelligence and see to its material needs); and the covert action complex. (If paramilitary operations must continue to be misassigned to CIA, then they too must be headquartered at Langley.)

In contrast, those engaged in espionage and counterintelligence must have working space that is as inconspicuous as possible. (It is worth noting that putting CIA in temporary buildings clustered around one side of the reflecting pool did not make its people invisible but did enable them to keep a very low profile.) The Agency's memory, its largely computerized records, should stay in Langley; but terminals, appropriately safeguarded, can be placed anywhere in the greater Washington area. Those older hands from the clandestine services who are known to have been publicly identified should also work in Langley, and they should not be reassigned abroad in clandestine capacities.

Newly recruited officers who will serve in the clandestine services should not be trained at identified training sites, but in a number of classrooms in various office buildings. They ought not to visit the Langley complex at any time. They should start living cover at the outset.

These cumbersome restrictions, which entail a complicated communications network, are "inefficient." As senior members of foreign intelligence services have remarked, Americans have a strong tendency to try to run a secret service like a business, using cost-accounting procedures, trusting equipment more than people, trying to force clandestinity into a tidy bureaucratic pattern, as though the product was automobiles, not secret information.

This will not work. We have tried so hard to make this misguided view an operating principle that we have very nearly transformed CIA from a secret service into a civil service. It is not enough to halt this process now. We must reverse it.

Concentrating the non-clandestine functions in Langley and in light cover groupings overseas will provide a most important advantage to the Clandestine Service: serious cover. If we make the separation carefully, the US and world press will continue to focus upon the CIA that it knows. Standing and *ad hoc* committees will continue to meet, regulations will be written and revised, payrolls will be made up, the heating and air-conditioning system will be improved. And the operatives of the new secret service will be able to get on with their demanding jobs.

The kind of thinking about the clandestine function that is integral to this paper will produce some headaches in the future if it is translated from theory to fact. First, shall we be able to draw into the secret service fledgling officers who are bright, courageous, adept in human relationships, linguistically qualified, and innovative, yet prepared to accept lifelong anonymity and the family strains engendered by deep cover? The answer, miraculously, is yes. Next, can the secret intelligence structure maintain that level of discipline essential to clandestine operations? Again, the answer is yes—because it must. Can the press be restrained from trying to identify locations used by clandestine personnel and printing such information, to the national detriment, for readers who cannot use it and would rather not know it?[5] Perhaps. The answer would be yes if the deliberate divulgence of highly classified information were legally punishable by penalties matching the gravity of the offense. Until such a law exists, the Clandestine Service must be good enough to avoid detection.

If the United States can create and sustain a secret service, its espionage or collection arm will pose only a negligible threat to our open society because it will function only abroad. But there is a significant concern that the counterintelligence element (the FBI and the CI component of CIA) might become a kind of Gestapo. In the press and in Congress, fear has been voiced that the FBI and the CIA may slip from scrutiny and control and become secret police on the fascist model, planting microphones on the unsuspecting, reading private correspondence, compiling dossiers on the innocent, and abusing the rights and freedoms that are our inheritance. Another version of the same apprehension is Senator Church's reference to a "rogue elephant." Most Americans reject the notion that a secret service has built-in guarantees against abuses because it consists of gentlemen who can be trusted. Alger Hiss was one of the finest flowers of the establishment. The British know that the old school tie is as likely to cover perfidy as is any other cravat.

Our first safeguard is the President. There can be no Gestapo without a Hitler. The specter of a rogue elephant is a chimera. The second safeguard consists of the rigorous selection, training, and supervision of personnel. Questions about possible abuse of authority may properly be included in polygraph tests routinely required of all who work in the Clandestine Services. The rules ought to be clear and should be stressed during training. Punishment for violations should be swift and severe. Secret service officers may contemplate ruefully the vast advantages enjoyed by hostile services working for non-democratic regimes, but they will not question the need to protect our freedoms. Under these conditions abuses might still sprout in some corner of the garden, but they will quickly be weeded out.

III.

If the US can create and maintain a truly secret service, it will consist of just two parts, as was said earlier: espionage, or foreign intelligence (FI) and counterintelligence (CI).

FI produces intelligence mainly from two kinds of sources: human and mechanical. So does CI. The chief difference is that CI is concerned with the security of secret American operations and the clandestine and covert activities of adversary intelligence services, whereas FI is concerned with a vast array of political, military, economic, and other information. Another difference is that CI is responsible for the security of both FI and CI sources and methods. FI has an obvious responsibility for sound tradecraft, for running clandestine operations clandestinely; but CI must oversee these processes.

The quirky problems that always arise in the management of human beings and a deep American preference for the technical have led to a proliferation of non-human intelligence instruments and a tendency to eschew human agents or at least to use them reluctantly. This drift is dangerous because technical sources (other than communications intelligence) can tell us only about hostile capabilities. They are mute about intentions.

Another major difference is that whereas FI produces intelligence for the use of many elements of government, CI is usually its own customer. When, for example, a defector from the KGB provides new information about the KGB's Second Chief Directorate, which is concerned with CI, the CI elements of US intelligence will not disseminate the product as though it were an Order of Battle report. They will restrict dissemination to the US counterintelligence community and, within that circle, to those with a need to know the identity of the source (who may still be in place) and the extent of his cooperation with us. The necessity of restricting CI information to those who need to know it obtains for other kinds of sources too. If the information came from an intelligence defector, the adversary service cannot be sure about how much he has told us unless we tell them. Whatever the source—a liaison service, a double agent, or whatever—the same rule holds.

It also applies to communications intelligence (COMINT). If we find a microphone in the office of the US ambassador to Ruritania and rip it out, we merely alert the adversary that he must use an alternative. But if we leave it in place as a channel for disinformation, we make it work for us. The consumer then becomes a hostile service.

Infrequently we have strayed from the rule that CI is its own consumer, with unfortunate results. For example, certain classified studies state much of what US intelligence knows about foreign services. The only protection afforded these sensitive counterintelligence data was inadequate (it depended entirely on formal classification). Initially the Clandestine Services resisted participation in a program that thrust into many hands sensitive information about the intelligence elements not only of bloc and non-aligned nations but of all countries, including those with whom the US had close liaison arrangements. In time the injudicious but powerful bureaucratic pressures on CI proved irresistible, and the dam broke. Almost none of the recipients could put such information to significant use. Whether any of these studies ever came into the hands of the intelligence services of other countries cannot be discussed here, but we cannot be sure that no such losses have occurred. Such papers went to a long list of customers in the US government, and they were sometimes sent abroad. The moral is that CI information is different from other kinds by virtue of the sensitivity of its sources and the fact that very few have a functional need to know it.

Another major distinction between FI and CI information is that the former usually has a much shorter life span. The balances of political power inside the USSR fluctuate; the economy undergoes swift ups and downs; but the KGB goes on. Consequently, records are more important to CI than to the other disciplines.

A final difference is that FI work is organized geographically, while CI is functionally organized. FI personnel become experts in one country or, at most, a small group of intermeshing, countries. The FI officer learns a foreign language, foreign customs and history, foreign laws, the geography of his area, and the rest. The CI expert becomes adept in double agents, the handling of intelligence defectors, penetration operations, and other matters in which geography is of little consequence.

The CI responsibility for the security of FI operations is not exactly matched by a parallel obligation towards CA operations because, as was noted earlier, these are not and cannot be clandestine. The CI role in the CA world concerns adversary CA more than our own. The reason is that almost all hostile CA operations are carried out by hostile secret services. A good illustration of counter-CA work is the study *Communist Forgeries*.[6]

This study exposed Soviet forgeries and other frauds in depth and on a world-wide basis. Soviet activity in this area dropped off dramatically for some two years. Such exposure of forgeries and related frauds also alerts the American academic world to the danger inherent in an uncritical amassing of source materials. Soviet and Soviet-inspired accounts of history and of current events distort the facts both through bias and through deliberate intent.

It is not suggested, however, that CI and CA should be disassociated. CA conducts its own file checks on potential recruits, just as FI does, to uncover derogatory information before a recruitment approach is made, to prevent recruitment of the same person for more than one element of US intelligence, and for other, similar reasons. CI, however, must check its own indices on behalf of FI and CA, because the sensitivity of some counterintelligence information precludes its incorporation in the general registry.

Next, experienced CI personnel should participate in the basic training of FI and CA officers. These new recruits need to learn at the beginning not specialized counterintelligence skills but an awareness of the hazards of conducting operations in foreign lands where adversaries are equally active. They need to acquire through instruction—and not solely by painful experience—a healthy skepticism, a probing attitude, a disinclination to grant credence to the merely promising or comfortable.

CI also has an obligation to share with CA as much information as it can about hostile clandestine and covert actions being conducted in areas in which American CA is also deployed.

Because of its extensive governmental, journalistic, and other contacts, CA inevitably acquires facts pointing to hostile control of influential citizens in other lands. Such information should, of course, be given to CI, which can best determine whether such persons should be identified to the appropriate liaison service, considered for possible doubling back against the opposition, exposed, or handled in some other way, such as defensive watch-listing intended merely to ensure that American intelligence does not stumble into blind associations with them.

IV.

It is both reasonable and prudent to assume that in the 1980's US counterintelligence will confront problems at least as serious as those of the past and probably graver. The chief intelligence adversary, the KGB, has never been in a stronger position. In fact, the damage that has been inflicted upon the FBI, CIA, and also military counterintelligence could scarcely have been more baneful if the Soviets had engineered it. To redress the balance, to make it possible to cope with the adversary operations that will be aimed at us in the future even more aggressively than they are now—and to mount sophisticated operations against the KGB—we do not need and should not rely on large budgets and complex organizational charts for the reconstructed Clandestine Service. We need a cadre of honed professionals.

This country rightfully expects of its Clandestine Service intelligence officers a generous measure of devotion. These men and women have chosen careers in which monetary reward is not a primary consideration, careers that result over the years in skills with scant marketability after retirement, careers that above all else require an ungrudging acceptance of anonymity. To those who accept we owe in return a fair chance to be effective. Those assigned to clandestine operations need work space that promotes operational security. They know that guidelines and restrictions will (quite properly) shape their work, but they consider (also quite properly) that these guidelines and restrictions should be formulated by those knowledgeable about the requirements of clandestinity. They have a right to expect that sources and liaison arrangements patiently cultivated will not be destroyed by the release of pin-pointing information to those who will not keep it secret. And they deserve to belong to a genuinely secret service, in which counterintelligence concepts permeate operations from the planning stage on.

Until the beginning of 1955, when the Counterintelligence staff was created, the CI function was almost trivialized in CIA. It was not treated as a co-equal clandestine discipline, but was instead buried in FI components and entrusted for the most part to employees of lower rank and less field experience. Under these circumstances it had degenerated to little more than record keeping, the accumulation and maintenance of files. Under the leadership of an unusually brilliant chief of counterintelligence and with the understanding support of the top echelon in the Agency's command, which knew how vital was the CI role, counterintelligence gained enough strength to be effective in CIA's headquarters. But it remained a staff element, not an integral part of the chain of command from the field to the center.

CI officers almost never went abroad except on infrequent temporary assignments. The very few who were assigned to tours overseas had to abandon their hard-earned expertise and become FI officers. Field operations lacked that added dimension that on-the-spot CI analysis might have added to them. CI officers, unable to work full time in their specialty, except at headquarters, were thus excluded from the circular flow of personnel that characterizes FI and is the systole and diastole of intelligence.

One advantage resulted. The CI officer acquired more and more specialized knowledge through continuity, and counterintelligence thus achieved a stabilizing effect upon operations. The CI officer tends to work within large time frames. Collection requirements shift continually, reflecting a constantly changing world. CA operations, too, are typically in flux. But such CI targets as the KGB neither die nor fade away. Hence, CI was less affected by the transitory and correspondingly more able to provide a kind of ballast, and to assert principle over exigency.

But this advantage can be retained in the new CS without denying to CI its rightful equality with espionage and covert action. Counterintelligence and those who embody it are not always popular with those responsible for FI and CA operations. Some see CI as forever blowing the whistle on operations that are promising but insecure, as always saying, "Yes, but," as stubbornly opposed to that spirit of "bash-on-regardless" that is imbedded in the American way. The result is that CI cannot gain the authority it needs through a voluntary grant by the other intelligence components. The monitoring and almost parental role of counterintelligence has to be decreed and supported by higher authority.

V.

Some guidelines are needed governing the relationships between the new clandestine service, for which the security of its personnel and operations must be a constant preoccupation, and the Center, the complex housing all of CIA's non-clandestine functions. It would be premature to try to discuss here the practical problems of safely housing this Clandestine Service, of blue-printing its table of organization, of planning secure and swift communications between the CS and the Center, of ensuring quick access to records while safeguarding sensitive materials against intrusion, and a vast array of similar problems. They can be solved, but in solving them we must grant no quarter to arguments of expediency. The administrative and support functions exist solely to help operations. As soon as the proper roles are inverted and the support tail begins to wag the operational dog, the effectiveness and the security of FI and CI diminish correspondingly. John Galsworthy once made a brief speech consisting of the observation that for too long Western civilization had made art the handmaiden in the house of life, in which she should by rights rule as mistress. It is also true that for too long we have made clandestine operations the manservant in the house of intelligence, where they should be master, as they once were.

Next to nothing has been said here about the military intelligence services, although their role in the total US intelligence program is vital. One reason is that this writer does not know enough about the subject. Another is that if this paper has practical consequences, if in particular the more martial of the functions now assigned to CIA are assigned to the military services, the areas of responsibility devolving upon G-2, A-2, Naval Intelligence, and DIA will be enlarged. The Clandestine Service would provide such assistance as it can, especially in the form of counterintelligence about adversary intelligence systems. Liaison between the CS and the Center, and also between the CS and the remainder of the US intelligence community, should be conducted by a liaison element of the CS.

In such a reorganized intelligence community the FI and CI halves of the Clandestine Service would be mutually supportive. CI would continue, for example, to run scrupulous records checks upon prospective FI and CA sources. In general, FI information that emerges from CI operations (as it does) would be passed to FI promptly, and the reverse would be equally true. There would be, as presumably there now is, a continuous interaction. For example, if a defector from an adversary service were to say that FI source X had come under the control of that service, FI and CI would decide jointly whether to drop the agent or try to play him back.

This fraternal cooperation cannot, unfortunately, characterize unreservedly the relationship between the Clandestine Service and the Center. Here, too, the British example is instructive. During World War II the English counterintelligence service, and the XX or Double-Cross Committee that was part and parcel of MI5, achieved not just superiority over the *Abwehr* and the *Sicherheitsdienst* but a mastery over German operations in the British Isles. What German agents in England did or did not do was determined in London, not Berlin. During those same war years the British Special Operations Executive (SOE) tried to run operations into the occupied countries on the continent in order to supply underground resistance fighters there with communications, supplies, and funds. The Germans controlled these operations much as English counterintelligence dominated German operations in England.

In essence, the English success was based upon MI5's ability to read coded German radio transmissions. In this way, MI5 knew in advance that some of the SOE operatives parachuted into Holland and other occupied territories were being sent into traps. But telling SOE the truth would almost certainly have resulted in precipitous action of such a nature that the Germans would have deduced the cause and changed the codes. The consequent losses for the Allies would have been far graver than those incurred through SOE.

A major function of counterintelligence is to protect clandestine sources against the peril posed by interaction with the non-clandestine. It would be incumbent upon the CI arm of the new Clandestine Service to give all the assistance to CA that the security of clandestine sources and methods will allow. Both FI and CI can furnish information pertinent to CA operations. FI can provide principally geographic or local data about the area of operations. CI can provide chiefly functional data about adversary CA operations in the same area. Assistance may also be forthcoming in such matters as cover for CA officers abroad. CA operations, in turn, do at times yield useful FI and CI information. But throughout this confluence the CI component must take care that the stricter security standards that must govern clandestine operations are not breached. Above all, the new CS must be scrupulous about the security of its environment, personnel, and operations, in that order.

Conclusion

The views that have been presented here are not new. They have been voiced by many CIA officers in the past, especially those who served abroad for extended periods on clandestine assignments. In fact, some of them constitute the cadre of a new or rejuvenated Clandestine Service. CIA has today, at various echelons of rank and experience, many officers working in clandestine operations who have not, to our knowledge, been exposed in the media or otherwise identified to adversary services. These men and women are the logical teachers and managers of tomorrow's CS.

It is suggested that the new service should grow very slowly. Some of CA's problems in its swaddling days as OPC (Office of Policy Coordination) arose less from the nature of covert action than from too rapid an acquisition of staff and agent assets. Throughout both its infancy and its maturity the CS must not be called upon to undertake assignments foreign to its own nature and capabilities or likely to jeopardize the secrecy without which a clandestine service cannot exist. The CS should also be exempted from the ministrations of oversight committees, which should deal with the Center.

Finally, the entire thrust of this paper may arouse in the minds of those reading it a question that has nagged at the writer as well. If these truths are sound, why were they not followed unswervingly by those who guided CIA's destiny: perspicacious and experienced men with a wide view of events?

There are two primary reasons. The first is that an intelligence service is just that—a service. It does not make policy. It may plead its cause with those above it in the national hierarchy, it may argue against a proposed course of action, but it may not say no. When in the judgment of its superiors the national interest requires that certain missions must be carried out and when CIA is designated as the action agency, then CIA has a restricted area of choice. What it *can* do is to select the Agency component best suited to the task. In particular, it can choose non-CS components to carry out non-clandestine activities.

The second reason why the compartmentation of the clandestine and non-clandestine functions was at times inadequately maintained was that the pressure placed upon the Director of Central Intelligence and upon his most senior lieutenants is intense. These people must orchestrate scores of dizzying complexity for a performance always scheduled for tomorrow. The DCI can adhere to principles designed for the long-range protection of the Agency (and thus for long-range results), despite the pressures of expedience, only if he is granted somewhat wider authority than the law now gives him. The discharge of his global responsibilities is as difficult and as vital to our future as is the role of the Secretary of State.

The past seven years have been harsh for the clandestine and covert components of the Central Intelligence Agency, but they are also instructive if we read them thoughtfully. If significant changes are not made, US intelligence will suffer further convulsions. If the reaction is to fight shy of clandestine operations because they are difficult to conduct, our government will be inadequately informed. If, for example, we cut back on the recruitment and employment of human sources and increase correspondingly our reliance upon technical means, we may learn more about hostile capabilities while learning less about hostile intentions, and we shall be more susceptible to deception because of the ingrained tendency to trust machines more than people.

If, on the other hand, we start now to build a secure Clandestine Service and if we devote to this task all the experience, energy, patience, and skill that we can muster, then we can fashion an instrument that will serve us well in the 1980's and in later decades. The task is simply to make sure that we have the right tools for the job, the right craftsmen to use the tools, and the right working conditions for the craftsmen.

Notes

1. For the sake of clarity this element, charged with all the functions currently assigned to CIA except espionage and clandestine counterintelligence, is hereafter called the Center.
2. This paper follows the CIA practice of using *agent* to mean not a staff officer of an intelligence service but a foreign national having a secret relationship with such a service and engaging in secret activity under its direction.
3. The KGB is believed to have "blown" agents deliberately to an adversary service in order to divert it from other sources who were in jeopardy and more highly placed.
4. Anyone writing down license numbers in the parking lots around the building can identify almost everyone who works there.
5. On March 2, 1980, ABC Television's "Issues and Answers" announced that a recent poll had shown some 73% of the American people in favor of *increasing* CIA's capabilities.
6. U.S. Congress, Senate, Subcommittee to Investigate the Administration of the Internal Security Act and other Internal Security Laws of the Committee on the Judiciary. Testimony of Richard Helms, June 21, 1961.

Discussants

Mr. Eugene Franz Burgstaller: Commenting on Counterintelligence, I inevitably reflect my own background, which excluded any direct involvement with, or assignments to the CI staff of the Central Intelligence Agency. I express the viewpoint of a station chief and of an officer who was concerned more with positive intelligence, in some instances covert action, than with counterintelligence per se, although obviously one can't be in the business that many of us have been in without having a fair amount of exposure to counterintelligence in one way or another.

I would like to endorse, first of all, the very lucid points which Mr. Smith made regarding the ill effects on counterintelligence, and, as far as that goes, upon positive intelligence as well, when senior administration officials turn to the CIA to solve annoying problems as they arise. This has been the pattern of many years now.

I think, for example, of the involvement of the Agency in narcotics-related intelligence collection. I certainly think of the involvement of the Agency in collection about terrorism while, on the one hand, I do not imply that there is no role for CIA and for counterintelligence in collecting intelligence on terrorist organizations and terrorist activities, I suggest that one can go too far in that direction, and that if one does, one does so inevitably at cost to the basic functions both of counterintelligence and of positive intelligence.

The chief of a Western European internal security service, a very competent, a very experienced, and a very intelligent individual, talking to a senior CIA official said, "I don't think that my organization should be involved at all, or certainly heavily involved, in the terrorist problem." The CIA official to whom he made this comment was rather taken aback and said, "Well, don't you regard terrorism as an important problem?" to which the European official said, "Yes, of course I do, but it is fundamentally a police problem in the sense that the actions taken in the effort to prevent an incident from happening, and certainly the investigation of the terrorist incident after it has taken place, are police functions. He continued, "The internal security services and, as far as that goes, the foreign intelligence services, should obviously contribute the pertinent information that they have to the responsible police elements, but they shouldn't be distracted from their fundamental job of counterintelligence. International terrorism, however important and unpleasant, and attention-attracting though it is, obviously is not comparable in seriousness to the efforts of the Soviet Union and its allies, and particularly to the operations and activities of the intelligence services of the Soviet Union and its allies, because these efforts are aimed at the fundamental subversion and ultimate destruction of the very fabric of our society and of all Western societies."

There is a great deal of truth to that. The usual international terrorist incidents are a serious nuisance and they can be very unpleasant. But they do not reflect, for example, on the part of, if you will, the Black September organization, any genuine interest in destroying or conquering American society. The intentions of the Soviet Union, of the CPSU, and of the KGB its "Sword and Shield," are as hostile as they have always been and, barring some major change in the nature of the Soviet Union, I think as they always will be. Their aim is certainly a serious one. The Western European official whom I cite pointed out that the resources of all of the Western counterintelligence services put together, are inadequate to the task of countering the KGB, and they propably always will be. The point of all this is that dilution of effort is bad for counterintelligence.

I would like to say that the two papers, excellent though they both are, left me with the feeling that it might be well to indulge in a few cautionary comments, in the light of my own experience. I will speak, in terms of the counterintelligence function as it has existed in the CIA, and specifically in the organizational component which we have always referred to as the CI staff.

There are other ways you can organize the CI function, but I certainly agree with Mr. Smith's comment that however it is organized, ultimately the atmosphere within which the CI component works and the quality of the personnel who are assigned to it are going to be the things that make the real difference, rather than the precise nature of its organizational structure.

I don't believe one should ever separate CI from the other functions which are assigned to an organization like the CIA, because very often the positive intelligence and the counterintelligence assets at the disposition of a Chief of Station in any country will be the most useful assets for exploitation in other areas, such as covert action, even perhaps selectively paramilitary operations of a circumscribed and genuinely discreet nature. Secondly, in 1951 I began my career in an organization called the Office of Policy Coordination (OPC). The OPC was then separate from the organizations which did positive intelligence and CI. In 1952, in the country in which I was then assigned, the old Office of Special Operations, the positive intelligence and counterintelligence component, and the OPC were merged. The experience I had in the following years reinforces my conviction that that was a sound move, that to have two American intelligence components in the field, one of them doing one thing or several things, perhaps, and the other doing other things, is an awkward and in many respects a dangerous organizational framework. That is not to say, of course, that we should break down compartmentation in any way that would be damaging. But I do believe they should remain together.

There is another reason why I think these things are important, and here I do draw upon my own experience, and that of fairly recent vintage.

When you deal as a Chief of Station (COS) with senior foreign service officials—this is true both for foreign intelligence services and foreign internal security services—they are not merely interested in counterintelligence. They will often be interested in other things—positive intelligence, terrorism, covert action. The ability of the Chief of Station to maintain a dialogue with them on those matters which they are legitimately interested in, and a meaningful dialogue will enhance, I am persuaded, their cooperativeness with him in the counterintelligence and selectively the foreign intelligence sectors.

Turning to another subject, Mr. Smith counterposes a centralized counterintelligence line unit against a toothless staff element. By the former I gather he means the kind of counterintelligence component that functions so independently that it becomes, one might say, an elite unit, which does not consult with other elements in the intelligence organization concerned on issues of mutual interest.

This subject has several component questions. For example, should the CI careerists, the members of this CI staff, deal directly with foreign intelligence services? Manifestly they should—but not as has happened at times in the past with the Chief of Station of the country concerned deliberately cut out of all knowledge of what was going on between the foreign service concerned and that CI staff component.

This did happen in the past and, in fact, on my last assignment it was still happening in a matter of admitted sensitivity. And while I was in that assignment there were changes in the CI staff at the Agency. Some of these changes may have been of dubious value, but one was certainly, from my standpoint as a COS, of inestimable value, that is, I was cut in on CI's operation, on this subject matter.

As soon as that happened I sensed a distinct feeling of relief on the part of the foreign intelligence chief concerned. I think he had found it embarrassing to have to treat this particular matter—although he did so very conscientiously—as though the COS in his country were somehow not to be trusted with knowledge about this particular activity.

I am saying I don't think that should be done. If we have a COS in a country who cannot be trusted with any knowledge at all concerning counterintelligence problems of interest between his organization and Washington and the service or services in the country in which he is the director or representative of, there is only one thing you should do—get rid of that particular Chief of Station and replace him with someone you can trust.

I don't think this was done in the past because COS's were not trusted, but it was an organizational thing, and however this component is set up in the future, I would enjoin those concerned to do so in a way that leaves the Chief of Station in the country concerned as an active participant in any dealings between the headquarters counterintelligence component and the foreign services with which he has to deal on a daily basis.

I might point out that though this did not happen in the country in which I had this experience, it is conceivable to me that if the COS were cut out of certain matters, the foreign intelligence service chiefs or the internal security service chiefs might be tempted in some cases to play both ends against the middle. In other words, I think it is organizationally disadvantageous to have a foreign official dealing with one component of, in our case, the Central Intelligence Agency, while he deals with another component on other matters without the knowledge of the COS who is, of course, his principal channel to the organization at home.

Another disadvantage may arise, if one makes of the CI component a sort of elite unit that overrides, in many respects the line units that are charged with collection of positive intelligence and other operational activities. If CI can override positive intelligence there is bound to be bad blood between the two. There will be jealousies. I know in a former era, in the 1950's, I really had no concept of what the CI staff did except that they were those guys down there behind locked doors. And there was almost inevitably, I think, a certain psychological compulsion on me, and I know on many others, to view these people behind the locked doors with very deep suspicion.

Whatever one thinks, as I say, about the changes that have been made—and they may have brought some harmful results—I felt that in my recent years in the Agency I was very much in touch with the CI staff, its senior officers, and I think the relationship which ensued was mutually advantageous as a result.

I concede the points made by Mr. Smith in particular as to the intellectually demanding nature of counterintelligence work, and I concede, of course, in that connection, that one does require a counterintelligence career service, people who work at this over a long enough period of time and over a sufficiently broad number of cases to develop a genuine expertise. Nevertheless, I would caution that such a career service should not again lead to two totally separate components. I think that the cross-fertilization brought about by having regular movement of personnel from your positive intelligence component to your counterintelligence component is a useful thing and will imporve, in fact, the performance of both components over an extended period of time.

Finally, I have just a few comments that arose in my mind as I read these papers. I would add that they are both extremely fine. I would say a most hearty amen to Mr. Pratt's stress on the absolute need to protect sensitive sources and methods. I think that whatever legislation is written must sanctify this aspect of intelligence work. I was concerned, as I read the proposed intelligence charter (S. 2284), and there was one phrase that really deeply distrubed me. That was the suggestion that the Senate and House Intelligence Committees should have access to any information they think they require.

In testifying before the Senate Committee I pointed out that as a Chief of Station I did not have to know the true identities of most of the sources my station ran—and I didn't know who they were. I had, obviously, knowledge in certain specific cases of who the individual source or contact was, but in others it was sufficient to me to know him by a code name and a description, for example.

And this really is the guts of our business. Foreign intelligence chiefs as well as individual sources with whom I have had occasion to speak almost inevitably get back to the point—and there is every reason why they should—of the confidentiality of the relationship between the intelligence service, the CIA, and themselves. If the day comes when that confidentiality is clearly gone, we simply will be out of business.

I am by no means convinced that there must be charter legislation. But if there has got to be charter legislation—it should make abundantly clear that the Congress respects and supports, in all respects, the protection of sensitive sources and methods.

I also feel there is much to be said for the argument for increased coordination and cooperation in the counterintelligence field among all United States Government elements concerned with that function, and perhaps specifically, obviously, between the CIA and the FBI. I think, from what I have heard that that collaboration and coordination has been on the increase, although I have not personally participated in the relationship. Certainly it is something all of us would support and should support.

Finally, I was very much struck by General Gazit's emphasis upon the relationship between policy, national strategy, and intelligence collection, including counterintelligence collection. And it seemed to me that the points he made—and he was speaking basically in the context of terrorist organizations and activities—that you do a better job of collecting intelligence and counterintelligence if you understand what strategy, what objectives, that intelligence is to serve.

But today in the United States, as several speakers in this Colloquium have pointed out, we have tied our hands behind our backs; we have sanctified the rights of individual US persons so extremely that, in my view, we have been inadvertently overlooking the rights of society as a whole. The primary obligation of our government, as of any government, is to the society as opposed to the individual members of it, which means not that you override individual rights but that you preserve individual rights through the preservation of the society itself. This is manifestly applicable in the field of counterintelligence as in many other fields.

Mr. David Ignatius: I want to turn first to Mr. Smith's paper, which I found very helpful. The only real criticism I have is that it speaks too delicately about what have become, over the last decade, some very emotional issues. I think Mr. Burgstaller helped move us away from the delicate phrasing with his comments, talking about the perspective that he had as a positive intelligence collector and Chief of Station, and some of the real-life issues that he faced in dealing with the old centralized CI staff.

From what little I know, the question that Mr. Smith deals with, the centralized line organization versus the decentralized staff is one that produced a great deal of internal tension, which has increasingly erupted into public discussion. The aftershocks from some of those debates are still very much with us.

Mr. Burgstaller makes clear what many people have observed: that from the viewpoint of intelligence collectors, the "old regime"—with its powerful, elite, centralized CI staff and very strong continuity of leadership—gave counterintelligence an inordinate kind of power. Clearly, some of these people would applaud the more recent change to the decentralized approach, feeling that this shift has helped restore a balance that was previously skewed.

I should say here that in the end, I think I agree with Mr. Smith; while you can make a case for the decentralized approach, recent evidence shows that it hasn't been working very well, and that a return to the old system may be warranted.

The second point that I want to make about Mr. Smith's paper is that while he is talking about the exotic work of an intelligence service, the issue that he is discussing—this question of centralized versus decentralized organization—is a classic, almost mundane management problem. The CIA is certainly not the first organization that has had to cope with this kind of management issue. Nor is it the first organization that has had to worry about individuals who held tenure for long periods of time and developed bitter rivalries. These are problems that arise every day in virtually every type of business.

I tried to think of a simple analogy for the CIA's organizational dilemma, and I came up with the following: Every corporation has a bunch of gung-ho division and plant managers out in the field, who are eager to invest a lot of money in new facilities and drum up new markets for their products. Hopefully, back at headquarters, the company also has a cadre of very disciplined accountants—skeptical, nasty accountants—who look at the plans that are brought in from the field and say, "This is scandalous. I can't believe these managers want to waste our money like this."

That kind of tension is in every business, and I think most businesses would want it to be there. That is the way the system is supposed to work.

Problems arise only if that accessory tension gets out of control, because top management has failed to keep it within constructive channels. In our hypothetical example, imagine that the plant managers in the field became bitter and began to blame the accountant back home for their own career difficulties, for the company's failures, and decided that "It's all their fault, the so-and-so's back at headquarters."

If you go beyond that, and imagine an outright revolt by the plant managers that dispersed this troublesome accounting staff away from headquarters and decentralized its functions, you can get a sense of how that could be a shattering experience, for any organization. And some of that disarray seems to have actually afflicted the CIA. In our example, the obvious answer is that superior management talent is needed at the top to reconcile the tension that is built into the situation. Sometimes that sound management has existed in the intelligence communtiy. Sometimes it manifestly hasn't.

In preparing these remarks, I consulted a former director who would be held in high esteem in this room and asked, "What is the best solution to the built-in tension between counterintelligence and positive intelligence? How can it be dealt with?"

He responded as follows: "It helps to think of the organization as if it's a court. In a courtroom, you would never want to dispense with either the prosecutor arguing his case or the defense lawyer rebutting it. They are both essential. If either was absent, the likelihood that you would reach the truth through the process would be reduced. But, in a sense, the key person isn't the prosecutor or defense; it is the judge who has to sit in judgment on the arguments and reach some decision in the end."

Again, sometimes that process seems to have worked in intelligence, where good decisions were reached by wise judges, and sometimes it hasn't.

I think the third issue that Mr. Smith raises is the question of continuity of leadership. We're all aware of the specific individual who dominated CIA counterintelligence for 20 years, but we can deal with the question in the abstract. For this, again, is the sort of management problem that has been the subject of reams of case study literature at Harvard Business School. Setting aside the personalities involved, it is really a mundane issue.

If you allow one person to run an organization or staff within it for an extended period of time, the risk of developing internal problems is enormous. If you were at GM or GE and saw the kind of continuity by such a strong personality, you would inevitably worry about detrimental effects. One typical management response, which was suggested in an earlier session, would be to rotate people in and out of that entrenched unit. And I suppose, generally speaking, that is a good idea. What you need, using Mr. Smith's phrase, is to avoid becoming "inbred" or "over the hill." As was said yesterday, speaking specifically about the counterintelligence function, "People who do this job for too long tend to lose their judgment."

The dilemma is that precisely because the need for an institutional memory is so special in counterintelligence work, counterintelligence may have a special need for management continuity.

Let's suppose that understanding the counterintelligence continuum required a careful, detailed reading of some 20 ''nut cases,'' which would show how the CI story had unfolded over several decades. Unfortunately, reading and mastering this case material might require nearly a decade. If so, the notion that you want to rotate CI people in and out, and follow sound, modern management theory, constantly ventilating the organization, may miss the point. By shuffling personnel, you might produce a series of eager management teams, none of which fully understood the work they were doing.

In my own business we have the same sort of dilemma. Reporters are supposed to be rotated frequently. Hopefully, for example, I will soon be rotated away from ever having to worry about intelligence coverage again. But there are some other parts of the *Wall Street Journal* which require continuity.

For example, we have an editor in New York who has been on the news desk for thirty years. Three decades of copy have flowed past him in an endless river. Every time a steel company raises prices or whatever, he has seen it happen thirty, maybe sixty times before. He knows exactly what it's worth. He knows how long the story should be, what should be in it, what kind of headline it should carry. He has seen it all; he has seen the whole range of the things that any organization cares about over and over again, and so he is able to exercise a quality of judgment that would be impossible if we were rotating people in and out of that job.

When I think about my own experience in a completely different sort of work, I'm willing to accept the possiblity that counterintelligence may be a special case, in which there may be reasons to avoid the normal management-rotation principle. Again, you need a wise judge on top who can decide how long is too long for someone to stay in one job.

I have one brief comment about Mr. Pratt's paper, which I though was generally excellent. I think that many outsiders might endorse his call for a genuinely ''clandestine'' service, and for pruning the other functions that have gathered around the CIA so as to preserve that clandestine role.

One simple step would be to abolish the name ''Central Intelligence Agency'' and the initials ''CIA,'' which today seem to exert a voodoo-like fascination for journalists, for Iranian mullahs and for half the world. Everybody might be a lot better off if that name and those initials disappeared forever from the landscape.

But, obviously, Mr. Pratt is talking about something a lot more subtle than that, and I think that he has sidestepped the heart of the problem. You could indeed create a "new" clandestine service but, to make this effort meaningful, you would have to solve the "old" problem of cover. No matter where you put this new organization, no matter how you initially hide it, how do you propose to hide each of your operatives? I don't think there are good guideposts in Mr. Pratt's paper to help solve that problem. My own sense is that, partly because of nosy newspaper reporters like me, cover is going to remain a very difficult problem.

Let me conclude by speaking just a moment about journalism because I know the press has bothered many of you over the years. I think that our contribution to a healthy American intelligence system will probably be quite limited—and that is putting it mildly. But I do think that, strange as it seems, the experience of the intelligence community over the last decade is showing that the First Amendment actually does work.

The costs of its working may seem to some of you too severe to bear. I hope not. But it has been my experience that a debate about intelligence that started off anarchic and vicious—as debates generally do—has ended up yielding a kind of balance. Today, journalists and the public they reach are more sympathetic to the missions of intelligence and more prepared to endorse the kinds of legislative steps that intelligence wants. In other words, out of the anarchic process of public debate, there is developing a national consensus that probably will support the kinds of things that the people in this room would like to see. Absent the anarchic discussion that we have had, I am not sure that that consensus could have been produced.

General Discussion

The discussion ranged widely, but continually returned to the central question: to what extent should the relationship between positive intelligence and counterintelligence be adversarial.

Several former intelligence officials from different countries treated the problem of cover and agreed that effective deep cover for the clandestine services is difficult and expensive but quite possible and worthwhile to achieve. One former official refered to a study done by his agency which found there had been very few difficulties with the sort of "fig leaf" cover afforded to officers and embassies, and few with the "suits of armor" given to ones under deep cover.

Rather trouble had arisen when something in between was tried. Another former official said that many of the adversary's successes in CI had come from lax security practices by American officers who feel too safe in countries of the free world.

Several former intelligence officials discussed at length whether there was such a thing as a *deformation professionnelle* which sooner or later would render career counterintelligence officers too skeptical to do their jobs. They agreed that great skepticism of one's own intelligence is necessary to do an effective job of CI, but argued that such skepticism could become detached from facts and become simply habitual or based on differences in personalities. CI officers whose job it is to question their colleagues' successes ought to intermingle professionally with them, by means of frequent transfers in order to minimize the role which personal conflict might play in their dealings. Another former officer thought that personal gamesmanship can and does intrude into all professional relationships, and that it is therefore a mistake to take more precautions against it with regard to counterintelligence than with regard to any other professional speciality. A third former official reiterated Mr. Ignatius' point that the relationship between positive and counterintelligence is akin to that of the defense and the prosecution in a courtroom. The key element in that relationship, he said, is the judge. Thus, he concluded the fruitfulness of the relationship between positive and CI is the responsibility of the CIA's top leadership.

A congressional staffer agreed with the courtroom analogy, but he argued that even the judge is not so importnat to what happens in a courtroom as is the entity which defines and assigns their peculiar role to the prosecution, the defense, and the judge. He argued that one must expect tension, both professional and personal, between officers engaged in positive and counterintelligence, but that one must therefore structure that conflict so that it will not end in the final defeat of one or the final victory of another side, but will be both continuing and constructive. He suggested the example of the United States Constitution, which had established the several branches of government so that they would continually conflict, but also so that all would survive each conflict and continue to check one another. A former intelligence officer disagreed, saying that no conflict should exist, and that if a CI officer explains that logic of his arguments to the positive collector or analyst whose judgment he is questioning, cooperation would result. When questioned as to why destructive quarrels had broken out in CIA between CI and other parts of the agency, this officer suggested that perhaps he had not been persuasive enough. Another former officer suggested that it took uncommon leadership to engender cooperation for two decades between CI and other parts of CIA, and that when that uncommon leadership ceased to be there, personal factors were allowed to predominate, and disaster occurred.

A conferee with executive experience in intelligence reasserted the need to structure our intelligence system so that when conflict occurs it stays within constructive channels. Another conferee with executive experience asked what would have happened had the designer and program manager for some of our most sophisticated satellite collection systems been confronted by Harris' thesis that those systems could well have been used by the Soviet Union to pass along disinformation. Mr. Smith and the conferee agreed that the particular individual involved would have eagerly investigated the possibility. But both agreed that this individual would be possessed of unusual doses of courage and integrity, and that the system ought not to depend for its normal functioning upon persons who possess abnormal virtues.

A former intelligence officer stated that our entire intelligence system depends on every officer being honest. A congressional staffer countered that honesty is not at the heart of the question. Rather, he said, everyone's habits, interests and propensities tend to shade their judgment. The purpose of the system should be regularly and continually to juxtapose each judgment so that the whole may be served. He contended that the juxtapositions have been less regular, less fruitful, and more destructive than need be the case.

CHAPTER EIGHT

Building for a New Counterintelligence Capability: Recruitment and Training

---

Paper:

Kenneth E. deGraffenreid

Discussants:

Dr. Robert Nisbet

Mr. Lawrence McWilliams

The question of what kinds of personnel should be recruited and how they should be trained to meet the needs of a new counterintelligence (CI) for the 1980's quite obviously presumes some agreement as to the need for an enhanced counterintelligence. But so far in the Congress and the intelligence community itself, there has been little agreement even to strengthen incrementally the sort of counterintelligence being done today. Much less is there commitment to a kind of strategic, multidisciplinary counterintelligence specifically designed to meet the total worldwide foreign intelligence threat to the United States.

CI recruiting and training are today almost certainly inadequate even for the narrowly defined mission that has been given to the CI entities. They do not even begin to address the needs of a national program of strategic multidisciplinary counterintelligence.

To be sure, there has been some tentative and isolated recognition of the need for better CI in the last year or so. But the definition of CI within the US government is too narrow to comprehend the kinds of things that would have to be done to meet the challenge of the 1980's. Currently CIA views counterintelligence as limited to providing support to CIA foreign intelligence operations. CIA has removed from the CI staff many of its traditional functions, such as the study of the international communist movement. Responsibility for collecting on international terrorism has also been removed from the CI function. Of course, counterterrorism is usually the function of the internal security services with which CI liaison officers cooperate.

The CI organization itself has been changed to that of a decentralized staff function in which each geographical unit is responsible for its own CI and each case officer responsible for his own CI awareness. The level of experience has also declined sharply. Following the firings and resignations resulting from the so-called Halloween massacre of 1978, virtually all of the CI specialists, and particularly those who had directed the CI operation for the previous twenty-five years, were gone. Above all, CIA does not believe it is responsible for meeting the total counterintelligence threat to the United States. Thus, under the CIA's view of its job, there is little need to analyze various approaches to the recruitment and training for the CI services. CIA is firing CI specialists, not recruiting them.

The FBI, on the other hand, while ostensibly elevating its foreign counterintelligence mission to the highest priority, has failed to increase the manpower or resources committed to CI despite a massive increase in espionage from the Soviet Union and from the increasing number of hostile states. Likewise, within the counterintelligence units of the military services, where the mission had rarely been more than tactical, counterintelligence functions have been deemphasized and reduced and files destroyed. The word has been passed that "counterintelligence can only get you in trouble."

Furthermore, it must be noted that neither the CI staff, the FBI's Intelligence Division, nor the military services have even gone outside their respective organizations specifically in search of people from civilian life with particular aptitudes, skills, or affinity for CI *per se* who would become CI specialists. Career CI officers of the CIA, FBI, and military services have come from the same pool as do other intelligence officers within their respective organizations. Following the pattern of the agencies as a whole, they are almost invariably volunteers.

Likewise, training for CI has tended to follow narrow lines, focusing essentially on the most basic counterespionage techniques and tradecraft. Formal CI training courses for career CI officers in both the FBI and the CIA are quite brief. Certain military CI training courses, while more lengthy, are even more narrow in focus, reflecting the limited function of the military CI effort. For many of the skills necessary to CI, little or no formal training is offered. For example, in-depth historical studies of counterintelligence cases for the purpose of isolating methods of operation are seldom formally undertaken. By contrast, the KGB's Juridical Institute of the Second Chief Directorate (Internal Security) is a four-year course in internal security and counterintelligence. And it must be remembered that those who had acquired this knowledge through experience are now in retirement and therefore unable to pass on this information. Also, there is no formal specialized training for CI officers on those technical collection systems often referred to as "National Technical Means" (NTM) of intelligence monitoring. Remarkably, few personnel in the FBI or even within the CIA clandestine service possess the security clearances necessary to have detailed knowledge of these highly compartmented systems.

Thus it seems clear that any discussion of recruiting and training for a new counterintelligence capability to meet the difficult and troublesome world of the 1980's must necessarily assume that a decision had been made to develop a national CI program whose broader scope would include NTM systems, counter-deception and protection against foreign intelligence threats, and which would cut across the jurisdictional lines of today's counterintelligence entities. In all likelihood it would include some functions now specifically excluded by the definitions contained in Executive Order 12036: i.e., personnel, document, installation, and communications security.

The mission and purposes of such a new CI would be threefold. First, in the broadest sense, identify, neutralize, and defeat the KGB's threat to the United States. That includes Soviet strategic deception of US intelligence collection systems and operations. Second, identify, neutralize, and defeat foreign intelligence efforts against US technology and the American economy. Third, to assist other elements of the intelligence community in responding to phenomena such as anti-American propaganda, terrorism, or the taking of American hostages. Such a new counterintelligence would require serious changes in the way things are done. While organizational changes might be needed, a variety of measures might do equally well. But whatever form a new CI structure might take, the most essential requirement for improved counterintelligence performance is the cultivation of a new cadre of skillful, wise, and dedicated CI experts and practitioners. Because this cadre for the most part does not presently exist, the role of recruiting and training is crucial.

A strategic multidisciplinary CI program will require a number of diverse practical skills. Most obvious is scientific and technical expertise. In spite of the shift in American intelligence to overwhelming reliance on technical collection systems, CI is today almost solely concerned with human intelligence operations and what might be termed classical espionage. There is currently virtually no application of CI procedures and analysis to the field of technical collection. As a result, there will be an immediate need for a large number of scientific and technical specialists who can provide the expertise for applying CI to the vast and complex realm of technical collection. An increase in the technical expertise allotted to CI would also benefit classical counterespionage. Heretofore it has suffered because it has generally made insufficient use of technical systems to check its hypotheses. Morever, the CI organizations have not possessed the technical expertise necessary for identifying and neutralizing foreign intelligence collection against US technology. Indeed, the US intelligence community at present lacks the structure, direction, and knowledge necessary even to guage the total foreign intelligence effort against US technology. At present there is not even a centrally-directed effort to protect US weapons from compromise during their development cycle from design through operational deployment. Any future MDCI effort would require a number of personnel with a high degree of technical expertise in the process by which weapons systems are developed and marketed.

Within the more classical CI functions, there is also a requirement for strengthening the basic professional skills of research and analysis. Long-term scholarly research that stresses painstaking attention to detail, to historical trends, and to *modus operandi* must be restored. Information and data processing specialists may be of assistance here, but the need now as always is for professional scholars who can master facts and relationships. On the operational side, there is increasing need to emphasize particular detective and investigative skills that are somewhat different than those of the foreign intelligence case officer and more akin to techniques developed for investigations of large-scale narcotics traffic or organized crime.

Among the most critical and difficult tasks facing the US intelligence community is the detection of strategic or geopolitical deception. Edward Jay Epstein, in a paper previously presented to this Consortium (published in *Intelligence Requirements for the 1980's:* Volume II, *Analysis and Estimates*) has usefully described two varieties of strategic deception. The first involves camouflage and concealment and aims at misleading an adversary with regard to an observable set of data. The second aims at distorting the interpretation of the meaning of the pattern of data that is received, rather than concealing or disguising the observable data itself. The latter is designed to mislead or confuse the adversary's cognitive processes. Because the success of deception depends on our sticking to conventional patterns of interpreting data, detection of deception could well benefit from what might be termed "studied unconventional thinking." Thus, following Epstein, it would seem wise to use cryptologists, game theorists, and even paranoids, confidence men, magicians, and financial swindlers to try to generate alternative explanations for perceived events.

To this list might be added theoretical physicists, mathematicians, and others who deal with systematic but unconventional thought. This is not to say that paranoia or a conviction for fraud ought to be made a prerequisite for employment in CI. But it does mean that a wider mix of skills and talents is needed. Finally, if counter-sabotage and counterterrorist functions are to be included within a new CI framework and a CI action capability mounted, there may be need for certain commando or unconventional warfare skills.

However, the truly essential skills required for CI are really qualitative. Skepticism, a well-developed historical understanding, an uncommon attention to detail, an almost tedious thoroughness, and a capacity for unconventional thinking are the ingredient qualities required for CI research and analysis. Furthermore, those who direct and carry out CI operations must also possess a strong competitive streak, imagination, gamesmanship, and a large measure of intellectual creativity.

The gathering of persons with these talents will not guarantee an effective and successful counterintelligence capability any more than will a new organizational structure. For above all else, American intelligence suffers from a lack of clear purpose and a lack of understanding of our adversaries. Technical skills and expertise in whatever abundance will not suffice to give the new CI the kind of direction it needs. Rather, it must be staffed and directed by those with strategic vision and for whom the adversary presents a competitive challenge that summons up a fighting spirit. Good counterintelligence, in short, demands wise, clever, and competitive people.

Certainly all these qualities remain ideals and can be measured and evaluated only subjectively. One cannot expect to staff any organization with ideal types alone. Nevertheless, people with these attributes are employed every day in other sectors of American society and are to be found all across this country. In fact no one can seriously doubt that this nation contains a large pool of all the skills, qualities, and attitudes necessary to establish a serious CI capability. During the Second World War, intelligence personnel were drawn from this nation-wide pool. In spite of a number of problems, it is possible to do so again. Today counterintelligence must compete for its personnel with other sectors of American society as well as with other areas of the government and other parts of the intelligence community.

Most immediately, the majority of those with the scientific and technical skills necessary to a serious CI capability must come from the government, particularly from the intelligence community and from among the career uniformed and civilian specialists of the military services. Many of these skills, notably those of the technical collection specialists, are esoteric and can come only from the intelligence community. But those technical specialists going into CI must be ones who have thoroughly appreciated the limitations and vulnerabilities as well as the strengths of the technical collection systems. One thinks here of the difficulty shown by some within the national intelligence community during the recent SALT debate in grasping the issues raised by Amrom Katz and others concerning the Soviet ability to cheat while avoiding detection by NTM systems.

Other necessary technical skills could well come from those within the military accustomed to working with full-threat analysis. Although such analysis is not popular even within the military, several US weapons systems are considered so vital that painstaking efforts have been made to protect their operational security. Those with such experience—for example, submarine officers, or SAC strategic planning specialists, or those with general operations security expertise—could be expected to understand counterintelligence and to contribute to positive improvement. Likewise, those who are engaged in the cat and mouse game of electronic countermeasures warfare often develop a cast of mind that could be useful in CI analysis. Also, within the services could be found most of the paramilitary or commando skills required for some types of counterterrorist capabilities.

However, it is immediately obvious that many, if not most, of the qualities that are needed for an aggressive and effective CI are not those which fare well in standard bureaucratic structures. Counterintelligence is a troublesome thing for an intelligence bureaucracy because its natural function is to question, to challenge, and to speculate. If CI works well, it naturally antagonizes the regularity, predictability, managerial tidiness, and agency (or even divisional) loyalties or viewpoints that are the very bones of bureaucracy. Also, it is true that for a variety of reasons, events of the last few years have discouraged energetic, competitive people from entering the military or the intelligence services. It is, therefore, in the private sector that we may expect to find many of those with the desired skills.

The academy has long been an important source of personnel for the intelligence community, especially for counterintelligence. Distinguished scholars with a variety of specialties must again be actively recruited. Their skills were invaluable to the World War II effort, and the need for them is greater today.

In spite of increasing bureaucratization and regulation, the business sector today contains the largest supply of bright, aggressive, and imaginative people who could make a significant contribution to improving counterintelligence. For example, the advertising industry, marketing firms, and the sales groups of a number of retail industries employ some of the nation's most operationally creative and talented people. Managers in these highly competitive markets consistently search for those with innovative ideas and the ability to apply them to aggressive sales campaigns involving the use of advertising (i.e., propaganda and deception), salesmanship, maneuver, and long-term strategic thinking. Significantly these strategies often aim quite simply at winning. Many of these people see themselves as engaged in a high-pressure, competitive, adversarial game being played for high stakes. These businesses routinely make use of sophisticated technical support measures such as data processing and operations research techniques while at the same time focusing on the less tangible and more political factors that influence the marketplace. They formulate hypotheses, test them, carry out operations, and don't stay in business unless they prove to be right. This mix of skills, attitudes, and motivations is precisely the one that could be useful in CI operations. A similar example is the electronics industry where intense competition occurs in some of the most sophisticated areas of high technology. Not only are these firms often engaged in defense and intelligence related work, but also they employ aggressive marketing strategies and techniques. The technical collection branches have long made use of experts from these industries; CI should now turn to this source for advice and for personnel.

There are other areas of the private sector where unique talents may be found. One that is not often considered as a talent source is the American labor movement. Traditionally labor leaders have possessed talents and experience developed in a highly competitive environment. They employ such skills as recruitment, persuasion, and propaganda and are possessed of a competitive world view as well as an established long-term adversary. They are familiar with lengthy struggles and often are not strangers to political manipulations that could provide excellent training for understanding the complex schemes of international politics.

A careful examination of other industries and professions would doubtless uncover many other sources of persons whose education and outlook could usefully be brought to bear on the strategic CI problem.

The recruitment of personnel from the sources suggested here would, of course, represent a radical departure from current practice. The bureaucratic structure and procedures of the US government would present severe obstacles to the employment of many of these people. Most significantly, the proposed new approach to quality recruitment would seek to attract the experienced and the accomplished rather than those just entering their professional lives. Presently, virtually all recruitment of professionals for the intelligence community occurs among young graduates of colleges or graduate or professional schools. Technically skilled personnel are usually recruited from among those who have received their formal training in the military services and have completed one tour of duty. The current practice, of course, is to look for those wishing to begin a full career. For certain skills and positions, however, the new approach would concentrate on those already pursuing their careers outside the intelligence field. The goal would be to attract mature individuals with the desired attributes to the counterintelligence profession in mid-career.

Putting aside for the moment the question of how such persons might be induced to make such a change, there are obvious and severe difficulties with this approach. Training, pay, advancement, and managerial practices are all dependent on the standard full-career pattern. Presently, young trainees enter government service following their formal education and acquire increased professional and managerial responsibilities and compensation as they gain experience and seniority. The permissible number in each grade-level is strictly controlled. Usually, the generalist and the manager advance most quickly. The new approach would involve bringing in highly qualified and highly paid individuals to serve tours as high ranking specialists. Opposition could be expected to be fierce.

Nevertheless, I believe that these and other problems could be solved. The cost of some career dislocation and of considerable trouble for personnel managers would be worth the gain to be derived from attracting skillful and competitive minds to a national CI effort. Clearly, this was the case in World War II. Moreover, there are several factors suggesting that such a new recruiting philosophy might be easier to adopt today than in the past. Today second careers are not uncommon. Indeed, the government itself has absorbed a sizeable number of retired military personnel who have then distinguished themselves as civilians. The intelligence community itself has made extensive use of this talent pool.

Also within some of the most successful and competitive business firms, it is now possible to find relatively young people who have reached top positions but who also have reached something of a creative plateau. Seeing nothing ahead but positions that take them farther away from operational assignments, they often are ready to apply their talents to new interests or careers. Such persons might not make CI a career but perhaps could enter laterally and remain for several years. They might be expected to bring, for example, some of the freshness of approach and alternate viewpoints that the President's Foreign Intelligence Advisory Board and the "B Team" brought to the national intelligence estimating process. The use of such temporary or "reserve" employees might be limited somewhat by security considerations, because many CI activities and particular operations are among the most highly compartmented in intelligence.

The most significant problem, however, is to attract these people to a career in counterintelligence once they have been located. How would this be accomplished? First, as has been indicated, the new approach to recruiting would have to be aggressive and would most likely be similar to the type of senior executive recruiting used by the American business community. Most persons outside the government would be located in this way. While this system would be time consuming and relatively expensive, it is perhaps the only way to locate those with certain of the less tangible but more important attributes.

Second, once located using criteria based on the general requirements, appeals to these individuals would have to be forcefully presented in view of the severe pay differential between the private sector and the government. Of course, attempts must be made to raise the pay levels, although not necessarily the grade structure, of the intelligence agencies. As a rule, the intelligence community, particularly within the military agencies, has suffered a one-to-two grade level disadvantage in comparison with the rest of the government. Pay raises here would help attract those presently working in government. On the other hand, for certain professions, such as the academic, government salaries are relatively high. For other sectors, particularly the business community, however, the new CI could not expect to compete for talent on the basis of monetary compensation. Appeals to other motivations must be made. Although it is often unfashionable to acknowledge the role of simple patriotism in motivating people, most Americans still feel a deep love of country. A number of people would come in if convinced that they could thereby tangibly help their country.

And some people simply thrive on challenge and competition. For them it may be necessary only to demonstrate the totality of the intelligence threat facing the United States. If it is true that the current US counterintelligence community does not quite realize what it is up against, it is also true that most Americans live in blissful ignorance of KGB and other foreign intelligence activities. Many citizens remain suspicious of Soviet activities. But a detailed explanation of the magnitude of the challenge could be expected to activate the reflexes of a weathered problem-solving executive. Many could be motivated for a career in CI if the degree of personal challenge and the worthiness of the enterprise were demonstrated. They must be shown that the CI problem would require the fullest use of their talent. Finally, the esprit of a new CI organization must be clear to the prospective employee. He must know that the people in the organization believe that what they are doing is worthwhile, that they are competent, and that they are capable of winning.

The question of what kind of training would be appropriate to a new CI capability is somewhat easier to answer. Among the first rules of intelligence (or of warfare for that matter) is to know your enemy. That must be the guiding purpose of a new CI training program. Formal training of the highest quality must be greatly expanded. Lengthy study of what is known of leading CI cases would provide the best method for training new recruits. Because the Soviets remain the primary adversary, formal CI training, in addition to traditional tradecraft, must focus on an in-depth study of the KGB, the GRU, and Soviet Bloc services and their predecessors. This training would not be complete without a high degree of familiarity with Soviet and Communist foreign policy and revolutionary action. Such courses, adequately drawing on all sources of intelligence data, do not now exist and would have to be created. Furthermore, they would have to be constantly updated and revised as new information bearing on old cases was developed. The research and analysis function would, therefore, play a significant role in the training and education of newly recruited CI officers.

Second, formal and extensive language training will be required. While the entire intelligence community suffers from a lack of language-trained personnel, this skill is particularly necessary for certain CI activities. High quality language training similar to that which used to be given by the Army at Oberammergau is surely required for the research and analysis staff as well as many operational officers.

Third, in order to achieve a serious CI capability, most CI personnel will require extensive technical training, especially on US and foreign technical collection systems. A general education program on the technical characteristics of US and allied collection and weapons systems targeted by foreign intelligence services must begin immediately. Likewise, technical specialists must be initiated into the world of CI, to its rationale and its tradecraft.

Finally, training and practical exercises in unconventional analysis and deception techniques should be added to the formal training courses for all CI personnel. In some ways, Americans are particularly vulnerable to deception which concentrates on their particular world view, and such awareness training could be helpful here.

Training for the new CI will be expensive and lengthy, especially at first. But it must be undertaken. In sum, training for a new CI capability must be thorough and intellectually vigorous. It must above all else educate people for a practical skill in a tough world.

Many of the suggestions presented here may prove to be difficult to implement, but the concept that underlies them is sound: to foster a broad, thorough, clever, and competitive approach to the foreign intelligence threat to the United States posed by its revolutionary adversaries.

Discussants

Dr. Robert Nisbet: Intelligence agencies, like any corporation, are in need of as much character—and I use that word in its old-fashioned middle-class sense—as they can get. Someone suggested that the recent revelations of Marchetti, Agee, and Snepp might be explained in terms of "male menopause." But I would interpret their behavior somewhat less charitably. It seems to me these men are simply venal. Intelligence agencies are just as much in need of character as AT&T or IBM or any of the other corporations whose executives I have occasionally sat down and talked with.

Our speaker referred to the duty, the heavy obligation, of discriminating, intelligent recruitment—and I won't repeat what he had to say. But I will refine the "out there," the private sector, and tell you that I think it is possible that the CIA through its history has made rather more use of recruits from the prestige universities, the Ivy League, than it should have made. In the event that you have been dazzled by Harvard and Yale or Berkeley or Wisconsin, I'd like to suggest you give a thought to a different area of academe.

I was Phi Beta Kappa National Visiting Scholar several years ago, and for the first time in my life I visited 15 or 20 colleges and universities that were very different than any I had ever been in. I was thoroughly familiar with the atmosphere of a Berkeley or a Princeton or Columbia. I was not, however, prepared for universities and colleges like Yeshiva in New York, Brigham Young University in Utah, Augustana College, Grinnell, and others. I am particularly directing your attention to the religious colleges and universities. I don't know of any religious college or university that has national stature, that appears high on the ranking lists of colleges and universities, but I became convinced that the young men and young women I met during the course of that year represent perhaps the best pool of good character traits in the country. There is never certainty of recruiting character, good character, but you should go to the areas where the probabilities are highest.

I have said in board rooms and conference rooms and corporations many times that if, as is quite possible, moral character as well as physical strength and a sufficient degree of intelligence is important, I would, with all admiration, with all historical gratitude to Harvard University and the University of California, Berkeley, suggest recruiting at Brigham Young or at Yeshiva. I have also suggested recruiting in areas that are heavily populated, for example, by the American Polish community, Roman Catholic Poles. It is not the ethnicity. It is not the religiosity that is in any way a factor; other ethnic groups would do as well. But it is important to get individuals who come from families that have become middle-class more or less recently, are proud of it, and are determined to maintain middle-class values to the limit of their ability, and to pound these values into their children.

Out in the universities the young people who supplied the recruits for the bombings and the riotings and the demonstrations in the 1960's were overwhelmingly children who had become bored by middle-class values. They had become bored by middle-class values because their parents had. And you will find more devotion today to the middle-class values that are absolutely fundamental to any organization—whether it is IBM, CIA, or a university—in certain ethnic or minority groups that have only recently achieved the proud level of middle-class status. There you are also likely to find the motivation to succeed and to make the agencies succeed. I don't think you will have much success in stimulating a motivation by glowing words about the Agency or the Bureau when your audience is bored by the very notion of success. Your best hope, I would say, is simply to pull your human materials whence the highest probability exists of finding a natural, instant response to the kind of values upon which an intelligence community simply has to be founded.

Mr. Lawrence McWilliams: While I cannot argue against any specific thing Mr. deGraffenreid has said, I feel as though he is talking of a wartime situation, a sort of "pie-in-the-sky" picture that we are never going to achieve. And I realize that while he said some facets of it may not be achievable, I believe a lot of it is not achievable. I feel he failed to take into account that a lot of the brains in the recruitment that he spoke about already exists in the intelligence community. I can't see, in the matter of national technical collection, for example, that the CIA or FBI should go out and hire a physicist or mathematician or whatever, then teach him CI, so that he will in turn teach a man of equal talent how to spot deception or disinformation. The CIA and FBI don't need CI help. They are thoroughly aware of what deception can do to their technical collection.

So while I feel we have to increase our skills, I do not believe we should build up a monolithic CI organization that ends up being worse than the separate entities we have right now.

One improvement we *can* make in the community—and in the last several years it has improved immensely—is more coordination. Right at the present time FBI training, for example, starts off with everybody being equal. We go out to all segments of society. Dr. Nisbet said, "Stay away from Harvard," or, "Don't put emphasis on Harvard." The FBI has never put emphasis on Harvard. He also mentioned Poles. We are all equal, but we are all from different facets of society, all different ethnic backgrounds, all different educations. It is not unusual these days to have Ph.D.'s coming in as agents.

There has been an argument within the organization: should we go out deliberately and try to get these individuals and bring them into CI? We say no. Because the basis of counterintelligence in the United States starts off, first, with a good investigator. That is the essence of it, a good investigator. No matter how well you do in collecting information from technical means, let's say, or developing an informant or a defector or an agent-in-place within the Soviet Embassy, if you don't have investigative skills you are going to blow the whole operation in nothing flat. So what happens within our organization—and I can speak basically only of that—is that these men come in. They have to go through the gamut of various operations. It used to be that in the long run they would sometimes drift into CI, or sometimes be dragooned into CI.

It is a different kettle of fish now. We now have training programs that are much more advanced than we ever had, let's say, seven or eight years ago. We solicit the field officers, every field officer in the country, for men who want to get into the field. This is not a one or two-year man. It could be up to seven or ten years' experience; he might be a Ph.D. from any ethnic background—it could be anyone. If he wants to come into CI we bring him to headquarters and start giving him specialized training.

Now, we have the basis of a good investigator to start with. That man has been out in the field long enough to conduct a couple of thousand interviews. He's dealt with drug dealers, with pimps, with everything imaginable. He has learned a little about the good and bad of life, the con artist, the sharpies, the gamblers. He has also, through these interviews, we hope, developed a certain instinct as to who is telling the truth and who is telling a lie. It is hard to define, but some develop an amazing capability to make such difficult determinations. These are the sorts of people we get in the CI field.

But the point I am trying to make is that while I cannot argue against any one thing in the paper, I just feel it is *so* futuristic that it cannot deal with the practicalities of the present.

My contention, I repeat, is that I believe a tremendous amount of our knowledge, our experience, is already in government in the FBI, in other agencies. Why can't we exchange it more?

In the matter of training, at one time within the FBI if we brought a CIA officer over to talk to us he probably wouldn't get out of the building in one piece! Now they come over in droves. And we go over to see them. Or we bring in the military, or the State Department. We bring in Soviet and Czech defectors. We utilize men who are already investigators and try to teach them as much as we can. But we don't give them a tremendous amount of history. We consider it a waste of time. If a man isn't interested enough—let's say he is assigned to work on Soviet operations—if he is not interested enough to start studying beyond what we teach him, maybe two or three days into the course, we haven't got the right man. You will find most of them become near scholars in it. They get really interested.

I have also heard, on the matter of CI, that it is considered one of the lowest rungs in the FBI. When I first came into it—and I happened to be in New York in my second office and they wanted to put me in the CI field—I had to have a special clearance from headquarters. If I had had just one mark against me, I couldn't get into it. It was elitist at that time. Unfortunately, it slid down. But at the same time you will find that three-quarters of the men that are in the field are still dedicated. They want to remain in the field.

We tried a career program, just for CI officers, to possibly handle the people we are talking about, to advance them in CI, and so on. Unfortunately, the way the Bureau is constructed—and a lot of people seem to forget this—we are only a part of what really is a police organization. Our head has never been a CI officer or an intelligence officer. He is an administrator. He's got to look after other branches. So we tried to make it separate; but it wouldn't work with the administrators. Fortunately, in the last few years with the DCI, we have a separate budget. Before that we never even had one. Now we have an intelligence budget which the criminal side cannot touch. That is progress, and these are facts of life the FBI has to face.

But I'd like to say this: The majority of the men that I worked with for many, many years love it—their love of CI transcended their ambitions, and they want above all to stay in CI. We have never really had a problem of dropouts. If they defect, it's in the first year or two or three, and then you go back and find out they were dragooned in and someone says, "You're going to Washington." But on the whole we don't face that problem.

Mr. deGraffenreid mentioned that the KGB gives four years of training to their intelligence officers. There is no doubt about that; they give them more sometimes. The fact is, they take them out of high school. The CIA and FBI take them out of the universities. But I would never use a Communist intelligence service as a model for a US service. I feel, with the independent thinking we have, that we are very much better off if we devise our own methods. And I think we have been fairly successful in the main.

I agree we need improvements. But I do not want to see the intelligence community so intellectualized that you forget that fellow that just wants to be an investigator. At the FBI we used to say, "Where on earth are the cops?" In other words, if everybody starts becoming ambitious, everybody wants to get to the top. In the end, there are no cops to catch crooks. The same is true in the CI field. There are many who want to remain, and it is the basis of counterintelligence within the US. I cannot talk about the sophistication of the Agency or the military needing scholars to the degree that Mr. deGraffenreid maintains. But in our field we do have analytical people—which is a relatively new innovation of the last five or six years. We never had analysis *per se* in the CI field. Now we have analytical units. But we coordinate a tremendous amount of that with other agencies. If we obtain scientific information, and we don't have the capability to understand it, we go to the CIA or the NSA.

I think we can improve the entire community if we develop this coordination to a greater degree. I'd like to see, as an example, a military CI officer brought into the FBI for a year or two, or a CIA officer brought in there for a two-year period to work in counterintelligence. The British do that. MI6 officers work in MI5, and vice versa. They get to know one another and understand one another. I think that would be a step forward. But we haven't yet achieved that in the US intelligence community.

General Discussion

Mr. deGraffenreid began by reasserting the need for an organization to do central counterintelligence analysis for the US government. Mr. McWilliams agreed that central CI analysis is needed and that the community once had something very close to it "until they destroyed it."

A conferee then criticized Mr. McWilliams' presentation for being limited by the horizon of the FBI's current and past practices. What is needed, said the conferee, is a greater willingness to learn from the experiences of foreign organizations and from the actual requirements of the job we have to do.

A current official of the intelligence community tried to define counterintelligence in ways that he hoped might be acceptable to current officials of the FBI, the CIA, and the CI components of the Department of Defense.

There was also a brief exchange on the question of which professions are most likely to produce people capable of spotting untrue statements. The participants agreed that those who most often use deception are likely to be most adept at recognizing it.

CHAPTER NINE

Legal Constraints and Incentives

Paper:

Arnold Beichman

and

Roy Godson

Discussants:

Professor Antonin Scalia

Dr. James Q. Wilson

Introduction

The law is not limited to prescribing "magisterial" standards for society. Statutes, executive orders, judicial decisions, and other acts of government having the force of law also shape society by providing subtle and not-so-subtle incentives for individuals both in and out of government to behave in certain ways. This paper seeks to examine the incentives now operating on people working in the field of counterintelligence. Based on our research to date, it appears that in order to foster success in US counterintelligence, quite different incentives ought to be operating. Our thesis is that, in recent years, official actions—and, just as important, inaction—at the highest levels of government have placed personal burdens on those seeking to make a success of US counterintelligence and are encouraging CI personnel to act in ways less beneficial to the United States than they might under different circumstances be inclined to do.

Success or failure in counterintelligence depends largely on the ingenuity of counterintelligence officers—their ability, for example, to notice and pursue significant anomalies in the data before them—as well as on the initiative and courage of sources of information. The quality of any counterintelligence service, then, follows almost directly from that which motivates its personnel—the CI analyst, the case officer, the agent or informant.

At the outset, we must recognize that counterintelligence contains powerful inherent disincentives to following out the logic of the CI process wherever it may lead—to question, to doubt, to serve as in-house naysayer, cynic, iconoclast, devil's advocate. It sets the CI officer apart from his own intelligence colleagues. Even the counterintelligence analyst, who is farthest removed from danger and betrayal, must constantly question the *bona fides* of sources and the validity of information that is usually hard-won and often unique.

Moreover, because he sometimes has information from defectors and sources that is not widely disseminated, he must question the judgment of other people in the intelligence community and in the government generally who rank much higher than he does.

The CI case officer's lot is even more difficult. He must decide to investigate, to surveil, to infiltrate, to carry out "experiments"—feeding data to certain results—in order to test hypotheses about whether certain persons have been deceived or used, or are actually working for the other side. The CI officer must realize that there is a good chance that any given hunch of his will turn out to be wrong and, recently in the United States, that someone will call his investigation stupid and illegal. Yet if he begins to operate on the basis of "benefit of the doubt" his usefulness is probably at an end.

The agent, source, or informant is in the most difficult position of all. If he is not in direct contact with the target of the investigation, he is liable to be accused of spying on the innocent. If he is in direct contact, any breach of security will probably cost him his reputation or his life. For example, Alex Rackley was killed some years ago when he was uncovered by the Black Panthers. Lester Dominique, a federal informant, was recently found bludgeoned, beaten with chains, and disemboweled with a machete. His name had been left inadvertently in open court documents.

In any case, the agent has to do the things required of anyone living in the environment he is penetrating. This usually is unpleasant and dangerous—and sometimes illegal. To all of this one must add the changing status of the counterintelligence operative in American life. In the 1950's his job was glorified in a television serial, "I Led Three Lives." By the 1970's some in the Establishment apparently agreed with the counterculture in deprecating the undercover man. E. Drexel Godfrey, a former senior CIA official, wrote in the January 1978 issue of *Foreign Affairs* that those in the business of corrupting others on behalf of the United States actually end up by corrupting our society. Randy Paul Young, writing in *High Times* in 1978, put this more trenchantly: "Everyone agrees that the informer waives the right to be called human and takes on the attributes of an insect, eligible only for ostracism, if not extermination."

Although details are classified, it appears that the size of the overall US CI program probably has not decreased in terms of manpower and money in recent years. Compared with the early 1970's, some parts of the CI community have been reduced (e.g., the CIA's CI staff and the FBI's domestic security program), but other parts have been augmented (e.g., the FBI's foreign counterintelligence staff and components of the Department of Defense).

Nevertheless, it is far from clear that the total resources devoted to CI are adequate for the magnitude of the tasks or that present levels of performance can meet the needs of the 1980's. The totality of the threat, as measured for example by increases in the presence of KGB and other hostile foreign operations in the United States and abroad, increased dramatically in the 1970's. (See, for example, the figures cited by Newton S. Miler in *Intelligence Requirements for the 1980's: Elements of Intelligence,* p. 51.) Moreover, perception of the threat has broadened to include technology and technical collection systems which require specially trained personnel and methods of coordinating specialists in human and technical matters.

In addition, as will be discussed, there appears to have been a decline in the ability and inclination to carry out CI in some areas. While there have been a number of reasons for this decline, it obviously cannot be due solely or primarily to the disincentives inherent in the discipline of CI: these always have been operative. Rather, it apparently is due not exclusively but in large part to the growth within both operative law and practice of positive inducements *not* to engage in the job of counterintelligence.

Specific laws, opinions of the courts, and regulations having the force of law are among the most obvious factors affecting CI operations. Some of these legal norms are clear-cut, and CI operatives now know they are not permitted to engage in activities that were considered permissible in the past. Other rules are nowhere near so clear-cut, and lawyers themselves argue about the meaning or implications of the rules and court cases. Finally, some rules were written intentionally to be vague to satisfy competing pressure groups and for other reasons. The effects, however, are the same. The CI operative has an incentive to stay safely back from the boundary of the law, especially where it is vague.

Perceptions about the rules and what is and is not expected of US CI appear to be another factor affecting performance. These perceptions may be even more important disincentives than the rules themselves. The totality—the laws, the court cases, Executive Orders, guidelines, the interpretations the CIA and other agencies make of these norms, and the hearings and statements of important legislators and their staffs—creates a legal and legislative climate that many retired CI officials and former informants indicate has been hampering performance.

This paper will first consider some of the major legal factors that seem to be affecting performance. Then it will describe some perceptual constraints on CI officers and assets. Finally, we will propose some positive regulatory incentives that might make for better performance.

It should be clear at the outset that we do not maintain that CI should be completely unencumbered by rules, standards, perhaps even by some outright prohibitions. These norms are necessary to protect the civil liberties of Americans. It is our contention, however, that the constraints and incentives that came into existence in the 1970's have been too narrowly focused—to the detriment of CI performance. We believe it is possible to devise a set of rules that can *both* assist the CI mission *and* protect civil liberties from potential abuse by the US government.

I. Legal Restrictions

We have found at least four categories of legal restrictions that seem to be adversely affecting performance. These restrictions are based in statutes, court rulings, Executive Orders, the Attorney General's and Department of Defense guidelines, and procedures established within the intelligence agencies themselves.

A. The identification of counterintelligence with criminal proceedings.

Criminal law assumes an adversary relationship between the government and anyone suspected of a crime. Because the law ought not to be "out to get" anyone, it is reasonable to demand that law officers show some evidence that an individual is engaging (or about to engage, or conspiring to engage) in criminal activity *before* they utilize intrusive investigatory techniques or seize evidence that could land that individual in jail.

Counterintelligence, however, deals with activities whose primary characteristic is not criminality but hostility to the nation's security. The purpose of counterintelligence is not to prevent crimes and punish criminals (although both may be spin-offs), but rather to learn about and to neutralize the activities of the nation's enemies. The relationship between the target of counterintelligence investigation and the investigator is not necessarily an adversary one. Whereas, except in cases involving organized crime and racketeering it is difficult to imagine the government having a legitimate interest in keeping tabs on wholly innocent persons, in the fields of intelligence and counterintelligence it is sometimes necessary to observe the activities of perfectly loyal citizens in order to learn about the activities of hostile intelligence services.

Moreover, the CI officer's relationship even with a hostile spy is not comparable to that between a policeman and a criminal. In many cases, gathering intelligence against and covertly influencing public policy in the United States is not a crime. Gatherers of intelligence are not in business for themselves. Punishing them is not what counterintelligence is all about. Rather, its tasks are to protect our own intelligence operations, to discover deception, to uncover secret political operations directed against the United States, and to keep spies and terrorists from being successful. Anyone who is discovered by counterintelligence officers to have committed a crime is punished under the criminal law. Any such punishment is by its nature extraneous both to the process and the purpose of counterintelligence, precisely because in CI matters there usually is no intention to prosecute. As the minority in the Senate Intelligence Committee's Report on the 1978 Foreign Intelligence Surveillance Act argued, the law's requirements for *ex parte* proceedings in order to obtain warrants for surveillance are a parody of criminal law. Others have pointed out that in the course of trials required to convict spies it is often necessary to reveal more information than the spies had actually succeeded in obtaining. In fact, counterintelligence officers generally argue against arresting hostile operatives. Once known, they become harmless.

Nevertheless, possibly because top US officials typically are more familiar with criminal and civil law than they are with intelligence, they have been receptive to the argument that any individual who is the subject of an intelligence officer's attention is *ipso facto* burdened, and that such a burden ought not to be placed on any person unless that person "has done something." Simply stated, the "criminal standard" for investigations consists of the requirement that high level officials certify that some individual or group is doing, has done, or clearly intends to do something illegal before permitting the investigators to carry out their investigation.

The Supreme Court, in the *Keith* case (1972), directed the Justice Department to obtain court orders before wiretapping persons for purposes of internal security and well-nigh directed the Congress to legislate similar requirements for foreign counterintelligence. In 1978 the Congress complied by passing the Foreign Intelligence Surveillance Act, which reduced intelligence and counterintelligence to terms familiar to criminal lawyers.

The intelligence charters proposed in 1978 (S. 2525) and the basically similar proposal introduced in 1980 as the National Intelligence Act of 1980 (S. 2424) sought to broaden the application of the criminal standard to cover the gathering of nearly all information on just about any person in the United States (citizens or aliens), and on many categories of aliens abroad. The Bill's provisions were crafted to require higher standards of evidence for "US persons" than for those who are not, lower standards for obtaining "third party records" than for using informants inside organizations, and so on. This complex welter of provisions and procedures is beyond our scope here. It is sufficient to note that the Carter and Ford Administrations, on their own authority, have been imposing most of the bill's requirements through Executive Order and the Attorney General's guidelines.

In 1976 President Ford's Attorney General, Edward Levi, issued two types of guidelines that have remained substantially unaltered throughout the Carter Administration. These guidelines regulate the FBI's CI activities in the United States. Apparently they also have been used by the CIA to guide the activities of its CI operatives when US persons abroad are involved. And they also have formed much of the conceptual underpinning of the Department of Defense CI guidelines.

Although these sets of guidelines are not identical, their main conceptual underpinning is the criminal standard—the notion that someone should not be subject to much, if any, investigation unless it can be demonstrated that he or she has, is, or probably will be imminently involved in a criminal undertaking. One set of guidelines, which is publicly available, pertains to "domestic security," as contrasted to "foreign counterintelligence investigations." It posits that a firm distinction can be drawn between the two. It then establishes rules or thresholds that cannot be crossed unless it can be demonstrated that a US citizen or resident alien actually has committed or is about to commit a crime, in contrast to advocating or discussing engaging in the violent overthrow of the government or the commission of terrorist acts.

According to these rules, as interpreted by the FBI, the Bureau cannot even *collect* the publications of a domestic organization (an organization composed substantially, but not exclusively, of US persons) unless there is "probable cause" to believe that a crime is imminent. Needless to say, other relatively more intrusive techniques, such as physical surveillance and mail cover (let alone mail opening) also cannot be undertaken. If the FBI comes across information to indicate that there is sufficient cause to believe that a group actually intends to violate the law (e.g., an allegation from someone that the group is buying explosives), it may slightly increase surveillance of the group or individuals and establish a "limited investigation." But it may not place informants in the group or use mail cover or electronic surveillance. According to the guidelines only when a "full investigation" has been authorized by FBI Headquarters, on the basis of "specific and articulable facts" describing the "(1) magnitude of the threatened harm; (2) the likelihood it will occur; (3) the immediacy of the threat; and (4) the danger to privacy and free expression posed by a full investigation," can an FBI agent use "intrusive" techniques and even then under various additional rules; moreover, the authorization for a full investigation must be renewed every 180 days.

One of the major problems with these rules is the catch-22 situation that makes it very difficult to obtain the information to justify a full investigation without first using the investigatory techniques that are expressly proscribed in preliminary or limited investigations. A second problem is that these rules impose considerable obligations on the field agents. To begin with, they have to write justifications for investigations. While there are advantages to requiring written justifications, there are also major disadvantages. FBI agents who may be good investigators may be reluctant to commit to paper hunches based on very imperfect data. Instead, it may be easier to drop the case.

Third, as is discussed in other papers in this volume, there is substantial evidence that terrorists and some of those who will eventually begin to work as agents of influence or spies for foreign powers are drawn to this work through legal political activities. When these individuals consciously decide to engage in illegal acts, they will begin to take precautions to ensure that they are not subject to surveillance. If they have not been identified or subject to any surveillance at an earlier and legal stage of their activities—i.e., if there is a weak or non-existing data base—the work of the CI operatives will be much more difficult later on.

Unfortunately for purposes of this analysis, most of the Attorney General's foreign counterintelligence guidelines and the CIA's rules for CI investigations abroad are classified. However, many retired FBI and CIA officials have indicated that the principles embodied in them are not substantially different from the domestic guidelines. They also have pointed out that the rules in the proposed intelligence charters (S. 2284 and S. 2525) would in many ways codify in law the Executive Branch rules that in fact have been governing CI against US citizens and resident aliens whether in the United States or abroad.

While not all FBI officials agree, these "domestic" and "foreign" guidelines have reportedly limited counterterrorism and counterintelligence operations to a criminal standard so strict that they have been interpreted as prohibiting surveillance of the Puerto Rican terrorists who were released after serving 25 years in prison and who vowed to strike again (and whose colleagues did so). The same guidelines have been interpreted to prohibit surveillance of a hypothetical known member of the Red Brigades who had entered the United States openly to raise funds for his brethren. The guidelines also reportedly require that the FBI obtain the Attorney General's permission whenever any informant must break the law in order to get or retain access to persons under investigation.

Also in the early 1970's, the Defense Department formulated the Defense Investigations Program that establishes guidelines for investigation by the military services, on the grounds that the military should not be engaging in domestic intelligence, and instituted the Defense Investigations Review Council (DIRC) to enforce these guidelines. According to the DIRC, the counterintelligence components of the Army, Navy, and Air Force are not to investigate persons not affiliated with the Department of Defense except under unusual circumstances and only in coordination with the FBI. If the FBI, usually because it is too busy, declines to pursue a case, or before the FBI has decided whether it is interested, the military services must show no interest in civilians, regardless of the CI threat these civilians might pose to the military. These controls are substantially continued under the current Executive Order.

In 1980 and Department of the Army and the ACLU agreed to settle a civil suit that the latter had filed against the Army's surveillance of an entity called the "Berlin Democratic Club" in Germany at the height of the Vietnam War in the early 1970's. The Army contended that particularly with US forces engaged in hostilities, it had every right to surveil a group that was actively sowing dissidence and disobedience to orders among US soldiers and that might also have been a place for recruitment of intelligence agents against the Army. Nevertheless, under the combined pressure of the judge and the ACLU, and doubtless mindful that something of the sort was being considered by the Congress, the Army agreed to institute regulations requiring its counterintelligence element to obtain a judicial warrant before using intrusive investigative techniques *even overseas* wherever "US persons" might be involved.

Recently, according to newspaper reports of a similar case, a US District Court held that a US citizen of Arab descent, who is the leader of a US-based PLO support group, had been subjected to unlawful electronic surveillance because the NSA and FBI had not shown that he had violated or was about to violate US law prior to initiating their surveillance. The Court then prohibited any agency from conducting electronic surveillance of US citizens *abroad* without first obtaining a court order comparable to the one mandated by the Foreign Intelligence Surveillance Act for Americans in the United States. Thus, by administrative and judicial fiat, henceforth American judges will direct that foreign laws (e.g. those relating to wire tapping) be broken!

The concept of "US person" was introduced into our legal vocabulary by S. 2525 and S. 2284. Anyone who—or anything which—qualifies as "US person" under the administrative and judicial measures that flow from the same set of concerns as these bills may be put under surveillance only pursuant to a court order following a finding that the information to be sought is "essential to the national security of the United States" and, given "extraordinary circumstances," can be acquired in no other way. Who *is* a "US person?" Citizens of the United States and permanent resident aliens, of course, regardless of whether they are registered as agents of a foreign power. But a "US person" also is any corporation chartered in the United States, or any corporation or group anywhere in the world (e.g., the Berlin Democratic Club), composed "substantially" of US citizens.

What do these legal provisions tell the counterintelligence officer and his agents? Generally, they signal that this nation does not want counterintelligence to burden anyone with attention unless something very like "probable cause" can be demonstrated. To that end, the government has established a series of hurdles to be cleared before investigations may begin. These hurdles raise troubling questions. Insofar as both guidelines and proposed legislation prohibit collection on so-called First Amendment groups—those engaged in literary or religious or political activity, and foreign agents are using precisely such groups as cover—a CI officer exposes himself to very serious scrutiny for proposing such collection. Such proposals as he does decide to make must be based on "facts or circumstances which reasonably indicate that the person is or may be engaged in a clandestine intelligence activity on behalf of a foreign power or international terrorist activity." How does one get such information without doing a lot of investigating? Yet if one investigates to get the "facts or circumstances," one may overstep the line. Does a group have enough US citizens to qualify as a "US person?" Who would want to risk five years in jail or a wrecked career to find out? Should we not expect that, as a rule, hostile intelligence operatives or terrorists will cloak themselves precisely in ways that put US CI officers in such "no win" circumstances? The answer is obvious. And it is deeply disturbing.

B. The "chilling effect" of current attitudes toward privacy and other formulations.

Recent court cases have held that individuals and corporations have property rights in information and that, moreover, they have the right to civil remedies for breaches of their privacy. Therefore, the informant who steals memoranda, tapes, or other information that does not indicate a crime but rather, let us assume, some clandestine financial connection with a hostile foreign power of group—that informant may be in deep trouble. It is not unreasonable in today's legal climate to imagine that the target may learn through the Privacy Act that an investigation by the FBI or CIA has uncovered his clandestine—but not illegal—dealings with the PLO or Cuba, and then charge that he has been damaged by this investigation and sue the government and the officer and agent responsible to recover those damages.

Privacy is an especially troublesome concept for intelligence. Staunch partisans of the Exclusionary Rule notwithstanding, there is little doubt that there is no absolute right to shroud the commission of a crime with a claim of privacy. The very existence of police, courts, and jails is intended to "chill" certain activities, e.g., murder, whether in public or in private. Indeed, the very word "crime" means a wrong which the public deems to be of general concern. However, most activities in which intelligence in interested do not necessarily involve crime. Certain civil libertarians regret that. As Thomas Emerson has put it:

> Although the intelligence agencies make widespread use of informers to infiltrate political organizations, the Supreme Court has declined to rule that such tactics constitute a search and seizure of information within the meaning of the Fourth Amendment. (The Center Magazine, January/February, 1974)

Nevertheless, the doctrine that, except for crime and economic activity, each person is surrounded by an impenetrable shroud of privacy is gaining ground. The ultimate source of this doctrine is beyond our present scope. Its proximate sources are declarations by the Supreme Court, especially by Justices Douglas and Blackmun, of a "penumbra" surrounding the Fourth, Fifth, and Ninth Amendments.

In the field of intelligence, an overriding concern for privacy has resulted in striking down the claim of "national security" as a justification for investigative activity. For example, in *Paton v. LaPrade* (D.C.N.J., 469 F.Supp. 773), Judge Lawrence A. Whipple ruled that "national security as a basis for the mail cover is unconstitutionally vague and overbroad." The reason is the belief that one's privacy is too sacred to be infringed upon except as a sort of punishment for something either done or clearly intended, and the corollary belief that no activity that is not a crime could be sufficiently serious. These beliefs have led to restrictions on penetration and surveillance of organizations and individuals who are themselves innocent (more or less) but who may be expected to lend support and companionship to spies and terrorists.

The growing belief in the sanctity of privacy has led lawyers in the three branches of government to choose against "chilling" the lives of those on the fringes of activities hostile to the national security and in favor of a corresponding "chilling" of counterintelligence activity. The priorities expressed by this choice are filtering down through the counterintelligence bureaucracy. These priorities encounter some resistance. But although any citizen is entitled to disagree with them, counterintelligence officers are obliged to comply.

C. Implications of the distinction between foreign and domestic counterintelligence.

Clandestine collectors, covert action specialists, and terrorists wishing to operate against the United States would be peculiar indeed if they divided their work neatly into two segments—that within the borders of the United States and that beyond. They would be stupid as well if, for some enterprises, they mindlessly used only US citizens while for others they used only foreigners. They would be triply stupid if they did this knowing that the CIA's small counterintelligence staff and the CI elements of the Armed Forces are excluded from domestic intelligence-gathering unrelated to their own personnel, and that the FBI's Foreign Counterintelligence operations usually take place only in the United States. They know as we all do that among the major problems and tasks of US counterintelligence none is more difficult than to coordinate information across this geographic, legal, and administrative chasm.

The US is probably the only major country in the world that does not now possess central counterintelligence files. It is the only one where those working on the same case cannot go to the same files and must consider whether, by sharing all the information they have, they might not be violating Executive Orders. None of this is mandated by the Constitution. In fact, the Drug Enforcement Agency (DEA), most of whose work consists of intelligence and counterintelligence both at home and abroad, without regard to geographical distinction, prides itself on taking no account whatever of the location of the intelligence target or of the suspect's nationality. The DEA, it appears, lets the nature of its intelligence work dictate the manner in which it is pursued.

Historically, it has been the task of counterintelligence to keep hostile intelligence services from taking control of one's own intelligence sources to make them at best useless and, at worst, fonts of disinformation. In the past, when the primary sources of intelligence were human spies, counterintelligence was an exclusively human discipline. As the technical collection services have grown, however, it is not at all clear that the discipline of counterintelligence in the United States has kept pace, either intellectually or bureaucratically. As a result, some very important CI questions may be receiving short shrift. For example, Soviet open literature fairly bristles with talk of the importance of deception in political-military affairs. The Soviets are said to know a great deal about our technical collection systems. Talk of the importance of telemetry fills the American press. Surely it must have occurred to the Soviets to send us some false impressions through technical channels. But in the United States we are told, at least until recently, that those who engage in CI neither know (or are cleared to know) nor are especially concerned about technical collection, while the technical collectors—who are either in the Defense Department or the CIA—know little about CI.

The key point here is that while there are several factors working *against* the integration of technical and human information in counterintelligence, until very recently only a little has been done to bring them together. Certainly the missions of NSA and of the FBI, defined by law and practice, have little overlap. The mission of the CIA, on the other hand, was the subject of bloody intramural battles. CIA's reduction of its own role in CI certainly does not inspire many at CIA to try to integrate the Agency's own CI work, particularly against Americans abroad, with the FBI's, much less to bring NSA into the business of counterintelligence.

The gulf between domestic and foreign CI in US practice also can be seen in the case of violent groups. The Puerto Rican FALN is composed primarily of US citizens and does its work and recruiting in the United States. But one of its sources of support, as from time to time it has publicly stated, is Cuba. Yet it appears that nowhere in the US government is there a single individual or working group charged with tasking collection and bringing together all of the collected information on the FALN. The FBI and CIA personnel both do painstaking and sometimes dangerous work on the subject; but each works in isolation, on the basis of information that is less complete than it could be but for bureaucratic and regulatory hurdles which separate them.

It also would not be surprising if hostile foreign services did not draw lessons from the United States' failure to prevent the horrors at Jonestown, Guyana. No law, no bureaucratic regulation actually forbade effective action from being taken against the leaders of the People's Temple. That organization broke US laws by shipping guns, tampering with the mail, and sequestering people. It gave "probable cause" for active interest by CIA by its frequent contacts with the Soviets. All of this was reported in the press. To this day it is still not clear what use, if any, the Soviets made (and are making) of the extensive network of the People's Temple. Yet several things the People's Temple did kept the US government officially ignorant of these activities. First, it cloaked itself in the veil (albeit thin) of religion. Second, it drew close to a major American political party. Third, it operated both in the United States and abroad. The CIA kept hands off because Jonestown, although abroad, was an American "thing." The FBI did not go to Guyana. In the United States, the Bureau did not want to touch such an obviously First Amendment group. And who could blame the officers of either agency?

D. Personal liability of CI officers and informants

It is true, as FBI Director William H. Webster, Jr., has noted, that

> . . . There has not been a single successful tort claim made against any special agent of the FBI for a violation of a citizen's constitutionally protected rights. (*New York Times*, 3/16/80).

But it is just as clear that the Supreme Court has said that personal liability of an FBI Special Agent or other counterintelligence officer does arise for a violation of constitutionally protected rights. This is the rule of law, whether or not the Court ever has spelled out in detail what those constitutionally protected rights might be. So far, the Court has failed to do so, and a Special Agent can never be sure that a decade from now his authorization of an informant's currently innocuous action will not result in an award of money damages against him personally.

The trial of W. Mark Felt and Edward S. Miller, both former high level officials of the FBI, on charges that they ordered "black bag jobs" in 1972-1973 in attempts to apprehend Weather Underground fugitives, has deeply undermined FBI morale. In 1970, in the case of *Bivens* v. *Six Unknown Named Agents of the Federal Bureau of Narcotics* (403 U.S. 388), the Court held that a violation of a citizen's Fourth Amendment rights "under color of this authority gives rise to a cause of action for damages." A $2 million suit is now pending against the FBI, brought by relatives of Ms. Viola Liuzo, stemming from the activities of FBI informant Gary Rowe.

In addition to criminal or civil sanctions, FBI Special Agents are subject to a series of administrative penalties. The 1974 Amendments to the Freedom of Information Act (FOIA) gave ". . . the U.S. Civil Service Commission authority to punish officials who wrongfully withhold documents from the public. . . ." (*The Nation*, 4/19/75, p. 464). Similarly, in the last several years, a series of internal FBI rules and regulations have been used to discipline scores of Special Agents for taking actions that, in virtually every case, were authorized by the White House and the offices of the Attorney General and the Director of the FBI.

Some FBI officials say that they have been reluctant to initiate investigations or authorize any but the most obviously safe activities. As one former FBI official put it, "the Washington headquarters has become merely a reactive organization. It merely reacts to the communications of local field offices." One former FBI Special Agent says that FBI Agents must work with "one eye on their objective and one eye on what personal legal consequences they may face" for carrying out their duties.

Consequently, counterintelligence work is one of the least popular assignments within the FBI. Why should a Special Agent freely choose to work in an area where he may be eventually punished, demoted, fined, investigated, or even imprisoned for following the orders of his superiors and established FBI practice? For most Bureau agents, chasing bank robbers or auto theft rings is both easier and safer than counterintelligence work.

If there is some question as to the liability of and danger to the FBI Special Agent, the danger to the FBI informant is most disturbing. In 1957, the Supreme Court ruled in the case of *Rovario* v. *United States* (353 U.S. 53) that the right of an informant to have his identity protected is not absolute:

> Where the disclosure of an informer's identity . . . is relevant and helpful to the defense of an accused . . . the privilege must give way.

The test the Court laid down to determine when an informant's identity should be disclosed leaves the question almost completely open to the particular judge sitting in a particular case. The Court ruled:

> We believe that no fixed rule with respect to disclosure is justifiable. The problem is one that calls for balancing the public interest in protecting the flow of information against the individual right to prepare his defense.

Each court is to act on the "particular circumstances" in each case. *Nowhere does the Court discuss or show the slightest concern for the physical security of the informant.* Freedom of the press is to be balanced against the right to a fair trial of a defendant. The fact that a "deep throat" may be cut in the process, literally or figuratively, does not seem to bother the Court.

This led, in the case of *Hampton* v. *Hanrahan* (__F. 2d __, No. 77-1698 (7th Cir., April 23, 1979) slip op. at 610670), to a court order that disclosure of a District Attorney's informant's identity was "essential to a fair determination" of the case. The Socialist Worker's Party case forced the Attorney General of the United States to go into contempt of court to protect the identities of 13 informants. In *ACLU* v. *City of Chicago* (No. 75 C3295 N.D. Ill.), the court ordered the government to disclose the identities of FBI informants and confidential sources to ACLU plaintiff's counsel. In a related development, the US Court of Claims forced the IRS to release the names of a confidential informant even though the IRS had promised to protect his identity; he, in fact, was fired from his job when his identity was disclosed.

An FBI Special Agent who works in Atlanta summed up the problem in these words: "I can't look a potential informant in the eye and truthfully say that I can protect him." (*New York Times*, 3/16/80, p. E5) This is precisely the source of a "chilling effect" on the willingness of individuals, organizations, and even foreign governments to provide information for US counterintelligence use.

II. The Effect of Perceptions

It is difficult to measure the effects on CI officers and informants of the Freedom of Information Act (FOIA), congressional involvement in intelligence in the 1970s, the clamorous leaks to the press from both the Congress and the Executive Branch, and the general unpopularity of counterintelligence within the intelligence community itself. Nevertheless, these effects must be recognized.

The application of the Freedom of Information Act to the intelligence agencies is an exclusively latter-day American phenomenon. There is nothing remotely like it in the Western democratic world. Britain and the Commonwealth countries have their Official Secrets Acts. Liberal Sweden prosecutes journalists for merely discussing the existence of a Swedish intelligence service.

Of course, FOIA allows—*but does not require*—properly classified information to be exempted from release. Indeed, official US policy is that mere classification is not enough for an exemption. All files must be searched in answer to each request, and a maximum effort must be made to declassify the answer. The FBI and CIA, together, spend over 400 man-years, every year, responding to FOIA requests.

Attorney General Griffin Bell, in May 1977, sent a letter to the FBI, CIA and other US intelligence agencies stating that:

> The Government should not withhold documents unless it is important to the public interest to do so, even if there is some arguable legal basis for the withholding. . . . The Justice Department will defend Freedom of Information suits only when disclosure is demonstrably harmful, even when the documents technically fall within the exemptions in the Act.

The CI-related problem here appears to be that there is a separation between the person who provides the information and the person who decides to release it. Only the provider of that information (and more than likely also the requester of it under the Act) know what is and what is not sensitive information.

An informant may, for example, tell the FBI that a certain individual keeps a post office box in a neighboring city. The 309 FBI officials working on the FOIA at FBI headquarters in Washington who must make a decision on what material to release under an FOIA/Privacy Act request will have no way of knowing that only the holder of the post office box and the informant know of its existence and that its only function is to receive payment for espionage activities. The declassifiers would judge it the most reasonable thing in the world to inform an FOIA/Privacy Act requester that he, himself, has such and such a post office box. How could that reasonably be expected to affect the national security of the United States? But the release of that seemingly innocuous piece of information identifies the informant beyond question.

Another way an informant could be identified is by comparing the typeface of informant reports released under FOIA. In the past every typewriter was unique. The typeface was as singular as any set of fingerprints. In the foreign espionage field, a hostile intelligence agency may well have the time and money painstakingly to compare samples of the typewritten letters of their contacts with material released under the FOIA.

Alternatively a former informant told us that while he was working under cover, one of his comrades had obtained under the FOIA and Privacy Act information, seemingly innocuous, but which indicated that there was a serious leak in the organizational network. The colleague asked our interviewee (who said he was actually the source of the information), if he would investigate. The former informant was so concerned with the information that he said he stopped working for the FBI and moved to another city.

Congress doubtless did not intend this sort of thing when it passed FOIA. It is surely unlikely also that the intelligence agencies that administer the Act mean to harm their sources. Intelligence personnel go over every page to be released and check to make sure that data on sources and methods are removed. But they make mistakes and they are perceived to make mistakes. It is easy to miss something important in millions of pages. For example, the FBI's typists are instructed to type individuals' names in all capital letters. In a recent case, an individual's name had been typed about 40 times in a series of reports. Thirty-nine times it was typed in all capitals and therefore blocked out. Once, it was typed as most people are used to typing names with only the first letter of each name capitalized. The unnamed Bureau official's eyes skimmed over the name and it was left in. Another source was identified, another FBI source who will never again cooperate with the Bureau. Officials who have only ten days under the law to check all of the possible files in which an individual or organization may be indexed are under pressure to act quickly. But this pressure produces quite another sort of incentive among counterintelligence operatives. Why, they ask, should they run such risks? FOIA provides no positive answers.

In the United States today, basically only one class of persons has an absolute ability to prevent information from being released under the Freedom of Information or Privacy Acts. That person is the informant himself. All he has to do to protect himself against the release of information is never to give it to the government in the first place. The problem of those who are legitimately concerned with counterintelligence is how to get the informant *not* to exercise this option. But how can we induce intelligent people to insinuate themselves among deadly enemies on behalf of a government which is unable to guarantee confidentiality under current law? There is no reason why anyone engaged in counterintelligence should be more loyal to the government than the government is to him.

To our knowledge, the Congress has not identified any counterintelligence officer or agent under cover. But, both by its very involvement in intelligence and by its record in other regards, Congress has given little comfort to those working in counterintelligence.

Congressional oversight of any agency rarely directs or forbids actions. Rather, oversight gives agencies a sense of what the people's elected representatives deem important and necessary and what they deem unimportant or improper. It is significant that, to our knowledge, the Congress has paid attention to counterintelligence only in hearings in which legislators have reproached the FBI's Cointelpro, and the CIA's operation CHAOS, and in the drafts of proposed charters for the FBI and CIA that require that the criminal standard (or something like it) be met and that a host of procedures be fulfilled before counterintelligence cases may be opened. Congressional staff members also have worked closely with administration officials in the FBI and CIA to finetune the restrictions.

Neither the staff members nor the legislative drafts nor the hearings have given working level officials in the agencies the impression that the nation would be displeased with them if their performance did not improve. Concern about performance, about the degree of coverage of foreign intelligence collectors, about the number of schemes for deception uncovered, has been quite absent from congressional discussion of counterintelligence.

Yet no counterintelligence officer could fail to be impressed by Congress's concern lest any counterintelligence activity deprive anyone of his rights. He could not fail to realize that any legislator who believed that a CI officer was acting improperly could leak information about the activity to which he objected. This has not yet happened and some would argue that, given especially the Congress's threat to censure its members who release classified information, such spiteful disclosure could not happen. But one is entitled to be skeptical, knowing that no member ever has been censured for disclosing classified information about other matters.

This is not to say that improved performance in CI necessarily implies carelessness about the rights of individuals but only to state the obvious—that any CI official who looked to Congress for guidance would in no way be inspired for the coutnry's sake to act beyond the stated concerns of Congress.

Leaks have become a substantial danger to all intelligence personnel but especially to those in undercover work. Publications like the *Covert Action Information Bulletin* and *Counterspy* have been using First Amendment freedoms to expose the names of US intelligence and counterintelligence personnel. At a press conference at the XIth World Festival of Youth and Students held in Havana in the summer of 1978, Philip Agee, who founded both publications, stated that he intended to:

> . . . make this publication a permanent weapon in the fight against the CIA, the FBI, military intelligence. . . . We know that the information and the research is there, crying out to be published and disseminated. . . . We will never stop exposing CIA personnel and operatons whenever and wherever we find them . . . . The CIA can be defeated. . . .

It is understandable to any counterintelligence official or agent that some people should be working to expose and wreck their operations. It is not especially troubling that some of these people should be Americans. But it is very troubling indeed that the US government does not bestir itself to punish such people or at least to use legal methods to put them out of business. One can scarcely fail to get the impression that it is more dangerous to work for the United States than to work against it. *The Nation* is opposed to outlawing activities such as Agee's. In an editorial on December 1, 1979, it argued against:

> . . . the dubious assumption that American investigative reporters are more effective and accurate than foreign counterintelligence operatives.

According to this sort of thinking, which has not been actively combatted by the Carter Administration, and which has been espoused by some members of the Senate Intelligence Committee, the right of the press to publish whatever it wishes is more important than the success of US counterintelligence, the lives of its personnel, and the national interests it serves.

It would be surprising if people who believe that their superiors do not care much either for their careers or their lives did not seek to protect themselves by reducing the scope of their activities—in a word, by going defensive.

III. Incentives for Better Performance

Counterintelligence cannot operate in the 1980's as it did before the mid-1970's because the laws, regulations, and attitudes that form the basis of its actions have changed. Today one cannot take for granted that officials and prospective agents will take an aggressive attitude toward their tasks. If the President and Congress want CI to have such an attitude, they must actively foster it. In the 1970's it became increasingly difficult for CI officers in the CIA to challenge major items of information developed by the clandestine service (DDO) or conclusions reached by the estimative analysts (NFAC). If we want them to do this we should tell them so and provide them with a certain amount of organizational independence. When cases involve US citizens one cannot expect CIA's CI officers to be guided primarily by the nature of the case unless they are given specific (and almost surely statutory) authority to pursue cases jointly with the FBI. One cannot expect the FBI to investigate support groups, without which spies and terrorists find it difficult to operate, unless FBI agents know that new norms have made this possible.

Therefore, to provide incentives for better performance in counterintelligence, we propose consideration of reforms like the following:

1. The authority and responsibility for counterintelligence should be vested either in the Director of the CIA, the Director of the FBI,

or in some other official. That official should be required to prepare a yearly estimate of the threat to the United States from hostile intelligence services and terrorists, including the numbers, functions, and purposes of personnel ranged against the United States in the several geographic and functional areas, as well as the measures being taken to neutralize those personnel.

2. National counterintelligence estimates should be produced, thus forcing the several agencies to work together; and regular dissemination channels should be established, probably separate from the ones for positive intelligence, by which these estimates would reach top consumers.

3. By statute or executive order, the counterintelligence service should be established within CIA, and possibly the FBI, and endowed with career prospects equal to those provided positive intelligence officers.

4. The law should make it clear that any prohibition against the CIA's involvement in domestic law enforcement should not be interpreted as inhibiting CIA officials from working on CI cases along with the FBI and the Department of Defense.

5. The laws and guidelines should provide authorization for the investigation of "support groups" and individuals with political ties to hostile foreign governments. Innocent people in such groups should be protected by provisions prohibiting the dissemination of information about them. They should not be subject to intrusive investigatory techniques (e.g., wiretapping and mail opening) unless it can be demonstrated that they are participants in foreign intelligence or terrorist activities. Proper and strict congressional oversight, which did not really exist until the late 1970's, would provide a high degree of assurance that these guidelines were being followed.

6. Consideration should be given to making it a crime for any person who has had authorized access—and perhaps for any US person, including a member of Congress—to deliberately and successfully reveal the identity of anyone working under cover for the United States with the intent to damage either that person or US intelligence.

7. The reach of the Freedom of Information Act should be limited in the area of intelligence.

8. Finally, it may be appropriate to consider a series of specific incentives for FBI counterintelligence officers.

One problem resulting from internal FBI procedures is the apparent view that every Special Agent can do every job and ought to be able to do so. People working on CI are transferred to bank robbery details and vice versa; hence, CI specialists are few. Moreover, key CI officials apparently now are forced to retire at age 55, just when they have become experienced, because if they were transferred to criminal work they might be too old to perform that task. These are but a few of the specific constraints that may be affecting the FBI's CI performance.

No one should be under the illusion that any task can be performed well if we simply give the people who are supposed to perform it the proper incentives to do their job. They may simply have forgotten how (or never knew), or they may be working against insurmountable odds. Nevertheless, we also should not delude ourselves into thinking that an inherently thankless task, which depends so much on the human factor, will be performed well unless we *do* improve the system of incentives for the people who are supposed to perform it.

Discussants

Professor Antonin Scalia: Let me begin by saying I do agree entirely with the concern of Beichman and Godson about the danger of overregulation of the intelligence community. Moreover, I even agree generally with their recommendations, although I would want to have some clarification, and perhaps I have some reservations about Nos. 5 and 6. Lastly, I agree entirely that not only are the laws that govern the intelligence community important but the perception of the laws that govern the intelligence community is important. But it is precisely on this last point that I feel I have to become intemperate.

An earlier discussion concerned Soviet deception of the United States intelligence operation. I am prepared to believe that that deception is very effective, having seen how effectively deceived the intelligence community has been concerning the laws that govern it, having seen how the (what might be called) civil liberation extremists have not only managed to mislead the community as to what the laws are, but have managed to enlist the community in misleading everybody else.

Let me give you examples from the paper, which I find misinterprets, misconstrues, or misrepresents statutes, court decisions, crucial constitutional doctrines, and guidelines.

First statutes. The paper asserts: "It is not unreasonable in today's legal climate to imagine that the target learns through the Privacy Act that an investigation by the FBI or CIA has uncovered his clandestine—but not illegal—dealings . . . ." Wrong. It is unreasonable. The Privacy Act, unlike the Freedom of Information Act, has a broad exemption, which both the FBI and the CIA can assert.

Then: "The 1974 Amendments to the Freedom of Information Act gave the U.S. Civil Service Commission authority to punish officials who wrongfully withhold documents from the public." Not true. Before the Civil Service Commission (now the Merit Systems Protection Board) can apply any sanction, the withholding must have been not merely "wrongful" but "arbitrary and capricious." The legislative history makes it entirely clear that a good-faith error will not suffice. Congress expected the provision to be invoked only "in exceptional circumstances." To my knowledge, in only one case has a court even invoked the procedure of referring a matter to the Commission for consideration of possible disciplinary action; and in no case has disciplinary action been taken! No employee honestly attempting to follow the law (as, I presume we agree, all should) need have any fear of this portion of the Act.

In any case, the Executive Branch has *always* had the authority (and, I would imagine, the obligation) to discipline employees for willful violation of the law; indeed, it has had the authority to do so even for mere negligence or error. The real fight in the 1974 Amendments was over whether this power should be given to the courts. The Executive Branch won that fight—and was very happy about winning it.

So much for the statues.

Now to court decisions. The paper describes the *Keith* case, which is a watershed in intelligence law, as well-nigh directing the Congress to legislate wiretapping requirements for foreign counterintelligence.

This is entirely wrong. The *Keith* opinion does state that "Congress may wish to consider protective standards for [security wiretaps] which differ from those already prescribed for specified crimes," and goes on to give some examples of the differences that might be appropriate. It concludes with the statement that this discussion "does not, of course, attempt to guide the congressional judgment but rather to delineate the present scope of our own opinion."

It is, to begin with, an exaggeration to describe this as "well nigh directing" the Congress to enact any legislation. But more important, the passage *does not refer to foreign counterintelligence wiretaps at all,* but only to *domestic security* wiretaps, which the *Keith* case held could not be conducted without a judicial warrant. The distinction is basic, and to overlook it displays—and propagates—great confusion.

The *Rovario* case is described as follows: "The Supreme Court ruled . . . that the right of an informant to have his identity protected was not absolute. "Where the disclosure of an informer's identity . . . is relevant and helpful to the defense of an accused . . . the privilege must give way."

Well, that is true in a way. But what you have to know is that all it means is that *if* the government wants to go forward with the prosecution it must reveal the informant's identity—not that it absolutely must reveal his identity. That is quite a different proposition. And it is indeed fair enough. It may be important to the government to withhold the name of an informant, but we are not going to convict an innocent man when the only person who might clear him cannot be disclosed. That is a sensible enough rule, and I don't think it should be described as a rule which says the right of an informant to have his identity protected cannot be safeguarded by the government. It assuredly can.

With regard to the *Hanrahan* case, the *City of Chicago* case, and a recent Court of Claims case, all are again loosely described as "ordering" or "forcing" disclosure.

But they do no such thing. All they establish is that *if* the government chooses not to make disclosure, it may be subject to adverse consequences. The point in question may be adjudged against the government, the government may be precluded from introducing other evidence, and so forth. That is far from an absolute requirement of disclosure—and it is also, by the way, far from new law.

The one case mentioned that might accurately be described as "forcing" disclosure was the Socialist Worker's Party case, in which the Attorney General was cited for contempt in failing to produce informants' files. But the paper neglects to mention that this judicial action was found to be wrong; it was reversed on appeal.

Another district court case, *Paton v. LaPrade,* is described as resting upon the belief "that one's privacy is too sacred to be infringed except as a sort of punishment for something either done or clearly intended, and the corollary belief that no activity that is not a crime could be sufficiently serious." The implication is that the decision—which found the Postal Service's regulation authorizing mail covers for "national security" reasons unconstitutionally vague and overbroad—would not permit mail covers for intelligence purposes.

That is simply not a permissible reading of the opinion, which in fact intimated that the FBI guidelines for mail covers (which of course include foreign intelligence and counterintelligence covers) might cure the vagueness of the Post Office regulation with respect to FBI activities. The *Paton* court's holding is accurately described by another court as follows: "(T)he Court did not find that a mail cover which was imposed because of legitimate national security concerns was invalid. Rather, it found a regulation permitting both legitimate and illegitimate mail covers to be unconstitutional." *Jabara v. Kelley,* 476 F. Supp. 561, 574 (E.D. Mich. 1979). The latter court, by the way, did explicitly address the assertion that a legitimate intelligence investigation stands on a weaker footing, as far as constitutional prohibitions are concerned, than a criminal investigation—and flatly rejected it. "(A) distinction based upon the type of investigation is without merit." *Id.* at 570.

Finally, as to the misdescription of court decisions, the paper asserts, that a "US District Court held that a US citizen of Arab descent, who is the leader of a PLO support group, had been subjected to unlawful electronic surveillance because the NSA and FBI had not shown that he had violated or was about to violate US law prior to initiating their surveillance." Judging from the description of the plaintiff's nationality (and only from that) this is an apparent reference to *Jabara v. Kelley,* 476 F. Supp. 561 (E. D. Mich. 1979). But the rest of the description is simply wrong. Perhaps the authors believe that the plaintiff was "the leader of a PLO support group," but the court's decision did not pertain to such a person. To the contrary, the decision was based upon the fact that there was not "any evidence to establish that the plaintiff or the domestic organization to which he belongs has been implicated in any way with a foreign agent or organization or acting in collaboration with a foreign power." The crux of the opinion was that "the defendants have failed to produce and could not produce any evidence which would establish that the transmission and examination of Jabara's communications was subject to the foreign agent or collaborator exception to the warrant requirement." That bears no resemblance to holding that it must be "shown that he had violated or was about to violate US law."

The same case is also described in the paper as having produced an order which "prohibited any agency from conducting electronic surveillance of US citizens abroad without first obtaining a court order comparable to the one mandated by the Foreign Intelligence Surveillance Act for Americans in the United States." The paper concludes that "thus, by administrative and judicial fiat, henceforth American judges will direct that foreign laws be broken!" But that is an extreme conclusion—and why would one want to believe it? The order in question is the work of a single district judge; it is being appealed; and it is quite obviously wrong. Before the Foreign Intelligence Surveillance Act was passed, a solid body of judicial authority held that even in the United States a proper foreign intelligence wiretap did not require a judicial warrant. The Act imposed a warrant requirement for domestic taps, but specifically excluded taps abroad. Thus, this lone district court order runs against the decisions of several higher federal courts, and against the judgment of Congress. It is more unlikely to survive, and to present it as the law is seriously misleading. So much for court decisions.

Let me now turn to crucial constitutional doctrines ignored in the paper. It states that: "In the United States today, basically only one class of persons has an absolute ability to prevent information from being released under the Freedom of Information or Privacy Acts. That person is the informant himself"—by never disclosing information.

If all this means to say is that only by failing to provide information can a potential informant completely assure himself against disclosure through human error or perfidy, then of course it is a truism. There is no other way to eliminate that risk. But if the statement is meant to imply that in no way does the *law* absolutely guarantee against *mandated* disclosure, then it is simply wrong.

In addition to the exemptions in the Freedom of Information and Privacy Acts that are, in theory, fully adequate to guarantee protection, there is the doctrine of Executive Privilege, which would enable the President to decline disclosure even if the exemptions did not exist. Now it may well be that the Freedom of Information and Privacy Acts unnecessarily increase the risk of erroneous disclosure—but that is a much narrower point.

What guidelines are misinterpreted or misdescribed in the paper? It says that the Justice Department guidelines are "so strict that they have been interpreted as prohibiting surveillance of the Puerto Rican terrorists who were released after serving 25 years in prison and who vowed to strike again . . . . The same guidelines have been interpreted to prohibit surveillance of a hypothetical known member of the Red Brigades who had entered the United States openly to raise funds for his brethren."

It is of course easy to make alarmist statements about guidelines that are not public; and even easier if one merely repeats how those unknown guidelines "have been interpreted" by some unidentified person. Since the guidelines are classified, all I can reply is that it would take an extraordinarily gullible person—or one who wants to believe the worst—to accept such an inherently implausible description of the unknown by the unidentified.

Later, the authors say: "Insofar as both guidelines and proposed legislation prohibit collection on so-called First Amendment groups—engaged in literary or religious or political activity, and foreign agents are using precisely such groups as cover—a CI officer exposes himself to very serious scrutiny for proposing such collection."

Yes, indeed, "insofar as" the guidelines and proposed legislation contain such prohibition—the implication being that they do. Once again, the guidelines are classified. But the accuracy of the description of them may be gleaned from the accuracy of the description of pending legislation. The proposed FBI Charter (which does not deal with foreign intelligence and counterintelligence) contains some restrictions in this regard; *the proposed Foreign Intelligence Charter does not.*

Another example. "(I)n the last several years, a series of internal FBI rules and regulations have been used to discipline scores of Special Agents for taking actions that, in virtually every case, were authorized by the White House and the offices of the Attorney General and the Director of the FBI."

Now, it may indeed be the subject of some factual dispute whether the agents' actions were so authorized—but the paper sets forth authorization as a fact. I assert categorically, on the basis of my participation in Justice Department deliberations concerning similar alleged misfeasance, that discipline would not be imposed if such authorization existed—unless, of course, the action in question was so clearly beyond the power of the authorizing official (for example, the rigging of a federal election) that no reasonable agent could believe the authorization valid. During Attorney General Levi's tenure, the Department publicly announced that it would not seek indictments against CIA officers for unlawful mail openings because those openings had been authorized by higher officials and had been undertaken in evident good faith. The paper's statement on this point is utterly in error in implying that good-faith reliance upon apparently valid authorization has been intentionally ignored by the Department.

What is the effect of all this misdescription? What good can come of it? I suppose that the good thought to come of it is emphasis of the threat—the dire threat—of overregulation.

But does that emphasis have to be achieved by exaggeration? There are plenty of areas that could be pointed to without exaggeration that make the case quite well. The Freedom of Information Act is one example. Some of the requirements of that legislation impinge too much on intelligence gathering and on the ability to preserve confidentiality of sources.

On the other hand, what bad comes of this exaggeration, or self-deception, or whatever else one wants to call it? First is the fact that you will not be taken seriously if you spout these notions of the law in discussions with those who want to impose further restrictions. You simply will not be taken seriously when you display such misinformation regarding the existing law. I recently saw a clear example of this phenomenon when, in my capacity as a consultant to the Committee on Law and National Security, a standing committee of the American Bar Association, I argued before the House of Delegates of the Association regarding the FBI Charter proposal. In the course of the debate, one gentleman obtained the floor who described himself as an ex-FBI agent. He might have had something good to contribute—but unfortunately, he began by saying that the effect of the proposed charter would be to prevent the FBI from getting at Communist cells throughout this country. That displayed the most basic misconception, because the FBI charter did not address the FBI's foreign intelligence and counterintelligence activities. So the speaker, who might have had good things to say and might have swayed the audience, could be neutralized with a single sentence: "I'm sorry, the gentleman is mistaken. The charter does not cover the FBI's foreign intelligence and counterintelligence operations." So basic was his error that he could be written off as an uninformed person. When you exaggerate and misdescribe the law, you do the same sort of harm to the good arguments you have.

The second bad effect is that you facilitate bureaucratic ineptitude. That is, you enable those who are messing up the intelligence operation unnecessarily to hide behind the law if you accept their misdescription of the law as correct. That is an old ploy. Any lawyer knows it.

For example, it is maintained in the paper that in settlement of a lawsuit the Army agreed to institute regulations requiring its counterintelligence element to obtain a judicial warrant before using intrusive investigative techniques overseas wherever US persons might be involved. Well, that was absurd for the Army to agree to, as you would know if you did not have some exaggerated notion of what the law requires. But if you muddy the waters by saying the law requires millions of things, you can't see the bureaucratic ineptitudes so clearly.

Another example appears where the clumsy operational division between foreign and domestic counterintelligence is blamed upon the law. But the law makes no distinction between domestic and foreign operations. It makes a distinction that is quite different, that is, a distinction between operations directed (domestically *or* abroad) against agents of foreign powers, and operations directed (domestically *or* abroad) against persons who are not agents of foreign powers. That is quite a different distinction. So to blame the inept separation of foreign and domestic counterintelligence operations—if it is inept, and I express no opinion on that—to blame that upon us lawyers. I'm sorry; the charge doesn't stick. And you are enabling those who like that ineptitude to run behind a cover that shouldn't be available to them.

A third bad effect of exaggeration is what might be termed its "chilling effect." Beichman and Godson express concern about not just the law but also the *perception* of the law. I assert it does not help the preception of the law when a group such as this—which obviously has the highest interest of the intelligence services in mind—suggests that an agent will be disciplined by the Department of Justice even when he acts in good faith on the orders of the Director of the FBI or the Attorney General; or that an agency employee acting in good faith takes a serious risk of disciplinary action by the Merit Systems Protection Board for wrongful denial of an FOIA request.

By suggesting such results, it seems to me you are helping to produce the very evil of timid intelligence-gathering you bemoan. Your task should be just the opposite—to debunk, rather than popularize, phony restrictions; to assuage, rather than encourage, groundless fears.

And that leads me to the last, and the worst of the effects. Constant misdescription will have the effect of changing the law. Most of the constitutional proscriptions we are operating under here are empty bottles. Phrases like "freedom of the press," "unreasonable search and seizure" have no precise content. What is "unreasonable"? It depends on what the society thinks is unreasonable. And any judicial decision is going to be informed by the common perception of these vague phrases.

Now if you yourselves—including the members of the intelligence community—accept and repeat as the common perception super-restricted views, you are going to facilitate judicial decisions which adopt those views as the law. If, for example, you ignore the doctrine of executive privilege and go about saying "it is impossible to withhold the name of any informant"—the courts are likely to take you at your word. Executive privilege does not appear expressly in the Constitution; from the structure of the document it has been assumed to exist. But if *you* are not willing to make that assumption, who else will?

I have two concluding comments. It seems to me that regardless of what the legal constraints are, you should not delude yourselves that a reduction of legal constraints or even a total elimination of them will relieve you of a considerable burden that I don't very often see the intelligence community willing to bear. That is the difficult burden of deciding for yourselves what the restrictions upon your activities should be if you don't want them imposed from outside.

You are prompt to say, for example, that there should be no absolute statutory restriction on participation in a felony. Fine. Let's say there is none. Somebody is going to have to decide, however, how far you can go in participating in a felony. Can you hold a machine gun and shoot down innocent civilians? Presumably not. Well, what else? *You* have to address these questions even if they are not addressed in the law. *You* have to think about them and decide. I have not seen that responsibility undertaken very seriously, and that is one of the reasons that such arguments fall on relatively deaf ears when you talk to the civil libertarians.

Finally, I want to say a word in favor of political sagacity, which is something that the intelligence community could use. When Attorney General Levi was passing upon requests for warrantless wire tapping under the President's constitutional power, he was unusually hard on those requests that sought surveillance of US citizens—not because there was any absolute constitutional ban upon such surveillance. It was not a matter of law; it was a matter of political prudence. He was able, during the worst years of the program against the intelligence agencies, to go up the Hill and say, "Ladies and gentlemen, not a single American citizen is now being wiretapped without a judicial warrant." That was worth a lot.

I think the intelligence agencies have to display similar political sagacity in deciding what they will and won't do, and in deciding whether to prosecute or not. I was mentioning in a private discussion earlier that I first became an aficionado of the FBI, like many of my generation, when I saw a documentary movie called, "The House on 92nd Street," which was about the Bureau's destruction of a major spy ring. Unfortunately, in recent times the only major intelligence and counterintelligence activities that come to public light are the errors and the abuses. And the public forms its judgments and makes its evaluations on the basis of those sad disclosures. Perhaps you should expose a major spy ring and go for criminal prosecutions, even at the expense of disclosing some of your sources, even at the expense of losing foreign agents you might otherwise "run," simply to bring home to the public the fact that, "There really are some major spy operations out there."

Dr. James Q. Wilson: Let me begin by saying that despite the apparently great difference in opinion that has been presented, there is in my judgment a broadly-shared set of understandings among the persons at this table. In speaking for myself, and I think in speaking for others as well, we are worried about a nation that has talked itself into believing that intelligence is not even a necessary evil; it is simply evil and not necessary, and that counterintelligence is something that we could dispense with because either there isn't a real threat or the cost of meeting the threat is too high. We have to counteract that.

We should make the best possible case as to why the problem exists and what has to be changed in order to get intelligence and counterintelligence back into vigorous activity directed at appropriate threats.

I am not a lawyer. I am a student of organizations, and over the last 20 years I have had occasion to study law enforcement agencies here and abroad, including the FBI, but not the CIA. Within the FBI, I have had occasion to become reasonably familiar with working conditions in the area of criminal investigation—to a lesser degree in organized crime and domestic security. I am not at all familiar with work in foreign counterintelligence. So what I will have to say constitutes in large part reasoning by analogy.

But I do think you can see, even in regular criminal investigative work, some of the same problems that we identify in the area of counterintelligence and intelligence. In all of these areas an agent—and I am now using the word "agent" to mean an FBI agent; an officer of the United States Government in a law enforcement capacity—is attempting to recruit an asset from the community of real or suspected bad guys. Without the ability to recruit that asset (an "informant" in FBI terms), and without the opportunity to exploit it and to build a case based on that information, the Bureau is left with little else but its well-known forensic laboratory, which I think everybody in the Bureau will be first to admit is, although admirable, inadequate to the problem of solving many crimes.

In my judgment, over the last five years there has occurred a decline in the willingness or ability of many agents to recruit and develop and use those assets. There has been, as we all know, a sharp decline in the number of domestic security cases that are being carried on an active basis. Indeed, the decline has been so sharp that the number of such cases, or at least the number of informants that are utilized for the purpose of maintaining those cases, is frequently classified for fear, if the fact were known, it would give aid and comfort to potential subversives.

This is an example of what Godson and Beichman talk about as perception trouble. There is a perception that you will get in trouble if you have these cases and these assets, and there is an understandable desire to avoid trouble. The difficulty is that more trouble is, in fact, avoided than actually exists, and the decline in the number of domestic security cases is all out of proportion to, and cannot be explained by, the Attorney General's guidelines on domestic security cases. These guidelines, after all, were not imposed on a totally unwilling Bureau. They were drafted with the active participation of senior members of the Bureau, and in the opinion of many are reasonable and workable. Unfortunately—or fortunately, depending on your view about these matters—far more cases were closed out than perhaps were necessary, given any reasonable interpretation of the guidelines.

There has been a decline in the recruitment of various kinds of assets. Many agents have told me, and they apparently have told Godson and Beichman as well, "I am not going to get involved with informant recruitment because you can get in trouble over that." I have had occasion to look at this phenomenon, and many of the persons saying such things are persons who had never recruited assets in the past. Therefore, what we have here is a cop-out. However, that doesn't make it any less a problem. It is always a problem when in any law enforcement agency, and the Bureau, I think, is no different from local and foreign police agencies. Only a few people are doing most of the work of the agency and many of the rest of the people are going along for the ride. In most field offices there are two or three skilled agents who have all of the good assets. If it weren't for them the office wouldn't have a whole lot to do.

Even though the problem often arises from a false perception, it is a problem. But the way to deal with the problem is to look at it candidly. I think the problem by and large is *not* to be found in guidelines or in court cases. For example, the *Rovario* decision, in which the court said that if you prosecute somebody on the strength of the testimony of an informant you cannot deny that person the right to cross-examine the informant, was handed down in 1957. In my judgment that decision could not be the cause of our recent troubles. That case, and subsequent cases, affected an agency's ability to use informants as the *sole* source for a case. This may be a serious problem to the DEA, but the Bureau has always had a tradition of not "burning" its informants and of building the actual prosecutable case out of materials that can be assembled from sources that can be divulged in the courts, including wiretaps where appropriate, without jeopardizing the identity of an informant. The fact that this case is 23 years old and that we only have had more recently this problem in developing and using assets suggests it is not the court case alone.

To be sure, the Socialist Worker's case, when it was first decided, sent a shock wave through most of us. It struct me as madness. But it was reversed. And in a system such as ours we are always going to have our share of eccentric judges. We have to hope the appellate process works, and usually it does.

The sources of the perceptions which do deserve our most serious concern are, first of all, the Freedom of Information Act. I think it can be shown, as the paper does, that without doubt the Act, as inevitably implemented by normal human beings working under tight deadlines, means that there are going to be a certain number of mistakes made and that those mistakes will be very costly.

I have interviewed a number of informants and a number of agents working informants, and there is no question in my mind, or their minds, that the Freedom of Information Act is a serious deterrent to the development and use of law enforcement assets, and I have to assume it also is in foreign counterintelligence, but I have to stress my personal knowledge does not run to that point.

The second source is that state of congressional and press opinion—not the content of the laws that have been passed but the barrage of investigations, often competing investigations by many committees, the continual drumfire of argumentation about the problem of individual rights and the absence of any organized counterveiling set of inquiries, investigations and press attention, at least until rather recently, to the problem of maintaining the security of the United States.

When the Director of the FBI or the head of the CIA was spending much of his time testifying before six, seven, or eight separate House and Senate committees in order to explain things, real and imagined, that happened in the past, a mood developed in each agency which is not conducive to taking the kinds of risks that any skilled law enforcement agent must take, and any skilled intelligence officer must take, if the work is to be done. There are precious few public rewards for taking risks, and if there is a high perception of great public costs for taking risks, then the risks are not going to be taken.

Finally, nobody has mentioned the curious role that the General Accounting Office is suddenly starting to play in our affairs. Traditionally, most nations have secret funds. British Prime Ministers have had them at least since the time of Pitt; the United States has had them since the time of Washington. Thomas Jefferson was very good at dispensing confidential funds for the furtherance of the interests of the United States or of the Democratic Party. But the General Accounting Office seems to be of the view that there is no such thing as a secret fund, that they ought to be able to investigate the use of all funds for all purposes. The GAO has said repeatedly, it would like to audit the Bureau's informant files to find out if all those informants are obeying the law and have signed vouchers for all the money they are receiving.

The GAO has not done this. I am cautiously optimistic it will not do so. But the fact that it is trying to do this, that this effort is highly publicized and supported by the chairmen of a number of important congressional committees, is, in my opinion, a mistake. The GAO has to come to the realization that it is not the sovereign source of accountability in American politics. The ultimate source of accountability, I think, is direct and manageable legislative oversight, not the General Accounting Office.

Unless we identify precisely the source of the problems and work at those problems, we are not going to address the real concerns of people who are reacting in an exaggerated way to the restraints upon them. Furthermore, if we identify the problem that law enforcement and intelligence agencies have today purely a problem of legal restraints, we will overlook the extent to which the organizations themselves have in some cases been deficient in designing recruitment and training programs and incentive systems that will produce aggressive effort.

In my judgment the level of training and the kinds of incentives and supervision given to agents to make them effective and productive in developing assets among groups for either intelligence or prosecutive purposes have been sadly deficient. There has been improvement. The FBI Academy is doing better at this now than it once was but, for a long time, the view there has long been that any agent can do anything, and that the training should essentially be legal training. If you were ask an agent going to his first office, "What did you learn about informants in Quantico?," he would say, "We heard about two days of lectures on how you could get in trouble with the law." They did not have the kind of experience and development in the importance of this, and the techniques for doing this. Training, I think, can only be conferred by persons who themselves are very good at this and who spend some time inculcating these skills in others.

I am concerned that if we focus too much attention on the restraint problem, which I take very seriously, and not enough attention to the training and incentive problem, we may discover the mood of the country will change—I believe the mood *is* changing—but that our performance will not increase proportionally. We will take the pressure off the system but the balloon will not expand to fill up the increased space we have allotted to it.

Let me touch on a quite different subject now, because I didn't think the comments in another session on the role of ideas in intelligence and counterintelligence came to a very satisfactory conclusion. We cannot say ideas must never be the subject of investigation. I don't deny for a moment that many of the most productive assets foreign agencies have developed in the US are people who have revealed nothing about their predispositions—chauffeurs, small-time employees of industrial and consulting firms, and the like, but I think this neglects two things.

First, it neglects the source and nature of terrorism. Terrorists, in my reading of history, reveal their intentions before they carry them out. They reveal them either by producing an ideology themselves or by responding to an ideology developed by others which states in not so subtle terms that the regime should be brought crashing down by whatever means lie ready at hand. Therefore, you have to take ideas seriously if you are going to be in a position to deal with those groups that wind up being the FALN or the Weather Underground or the SDS or the Black Panthers.

The distinction we want to make is the distinction between ideas as the *objects* of investigation and ideas as the *reason* for investigation. I think it is quite appropriate that ideas be a *reason* for investigation, they are a trigger, one among many, alerting us to the need to take a closer look at something, to make a preliminary inquiry, to find out if there are grounds for opening a substantive case. That is different from saying, "We want to investigate ideas and the people who hold those ideas because we think these are bad ideas and we want to chill the expression of those ideas." That distinction is often hard to maintain in practice, but at least it points to a complexity which often is lacking in the consideration of the difference between ideas and action.

The other reason for raising this is because I think one of the things that we are neglecting is pre-employment screening of candidates for federal employment. The proposed FBI Charter doesn't really address this question. There has been a tendency to shift pre-employment screening to the Office of Personnel Management, and away from the Bureau. Now, that may be a quite reasonable procedure, but we should not carelessly hire people for sensitive positions who have spent a large part of their lives engaging in the company of others in the denunciation of the United States and all it stands for. But to know when that has happened, one has to have and maintain a fairly substantial institutional memory as to who these others are, what kinds of ideas are regularly in circulation, which ideas are harmless, and which ideas have been known to lead to subversive action in the past. I have a feeling that such institutional memory is being degraded.

Let me conclude that, after having said all that, I find myself in substantial agreement with most of the recommendations which Godson and Beichman have in their paper.

I heartily endorse the notion we must modify the FOIA. I believe the best signal that must be given to the intelligence community now is to abandon the efforts to write a CIA charter that looks like a cross between the Federal Penal Code and the windfall profits tax legislation—page after page of, "Thou shall not."

I don't see why a CIA charter couldn't be written in ten double-spaced pages focusing on what we want intelligence to do for the country. And if it appears that that is the way Congress is going to frame the debate, I think we will see some changes in perception without changing a single court opinion or a single guideline.

This requires some Members of Congress to make some changes in cherished and entrenched positions about the "Thou shalt nots" to which they are wedded. I think their legitimate concerns can be met by the legislative oversight process, limited in my opinion to two committees, one in the House and one in the Senate.

I also agree that that oversight provision should not require the divulging of the identity of sensitive sources and methods. I think that is of the absolute essence for both the Bureau and the Agency.

General Discussion

The discussion revolved around the accuracy of Professor Scalia's remarks. At the end, a conferee regretted that so little attention had been paid to the recommendations of Dr. Godson and Dr. Beichman.

Professor Scalia's general point, that it is detrimental to talk as if restrictions were more stringent than the letter of laws on regulations says they are, found broad agreement. A consultant, who is also an attorney, voiced frustration at the intelligence agencies' habit of reading laws and regulations so as to minimize their own authority—

and therefore their own vulnerability. A scholar who had read the relevant memoranda also noted that the agencies had gone out of their way to present foreign governments with the most disquieting interpretations of the Freedom of Information Act. Also, the agencies have interpreted the FOIA much too liberally. Given this attitude toward laws and regulations, said that scholar, it is difficult to see how much good can be accomplished merely by loosening "standards" for intelligence activities. How can one explain, he asked, the fact that CIA is asking for exemptions to the FOIA while conceding that even if its requests were granted it would continue to supply Philip Agee and others like him with their own files? The scholar concluded that the people at the top of the intelligence community appear afflicted by moral confusion about their own purpose. This is why the intelligence community has never argued before the congress for the sort of mandate it needs to do its job. Rather its words have been aimed at placating people who cannot be placated.

A congressional staffer added some further examples of the agencies' timidity. He said that when confronted with a statement by the American Civil Liberties Union that, according to its interpretation of the law the FBI is allowed to collect the open publications of organizations which advocate violence, the FBI's official representative stated that the FBI would still feel itself legally prohibited from such collection.

There was widespread disagreement with several of Professor Scalia's specific arguments. A scholar pointed out that the FBI does *not* have a general exemption under the Privacy Act. A congressional staffer supported the paper's remarks on the *Keith* case, pointing out that the court having regulated domestic security wiretaps and having noted that wiretaps made on the grounds on national security were not amenable to the same type of regulation, urged Congress to pass something like the Foreign Intelligence Surveillance Act. He agreed with Professor Scalia that the courts cannot actually *order* Congress to pass a law, but he recalled that the court's recommendation weighed very heavily at every stage of the Senate's deliberations on the law.

Several congressional staffers disputed many of Professor's Scalia's contentions. For example, one stated that identified terrorists who were *not* known to be about to commit a crime could be surveilled. Testimony by a responsible official of the FBI showed that the Puerto Rican terrorists who had been released from the penitentiary after twenty-five years and who had vowed to strike again could not be surveilled under existing law. The same FBI official had also excluded surveillance of a hypothetical known member of the Red Brigades, as long as he was not known to be about to break US law. Professor Scalia countered that, upon reflection it might be a good idea to restrict surveillance of domestic groups who merely advocate violence. The recently released Puerto Rican terrorists, he said, were probably harmless. A second congressional staffer replied that just a few days after the released terrorists had made their threat, American sailors on a bus in Puerto Rico had been shot at, and the perpetrators never caught. The congressional staffer also argued that were all law enforcement agencies under the Attorney General's guidelines (which Professor Scalia as an Assistant Attorney General had helped to draft), terrorists could be more successful than they now are. He mentioned a case in Maryland, where the FBI had judged that existing guidelines prevented it from placing an informant in the Ku Klux Klan because the Klan was threatening violence in general. But the Maryland State Police, not similarly constrained, had placed an informant in the Klan and was thus able to foil attempted bombings at the home of a Congressman and at several synagogues.

The first congressional staffer agreed with Professor Scalia that a recent district court order requiring that court orders be obtained before Americans abroad could be wiretapped was very bad decision. But he strongly disagreed with the contention that the decision was "absurd." Rather, he said, the decision closely followed the text of a proposed intelligence charter, S. 2284, which had the official support of the Carter Administration and of certain groups in Congress. The court, as indeed much of the intelligence community, was behaving as if S. 2284 had already been passed. The staffer concluded that the restrictions upon intelligence are affected by a legal climate—the very definition of which is a field occupied by legislation, proposed legislation, judicial decisions and executive interpretations all tending in similar directions.

A journalist and a lawyer differed sharply on the value of legislative standards for initiating intelligence activities. The former contended that legislative charters consisting of standards would mire in endless legal discussion many bright people who should be concentrating on their jobs. He noted that excessive intrusion of law into other areas of society in recent years had diverted much useful energy from substantive to procedural concerns. The lawyer argued that standards can be implicit or explicit, and that where troubling legal questions may be present, the best course is to write explicit legal standards so that everyone will know where he stands.

APPENDIX I

"Directive to the London Station No. 59"

John Bruce Lockhart

Editor's Note:

The author of the "Directive to the London Station No. 59" is John Bruce Lockhart, formerly with the British Foreign Office. Of course, it is not an authentic document. Indeed, it is deliberately overstated, but based on his experience with intelligence matters, the author believes it is a plausible representation of the kind of directive that is sent to important KGB stations.

Directive to the London Station No. 59

Contents

Dear Comrade Colonel,

Annual Directive No. 57 laid down certain variations within our constant strategic framework. Comrade General Zurov has authorised me to inform you that he is satisfied with the way you have implemented this Directive. Directive No. 58 was essentially an instruction to continue on the lines of Directive No. 57. However there have been major developments in different parts of the world in the last twelve months, so that this Directive—Directive No. 59—includes certain changes of emphasis that you should note carefully.

The strategic objectives of the Central Committee, and the essential role of the KGB in achieving these objectives remain constant.

We have had some outstanding successes. Our progress has been substantial in Africa, Afghanistan, Iran, the establishment of a naval base in Aden, the steadily increasing influence of the militant Left in Britain, in Parliament, in the Trade Unions, in education circles, and the increasing undermining of the central patriotic will of the British people. There have also been new problems, connected with ideological conflicts raised by détente, Eurocommunism and, of course, China.

You have recovered well from the Douglas Hume disaster of eight years ago. The main change in your Directive is that in the past we have instructed you to use your initiative only in matters concerning Britain, and simply to obey our orders as regards non-British targets in Britain. We now wish you to regard London as one of the main centres of world revolutionary movements and terrorist conspiracies. The approval for specific operations will have to come from me, but you now have the right to suggest any operation against any authorised target of any nationality residing in or visiting Britain. The changes in organizational structure that this great potential will involve are so complex that you will soon have to come to Moscow for a week's discussion. Until then you should concentrate on the British target.

Comradely greetings,

Ivor Kurakoz
Director of Western Europe Department
KGB HQ Moscow
September, 1979

THE KGB DIRECTIVE NO. 59 TO THE LONDON STATION.

1. STRATEGIC AIMS.

First to destroy Parliamentary Democracy in Britain and replace it by a People's Socialist Democracy.
Second to exploit Britain as a base for operations against other non-socialist countries throughout the world. These will include action, propaganda and intelligence.

2. KEY OBJECTIVES TOWARDS ACHIEVING THESE STRATEGIC AIMS.

As regards the first strategic aim, the four key objectives remain the same:

(a) To inflame class hatred by all possible means. Where no class hatred exists, the myth must be made to appear a reality;

(b) To undermine the total economy; and in particular to destroy the prosperity of industry through the continued penetration of the unions, and the consequent exploitation of the strike weapon;

(c) To undermine respect for authority and all established bourgeois institutions; and

(d) To initiate and support all possible action leading to increased inflation. It is the Central Committee's view that nothing destroys the mainspring of the capitalist bourgeois state more effectively than inflation.

As regards the second strategic objective, this is being given to you as a responsibility for the first time. There are two factors involved in this:

(a) The enormous increase in 'visitors' to Britain. Even allowing for the competence of British security forces, the scale in number of 'tourists' cannot be controlled. In addition, the open door provided by Eire gives any revolutionary or illegal entrant almost free access to Britain.

(b) As the result, London has developed into the main conspiratorial centre in the world. Assassinations of senior foreign officials, and of British Members of parliament in Britain would have been unthinkable five years ago. This is not so today. We would be foolish not to exploit this freedom of action.

3. MAJOR TACTICAL CONSIDERATIONS.

Comrade General Zurov wishes me to stress certain points on several aspects of your work towards the achievement of these key targets:

(a) *The Labour Party and the Unions.*
Unlike France, Italy, Spain, and even West Germany, it has long been clear that the CPGB has no chance of achieving power through the ballot box. Since 1972, however, when the Labour Party Executive Committee decided to allow members of 'proscribed' parties to join the Labour Party, the central point of our tactical plan has been the penetration of the Labour Party and the trade unions. This has been a basic target since Directive No. 26, but the 1972 change in the policy of the Labour Party Committee made this much easier to attain. We are pleased with the progress you have made.

Indeed our present strength in the unions is such that we could bring the country to a halt through a general strike, if we so wished. However this might not necessarily be to our advantage, and you are expressly forbidden to orchestrate a general strike without specific orders from Moscow. You should concentrate rather on continuing to manipulate the election of militant left wing socialists as Parliamentary candidates, and to other key organizational positions. The recent election by the National Executive of the Labour Party of a well known Trotskyist as head of the Labour Party Youth Movement was well conceived and well executed.

I must, however, warn you that the British people are becoming increasingly aware of revolutionary influence in Britain, and the highest standards of security must be observed. The increasing awareness of the British may well lead to the creation of a forceful, nationalist, urban, proletarian right wing movement based on the present National Front. The penetration of this National Front is an obvious objective.

In this context you must ensure that the CPGB survives. In the first place it provides us with operational assistance. In the second place its apparent smallness and ineffectiveness reassures the British, and this is important.

Finally you should continue to penetrate and influence the unions and the Labour Party by the three classical methods:

1. The placing in key positions of open left wing militants devoted to revolution. These are your principle 'agents of influence.'

2. The placing under deep cover in key positions of those with no outward connection with the Left. These can act as 'agents of influence' or vital 'intelligence agents' at times of crisis.

3. The befriending, fostering and grooming of left wing idealistic fellow travellers who for their own motives believe in our role. Their importance has repeatedly proved itself. You will remember that Comrade Stalin always referred to them as 'my useful idiots.'

(b) *The Penetration of British Institutions.*
The Labour Party and the trade unions must be the prime target, but you must not forget the importance of the strategic attack on all institutions at the heart of British society. We would stress in particular local government at all levels, educational institutions—the universities, the colleges of further education and the schools, all elements of the central civil service, and of course the media in all its forms. I will deal with the media in para 3 (d).

It is doubtful whether Britain will reach a 'flash point' of revolution. If we continue our 'long march through the institutions' our objective of a People's Socialist Government in Britain may arrive almost without resistance. This is why we seek no dramatic confrontations, and no general strike. Throughout this 'long march' your agents must argue the intellectual reasonableness of Marxism, and how it provides a serious, respectable political and economic alternative to present British bourgeois policies.

(c) *Non-Communist Revolutionary Groups.*
The guidance given in Directive No. 57 remains valid. The importance however has increased because, though we may

regret it, the anti-Soviet revolutionary elements have increased their influence faster than we have increased ours. Our policy remains clear. Groups such as the Trotskyists, International Marxist-Leninists, Anarchists, International Revolutionary Socialists, etc., even though they are anti-Soviet, serve our strategic interests admirably. It is entirely to our advantage to have these groups doing our work for us, and bearing a large part of the odium that would otherwise be turned against us.

However I must repeat that they are never allies. In every revolutionary movement in Britain you must have one deep penetration agent, so that you know exactly what their plans are. You must in addition have able men who are in overt contact with each of these groups so that the means of communication are available to us should it be necessary. You have made good progress in this area, but it becomes of ever increasing importance.

(d) *Television and other Media.*

As mentioned in 3 (b) above, our influence over the communication media remains a major objective. Television in particular is the door to political power within every house. You must gain as much influence through agents of influence over the television as you can, while not forgetting the supporting role of the radio and the newspapers. Within the framework of the objectives given earlier in this directive, your priorities remain unchanged:

1. You should use your influence to bring into disrepute and ridicule:

The Monarchy.
The Law.
The Church.
The Police.
The Armed Services, and in particular the Officer Class.
Property Owners and the Management Class in industry and commerce.
Members of Parliament, and in particular Social-Democrats.
Concepts such as patriotism, loyalty, courage, the virtue of hard work, elitism in education, the family.

2. Class distinction should be stressed in every possible context.

3. The views of all those seeking to abolish wage restraint should be supported.

4. References to the Soviet Union should be invariably friendly, stressing our sporting, cultural and technological superiority. The Soviet desire for world peace and our policy of détente should also be stressed.

5. On international affairs the guidelines remain the same. Any country or institution working against Soviet influence should be denigrated. This particularly applies to the policies of the US (and especially CIA), NATO, the EEC, and now of course as a top priority the People's Republic of China. This latter problem we will discuss in Moscow.

(e) *The General Election and the Labour Party.*
The election must take place this year. When it does your instructions are to take every step you can to see that 'Left Wing Militants' are elected as Labour Members of Parliament. In Directive No. 57 we instructed you to infiltrate the executive committees at the constituency level in order to achieve the maximum influence over the choice of Labour candidates. In this you have been reasonably successful.

If Labour loses, you should discourage any attempt to divide the Labour Party, and so create an independent Militant Socialist party of the Left. The evidence does not show that the working classes will support the Militant Left at the ballot box, and you risk turning a fundamentally favourable situation into a position of isolation. You are to orchestrate every instrument of influence—front organizations, agents of influence, the 'useful idiots', even the penetration agents, to ensure that no split happens. You must understand that if Labour loses the election, it is General Zurov's view, and the view of Comrade Ponomarev, that the Socialist Left will be able to take control of the Labour Party during the years of opposition, provided only that it remains within the Party. You should remember Comrade Lenin's advice to the German Communist Party 'you should support all parties of the Left, but as the rope supports the hanged man.'

(f) *Ulster, Devolution and Racialism.*

Any development that weakens the national will and sense of purpose of Britain is a development to be encouraged. This we have made clear in many previous Directives, but we criticize ourselves that we did not sufficiently stress to you, the importance of devolution. The results of the referendums in Wales and Scotland were disappointing. But Ulster remains of vital importance. It is a running sore, a permanent threat on Britain's flank. We will however retain control of operations in Ulster from Moscow in spite of the new international responsibilities we intend to give you. Ulster is a truly international operation which it is your task solely to facilitate when ordered.

Racialism comes under the same group of problems. Your influence must be used in every way to encourage racial prejudices. That these exist strongly among the working classes in Britain has long been accepted by us. But in addition to working on the prejudices of the British working classes, you must increasingly infiltrate the coloured immigrant population, and encourage militant anti-white movements. We have for some time been training, in various institutions near Moscow, Indians, West Indians, Arabs and Africans in the skills of subversion and *agitprop*. We have also trained terrorists. We will not, however, send you the terrorists unless you can make a specific convincing case. The ever increasing number of coloured citizens and immigrants in Britain creates its own time-bomb within the bourgeois parliamentary system. Race hatred, like class hatred, should always be encouraged: but you will initiate no terrorism or assassination without specific authority from me.

4. INTELLIGENCE TARGETS.

Since Directive No 1, (now in the Kremlin's National Collection of 'Sacred' Documents), intelligence on the plans and policies of Imperialist Britain has been amongst the highest of our priorities. The diminishing world role of Britain, the collapse of any national sense of purpose have inevitably reduced the importance of this task. Finding and placing intelligence agents in Britain is now of less importance than finding and placing of agents of influence. Nevertheless the long term importance is still there.

The intelligence targets remain broadly as stated in Directives 38 to 58. They are:

1. Industrial and Technical Intelligence: research and development.
2. Political Intelligence: plans and policies of the Foreign Office, of the Conservative and Liberal Parties, and of the National Front.
3. Defense: technical weapon developments (the British still have great inventive capabilities); NATO plans; contacts with America; chemical warfare research.
4. The British Intelligence Services.
5. Soviet Citizens in the U.K.
6. All visitors and residents from the Chinese Republic, and all negotiations between Britain and the Chinese Republic at any level, in any field.

5. CONCLUSION.

Much is working in our favour in Britain. Comrade General Zurov regards London now as possibly the most important KGB station in the world. He believes the next twelve months will be critical in Britain. Our first objective of destroying parliamentary government and replacing it with a People's Socialist Democracy has come appreciably nearer. You have done well, Comrade Colonel, but remember *no dramatic action*. Time is on our side.

APPENDIX II

Consortium for the Study of Intelligence

Origin and Purpose

During the past decade, there has been a flood of material dealing with intelligence, particularly American intelligence and its relationship to national security and U.S. foreign policy. Some of this information has been made available in the writings of former intelligence officials. Other major sources include Congressional documents resulting from oversight activities, and documents released under the Freedom of Information Act.

As a result it has become increasingly possible to undertake objective, scholarly and unclassified research into the intelligence process and product, and to examine their relationship to U.S. decision making.

In light of these new circumstances, a group of social scientists from several academic institutions decided in April, 1979, to create a CONSORTIUM FOR THE STUDY OF INTELLIGENCE (CSI). Its membership includes political scientists, particularly specialists in international relations and U.S. foreign policy, historians, sociologists and professors of international and constitutional law.

CSI set for itself the following purposes:

(i) To encourage teaching on both the graduate and undergraduate levels in the field of intelligence, as it relates to national security, foreign policy, law and ethics.

(ii) To promote the development of a theory of intelligence—What is it, and what is its place in American national security policy? Comparative analysis with the practice and experience of other nations will be emphasized.

(iii) To encourage research into the intelligence process itself—analysis and estimates, clandestine collection, counterintelligence, and covert action; and to determine the feasibility of measuring efficiency or setting standards of efficiency so that the product can be improved.

(iv) To study the tensions between intelligence activities and the democratic and constitutional values of our society, and to seek the development of principles and methods for reconciling the two.

For various cultural and political reasons, the study of intelligence has too often been regarded by academicians as *ultra vires*. Their self-exclusion from the subject has inhibited an understanding of this significant instrument of the modern nation-state.

APPENDIX III

Colloquium on Counterintelligence

April 24-26, 1980

Washington, DC

List of Participants

Mr. Daniel C. Arnold
Former Chief, Evaluations, Plans and Design Staff, DDO, CIA

Mr. Frank R. Barnett
President, National Strategy Information Center

Captain Richard W. Bates, USA (Ret.)
Vice President, Association of Former Intelligence Officers; Former Commandant, Defense Intelligence School

Dr. Richard K. Betts
Brookings Institution

Dr. Arnold Beichman
Freelance Writer; Professor of Political Science

Dr. Richard Bissell
Managing Editor, ORBIS

Mr. Ladislav Bittman
Formerly with the Czechoslovak Intelligence Service

Dr. Adda B. Bozeman
Professor of International Relations, Sarah Lawrence College

Mr. William A. Branigan
Former Chief, Soviet Counterintelligence, FBI

Mr. Eugene Franz Burgstaller
Former Chief of Station, CIA

Mr. Robert Chapman
Former Chief of Collection, Latin America, CIA

Dr. John G. Chomeau
Chief, Analysis Training Branch, Office of Training, CIA

Dr. Ray S. Cline
Executive Director, Georgetown Center for Strategic and International Studies; Former Deputy Director for Intelligence, CIA

Dr. Angelo Codevilla
Professional Staff Member, Senate Select Committee on Intelligence

Mr. Kenneth E. deGraffenreid
Professional Staff Member, Senate Select Committee on Intelligence

Dr. John J. Dziak
Senior Soviet Specialist, DIA

Dr. Edward J. Epstein
Center for Research on International Deception

Mr. Jean Evans
Professional Staff Member, Senate Select Committee on Intelligence

Major General Schlomo Gazit
Director, Israeli Military Intelligence, 1974-1979

Mr. Richard H. Giza
Professional Staff Member, House Permanent Select Committee on Intelligence

Dr. Roy Godson
Associate Professor of Government, Georgetown University; Research Associate, National Strategy Information Center

Mr. James H. Guirard
Administrative Assistant to Senator Russell Long

Lt. Colonel John Guenther
Special Assistant to the Director of Intelligence, USMC

Mr. Samuel Halpern
Former Executive Assistant to the Deputy Director for Plans, CIA

Dr. Michael Handel
Center for International Affairs, Harvard University

Dr. William R. Harris
The Rand Corporation

Rear Admiral Donald P. Harvey, USN (Ret.)
Senior Scientist, TRW; Former Director of Naval Intelligence

Dr. Roland Herbst
R&D Associates

Mr. David Ignatius
Wall Street Journal

Mr. George Kalaris
Central Intelligence Agency

Mr. Roger Kaplan
Program Officer, Smith Richardson Foundation

Mr. Merrill T. Kelly
Special Assistant to the Assistant Chief of Staff for Intelligence for Human Systems, USA

Ms. G. Elizabeth Keyes
Professional Staff Member, House Permanent Select Committee on Intelligence

Mr. Wilfred Koplowitz
Former Chief of Station, CIA

Mr. William Kucewicz
Editorial Page Writer, Wall Street Journal

Mr. Charles M. Lichenstein
Counsel to the Public Broadcasting Service

Mr. John Bruce Lockhart
Formerly with the British Foreign Office

Mr. Patrick G. Long
Associate Counsel, House Permanent Select Committee on Intelligence

Hon. John O. Marsh, Jr.
Mays, Valentine, Davenport, and Moore; Former Counsellor to President Ford

Mr. David Martin
Consultant to the American Bar Association Committee on Law and National Security

Mr. Lawrence McWilliams
Former Chief of Foreign Counterintelligence Training, FBI

Mr. Newton S. Miler
Former Chief of Operations, Counterintelligence Staff, CIA

Professor John Norton Moore
Director, Center for Oceans Law and Policy, University of Virginia Law School

Rear Admiral William C. Mott, USN (Ret.)
Chairman, Advisory Committee, ABA Committee on Law and National Security; Vice President, National Strategy Information Center

Dr. Robert Nisbet
Resident Scholar, American Enterprise Institute

Mr. James E. Nolan
Section Chief, Intelligence Division, FBI

Lt. General William Odom
Military Assistant to the Assistant to the President for National Security Affairs

Dr. Richard E. Pipes
Professor of History, Harvard University

Mr. Donovan Pratt
Former Director of Research, Counterintelligence Staff, CIA

Mr. Alfred S. Regnery
Legislative Counsel to Senator Paul Laxalt

Mr. Raymond Rocca
Former Deputy Chief, Counterintelligence Staff, CIA

Mr. Herbert Romerstein
Professional Staff Member, House Permanent Select Committee on Intelligence

Professor Antonin Scalia
University of Chicago Law School; Former Assistant Attorney General

Dr. Paul Seabury
Professor of Political Science, University of California, Berkeley

Mr. Theodore G. Shackley
Former Associate Deputy Director for Collection Tasking, CIA

Mr. Dennis P. Sharon
Minority Counsel, Senate Select Committee on Intelligence

Mr. David Shaw
Professional Staff Member, Senate Select Committee on Intelligence

Mr. Norman L. Smith
Former Deputy Chief of Operations, Counterintelligence Staff, CIA

Dr. Richard F. Staar
Director of International Studies, Hoover Institution on War, Revolution and Peace

Mr. Daniel Southerland
Christian Science Monitor

Mr. David S. Sullivan
Former Strategic Analyst, CIA

Mr. P. L. Thyraud de Vosjoli
Former Chief of Station, SDECE

Major General Edmund R. Thompson, USA
Assistant Chief of Staff for Intelligence, Department of the Army

Dr. Michael Uhlmann
Former Assistant Attorney General

Mr. Joe Volz
New York Daily News

Mr. W. Raymond Wannall
Former Assistant Director, FBI, Intelligence Division

Mr. Edwin Warner
TIME, Inc.

Dr. Allen Weinstein
Professor of History, Smith College

Dr. James Q. Wilson
Professor of Government, Harvard University

Mr. Arthur A. Zuehlke, Jr.
Soviet Analyst, DIA

INTELLIGENCE REQUIREMENTS FOR THE 1980's

Published by the National Strategy Information Center, Inc.

Distributed by Transaction Books, New Brunswick (USA) and London (UK).